"The authors generate a novel 'balance
tional relations grounded in practice, :
should help US decision makers better
parts, but the theory is also usefully presented as a general resource availa
ble to all states that choose to adopt a relational foreign policy."
— **Cameron G. Thies**, *Arizona State University, USA*

"This book courageously establishes an innovative theory that is conceptually and culturally different from existing Western theories of international
relations. It also provides appealing reinterpretations of the relationships
between China and the United States and between mainland China and
Taiwan."
— **Wang Jisi**, *Peking University, China*

"The temptation when looking beyond 'Western IR theory' is to code the
potential contributions of thought that is grounded in experiences outside of
Western Europe and North America in terms already familiar to the mainstream: as a new 'ism,' as support for one or another existing school of IR
thought, or as a completely distinct way of thinking about international affairs that serves as a comprehensive rival. This book avoids that temptation,
producing instead a detailed engagement with dominant Anglophone IR
that is grounded in the Confucian heritage, foregrounding 'improvised resemblance' as a foreign policy strategy that doesn't fit neatly of the existing
categories that Anglophone IR thinking provides. The result is a bit disqui-
eting, but for a profound purpose: to explore the tissues of resemblance and
distinction between so-called 'Chinese' and 'Western' IR, and to perhaps
afford us a better grasp of both."
— **Patrick Thaddeus Jackson**, *American*
University, USA

China and International Theory

Major IR theories, which stress that actors will inevitably only seek to enhance their own interests, tend to contrive binaries of self and other and 'inside' and 'outside'. By contrast, this book recognizes the general need of all to relate, which they do through various imagined resemblances between them.

The authors of this book therefore propose the 'balance of relationships' (BoR) as a new international relations theory to transcend binary ways of thinking. BoR theory differs from mainstream IR theories owing to two key differences in its epistemological position. Firstly, the theory explains why and how states as socially-interrelated actors inescapably pursue a strategy of self-restraint in order to join a network of stable and long-term relationships. Secondly, owing to its focus on explaining bilateral relations, BoR theory bypasses rule-based governance. By positing 'relationality' as a key concept of Chinese international relations, this book shows that BoR can also serve as an important concept in the theorization of international relations, more broadly.

The rising interest in developing a Chinese school of IR means the BoR theory will draw attention from students of IR theory, comparative foreign policy, Chinese foreign policy, East Asia, cultural studies, post-Western IR, post-colonial studies and civilizational politics.

Chih-yu Shih, the primary author of this book, teaches international relations theory, anthropology of Knowledge, and cultural studies as National Chair Professor and University Chair Professor at National Taiwan University. Access to his current research—Intellectual History of China and Chinese Studies—can be found at http://www.china-studies.taipei/ Together, his writings on IR theory, intellectual history, and ethnic citizenship challenge familiar social science and humanity categories. His co-authors—Chiung-chiu Huang (National Cheng-chi University), Pichamon Yeophantong (University of New South Wales, Canberra), Raoul Bunskoek (National Taiwan University), Josuke Ikeda (Toyama University), Yih Jye Hwang (Leiden University), Hung-jen Wang (National Cheng-Kung University), Chih-yun Chang (Shanghai Jiaotong University), and Ching-chang Chen (Ryukoku

University)—have all published critically on Asia in IR in general and on China, Japan, Taiwan and ASEAN in specific. They have come across each other through different joint projects involving critical IR, post-Western IR, homegrown IR, global IR, Asian IR and Chinese IR. Their careers include professional posts in India, Germany, Thailand, Japan, the US, Taiwan, the Netherlands, Australia, and China.

Chiung-chiu Huang is Associate Professor at the Graduate Institute of East Asian Studies, National Chengchi University, Taiwan.

Pichamon Yeophantong is an Australian Research Council DECRA Fellow and Senior Lecturer at the School of Humanities and Social Sciences, University of New South Wales at the Australian Defence Force Academy, Australia.

Raoul Bunskoek is a Ph.D candidate in the Department of Political Science at National Taiwan University, Taiwan.

Josuke Ikeda is Associate Professor at the Faculty of Human Development, University of Toyama, Japan.

Yih-Jye Hwang is Assistant Professor at the Faculty of Governance and Global Affairs, Leiden University College, The Netherlands.

Hung-jen Wang is Associate Professor at the Department of Political Science, National Cheng Kung University, Taiwan.

Chih-yun Chang is a Research Fellow at the Department of History, Shanghai Jiaotong University, China.

Ching-chang Chen is Associate Professor at the Department of Global Studies, Ryokoku University, Japan.

Worlding Beyond the West

Series Editors: **Arlene B. Tickner**, *Universidad del Rosario, Colombia*, **David Blaney**, *Macalester College, USA and* **Inanna Hamati-Ataya**, *Cambridge University, UK*

Historically, the International Relations (IR) discipline has established its boundaries, issues, and theories based upon Western experience and traditions of thought. This series explores the role of geocultural factors, institutions, and academic practices in creating the concepts, epistemologies, and methodologies through which IR knowledge is produced. This entails identifying alternatives for thinking about the "international" that are more in tune with local concerns and traditions outside the West. But it also implies provincializing Western IR and empirically studying the practice of producing IR knowledge at multiple sites within the so-called "West".

For more information about this series, please visit: https://www.routledge.com

China and International Theory
The Balance of Relationships

Chih-yu Shih
and
Chiung-chiu Huang
Pichamon Yeophantong
Raoul Bunskoek
Josuke Ikeda
Yih-Jye Hwang
Hung-jen Wang
Chih-yun Chang
Ching-chang Chen

Routledge
Taylor & Francis Group

LONDON AND NEW YORK

First published 2019
by Routledge
2 Park Square, Milton Park, Abingdon, Oxon OX14 4RN

and by Routledge
605 Third Avenue, New York, NY 10017

First issued in paperback 2020

Routledge is an imprint of the Taylor & Francis Group, an informa business

British Library Cataloguing-in-Publication Data
A catalogue record for this book is available from the British Library

Library of Congress Cataloging-in-Publication Data
A catalog record has been requested for this book

ISBN 13: 978-0-367-73078-9 (pbk)
ISBN 13: 978-1-138-39050-8 (hbk)

Typeset in Times New Roman
by codeMantra

Chapter 2 is a rewrite of "Affirmative Balance of the Singapore-Taiwan Relationship: A Bilateral Perspective on the Relational Turn in International Relations," *International Studies Review* 18(4).

Chapter 3 is a rewrite of "China's Quest for Grand Strategy: Power, National Interest, or Relational Security?" *Chinese Journal of International Politics* 8(1).

Chapter 7 is a rewrite of "The Rise of China between Cultural and Civilizational Ratinoalities: Lessons from Four Qing Cass," *International Journal of Asian Studies* 14(1).

Chapter 10 is a rewrite of "International Relations of Post-hybridity: Dangers and Potentials in Non-Synthetic Cycles," *Globalizations* 14(4).

Chapter 12 is a rewrite of "Re-worlding the 'West' in Post-Western IR: The Reception of Sun Zi's the Art of War in the Anglosphere," *International Relations of the Asia Pacific* 18(3).

Contents

List of figures

List of tables

Preface

During the development of the balance of relationships (BoR) as both a theory of the international system and of strategic agency, we faced the challenge of engaging in and contributing to two major dialogues at the same time—international relations theory in general and the relational turn, in particular. Further complicating this challenge is the fact that the second dialogue involves a readership across the Anglosphere and the Sinosphere, with both spheres similarly focusing on why and how relations are necessary in international relations, but from different cultural backgrounds. In light of this, our intention is for our theory to transcend the familiar binaries of China and the West; great and small powers; rationality and relationality; as well as those reflecting political rivalries. Nevertheless, our primary purpose is to illustrate how Chinese intellectual resources can enhance the understanding of international relations and foreign policy practices everywhere. Through doing so, we hope to tackle the misreading and misconstruction of Chinese international relations. Our writing thus seeks to construct bridges across seemingly incongruent epistemological traditions.

This book offers a composite agenda that compares and reconciles relational imaginations of different kinds through the notion of the balance of relationships. We have opted to focus mainly on unpacking the concepts, ideas and epistemology that undergird BoR theory, and as a result, had to take out extensive empirical case chapters. Nevertheless, we do rely on real-world examples to determine BoR's scope for potential application, with the aim of making sense of empirical phenomena that familiar IR theories struggle to explain.

Such a double-headed mission complicates not only the writing but also coordination among the authors. I am grateful to my eight younger colleagues who fearlessly agreed to join the collective writing of this book, which trespasses multiple fields and critically moves outside familiar scopes of thinking. Our professional teaching spreads over the disciplines of political science, postcolonial studies, modern Chinese history, intellectual history, philosophy, East Asian and Chinese studies, and ethnic studies. In terms of nationality, we come from Japan, the Netherlands, Taiwan, and Thailand. We have received doctoral training or taught in Australia, China,

Germany, India, Japan, the Netherlands, Thailand, Taiwan, the UK, and the US, for extensive periods in each of our careers. All of these factors meant parallel and long processes of negotiation and coordination. However, as the existence of this work now shows, in the end we managed to merge all these diverse perspectives together and establish a balance of relationships among ourselves.

We realize that it is unconventional to have nine coauthors as opposed to nine authors of separate chapters. I rather enjoyed the processes of cooperation and coordination, however. Being the common denominator who initiated the idea and writing of each chapter, my coauthors joined at different stages upon my invitation and inevitably contributed across the writing of all of the different chapters. We interacted intensively, and at least five of us participated in finalizing all the chapters. Relying on our other collaborative projects or workshops, I was able to organize occasional meetings with all eight coauthors over the past few years. Major funding for the writing of this book was, nevertheless, received from a three-year grant from the Ministry of Science and Technology of Taiwan that I received from 2014 to 2017. A few summer and winter camps specifically contrived to introduce the balance of relationships to younger generations were also organized by the Center of International China Studies at the Chinese Academy of Social Sciences, the Division of Area Studies at the University of Tokyo, the Department of Political Science of the National Taiwan University, and the Institute of International Relations of Shanghai Tongji University.

With the support of the editors of Routledge's *Worlding the West Series*, through the publication of this book we hope to engender passion and a strong interest in the Anglosphere to reflect on China and international theory in even more comprehensive and sophisticated ways.

Chih-yu Shih

Introduction

Relating China to international relations

The international as relational

This book proposes the 'balance of relationships' (BoR) as a new international relations theory (IRT). Relations between actors exist in imagined resemblance of each other in terms of kinships, geo-cultures, languages, values, norms, customs, memories, institutions, networks, threats, commitments, and most pragmatically, interests. 'Relationship' is conceived here as a process of mutual constitution that reproduces imagined resemblance, where actors self-identify with others on the basis of a Wittgensteinian network of perceived similarities overlapping. Resemblance enables an imagined collective identity to constitute the self-identities of resembling members. This runs contrary to the premise of anarchy in mainstream IRT, which denies the relevance of resemblance. The Chinese version of relational theory is primarily founded upon Confucian thought, but also complemented by concepts and perspectives originating from Buddhism, the Kyoto School of Philosophy (KSP), and the cyclical view of history. It also speaks to the 'relational turn' in IR theorizing, which underscores how human relations matter to a deeper understanding of social action (Qin 2018). BoR brings to the fore three attendant concepts: practice, self-restraint and bilaterality.

BoR theory differs from mainstream IR theories—namely, neorealism and neoliberal institutionalism—as a result of two key differences in its epistemological position. First, rather than accepting the conventional view that the international system is characterized by states driven by a self-help imperative, the theory seeks to explain why and how states as socially-interrelated actors inescapably pursue a strategy of self-restraint, in order to join a network of stable and long-term relationships. Second, owing to its focus on explicating bilateral relations, BoR theory bypasses rule-based governance. All nations have their own ways of engendering resemblance and, as such, implementing BoR in principle. However, not all states will engage in it at all times.

Defined as the condition of nations being related to one another, this book posits 'relationality' as a key concept of Chinese international relations; however, argues that it can also serve as an important concept in the theorization of international relations, more broadly. We argue that the loss of relationality can result in systemic ontological insecurity. BoR is thus pertinent to the relational IR research agenda, as it tackles the thorny question of how the logic of relationality affects state behavior. As countries draw on cultural memory and a need for conflict resolution to cultivate relations, BoR consequently brings into sharper relief a system of states seeking to synchronize their imagined resemblance. It also speaks to the policy adopted by certain states to ensure that resemblance exists between them. Accordingly, BoR involves the construction of an image of ideal resemblance between state actors, and underwrites the social cognitive obligation and psychological drive of states to strive for or maintain this ideal.

By definition, BoR refers to the process of establishing and maintaining mutual obligations between state actors. Following from this, BoR challenges mainstream IRT in three key ways. First, it proposes that acts of confrontation and compromise do not necessarily happen in accordance with the balance of power considerations or rule-enforcing governance. As a result, one can anticipate occasions where a weaker party in an asymmetrical relationship might try to put on a show of determination, whereas the stronger party might conversely behave in a compliant manner. Second, BoR advances the expectation that states do not always pursue "apparent" national interests. Sacrificing interests to restore relational balance embedded in an imagined resemblance (i.e. rectifying a relationship) is not an uncommon phenomenon, and certainly one that is not unique to a particular country (Fierke 2016). In light of this, BoR proceeds on the assumption that relational balancing takes place when an actor seeks out compatible or converging expectations with another actor, and then acts accordingly. This may be in the form of, for example, reproducing extant relationships through rewards or sanctions, or through acts of relational adjustment such as signaling and enforcing.

The third challenge that BoR mounts against mainstream IRT concerns its appreciation of the ubiquity of relationality in international politics. Despite the emerging body of scholarship on this topic, contemporary IRT has yet to deal sufficiently with the coexistence of relationality and power. This is largely due to the fact that Western IRT remains firmly grounded in philosophical and analytical traditions that tend to favor logical consistency, as well as a linear or teleological understanding of historical progress. However, as this book demonstrates, dialectics is by no means anathema to the Western tradition, being similarly embedded within Chinese, Japanese, and Indian philosophical traditions that adopt a cyclical theory of historical development. It is in this way that relationality exhibits broad resonance and applicability across different historical and sociocultural contexts: the Chinese proclivity for non-interventionism and cultivating bilateral strategic partnerships is not exclusively Chinese, but could equally be conceived as East Asian, Asian or even Western as well. In revisiting

Chinese philosophical traditions and their modern implications, this book also anticipates the (re)discovery of bilateral and relational sensibilities in Western IR.

In sum, this book argues that relations cannot exist without the creation of imagined resemblances between actors. These imagined—and socially constructed—strings of resemblance commonly constitute the identities and interests of actors, enabling them to build networks to address collective concerns, monitor non-compliant behavior, and most importantly, allow for predictions of how resembled others will act. BoR thus challenges and builds upon mainstream IR theorization by conceptualizing relationality as the prevailing condition, alongside anarchy, that defines international politics. In other words, anarchy serves to set one prior relation that fundamentally configures all others—albeit to varying degrees. Echoing the Wendtian notion that 'anarchy is what states make of it' (Wendt 1992), how, where and when anarchy is 'practiced' depends on the decisions of the (state) actor in question. If in international anarchy states resort to self-help in order to survive, then the logic of relationality is one that prompts states to seek the maintenance of relations in order to mitigate the self-help effects of imagined anarchy.

While the use and accumulation of power are perceived as key to state survival from a neorealist standpoint, the BoR framework acknowledges how states may be reluctant to exercise power under certain conditions—more specifically, if doing so should jeopardize their relationships and, by extension, ontological security. It is in this sense that states can simultaneously imagine both anarchy and relationality, with both serving as intellectually universal principles, despite the fact that mainstream IRT remains primarily biased towards anarchy.

China and confucian relationality in the post-western world

The Chinese experience aptly captures the nexus between relationality and power, especially considering China's preoccupation with the exercise of bilateral and dyadic diplomacy. Employing a BoR lens, this book will review how and why Chinese leaders adopt bilateralism to explain Chinese foreign policy and, in so doing, why and how bilateralism is essential to IR theorization more generally, which has tended to focus on multilateralism and systemic-level theorization. In particular, this book will uncover the strands of East Asian history and philosophy that make the bilateral frame intuitive through empirical examples. The concept of relationality enables theorists to uncover a rationality of IR that does not necessarily follow the logic of power or national interest calculus. The ontological challenge that bilateral relationality poses to mainstream IR concerns how the act of imagining and reproducing resemblance in others epistemologically equalizes parties within the BoR, such that their subsequent interactions do not proceed according to relative power differentials. Conceptions of imagined resemblance between actors, in this way, allows for the mutual constitution of the actors involved. A breach in a relationship thus calls for remedies to either restore the imagined resemblance or construct a new one. This calls for self-restraint, which in this book refers to prioritization of perceived common interests, as well as the interests of certain others over one's own self-interests.

Contemporary bilateralism seen in Chinese foreign policy has multiple sources. Confucianism instructs Chinese political actors to assume the reciprocal role in bilateral dyads, as reflected in the notion of kinship, so as to achieve order. The KSP, which philosophizes IR away from multilateral rules and yet relativizes them according to spatiotemporal conditions, further complicates the binary of East versus West. Both Confucianism and the KSP are perceptive of the value of self-restraint. In this regard, the lingering influence of Buddhism across Asia provides a tacit logic for the reluctant participation of Asian states in the interventionism that is involved in multilateral regime-building.

Indeed, for Sinophone thinkers, relationality has always been more intuitive than anarchy. (Here, even anarchy is considered relational; disorder or ungovernability would come closer to serving as the antonym of relationality.) Relationality not only underlies Confucianism but has also served as a guiding logic for Confucian scholars seeking to explain the rise and fall of regime (or rather, dynasties). Confucianism seeks to instill a moral consciousness within the ruling elite and ensure that duties are performed as prescribed by their specific institutional roles. Confucius, given his belief that human nature is essentially good, asserted that moral consciousness arises from the benevolence of kings and their officials. And to promote benevolence, Confucius turned to blood kinship, identifying it a central consideration in his institutional design.[1] Here, an actor seeking to establish and maintain their legitimate position within a kinship circle must first cultivate and practice self-restraint with respect to other actors, in accordance with the reciprocal obligations expected of their social role. To this effect, Confucius posited that voluntary self-restraint, as expressed through observance of rites and displays of benevolence toward others within one's kinship circle, was crucial to the restoration of order. Indeed, as a member of the broadest kinship circle (i.e. the state), rulers are expected to practice self-restraint in both the governance of the state and in their relations with other states, thus rendering expansionist policies unnecessary, if not outright harmful. The legacy of Confucianism is such that subsequent followers of Confucius likewise stressed the importance of rituals. Legalism, for one, focused on how strict laws were necessary to enforce the fulfillment of duties. However, within the legalist tradition, self-restraint became compulsory instead of spontaneously voluntary.

Confucianism, like other Chinese classical schools of thought, featured a proto-IR focus from the very beginning, considering how it had emerged as a political philosophy to help recover order under All-under-Heaven (*tianxia*) from the chaos of the warring states period (roughly three and half centuries before 221 BC). Prior to this period, kingdoms were feudal domains that the Zhou emperor had bestowed upon his kin. But because the emperor failed to earn the respect of his kin, soon enough they declared their respective kingship after receiving the lands. The warring states period marked a transition from a hierarchical world order, dominated by a few kings, to a (dis)order characterized by numerous competing powers—a situation not unlike those that eventuated following the collapse of the Concert of Europe or the end of the Cold War. What had distinguished Confucianism from other contending schools at the time, and which arguably led it to rise in popularity among the Chinese elite, was its emphasis on morality. It did nevertheless share an important goal with the other schools: that is, the restoration of order through the rectification of 'names'. Names, as the argument went, provide individuals with a clear role conception in relation to each other as well as a code of propriety, with the latter serving as the basis for orderly social interactions.

Classic Confucianism and contemporary post-Western IR face a similar predicament that tasks them with a comparable mission: the breakdown of hegemonic order and the quest for a post-hegemonic order that is not unilaterally enforced by a hegemonic center. Post-Western IR attends to the geocultural distinctiveness of each site in the re-appropriation of hegemonic order for the individual purposes of all sites, and in the process, hegemonic order comes to be exposed as no more than a provincial site called the West (Tickner & Blaney 2012, 2013). To achieve post-Zhou identities, Confucianism drew upon nostalgia for a bygone utopia as its reference point to appropriate Zhou values and institutions. However, post-Western IR invariably relies on the retrieval of a large variety of nostalgias, each embedded in their own sited genealogy and defying efforts at hegemonic theorization to incorporate, synchronize, and convert. Incidentally, the advocacy of the Chinese School of IR shares the same Confucian nostalgia for either a relational order (Qin 2018) or a benevolent hierarchy (Yan 2011). In light of the post-Western determination to resist any plausible hegemonic order, the propensity of the Chinese School of IR towards establishing a hierarchy-based theoretical framework is old-fasiotned.

Confucianism copes with the conditions of anarchy as disorder by endeavoring to control and mitigate them. The conviction that anarchy as disorder should—and can be—controlled lies with the imagined state of nature, as depicted in the ancient classics that existed over a thousand years prior to Confucius. For Confucianism and contemporary neo-Confucianism, anarchy as disorder is not the state of nature but a corrupt reality that must be controlled and changed. Revisiting Confucianism in the 21st century can inform both post-hegemonic and post-Western theorization. Post-hegemonic and post-Western theorization are preoccupied with anarchy, although the former as a state of nature, rather than a deviation from it, to be controlled and the latter in its pursuit of multiple sites of genealogy each rooted in their own geocultural distinctions. But while Confucian concepts such as benevolence and name rectification may resonate with the post-Western notion of geocultural genealogy (Shih 2010), such a concept can also bring forth the specter of another hegemonic theorization that might result in the naming of duties around the world (Callahan 2008).

To a certain extent, Confucius and his contemporaries managed to deal humanistically with the vagaries of international and domestic politics. Self-restraint was their advice for kings to maintain order internally and attain a good reputation internationally. For a king and his state to exercise self-restraint, this would not only prevent them from becoming tyrants domestically, but also reduce the chances of them being perceived as a threat in terms of foreign policy. Self-restraint, in this sense, would serve the goal of pacifying relations among the warring states, with them reassuming their named duties within an order represented by the 'selfless' Zhou emperor. This ultimate goal speaks to what Confucius referred to as 'the Way' or 'oneness', a state where peaceful coexistence is achieved as a result of all actors behaving in a self-restrained way (Ivanhoe 2004: 197). Such an ideal state has its Western counterparts, for example, the ideals of critical peace (Behr 2014) or a world government (Wendt 2003), both of which obscure the international from the internal. Indeed, transcending territorial boundaries seems to characterize all post-hegemonic versions of the ideal state—whether Confucian or post-Western. However, to achieve Confucian peace, the focus is on establishing bilateral resemblance between states, as opposed to a multilateral commitment to humanity.

The relational turn reconsidered: unravelling the Chinese sources of an international theory

Aside from challenging mainstream IR theorizing, BoR stands to contribute to Western relational thinking, which is likewise biased in favor of multilateralism. The relational turn in the study of international relations is indebted to a number of intellectual strings, most noticeably the feminist ethics of caring (Chodorow 1991, Redshaw 2013, Robinson 1997, Stern & Zalewski 2009), Bourdieu's conception of field, (Adler-Nissen 2014, Berling 2012, Bourdieu 1977, Bourdieu & Wacquant 1992, Senn & Elhardt 2013) and network sociology (Cao 2009, Hafner-Birtpm, Kahler & Montgomery 2009, Maoz et al., 2006, Nexon & Wright 2007). Common to the literature on the relational turn is its focus on processual analysis in order to understand how practices reproduce, evolve, and change (Jackson & Nexon 1999). All structures, or imaginations of structures, are arguably constituted by imagined prior/unowned resemblance, which in itself is composed of multiple practices of relationship-building between embedded national actors at various levels and sites. As such, agents—as they select and practice rules in the international political realm—are conditioned by the prior relationships that exist among and between national actors. However, the relational turn posits the impossibility of national actors to be completely autonomous. National actors will invariably incorporate, consciously or unconsciously, imagined resemblance as it defines the parameters of their self-understanding, self-expectation, and self-enactment. Even self-help, rivalry, and imperialism are relational (Campbell 1992, Guillaume 2002) in the sense that they emerge and occur meaningfully only when performed before a waiting audience.

Appreciating the relational turn thus underscores the importance of understanding how structures and rules bind, or fail to bind, actors to each other. It also raises questions in relation to the rise and fall of certain norms and institutions, the formation of legitimacy among groups of actors, and the plethora of constitutive ways through which agential identities come into existence.

Despite its distinctive ontology, the relational approach does echo realism and liberalism in two important ways, and through which the pursuit of BoR can provide opportunities for further critical reflection. First, the relational approach highlights the significance of self-identity and, in particular, on how self-subjectivity necessarily appropriates imagined resemblance to achieve self-understanding or even enhance self-fulfillment. The epistemological concern of the relational approach therefore coincides with other research agendas that focus on the autonomous state, albeit with the qualification that no state can be truly autonomous in reality. Here, relationality ontologically accepts the lingering cliché of the self-other relationship to make a meaningful self-identity (Shih 2010).

Second, the majority of scholarship on the relational turn has often insisted on a multilateral frame of analysis, where prior resemblance comes to constitute the identities and strategies of individual states and dyads of states (Dorff & Ward 2013, Ward, Siverson & Cao 2007). The analytical potential of caring, usually embedded in specific relationships (Gilligan 1993, Jaggar 1995, Tronto 1993), is one that is yet to be fully developed. As a result, the relational perspective is inclined towards contemplating the contribution of relationality to the formation of national self-identities, while acknowledging that such identities are not teleological (due to the fact that states are driven by different purposes), unilateral (states demand feedback), or convergent (states constantly interpret and practice to continuously bifurcate). A lacuna exists with respect to the imagined dyadic resemblance in which states develop their own patterns of interaction, whether by enabling one another to bypass rules, norms or social networks supportively, or by acting recalcitrantly with the expectation of tolerance. Imagined dyadic resemblance serves as a type of improvised and negotiated resemblance, one which ontologically equalizes two parties whose practices, defiant of a power calculus, could be explained. Such non-multilateral relationships are central to neighboring countries, a local actor and an arriving major power, or any two civilizational, economic, and security stakeholders. These relationships are seen to exist almost everywhere at all times.

Confucianism provides a generalizable clue as to how to move beyond the preoccupation of the relational approach with self-subjectivities and multilateral relationalities. On the one hand, Confucian relationality constitutes self-identity by restraining or even renouncing self-subjectivity. The improvisation of this relationship does not aim at self-fulfillment; rather, it advocates for a greater social self to the effect that neither party involved can act without considering the other's interests or feelings. The actors improvise and consider their co-dependency intuitively. Consequently, self-fulfillment or any egocentric self-understanding becomes counter-productive to survival under circumstances where it exposes the state as an apparent target to be balanced against, converted, or invaded. This logic of practice, while not unique to Confucianism, is well-suited to Confucian thought that opens up an epistemologically-oriented relationality, which is practically familiar and yet under-theorized.

On the other hand, Confucianism is particularly sensitive toward how two related selves can compromise to give rise to a greater dyadic self-identity. The relational self thus requires a reflexive agent, with greater self-consciousness or -imagination—as opposed to a pregiven subjectivity—constituting its identity. Confucianism examines how the construction of a role that reflects such a higher-level self can further transform a multilateral condition into a bilateral relationship. For example, through Xi Jinping's proposition of developing a new "type of major power relations" with the United States (US), Beijing arguably seeks to establish resemblance with Washington on the basis of a common role obligation of respecting each other's core interests. This bilateral proclivity further explains how countries, when in a multilateral context, may opt to not assume a position on an issue. Here, there are three possibilities: inaction in the form of absence or abstention to avoid embarrassing bilateral relations; posting a model for the audience to emulate in a suggestive but non-interventionist manner; and mediation between contending positions. Even so, a dyadic relationship enables all kinds of creative arrangements to allow for the formation of an active, greater self-consciousness. In contrast, within a multilateral setting, such creative arrangements are more difficult to fashion given the number of different parties involved.

In sum, BoR theory speaks to the relational turn in current IR scholarship through the shared ontological assumption that relations precede the state. It also stresses the seven following principles:

1   Universality: Self-restraint is a universal feature of IR, rather than an attribute primarily applicable to Western liberal states.
2   Consciousness: BoR explains how and why states consciously manage their relationships. Western relational IR explains state actions and interactions without requiring them to consciously understand how their purposes are relationally constituted.

3   Bilateralism: Bilaterally improvised resemblance, as opposed to prior multilateral resemblance, is the indispensable focus of the study of relationships. In the relational IR literature, prior/unowned relations constitute national self-identities, and a state within a BoR context navigates multiple bilateral relationships.

4   Sociology: Relationality involves the intersubjective processes of role-taking and altercasting, as well as the psychological processes of identity creation. The latter may reproduce state-centrism oriented towards self-fulfillment and the reproduction of the 'self-other' relationship, but which sits alongside BoR theory's focus on the emergence of a greater self-consciousness.

5   Cyclicality: The improvisation of bilateral relations is a dialectic and non-synthetic (i.e. layered) process, and is founded upon cyclical imaginations. It thus differs from mainstream IR theories that are largely predicated on a teleological and linear understanding of history, and oriented towards the construction of synchronizing, universal rules.

6   Possibility of exiting a relationship: Bilateralism permits state actors to exit a relationship or concede to a certain status quo. BoR focuses on the ways through which actors exercise patience, instead of striving for unenforceable resemblance. This emphasis contrasts with synchronic and systemic conceptualizations of relationality that create resembling states.

7   Judgment: This is an intrinsic element of BoR theory that allows for a considerable degree of epistemological fluidity not currently recognized in the existing IR literature. In practice, all states may, depending on their normative judgments of the prevailing situation, shift between activating BoR, BoP or another such mechanism.

Structure of the book

This book flows from the theoretical propositions of BoR, through a history of thought that situates BoR—along with the processual mechanisms that states practicing BoR rely on to make judgments—within a broader philosophical lineage, and finally toward a post-Western analysis of a geo-cultural site that is necessarily constituted by relationality. The book enriches contemporary IR theory in three fundamental ways: first, it adds a temporal sensibility to the exclusively spatial curiosities of current theorization models. Second, it treats human judgment as an important component of theoretical explanation. Third, it diminishes the artificial divide between the West and China into a universally-plausible system of dual epistemologies, with each activated and suppressed depending on the prevailing context.

Chapter 1 begins with the core theoretical propositions of BoR. BoR is conceptualized here as a system within which reciprocally-related states avoid the implications of anarchy/disorder by stabilizing long-term inter-relationships through self-restraint. Self-restraint is thus considered as a rational strategy. Here, a state might readily concede or compromise once it has determined whether the other party's intentions are benevolent or not malicious; or it may choose to confront the other party when the converse is perceived. When negative intent is observed from another party, a state may also be moved to restore the jeopardized relationship—either amending or destroying it altogether. The decision to concede or confront is, therefore, not based on a judgment of relative power, but rather on the perceived sustainability of the long-term relationship. BoR functions best in bilateral interactions, where improvisation of ways of self-restraint bypasses multilateral rules to cope with grievances, inconveniences, or sanctions that may be caused in a multilateral setting. A BoR-based system of states amounts to a network of multiple bilateral relationships, reminiscent of those that similarly exist in the domestic political sphere.

Such a relationship-driven system neutralizes the absolute concern for power that exists under realist projections of international anarchy. Assuming that all states have an interest in maintaining stable and secure relationships, the size of a country ceases to be a primary determinant of expected behavior. Chapter 2 demonstrates this by reviewing how small states can be equally active actors in the face of (materially) stronger states. It also questions the conventional IR wisdom that small states invariably prefer multilateral interaction to bilateral ones. This case further challenges the findings of both the Western and Chinese relational turns, where the construction of relationality is seen to result in positive emotions. This chapter reveals how small states—and states in general—are sensitive to how the other party evaluates their performance and responds, with anxiety serving as the predominant emotion. As such, exchanges like gift-giving become a common approach to affirm and reaffirm goodwill. Only when the personalization of a relationship occurs, does IR inspire passion. Even so, personalization is not a necessary condition for BoR to take place and succeed.

Nevertheless, major powers differ from small states insofar as they have the option to also act on behalf of the global community, whether in enforcing or undermining specific international rules. Chapter 3 compares the 'stylistic' differences between the grand strategies of two major powers—the United States and China—and demonstrates two different types of altercasting in relational politics. The identity-based grand strategy that the United States adopts exerts rule-based altercasting that calls for intervention. In comparison, the relationship-based altercasting that China adopts avoids rules. The grand strategy of a relational actor is to achieve as much acceptance as possible among its peers, as opposed to bringing about a particular world order. This contradicts neoliberal IR thought, especially its proclivity toward interventionism.

BoR makes up a universal system, even though not all states explicitly or consciously adopt relational sensibilities. Chapter 4 illustrates how BoR is an intellectually accessible resource to all states, insofar as proper drivers are present to generate a shift in their ontological imagination. This chapter enlists the KSP and its philosophical concept of nothingness to show how BoR, together with the postcolonial and nothingness schools, integrates an aversion to the practice and theorization of IR, as embedded in a rule-based order. Moreover, a rising power that lacks a fixed conception of world order and a declining hegemonic power lacking the ability to enforce it are inclined to implement bilateralism. With shifts among ontologies discursively possible, a cyclical perspective on history becomes a plausible substitute for a teleological view.

An additional intellectual resource from the Chinese, and broader Asian, context—Buddhism—further clarifies Chinese understandings of relationality and self-restraint. This is exemplified in Chapter 5 through an examination of China's quest to good governance under strict government control, whilst also insisting on a non-interventionist policy regarding other state's failing governance. Neo-Confucian thought in modern Chinese history, and the Xi Jinping leadership in the 21st century, have adopted the Buddhist wisdom that only the transcendent mind can avoid reductionism in materialism, and that the transcendent mind can only be achieved internally. This, in part, resonates curiously with the Chinese notion that meaningful intervention can happen through domestic struggle. Such a view that paints the state of nature as being characterized by suffering, and of transcendence as occurring in cycles, speaks to a relational theory that values patience and long-termism over immediate, short-term responses.

Just as Buddhism enables internal activism, so Confucianism discourages external activism. This underlying concept of patience gives rise to the temporal dimension of relational thought that is largely overlooked in Western IR theories, which tend to be more anchored in the logic of spatiality. Global governance, for one, breeds a proclivity towards interventionism that seeks to synchronize practices across borders. Predicated on a liberal governmentality that treats sites as a simultaneously existing presence, global governance makes the external grafting of international institutions onto domestic ones possible. By contrast, Confucianism advocates for a conservative, non-interventionist philosophy that emphasizes the construction of localized orders. It is open to accepting any type of functioning order, focusing more on the importance of (re)establishing order from disorder. In light of this, Chapter 6 unpacks the idea of Confucian governability, which brings into relief the notion that countries have a prior responsibility to wait, contending that an (over)emphasis on the responsibility to protect can be dangerous as it can impede spontaneous, local forces of order restoration. Here, Confucian governability acknowledges the impossibility of a perpetual peace, but remains optimistic that order can continue to emerge from disorder in a cyclical pattern through the maintenance of a legitimate working relationship.

Given that BoR is intellectually accessible and applicable to all countries, the decision to adopt a relational foreign policy, as opposed to a realist or liberal one, can prove to be almost intuitive. Chapter 7 draws on four cases from the Qing Dynasty to illustrate how cultural memory had acted as a mechanism that framed China's experiences of joining European international society. Cultural memory is shown to orient China towards a choice between developing a civilizational relationship that encourages mingling, and a cultural relationship that reproduces the binary. The cultural memory mechanism displayed at the moment of China's entry into international society in the 19th century is repeated with China's decision to participate in global governance in the aftermath of the Cultural Revolution. Cultural memory provides a frame to analyze what relational orientation is to be deemed rational in the long-term, even when it defies the logic of power politics. For example, a decision to confront in the 1860s, despite the certainty of losing, worked to preserve the imagined binary of China and the West. The practice has since undergirded a relational position that re-emerged repeatedly over the course of the next century.

Confronting a stronger party to rectify the relationship—or at least make a statement that encourages future efforts to restore just relations—is not usually expected in practice. The lack of opportunity can be intimidating, such that even countries cognizant of the importance of relational security may still yield to the calculus of power. Chapter 8 identifies three psychological mechanisms that enable weaker parties to adopt a confrontational approach in order to restore a relationship that is considered to have been violated by the other party. The first mechanism is 'efficacy for peace', referring to the weaker party's sense of being able to control the unfolding of the situation and ensure the continuation of peaceful relations. The second is the 'determination mechanism', which enables the weaker party to resist regardless of the outcome. The third is the 'legitimacy mechanism', whereupon the weaker party's decision to resist is imbued with political correctness and lawfulness.

The subjective nature of relationality ironically emphasizes the intersubjective process of altercasting, which in turn speaks to the unilateral tendency of countries acting on behalf of the bilateral or greater relationship. While nations mediate the effects of international anarchy as disorder by securing stable relationships, the stronger power may still rely on its internal resources to carve out portraits of resemblance that define the 'proper' practices of relation. Chapter 9 examines two kinds of unilateralism in relational IR: the first is uni-multilateralism, as represented by the US, where a unilateral approach is adopted in order to achieve a multilateral order. The other is uni-bilateralism, represented by China, where the unilateral approach is used to promote a bilateral order. China's application of uni-bilateralism sheds light on how relationality remains an unresolved puzzle in practical terms, considering how the other party is unlikely to appreciate the practical contradiction between the approach and the pursued order.

The last section addresses the equivocal identity of BoR as a theory. The first question it poses is whether or not BoR constitutes a non-Western theory. At a time when there is a call for a global IR discipline, coupled with the growing acknowledgment of non-Western IR's significance, how can the Chinese cultural underpinnings of BoR be recognized as non-Western? Given the postcolonial celebration of hybridity, which is central to global IR's promotion of sited identity, its agential appropriation of Western IR for sited purposes, and the consequential re-worlding of these sited identities, the temporal sensibility and cyclical view of history adopted by BoR can hardly belong. On the contrary, BoR implicitly identifies the dangers of highlighting sitedness, cautioning against an obsession with difference, spatiality, sited integration, and synthesis. Chapter 10 enlists post-hybridity to remind us of the dangers of reductionism in the construction of sited identity. Post-hybridity favors the notions of multilayeredness, cycles, and resemblance, so as to enable the conceptual flexibility required of role-playing, epistemological shifts, and self-restraint. BoR is thus an uneasy partner of post-Western IR.

A post-hybrid or post-Western identity is unnecessarily acceptable in the post-colonial world. As China rises, rival Taiwan lost the economic and strategic advantages it once enjoyed during the Cold War. Its 'advanced' economic status vis-à-vis China used to be defined against an Anglophone standard taken from capitalism, democracy, and the Western alliance system. Increasingly, such a sense of superiority suffers as China rises and has received compensation from an intellectual indebtedness that is owed to Taiwan's highly Americanized IR. In Chapter 11, the denial of any plausible Chinese IR and downplay of its relevance from the Western IR perspective is examined with respect to Taiwan's quest to establish a relational dichotomy between China and Taiwan qua the West. It sets up the correct relationship between Taiwan and China to be one of civilizational hierarchy with Taiwan on top. By contrast, Chinese IR is intellectually threatening because it may expose Taiwan's unwanted (by some, not all) Chinese identity, one which could undermine Taiwan's current strategy of distancing itself from China. BoR, if applied in the Taiwanese case, is thus an uneasy partner of Chinese IR.

The last chapter of the book takes on the general and universal appeal of BoR theory. It also seeks a plausible place for the theory within Western IR, in addition to its multiple and fluid non-Western, Chinese, and non-Chinese identities. Likewise, espousing the ideas of relationality, self-restraint, and non-linear historiography, the notion of *tianxia*, which is extensively discussed among Chinese scholars, has made its way into the Western scholarship. However, this concept has failed to attract sufficient support, and it has even incurred animosity within certain circles. Hence, this chapter explores the journey of *tianxia*, along with Sun Tzu's classic work *The Art of War*, as two examples of Eastern theories travelling to the West. Four routes of this journey are identified—outdated, collusive, exotic, and contemporary. BoR, if it were to become accepted as a general theory, is thus an uneasy partner of Western IR.

Note

1 See Confucius' discussion on benevolence and filial piety in the chapter on "Xueer" in *The Confucian Analects* (Author n.a.).

Part 1
Balance of relationships

1 Relationality versus power politics

As China's power grows, it is worthwhile to examine if current IR theory can explain its relations with major powers, such as the US and the EU, and smaller neighboring states. In the spring of 2013, when the then newly-inaugurated leaders of two great power nations—Chinese President Xi Jinping and US President Barack Obama—met, Obama had raised a range of global governance issues related to human rights, climate change and cybersecurity, whereas Xi sought to promote his notion of a "new type of great power relations". Obama's strategy seemed to be predominantly grounded in idealism, as he pushed for universal criteria to guide each governance issue, and possibly by a degree of realism, motivated by a desire to impose more pressure on a rising US competitor. Regardless, Xi seemed uninterested in negotiating these universal principles of governance and appeared almost insensitive to the relevance of different values to the Sino-US relationship. Rather, he suggested that the two powers establish an amiable relationship independent of their differences, one that avoids the confrontation expected of a possible power transition within a bipolar system (Calmes & Myers 2013).

At almost the same time, a similar if not sharper contrast between universal principles and relational concerns could be found in the China–European Union (EU) relationship, exemplified by the chronic issue of the arms embargo (Ministry of Foreign Affairs of the People's Republic of China or PRC 2013). In the face of China's unsatisfactory human rights conditions, the embargo served as a strategy to actualize the EU's self-image of being a "normative power" (EU Official 2003). However, for China, a bilateral relationship can never be normal under the circumstance of an embargo. The EU's pursuit for a rule-based international society may prompt suspicion that China has never been judged as an equal of the EU (Kavalski 2013).

In addition to failing to respond with any defensive counter principle to cope with US and EU pressure, China—viewed as either a global bipolar power or a hierarchical regional power—tends to deny its own legitimacy of pursuing unilateral control over smaller neighbors. For example, China has refused to intervene in North Korea, even when facing the provocation of nuclear proliferation. A popular realist explanation suggests that China needs North Korea to balance against South Korea and the US (Bajoria 2010). This account fails to explain why China is far from effective or sufficiently active in assuaging North Korea's recalcitrance to rejoin the negotiation table in earnest. Rather, China shifted towards a strategy that sought to engage and work with the US. Alternative realist wisdom suggests that this can be explained by China's desire for North Korea's natural resources; however, this explanation is undercut by the fact that China actually supplies natural resources to North Korea (Lin 2009). Contrary to these speculations, US President Donald Trump affirmed that Xi had once briefed him about his difficult position, revealing that the difficulty laid primarily in the long and complicated relationship between Beijing and Pyongyang (*Wall Street Journal* 2017).

Moving southwards, China appears entangled in a maritime dispute with Vietnam, yet the dispute has not prevented a bilateral agreement of strategic partnership between the two governments and a joint drill of maritime rescue between the two navies from taking place (Ma 2012). Even more strikingly, China's relations with Myanmar have survived the ideological incongruence, contradicting size, opposing alliance, border and ethnic disputes, global intervention, and internal upheavals on both sides, to the extent that Myanmar has not resorted to either balancing or bandwagoning (Roy 2005). Their bilateral relations call for an unconventional explanation.

Contrary to Washington's perceptions, increase in China's power has not pushed it to commit to an idea of establishing a sphere of influence, including the South China Sea where Washington has perceived a China threat. China's rebuttal hinges on the claim that no incident has ever occurred in the area that hinders free passage, reflects the logic that ensuring free passage has nothing to do with power. Instead, China is inclined toward the dyadic arrangements between China and each of all others. China's stylistic pursuit of bilateral relationships with smaller neighbors as well as the ASEAN is consistent with its stress on bilateral relationships with the US and EU, regardless of the power status of the other side, although the issue area and substance of the relationship sought in each case vary.

According to the conventional wisdom, the foreign policy of all nations, including China, is driven by energy security (Collins et al. 2008, Copeland 1996, Lampton 2008, Ziegler 2006), China's insistence on non-interventionism to the effect that it has lost vital sources of energy, as in the case of Libya (Piao 2011) is hard to explain. In Africa, China gave its consent to UN intervention in Sudan and Liberia in 2003 and 2007, despite them being China's major suppliers of oil and timber, respectively. Notably, China's consent was given only after securing the approval of regional organizations (i.e. the African Union and the Economic Community of West African States). These regional organizations, which appear so marginally in mainstream IRT, have proven critical to the settlements reached between China, the UN, and local authorities.

A theory to explain a rising China's consistent practices of gift-giving as well as its relative disinterest in global governance principles is thus needed. Explanations from within China draw on the notions of peaceful coexistence, a harmonious world, and a peaceful development; however, these fail to explain cases where China has not hesitated to resort to limited sanctions or coercion. Neither Vietnam, the Philippines, nor Taiwan is likely to characterize China's maritime policy as harmonious. Nevertheless, China has demonstrated a seemingly counterintuitive refrain from taking territories where it has an upper hand, as in the case of North Korea and Myanmar, while exercising military determination where it has no capacity or even intention for immediate take over, as in the South China Sea, East China Sea, or Taiwan Straits.

This chapter explains theoretically the relational concerns in Chinese foreign policy and their implications for understanding IR. We argue that Chinese foreign policy is guided by the principles of BoR, and relationship is defined as the process of mutual constitution. States achieve mutual constitution by way of improvising imagined resemblances between them. BoR stresses the key concepts of practice, self-restraint, and bilaterality. It reflects a systemic commitment by states to avoid disorder under anarchy by seeking long-term reciprocal IR, regardless of prior differences in values, institutions, and power status.

BoR differs to BoP, where self-help typically characterizes foreign policy. Self-restraint is what informs foreign policy under BoR. A state relies on self-restraint to acquire all kinds of relationships and may revoke self-restraint to rectify a relationship that is perceived as unsustainable or wrong. In addition, offering of benevolence makes a proactive kind of self-restraint. This is called gift-giving in the Sinosphere, but we argue that BoR transcends Chinese conditions. Through this facilitation of self-restraint, the relational constitution of the state reduces disorder between separate states. BoR theory surpasses civilizational divides and the epistemological gap between rationality and culture by always searching for localized or even individualized routes to access BoR.

Most theories perceive IR as structures independent of the maneuvering of individual nations. Specifically, these theories always consider power as a property, never a relation (Baldwin 2004). Alternatively, BoR considers a state as the agent of relationships. We reiterate Giddens's (1984) structuration theory and perceive BoR as a structurational mechanism recognizing the relevance of strategic choices of a state in reproducing or revising IR to constantly redefine the state, through the multiple and changing dimensions of relationality. Nevertheless, we do not treat the agent as a pregiven. Rather, we consider the agent as a constituted identity, rendering agential identities unstable at best and contingent upon the relationships incurred. The notion of "relationship" treats the phenomenon of the double standard in all countries' foreign policies as a systemic necessity. This treatment provides a universal frame to explain inconsistency in foreign policy, which other IRTs easily throw into the theoretically irrelevant category of idiosyncrasy or hypocrisy (Hui 2005, Yan 2011).

Self-restraint: statist and Confucian

IR can be more conveniently dealt with where states perceive resemblance to one another in terms of their shared identity, rules of conduct, or necessities of power. Contemporary IRTs emphasize these imagined strings of resemblance between states. However, at times, states may defy a presumably shared identity, agreed upon rules, or power structure. Instead of reducing these incidents to idiosyncratic reasons, BoR theory aims to explain how these cases of defiance or double standard follow a plausible logic that is equally, if not more, convincing and attractive to states in the face of unwanted disorder in the imagined condition of anarchy. Imperfect politics of identity, rule making, and structuration compose a systemic incentive for states to resort to the strategy of BoR. By opening the state to relationality, IRT informed by BoR presents the rationale for a predominant number of those acting in the name of the state to deviate from the established patterns registered in other strings of IRT.

Our relational sensibilities are distinct from other positions arising out of the relational turn in social science. The relational turn generally disputes substantialism that regards actors or agents as ontologically pre-given (Crossley 2010, Donati 2010, Emirbayer 1997). However, no consensus has been reached on the extent to which actors are external to the process of engaging in reflexive or even subconscious selection to remain being a self (Burkitt 2016, Depelteau 2008, 2013, Selg 2016). The relational turn in IR has not attended to such a debate in which the literature consistently treats states as reflexive actors or agents (Breiger et al. 2014, Cranmer, Heinrich & Desmarais 2014, Perliger & Pedahzur 2011). Chinese scholars subscribing to Confucianism would handle such a debate hypothetically by assuming that all agents and actors are part of the little selves together making an unthinking greater self. Little self is relational in the sense that the imagined greater self, by its own nature, constitutes each little self, which is capable of reflexive decision making. The reflexive decision making of a little self indirectly aids in actualizing the greater self in one way or another.

The Anglophone agenda with respect to the relational turn practically analyzes how actors are likely to behave according to their relational constitution, as informed by an imagined prior resemblance. By contrast, the Chinese agenda is preoccupied with how actors consciously contribute to the construction and reproduction of an imagined greater self, embedded in shared ancestors, which is too thin to guide actions without constant improvisation of relations in accordance with occasions. On the Chinese agenda, the agency of the actor lies in reciprocating between little selves to reproduce imagined resemblance that defines the greater self. Reciprocating symbolizes the existence of only one collective self. This certainly needs reconfirmation from time to time. The caveat is that abortion of reconfirmation could incur political control. Without conscious reconfirmation, however, the little self could lose reflexivity and harm the greater self and all other little selves constituted by the greater self.

Nevertheless, an implicit consensus exists between the Anglophone and the Sinophone relations. That is, no state can afford to practice pure unilateralism, not even the US during the prime of its hegemony or China during the peak of the Cultural-Revolution autarky. Unilateralism has only been applicable in the short-run and on specific issues. Moreover, it often exists more in rhetoric than in practice, being ultimately reliant on altercasting, which cannot occur in isolation from other actors. This book regards self-restraint as a meaningful point of connection between the two epistemologies. The universal virtue and practice of self-restraint, epistemologically differently informed at various geocultural sites, testifies to a systemic force everywhere that allows only those capable of self-restraint to survive evolution. Translating the meaning of Confucian self-restraint philosophically and empirically is key to the Confucian contribution to IR theorization.

Self-restraint serves as a norm that has been emphasized in statism and communitarianism, and it is similarly treated as a virtue in Christianity and Confucianism. Nevertheless, disparities exist between them in philosophical, institutional, and practical terms, resulting in diverse foreign-policy motivations. The liberal understanding of self-restraint acknowledges individuals' prior given rights to pursue their respective interests. It functions most powerfully among resembling strangers belonging to the same community of practice, where it serves to organize individuals into synchronized role players, in order to prevent them from encroaching on others' rights. Reaffirming the notion of mutual and self-respect, liberal self-restraint confirms the self-worth of every actor, hence the reproduction of an imagined self-subjectivity that independently determines national identity and confidently expects acceptance.

Relational identification confirmed by the voluntary observance of certain unowned, yet established, values and procedures among strangers ensures relations among these actors through the practice of shared norms. An implicit metaphor of domestic civic nationalism is noted, whereby citizens of different ethnic backgrounds develop joint loyalty to a state that enforces a particular set of social procedures irrespective to ethnicity. At international level, without a central authority to regulate interstate relations, self-restraint reflects the needs of states to mitigate anarchy and the potential disorder that comes with it. Constructivism falls back on this understanding of state agency to arrive at the realization that self-restraint is rational. However, for those cases where prior resemblance is lacking in general or inadequate in context, BoR adds the study of improvised relation to the relational turn. Without a prior consensus on rules or norms, enactment

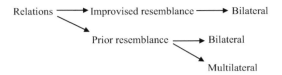

Figure 1.1 Two Kinds of Relationality
Source: Authors

of resemblance has to almost entirely rely on gift giving of all sorts, such as zero interest loan, territorial concession, or support in an event. A properly devised benefit for the other state symbolizes and enacts resemblance of certain role identities, e.g. comradeship, brotherhood, and partnership, whose prior consensus is thin (Figure 1.1).

Confucian self-restraint is such an acknowledgement of a "greater self" whose survival and wellbeing are the utmost priority. This greater self is practically thin and usually expressed through and reinforced by the metaphor of family. Confucian self-restraint incurs self-sacrifice, so it does not involve a reciprocal duty to exchange one's own rights with those of equal others. Rather, it is an absolute duty to ensure the survival of the greater self and thus requires the suppression of self-worth. This sense of duty necessitates the reciprocal self-restraint toward others, who presumably resemble one another in terms of their relationship with the greater self. Self-restraint that contributes to other little selves is always idiosyncratic, as opposed to communities of strangers abiding to universal values and procedures. Relational security arising from belonging to the greater self transcends differences in ethnicity, regime type, power, and religion. The coexistence of differences is preserved by shunning the synchronization of specific thought foundations, such as liberalism.

Multilateral settings deprive Confucian actors of the legitimacy to pursue their own interests or enforce an allegedly universal value, lest these policies damage the greater self-identity among varieties. Consequently, Confucian self-restraint becomes a ritual in addition to a virtue. It is a required ritual in multilateral settings so as to reproduce relations among varieties. A bilateral setting makes only a slight difference from a multilateral one to a relationally minded liberal who exerts self-restraint, as the same procedures and values are observed to apply to both contexts, governing how an actor relates to strangers and associates alike. Under Confucianism, an actor achieves relational security through a shared practice of self-sacrifice, usually incurring specifically crafted gifts or favors. The exercise of self-restraint—understood as either concessions or sanctions in this book—vis-à-vis another specific state is tantamount to an invitation to form or reconfirm the existence of a specific greater self with the target state.

A cyclical view of history results from the use and withdrawal of self-restraint, with the former aimed at consolidating the greater self and the latter at rectifying a distorted greater self. Resembling little selves are equalized in their reciprocal contribution to the greater self. BoP can be deliberately disregarded at any moment to demonstrate the determination to ultimately protect the greater self. The stronger party can appear timid and the weaker party, aggressive. This is why the system of BoR can neutralize power disparity.

Theoretical propositions of BoR

The BoR addresses the dynamics of how two actors keep each other engaged in their imagined resemblance, constantly improvised by and for them to address general situations or in the face of a particular perceived incongruence. BoR, which is typically rationalized by Confucianism in China, is both a system that defines and constrains China as state in the world and a strategy that maintains balanced relationships for China. Here "system" denotes the universal need and capacity of nations to have stable relations with each other (Pan 2018). BoR is a major processual mechanism to reify the agency of state in imagining and crafting resemblance to constitute an inalienable part of the state. In particular, under the Confucian condition, BoR harmonizes a bilateral relationship more manageable than a multilateral relationship since the pressure for rule-binding is much less in the former situation. For subscribers of Confucianism, greater self-consciousness in a multilateral relationship exists between the mutually self-restraining head of the greater self and each little self, not abstractly among all the self-restraining related strangers as imagined by communitarianism domestically or relational statism internationally. Rationality of the little self prioritizes the welfare for the greater self. The little self calculates, but not as a distinctive entity external to the greater self. Rather, its calculus is a simultaneous testimony to greater self-consciousness.

China's pragmatic appeal to and reliance on relational epistemology have dragged the country to a peculiar version of realist BoP. In terms of relationality, China's quest for security cannot involve an expansion of its own influence or an increase in its own capacity for control without harming its many dyadic relationships. Immediate and concrete gains are thus considered less useful than stable relationships, which are often achieved even at the expense of such immediate and concrete gains. To that extent, even harmony can be legitimately renounced immediately if the purpose is to restore a relationship. Throughout modern history, the Legalist wisdom, which supplements Confucianism [in China], taught to rely on severe punishment during times of chaos.

Using the ubiquitous and spontaneous need for stable relationships as basis, we propose the following three principles of BoR for any two actors to craft a pragmatic resemblance in terms of their common interest calculus, especially during a dispute, as if they can always improvise for a stable relationship.

1   When a condition is perceived as potentially threatening, resort to compromise to repair it. This strategy is to balance an almost revoked resemblance with enhanced self-restraint to restore the relationship as if it was never under challenge. Self-restraint aims at enabling the other relational self to similarly exert self-restraint.
2   When a condition is perceived as already directly threatening, resort to breakup to start anew. This strategy is to balance the breach of relationship by revoking China's self-restraint. This revoking of self-restraint is intended to destroy a corrupt relationship so that follow-up improvisations of new resemblance can only move toward an improved relationship.
3   When a condition is perceived as indirectly threatening, resort to a mix of punishment and repair to rectify it. This strategy is to balance the revoked resemblance with enhanced self-restraint in one (issue/geographical) area or period and the revoking of self-restraint in another. China's act of balance aspires preservation of flexibility to prepare for the situation to improve or exacerbate it.

BoR explains the limited relevance in Chinese philosophy of differences in ideas, institutions, identities, and material forces as key variables in IR, because these can readily be disregarded for the sake of long-term stability. BoR is in direct contrast with the pursuit of a synchronized world or regional order. *Synchronization* is the derivative of rationalism and universalism, and it informs most general theories in IR. Synchronization refers to the simultaneously executed or promoted diffusion of a pattern of rationality embedded in an idea, an institution, a collective identity, or a perceived arrangement of material force. Synchronization is a process whereby unrelated national actors conjunctionally fulfill their systemically (or, alternatively, relationally) assigned functions in order to interact rationally. By contrast, BoR is a systemic belief exempt from synchronized rationality. It shuns varieties, each embedded in its geo-cultural trajectory and its relational history. BoR prescribes ontological irrelevance and epistemological sensibility for China in the imagination in which all are bound to relate in their own forms that are inevitably transient. Ontology refers to what constitutes the agent, whereas epistemology is how the agents understand.

BoR predicts that national actors will not consistently adhere to any specific synchronic ways of rationality in the long run. Rather, national actors will always try to achieve stabilized bilateral relationships regardless of how deterministic or opportunistic they may appear in their pursuit of security, prosperity, global governance, and peace. Thus, Chinese foreign policy may appear to be deliberately making multilateral relations volatile, because a multilateral frame is usually dependent on certain universal rules in order to function. Chapters 2 and 9 attend to the bilateral nature of IR in general and BoR in particular, implying inconsistency in enforcing one's own values when facing different countries at different times. This nature is also elucidated when the different style of grand strategic thinking between China and the US is compared in Chapter 3.

Chinese BoR as a systemic principle

Long-term rationality of non-apparent interests

Given Confucianism's proclivity for long-term and relational thinking, Confucian lessons for foreign policy tend to contradict mainstream IRT. Orthodox approaches share the same epistemological individualism that focuses on a state. Each of these schools of thought perceives the foreign policy of all states as in pursuit of a synchronized set of national interests, which includes structurally determined security and power for realism on the one hand (Waltz 1979), and welfare and institution for liberalism on the other hand (Keohane & Nye 1987). The synchronic kind of national interests also includes non-structured, mutually negotiated, but collectively applicable goods for constructivism, such as Wendt's (2003) Kantian culture of anarchy. To a certain extent, the English School adopts societal thinking and emphasizes the impacts of diverse civilizations and cultures (Bull 1977, Buzan 2004). However, concerns for common rules and systemic stability continue to echo the synchronic style of theorization despite that the English School's definition of the international system allows room for a state to manipulate relationships (Bull 1977), learn gradually, and assimilate eventually.

In comparison, Confucianism is concerned with the preparation of foreign policy for relationality, mutuality, embeddedness, and contextuality, unfailingly making Sinicization, historical and contemporary, an all-directional movement void of destiny (Katzenstein 2012).[1] Accordingly, China is hardly a distinctive analytical entity (Callahan 2004). These cultural processes either introduce or rejuvenate Chinese worldviews as defined by the values of harmony, group orientation, and *guanxi* culture (Qin 2009a). *Guanxi* is particularly pertinent to BoR. It refers to the cultural belief, as in the tradition of sociological literature on network theory (Archer 1996, Eliasoph & Lichterman 2003, Vaisey & Lizardo 2010) that nations cannot survive without coupling their existence to one another in certain mutually agreed and practiced relationships. The quest for *guanxi* makes self-restraint an intrinsic component in any rational, bilateral exchange. Here, we follow the constructivist call to establish the link between ideas and rationality (Finnemore & Sikkink 1998) and examine the Chinese foreign policy that serves non-apparent national interests.

Non-apparent national interests are interests that presumably secure apparent rational/national interests in the long run. One particular non-apparent interest refers to control over uncertainty in relationships, which is aimed at stabilizing these apparent national interests. Stabilized relationships presumably exempt China from uncertainties, compelling Chinese leaders to constantly test the intention of others. The archetypal interest of IR liberalism in institutionalization likewise lowers the transaction cost of negotiation in the long run (Keohane 1984, 1987). The Confucian emphasis on stability is methodologically consistent with IR liberal rationality that neutralizes the uncertainty caused by distrust. Even realist IR has a similar emphasis because one of its pedagogical models, the prisoner's dilemma, prefers cooperation over betrayal, although by betrayal one loses less in the short run (Axelrod 1984). This kind of long-run calculation is consistent with the notion of hedging, which does not produce any immediate gain other than risk-averting utility.

Although all are capable of long-term calculation, the major difference between the Chinese BoR and other IRTs lies in the former's readiness to avoid specific standards of calculation. The logic of apparent national interests under liberalism and realism requires a clear and universally applied base of calculation, such as power or wealth. However, Confucian disciples may at times believe that no calculation is long-lasting enough, making calculation and its base trivial. Patience, instead of justice or order, is sought for when there is no evident solution to an embarrassing setting of incongruence. Reliance on a stabilized relationship, compared with calculation of interest for any length of time ahead, is always a culturally preferred approach of Chinese foreign policy. Chapter 7 discusses the logic of cultural memory to illustrate the ultimate relational security, reproducing the cultural belief that states cannot survive without coupling their welfare, leadership, and security to one another. Self-restraint is rational and relational simultaneously.

Chinese strategic calculus can also be realist. Alastair Iain Johnston (1995) formulated a strategic culture argument based on his investigation of China's *Seven Military Classics*. He concluded that the parabellum paradigm may be observed in both the Chinese classics and Ming dynasty practice. Yuan-kang Wang (2010), along with Johnston, further demonstrated that pedagogical nurturing is not required for Chinese literati to adopt realpolitik thought and practice and advocated that realism is an inescapable imperative, independent of cultural construction. Hui (2012) concluded that Chinese culture is made up of more than just Confucianism, which makes pacifism far from dominant in Chinese foreign policy making.

Nevertheless, the parabellum paradigm is not a culturally preferable solution to Confucianism's quest for security, probably because it only addresses an emergent need. If Confucian long-term calculation relies on the conviction that stable relationships should always prosper in the extreme long run, then a pattern of foreign policy in frequent violation of mundane calculation is expected. Moreover, whether the totality of national interests in the long run is calculable is not a question of rationality in itself but rather a matter of cultural memory, which breeds a different attitude toward time. In the case of Chinese foreign policy, a stabilized relationship is taken as a convenient and reassuring indicator of long-term national interests. The non-apparent national interests that guide China's rationality are primarily long-term conditions in which all countries' apparent national interests will have a stable, that is, relational foundation to build on, meaning they are not immediately subject to estimation. In short, all are bound to relate, so they must craft relations out of all imagined kinds of resemblance to oblige mutual favors, exemptions, and, at times, sanctions.

Since the national interest calculus is centered on the preservation of stable relationships to minimize future uncertainty; the ways to convince other states of one's sincerity toward stability becomes critical. In practice, as illustrated by the examples in later chapters, peaceful harmony is achieved only if both sides apply self-restraint in a mutually compatible and trustworthy manner. Self-restraint that is unilaterally practiced and imposed by China can be ironically threatening or confusing to other parties. Such kind of altercasting is discussed in Chapter 3 and its resulting style of uni-bilateralism is elaborated in Chapter 9. China has demonstrated its ability to resort to confrontation, including violence, from time to time when necessary, even from a weak position to show its determination to restore what it perceives to be a proper relationship. Other case studies are available in Chapter 7 and empirical tests in Chapter 8. Neither of these clues—compromise and confrontation—appear rational from the viewpoint of apparent national interest, especially in a power asymmetry where the solution should allow little room for flexibility.

Non-interventionism

China values stable relationships, therefore it will not support the type of intervention that is designed to enforce global synchronicity according to certain types of regimes (Wang & Rosenau 2009). Chapter 6 sheds light on how this is historically as well as philosophically sensible. According to David Kang (2007), China does not use intervention in neighboring countries for the purpose of conquest or the achievement of hegemony. He concluded that when China was strong, the East Asian international system remained stable and peaceful; by contrast, when China was weak, chaos and conflict was rife in East Asia. China has rarely used force to intervene in other countries (Jacque 2009). In the rare cases where force was used, China's main purpose was to restore the hierarchical relationship that had been allegedly disrupted by the target state.

Nevertheless, investment in hard power is always wise at any given moment, because bilateral relationships can continue to break down or hegemonic power can still coerce bordering states. This combination of pragmatic preparation for confrontation and pragmatic renouncement of benefits for the sake of any particular relationship is the same reason that once led the late Lucian Pye (1990) to misperceive that China perplexingly tolerates cognitive dissonance and subsequent generations of strategic culture to debate whether the Chinese have a peaceful strategic culture (Buzan 2010, Hui 2008, Johnston 1995, Mearsheimer 2006, Wang 2010).

The Chinese apply force in dealing with international crises primarily for its symbolic meaning rather than for enforcing multilateral rules, though. Whenever China, either the PRC or the imperial dynasties of the past, has resorted to military force, the country has hardly reaped substantial gains. Instead, force may be perceived as an effort of China to restore a relationship that symbolizes mutual resemblance of a certain kind. According to Adelman and Shih (1993), several meanings may be attributed to China's use of force, including eliminating a challenge to China's belonging to the greater self, signifying China's disapproval of certain events that disrupt existing relationships, signaling the emergence of a new role-identity that calls for a different relationship, managing the disruptive event by targeting an indirect target, and searching for a little self-identity to adapt to a problematic relationship. Violence is typically conceived as self-discipline or self-rectification, implying that China and its targets must have first composed a greater self in the Chinese worldview before violence can be justified in China's own eyes (Shih 2010).

John Garver (2006: 123) took a similar view in his investigation of the causes of China's war with India in 1962. He concluded that China decided to attack India because of "a belief that India's leaders did not appreciate the fact that the People's Republic of China was a 'new China' that had 'stood up' and, unlike pre-1949 'old China,' could no longer be 'bullied' and 'humiliated' by foreign powers."

Pragmatism and bilateralism

In the age of global governance, the pragmatic purpose of BoR is to find a plausible solution to the dilemma between (1) the quest for stable borders, which intervention would undermine, and (2) the quest for recognition by the global powers, which resistance to intervention would undermine. No state can avoid the synchronizing demand of global governance led by major powers, despite that the fundamental concerns for natural rights of human being that undergird resemblance between global governance nations can be perceived to be hypocritical. China has to learn to cope with interventionist forces by supporting them to the extent that is minimally required to join prior imagined resemblance between Western nations.

Since Chinese pragmatism is relational, thus defining China's style of soft power, it contributes to crafting a reputation for never deliberately standing in the way of any other state's goals. In this way, Chinese leaders wish that China may be acknowledged as non-threatening by others, even those who may dislike Chinese values or institutions. Consequently, Chinese authorities are consistently disinterested in how they differ from others as long as China achieves its acceptance by others. This suggests China's sanctions against a perceived violation would never last forever, even if no adjustment is made on the other side. The expectation that China will yield eventually and retreat from sanction policy provides an incentive to the other party to stay within a Chinese agenda. This is the essence of Chinese soft power. Chinese soft power is contrary to American soft power that prevails in IRT. American soft power emphasizes the capacity of the US to synchronize ways of rational thinking of other nations into following American values and institutions voluntarily, even if these nations may dislike the US. This disposition for synchronizing requires epistemological curiosity to discover how differences can be transformed. In contrast, BoR discourages curiosity.

In addition, BoR theory favors bilateral relationships over multilateral ones, although the theory does not preclude the multilateral BoR. It is a system composed of multiple bilateral relationships. To lead or even participate in multilateral relations requires an intervening attitude regarding how to synchronize domestic practices of all the countries (Carlson 2005), unless all relevant parties are applying BoR at the same time, as illustrated by the ASEAN (Nair 2019).[2] Any notion of the right values or procedures positions countries against one another, thus dividing them into followers and revisionists. Whenever there is a perceived revisionist, there is perceived confrontation. To enhance one's relational security, one minimal strategy is to avoid testing if anyone else is becoming a revisionist.

Engaging in bilateral relations denotes a simultaneous neutralization of multilateral synchronization so that the scenario of global interference with domestic or bilateral relationships can generate only a minimal threat. Accordingly, China does not have to resist the hegemonic order imposed by a superpower if all countries bordering China do not have to take sides between China and the superpower. Despite the compliance of a neighboring country with the hegemonic request for cooperation, it will not seek a change in its already crafted relation with China. Note that the reproduction of hierarchy in IR is usually bilateral (Lake 2009). All-round stabilized bilateral relations, though hierarchical, along the borders will resolve the threat of containment by the US. China's own bilateral relationship with the US can remain maximally non-confrontational. A bilateral relationship benefits both sides if it does not fluctuate according to the perceived power shift or emerging alliance reformation in a multilateral setting. One incident that shows salience of bilateral relationships is the case of Beijing commenting on the arms sales by Russia to India: "Both India and Russia are China's friendly neighbors.... China welcomes the growing friendly relationship between India and Russia and believes that the growing of their bilateral relationship is conducive to the world's peace and stability" (EWS 2012).

One notable Confucian dictum is particularly relevant here. Confucius recommended that a father cover for his son and a son cover for his father to achieve integrity for both. This understanding of integrity is incompatible with the request for consistency in striving for a just social order, because personal kinship has the higher priority than social justice. The resemblance of kinship does not necessarily incur liking, but it involves role-duty that requires performance. The dictum implies that Confucian relationality, embedded in such practical trust, is essential to the integrity of personality and keen to dyadic roles in question rather than any abstract duty of a member citizen toward the entire community. Relationality at all levels should simultaneously contribute to the constitution of selfhood. Nevertheless, highly contextualized and temporal bilateral relationality receives stronger care—for example, loyalty to the emperor during war is superior to filial piety to the father.

Each stable bilateral relationship has its own history and distinct features, and this is why the salience of bilateral relationships inevitably causes inconsistency between the bilateral relationships with different countries and even characterizes US foreign policy. US foreign policy often suffers the charge of hypocrisy due to its apparent use of double standards. Concluding that the US does not actually care about principles is misleading, because the BoR rationality certainly demonstrates greater tolerance towards defensive actions of allies than defectors, who tend to be placed under greater scrutiny (Gupta 1971). This is particularly relevant to both the US and China today. As a rising power experiencing expansive interactions, China cannot practically enforce any value consistently. The rebalancing of US in Asia also has to avoid promoting a single value to negotiate support from a whole range of partners. Chapter 4 presents an ontological explanation of this inevitable limit and the implications for understanding the BoR of rising and declining powers. Whenever there is a will to retrieve the loose reciprocal relationship, there is regression toward BoR.

Implications for IRT in general

The idea of BoR, originally derived from Confucianism, is to extend the horizon of BoP. BoP prescribes a state facing the rise of another power to engage in either balancing or a deviant strategy of bandwagoning. Balancing is aimed at defending against the potential aggression exerted by the rising power to maintain one's own security. Bandwagoning is aimed at joining the side of the rising power to avoid becoming its target. The goals of BoR, like BoP and bandwagoning, also include the preservation of the security of the state. Although both strategies focus on national interests, such as survival, security, and economic benefits, among other things, BoR does not take such interests as priorities or immediate ends. The belief that rational states should persevere to establish harmonious relations is the distinctive feature of BoR.

A state applies the strategy of BoR to remain connected and avoid anarchy. Anarchy is a systemic culture of independent states pursuing self-help but suffering disorder, the most extreme form of which is outbreak of war. The state wants to avoid anarchy so that it does not have to assume the enmity of other states. How to achieve the better BoR is a skill that enables parties of a relationship to craft and reproduce resemblance so as to transcend their prior differences in power, values, institutions, and so on. Each BoR is a model of practice in itself. It may lay down apparent and immediate national interests for the preservation of relationships. By contrast, the strategy of BoP or bandwagoning is often triggered by fear that external powers will threaten a state's survival. Such rationale is similar to what Thucydides described thousands of years ago—the same idea the classical realist assumption in IR theory has unremittingly followed: "The strong do what they can and the weak suffer what they must" (1874, 1996: 351–356). The motivation that underpins the BoR is completely different.

If anarchy is a system of no central authorities in which a state in solitude is compelled to adopt a self-help strategy, then relationality must be a system in which the state, protected by reciprocal self-restraint, is inclined to avoid the disruption of relationships (Qin 2009a, 2009b, 2011). Under anarchy, the foundation of strategic calculation is the capability and relative weakness in physical power resources as indicators of danger. If realists believe that states must live in anarchy and thus cannot help but resort to BoP for survival, then they can alternatively avoid disorder by acknowledging and then reproducing reciprocal relationships so that self-help actually means mutual help. The same fear toward potentially violent disorder of anarchy leads to the systemic culture of BoR on which they can rely to stay away from the challenge of survival. BoP is a systemic aptitude for realists to live with anarchy as nature, whereas BoR is a systemic resource for the rational state to avoid or suppress anarchy/disorder as an undesirable but not inevitable condition. They are parallel to each other, and abortion or failure of either leads to strategic thinking leaning toward the opposite.

If a state subscribes to a specific value (e.g., liberalism) or institution (e.g., capitalism) and acts with determination to synchronize ways of thinking of all other nations to operate IR accordingly, then BoR will predict that its determined pursuit will not continue in the long run. Under the systemic condition of BoR, nations that seek to diffuse a distinctive value or institution always require coordination with other nations and therefore inevitably act inconsistently when coping differently with complying and revisionist actors that coexist. All the inconsistencies are harbingers for the undergirded force of BoR, which pushes one to compromise on deviant behavior of a perceived ally. BoR is a peculiar systemic belief that pushes all the other systems to face their limit. There can be instances in which states stick with a particular way of rational thinking at the expense of bilateral reciprocity. However, they are always capable of retrieving reciprocity through self-restraint in the aftermath of—or during an interval in between—moments of rationality. BoR enables states to recover from exhaustion or uncertainty caused by over-commitment. Other systems of rationality based on power, institutions, or identity always need to retrieve specific bilateral relationships where systemic constraints fail to provide guidance. Chapter 4 discusses the process philosophically.

Compromises and confrontations that deviate from synchronizing forces attest to the systemic culture of BoR. Compromise is a prevalent practice anywhere and anytime. Compromise with a complying state can secure its continued support, whereas compromise with a revisionist state can stimulate feelings conducive to either future synchronization or future relationships. The latter is usually deemed as peaceful evolution or engagement. Whether compromise necessarily involves human judgment and how much to compromise compel one to think in the long and relational terms. The quest for relationships is too strong to allow synchronization to continue consistently, indiscriminately, or teleologically, alluding to relational security as a systemic incentive, and the aforementioned phenomenon of double standard and hypocrisy as a bare systemic necessity. As an indicator of the failure of a state to comply with BoP theory, inconsistency in enforcing a value or rule is actually intrinsic to BoR, because judgment and its undecidable consequences are its systemic parameters. Even the national leaders who subscribe to BoP tactics will find it rational to act with self-restraint. Joseph Nye (2013) claimed that such a policy ought to "ensure that China doesn't feel encircled or endangered.... Sometimes America's power is greater when we act with others rather than merely over others" (p. A19). Nye believes that even a superpower is capable of self-restraint for an unspecified benefit to accrue in the future.

Theoretically, BoR can be a strategy relevant to states of different power capabilities. Empirically, BoR becomes the main theme of foreign policy more easily in states whose domestic culture (politically and socially) provides strong support for the application of such a relationship-oriented strategy. BoR emphasizes the importance of reciprocal interaction and self-restraint in one's effort to craft resemblance. The goal of harmony does not signify the ethical and virtuous aspects of a state's actions. On the contrary, achieving harmony is a comprehensively realistic consideration with the hope for more future gains or less future losses by preserving positive relations with all concerned parties. Once the systemic necessity of BoR is consciously acknowledged, BoR can compose a strategy with a genuinely pragmatic logic that seriously takes national interests into account. Such logic treats the sequence of interests differently. Under BoR, every option should be pragmatically possible as long as balanced arrangements are made. Pragmatism is translated into adapting to both international conditions and the conditions of others in order to ease their worries about one's own intentions. Each nation is deemed to deserve distinctive arrangements, which are marginalized with multilateral relations whereby a universal type of norm is called for.

Indication of BoR as a general system

Quest for relational security is not merely limited to the style adopted by China or other Confucian societies, granted that Confucianism is the

Chinese way of practicing BoR. Such a quest is also neither necessarily peaceful nor necessarily violent. BoR is prevalent all over the world and throughout history. Nevertheless, scholars have not yet acknowledged BoR as systemic behavior. The reason they are hesitant to acknowledge it is two-fold: BoR predicts inconsistence rather than synchronic ways of rational thinking, and BoR guarantees no systemic consequence. In addition, the multilateral repercussions of bilateral relationships are often indirect or slow. Both compromise in a stronger position and confrontation in a weaker position provide political statements about what should be the proper relationship primarily bilaterally. However, the view on what resemblance exactly constitutes both parties is necessarily improvisational over time. All of the above are probably the reasons why although states resort to BoR all the time, students of IRT are yet to be prepared in considering BoR as a systemic culture, albeit a system of inconsistency.

Considering the notion of relational balancing to be universally defined as the pursuit for a practically governable pattern of mutually agreed reciprocal tolerance, BoR is demonstrated to be neither new nor restricted to a few Confucian cultural areas. Nevertheless, IRT has failed to acknowledge its ubiquity and longevity. Yet it is important to note that discussing how universally applicable BoR can be in IR misses the point of studying BoR; as it is mainly bilateral and contextual. Whether a stable bilateral relationship can emerge is the result of both coincidence and volition. The Confucian culture, which cherishes long-term reciprocal relationships, prepares Confucian leaders to imagine and craft a kin kind of resemblance instead of BoP or balance of interest. Each culture has its own route to such a realization, and this is why BoR differs from repeated prisoners' dilemmas or transaction–cost institutionalism, both of which advocate a synchronic measure of rationality.

Through the BoR perspective, contending explanations and meanings alternative to mainstream IRT can be derived from familiar events. The Christian tradition that emphasizes ontological integrity rather than a relational self can still incorporate BoR as long as a nation judges that the pursuit of BoP does not yield any apparent result. In 2005, the US promised Democratic People's Republic of Korea, designated by the US as a terrorist state, not to attack it with either nuclear or traditional weapons (Cha 2009). Although the BoP between the US and North Korea is asymmetric, such a rigid pledge nonetheless contradicts the realist calculus of balance of threat. Neither was the US goodwill with North Korea a move to balance a rival China, as China strongly encouraged such a show of benevolence. In 2018, North Korea relied on the reciprocal relationship with South Korea and commissioned the latter to take advantage of its reciprocal relationship with the US. Finally, the US agreed on a reciprocal talk with North Korea via South Korea's mediation. The US was able to apply BoR. In 2003, the US invaded Afghanistan and then Iraq on the grounds that these countries trained terrorists and possessed weapons of massive destruction (on conspiringly false evidence), although neither country was capable or intentional of a war with the US. Such a behavior was incompatible with either realism or idealism. BoR is necessary because BoP does not provide sufficient explanation.

Apparently, realism has not been an exclusionary principle of IR for the US facing the rise of China. Since 2011, the US has adopted the strategy of rebalancing toward Asia. Practically, it has included both partnership building with Myanmar, Malaysia, and China, on the one hand, and realist balancing against China vis-a-vis cooperation with Japan, the Philippines, and Vietnam on their maritime disputes with China, on the other hand. BoP and BoR together characterize the endeavor of the US to remain influential in spite of relative power decline. The Falklands War of 1982 between the United Kingdom (UK) and Argentina is another example. The US made the victory of the UK possible even at the expense of the long-held national interest of refusing any European force to interfere with American affairs. Rather, via a long-term BoR with the UK, the US had its "main overseas partner in the Cold War sustained and strengthened for the long struggle ahead" (Osullivan 2012: 11). "The long struggle ahead" primarily involves non-apparent national interests.

For a nation practicing BoR, determining how threatening a condition is requires judgment on the possibility of recovering from lost reciprocity. This judgment should be based on both the strength of extant reciprocal relationships and the resources available for carrying out punishment and compromise. Different leaderships may arrive at different judgments under similar conditions. Therefore, once consciously acknowledged, BoR, aside from being a systemic culture, is also a skill, an attitude, and a decision. All nations practice BoR to some extent when a crisis is judged present. Judgment on the nature of the threat to the existing reciprocal relationship is critical in the play of BoR. On the contrary, BoP theory is presumably an analytical tool used by scholars to explain IR without referring to the specific. Unlike BoP theory in which policy options are considered structurally constrained, the nature of BoR requires judgment and improvisation. Policy makers need to rationalize whether a particular situation is a total threat that requires total breakup of a relationship or a minor threat that requires only pampering to repair. What guides a policy choice is not only the power change but also the judgment on the specific conditions of relationship.

Confucianism is not at all required to exercise BoR on a global governance issue. A major power may refrain from intervention when it judges that a challenge to its desired order can be improved if a relationship can be established. This is how China was able to contrive the framework of the Six-Party Talks to bring the US together with North Korea to the same table. The US went along, despite the prevailing criticism or the lack of any result.[3] The rationale to support the Talks could not be that it did not have the capacity to impose sanctions on North Korea, but it had to be because BoP provided no pragmatic solution. At the limit of BoP, a relationship with

North Korea and/or China, once emerging, could bring a longer-term solution. North Korea, in comparison, has never hesitated to threaten the much more powerful US in order to demonstrate its disapproval of a perceived act of betrayal by the US.

Another example of dissolving a multilateral crisis through enhancing a bilateral relationship is when the UK rushed to recognize the People's Republic of China in 1950 at its birth, despite the major threat of communism at that time. The early bird effect successfully dissolved the potential crisis of the PRC's taking over the British colony of Hong Kong. Preventing the loss of Hong Kong at the time exempted the UK from the image of decline and also delayed the domino effect on its multilateral empire of African colonies and elsewhere. The British were not subscribing to BoP in the emerging bipolar system that should have required disciplinary following of the US or taking the advantage of China at its vulnerable moment. Rather, investing in a long-term relationship was prioritized. By contrast, even if the capacity of a major power to intervene is insufficient, intervention will nonetheless proceed if the violation of its order is judged as direct. After all, according to BoR logic, an apparently bad relationship has to be renewed by destroying it completely. The US intervention in Iraq, neither a major power nor an owner of energy, exemplifies the BoR principle of restoration through destruction, and yet incurred noticeable criticism from leading realists (Waltz et al. 2002). The criticism testifies to BoP being simultaneously normative and BoR, equally analytical. The normative choice of the policy logic comes before the analytical function.

Conclusion

The grievance of China toward the EU's arms embargo and its desire to promote a new type of great power relationship with the US are not China-specific attitudes. Both are attempts to explore a long-term relationship by asserting the importance of transcending universal rules. The same relationship easily exists between personalities in the US or the EU, or between political parties in the former Soviet Bloc, for example. The US and the EU can achieve a better relationship with China, by restraining the application of rules in China's favor or adopting a respectful attitude. Accordingly, China is presumed to respond with self-restraint by improving its record with the EU and the US.[4] China reacts to recalcitrant smaller neighbors differently, each with a specific combination and sequence of compromise and sanction, which intends to show a related partner's self-restraint and determination at the same time, albeit not always convincingly. China's concerns for reputation and credit can be found in nations around the world, often exceeding the bounds of apparent national interests. Finally, China's reliance on regional organizations in Africa to legitimize its own participation in the UN's intervention attempts to balance relationships between the interventionary force and the target state. A similar practice of avoiding choosing sides, which usually involves no immediate goal, has been the everyday task of US diplomats all over the world.

The co-existence of BoR and BoP as parallel systems in international politics resembles the parallelism of political and social systems in domestic politics. Such a situation is not extraordinary because the quest for stability and certainty embodies the desire to avoid the potentially violent disorder of anarchy. On the one hand, BoP is only necessary when a reciprocal bilateral relationship is not foreseeable. On the other hand, the reciprocal bilateral relationship provides a solution to cases where BoP fails to successfully coordinate IR. Conversely, a failed BoR practice can also lead to BoP or bandwagoning. The decision to enter a particular system depends on judgment, but the decision itself is inescapable. Together, BoP and BoR provide a more comprehensive understanding of the overall system. Theoretically, BoR is not necessarily present or cognized universally, but practically, it is inevitable, pragmatic, and therefore universally possible. In this sense, BoR is a theory that is readily retrievable anywhere and anytime and a system of relations ubiquitously present.

Notes

1 For Confucian legacy in China's dealings with the world, see Fairbank (1968).
2 The most famous and controversial principle in the ASEAN Charter is Article 2.2 (e), which states that all ASEAN members should obey the principle of "non-interference in the internal affairs of ASEAN Member States." The ASEAN Charter can be downloaded here: http://www.asean.org/archive/publications/ASEAN-Charter.pdf.
3 Christopher Hill, former Assistant Secretary of State to the Bush Administration and US chief representative to the Talks was quoted by Zhu (2011) saying that "the North Koreans lied to the US" (p. 192) and to all Six-Party participants. Hill said there was "absolutely no value" in restarting Six-Party Talks so that "the North Koreans can go and lie to us again" (p. 192).
4 Remember, for example, Xi acquiesced on US surprise missile attack on Syria at Trump's party on April 7, 2017 after the latter's granddaughter recited Chinese poems for the extremely impressed guest. "Trump tells Xi of Syria Missile Attack over Thursday Night Dinner in Mar-a-Lago," South China Morning News April 8, 2017 at www.scmp.com/news/china/policies-politics/article/2085954/trump-tells-xi-syrian-missile-strikes-over-dinner-mar Access August 13, 2017.

2 Relational policy
of small states

Introduction

Small states are an important focus in relational theory given that state actors have always made sense of their world through mutually constituted relationality, regardless of their size or level of power. Chapter 2 applies BoR to the study of the foreign policy of small states, with a particular emphasis on the bilateral, processual, and emotional dimensions of the theory. In doing so, BoR theory critically joins the relational turn in both Western and Chinese IR to resolve the bias toward multilateral and structural analyses. The applicability of BoR to major powers and asymmetric relations will be further discussed in Chapters 3 and 8, respectively. The aim of Chapter 2 is to account for the rise of non-competitive relationships and the BoR practices that result in it. Such practices reveal the agency of leaders, and how the relations thus engendered can stay beyond their initial purposes. Finally, the chapter demonstrates how 'gift giving' can fashion resemblance and enable deeper relations between countries whose prior relations had been thin.

The chapter begins with a brief comparison between the relational turns in Chinese and Western IR. It describes the emotional aspect of the relational turn and argues that Chinese relation is more focused on anxiety than passion. It uncovers the bilateral sensibilities of relational IR to offer a critique on the predominantly multilateral concerns of both Chinese and Western IR. The ensuing case of the Singapore–Taiwan relationship highlights three theoretical possibilities in BoR: (1) a bilateral relationship enables two unfamiliar countries to engage effectively in affirmative rather than defensive interaction; (2) affirmative relations are conducive to the development of positive passion; and (3) the positive affect easily trickles down to the personal level in a bilateral relationship but enforces no necessary condition of relations at the state level.

Theoretical significance of the Singapore–Taiwan relationship

By any realist standard, Singapore and Taiwan are small states on the world stage. During the Cold War, the US was viewed as the most dominant force supporting the anti-Communist regimes of these two regional allies. However, Singapore and Taiwan were not in close contact with each other during this period. The Shanghai Communiqué signed by Washington and Beijing in 1972, however, changed the situation. Following the Communiqué, the two anti-Communist regimes began to consider each other as potential allies and initiated a mutual engagement without prior encouragement from the US. They also enhanced their mutual relations within a very short period of time. Through closer acquaintance with Chiang Ching-kuo and his top officials in Taipei, Singapore's former Prime Minister Lee Kuan Yew (LKY) changed his previously suspicious attitude toward Chinese culture and became an enthusiastic advocate of Asian values. The bilateral relationship continued smoothly until the mid-1990s, peaking in 1993 when Singapore hosted the first official talk between Taipei and Beijing. Taipei continued to provide military training to Singapore's army well into the second decade of the new century. This military arrangement allowed Singapore to not exclusively depend on major powers or seek military training sites in other countries within a region that had not wanted to alienate Indonesia or Malaysia.

Anthropologists have shown that weaker actors are capable of transcending power and self-interest through their insistence on fair prices and surplus-sharing to survive in a subsistence economy (Randall & Charlesworth 2000; Scott 1976). Small states also contribute to the global system when they strike deals, interact stylistically, and generate moral incentives irrespective of their power limitations (Ingebritsen, Neumann & Gstöhl 2006). The "non-competitive" nature of the Singapore–Taiwan relationship between 1973 and 1996 was one where the two countries did not seek power or status competition, nor the interest-based reciprocity, and precisely for this reason, the relationship bears both theoretical and practical significance. Theoretically, neither side had a specific policy goal in mind to begin their kinship-like partnership.

With the traditional focus of IRT being on competition, estrangement and defense, the desire for stability and ensued improvisation of self-restraint as well as gift-giving within an imagined anarchy remains unsatisfactorily unexplained. International theories that are primarily multilateral theories have not focused, at the theoretical level, on bilateral relationships that constitute almost all international processes (Moran 2005). The evolution of a lukewarm relationship to one of mutual trust and care requires a processual analysis in order for students of IR to appreciate the relational nature of their subject-matter. The case of Singapore–Taiwan relations illustrates a non-competitive relationship—that is, a practical theory of diplomacy and bilateralism.

Non-competitive bilateral relations has the potential to provide rich insights into the Western and Chinese relational turns in IR theorization. Processual analysis indicates how the leadership of either country had sought to achieve no immediate national interest objective, but were instead interested in a 'rational' strategy aimed at developing a reciprocal relationship where a trustworthy partner would come to one's assistance in times of need.

They did not tackle any immediate threats, although both were clearly anxious when East Asian anti-Communist sentiments were undermined, a result of the reversal of the US's China policy during the Nixon administration. However, bilateral cooperation was not intended as a strategy to deal with the US as a potential threat. Moreover, the security concern over China's potential enmity was viewed not as an imminent threat but as a long-term one. This fact rendered the emerging bilateral relationship a noteworthy one, as it did not focus on any apparent security issues shared by either party.

Indeed, both sides managed to discover ways to provide mutual support. This processual mutuality was not a matter of exchange, but it did resemble the act of gift giving: both states improvised carefully considered gifts proper for the other side. Such attempts at pleasing each other, especially at the beginning of the relationship, reflect their anxiety toward the lack of a relation beyond the thin resemblance created by a common anti-Communist front.

The personalization of the bilateral relationship between the two states surfaced as the two leaders, Lee Kuan Yew and Chiang Ching-kuo, together with Chiang's advisor Shen Chang-huan, developed strong 'bonds' between them. The processual nature of IR is most vividly captured in the agency of leaders in new relationships that exist at the margins of the global power structure. As neither side worried about the defection of the other, and with both parties holding a degree of respect for each other, 'passion' replaced anxiety. Although personalization is a generalizable route to a more passionate relationship, BoR does not rely on personal emotion. LKY could disregard the treatment of pro-independence leaders, like Lee Teng-hui, who succeeded Chiang, and continued to make straightforward comments on issues he believed were in Taiwan's interests.

The Singapore–Taiwan relationship provides a potentially generalizable case of BoR, where bilateral relations inform the processual characteristic of state identity. As a result, Taiwan's Confucian values and resistance to China have both reconstituted Singapore's self-identity. The bilateral relationship of Singapore and Taiwan has its own momentum independent of multilateral IR. The case further shows the tenacity of BoR even after personalization ceases to reproduce passion. Self-restraint in terms of gift giving continues to characterize Singapore's Taiwan policy, which is so noticeable that even China was willing to rely on its improvisational characteristics during the Xi Jinping–Ma Ying-jeou Summit between China and Taiwan in 2016.

Connecting Western and Chinese IR

Relational turn

The relational turn in IR literature, as mentioned in Chapter 1, features an ontological divide. The relational turn that abides by a statist ontology perceives relations as social and cultural capital (Slaughter 2009: 113). A statist relational analysis advocates the substitution of connectivity for material strength. Connectivity, which is similarly measured in military, economic, and cultural terms, is arguably a fungible power resource. According to network statists, a wider network of social capital always works to constrain any mutual relationship (Hafner-Burton, Kahler & Montgomery 2009; Moaz 2011). The other side of the divide asserts relational ontology and believes that relations come before states (Jackson & Nexon 1999). Relations exist in imagined prior or unowned resemblance that undergirds ensuing relations among seemingly autonomous actors. This perspective emphasizes processes and analyzes how such processes constitute states. For example, one's "narrative sociability" in an initial encounter with a group can define not only one's subsequent relationship with the other members of the group, but can also perpetuate one's own identity (Neumann 2011). This perspective can be applied to China's (forced) entry into European international society during the Qing Dynasty (as discussed in Chapter 7), and is equally evident from the dynamics of 'group belonging' where membership in a security community often results in self-restraint becoming an intrinsic quality of the state (Adler 2008).

Studying small-state diplomacy can reveal how epistemological equality can be achieved through the relational and practice turns in IR. This is because the attributes of the state—primarily power (but not limited to it)—allow for process and relationality to the effect that greater states, much like smaller ones, become relationally constituted and process driven. By exercising self-restraint, the evolving self-understanding, mutual expectations and behavior of the greater power can be constituted by the smaller power, and vice versa. For example, Chinese practices of enacting self-restraint as the greater power is evinced by Beijing's Hong Kong, Taiwan, North Korea, and Vietnam policies (Womack 2006, You 2001) that stress concession. China could have pursued a much more hardline approach; however, the target smaller states served the purpose of reinforcing China's self-role identity as a benevolent center. By contrast, US practices of acting as the greater power by renouncing self-restraint can be seen from its military actions in Grenada, Libya, Panama, Iran, and Afghanistan. Such action reproduces the US' identity as the guardian of the hegemonic order. In other words, how much room a great power allows its weaker counterparts to maneuver ends up defining the parameters of great power-hood.

Between the use of multilateral and bilateral tools, a weaker party usually prefers the former in defending against the imposition of rules by a stronger state (Cha 2012). However, the disadvantage of a multilateral frame for a weaker party is that it is less likely to succeed in acquiring gains from a stronger party without the support of the majority. Depending on what its goals are, the weaker party would be better positioned to combine the use of both multilateral and bilateral approaches.

Even among smaller powers, the bilateral relationship may have broader implications for IR theorization and the diplomatic behavior of a greater power. This is because the function of the relationship can be clearer where confrontation is less likely and their relationship indirectly, yet practically, affects the machinations of the greater power. Enhanced cooperation between Singapore and Taiwan, for example, served to (indirectly) reproduce China as a Communist threat in ideological terms, such that the rapprochement between Washington and Beijing appeared more a decision made on the basis of power expediency, as opposed to the US' abortion of its anti-Communist policy.

Even so, the idea that states are relationally constituted may be too general a proposition to explain the peculiarities of the Singapore–Taiwan partnership. To improve relational analysis, Daniel Nexon (2008) identified three specific mechanisms that lay the groundwork for resemblance: network (also see Böhmelt 2009, Freeman 1979), field, and discourse. These mechanisms, however, remain inadequate for explaining the evolution of the Singapore–Taiwan relationship. Nexon's network analysis would acknowledge the common alliance with the US; however, Washington was not responsible for encouraging the Singapore-Taiwan partnership. His field analysis would highlight the geo-proximity and dense Chinese populations in Singapore and Taiwan, arguing how this common denominator could facilitate the potential expansion of mainland Chinese influence into either country. As such, this shared characteristic rendered them strategically and psychologically sympathetic to each other. However, such anxieties should have been more evident during the Cultural Revolution than in the aftermath of the Sino-Soviet rift and the Shanghai Communiqué. Yet, no such association was attempted during the heyday of the rift or revolution. Singapore also remained extremely cautious when the situation in China was reversed, opting not to establish diplomatic relations with Beijing until 1990. In contrast, Tokyo, Kuala Lumpur, Bangkok, and Manila had all moved beyond the containment policy between 1971 and 1975 by exchanging diplomatic recognition with Beijing. Finally, discourse analysis would serve to reveal the motives of Taiwan and Singapore in forming a relationship to protect against anti-Communism, which had been undermined by the Shanghai Communiqué. However, the picture remains an incomplete one considering Singapore's then aversion to its Chinese identity that contrasted sharply with Taipei's efforts to align its identity with the Chinese cultural renaissance. In this way, their association could be seen as in discursive terms as contradictory to their purpose of consolidating a legitimate, working relationship. The growth of a passionate mutuality between Singapore and Taiwan in the early 1970s, therefore, suggests that non-competitive bilateral relationality is undertheorized.

As previously mentioned, the 'relational turn' in IR has reached Chinese IR studies through Qin Yaqing's body of work (Qin 2010, 2012). Specifically, Qin referred to Thaddeus Jackson and Daniel Nexon's processual relationalism to situate his relational studies (Qin 2009). Qin was also inspired by the Confucian relationalism of the indigenous psychologist Hwang Kwang-kuo (Hwang 1987: 944–974, Qin 2011, 2012). Their Confucianism further emphasizes the difference, instead of similarity, of Chinese relationality. The difference in sensibilities indicates an ontological interest that contradicts the claim of processual relationalism that would shelve the ontological pursuit (Kavalski 2018). However, for both Qin and Hwang, Chinese uniqueness or exceptionalism does not mean that these cultural resources are not scientifically universal in epistemological terms (Hwang 2013: 105–112, Qin 2012: 75–77). They enlisted the notion of the 'greater self' to convey how the personal self, submerged in a variety of relational selves that together contemplate the personal self as the 'little self' or 'lesser self' (Ho 1998, Hwang 2012, King 1985), is an intrinsically constituted process. Although their relationality is allegedly a multilateral tool of analysis, their analytical frame predominantly adopts bilateralism.

Hwang's (1987) scientific sensibility first appeared in an article on *renqing* (benevolent emotion) and face, in which he presented a type of relationality consisting of the interaction between two abstract roles—a petitioner and an allocator. He proposed two rules on resource allocation, one based on need (kin-oriented) and another on interest (rational). The need rule carries a positive affect, whereas the interest rule resonates with the cool-headed calculus of social capital. Between the two is the mixed rule in which an interest-driven petition improves its plausibility by enlisting a kinship metaphor based on gift giving.

In Hwang's formulation, relation is both ontological as a need and strategic to the extent that relation is incurred in the interaction through the metaphor of kinship. This strategic relation, which takes advantage of ontological relationality, echoes Qin's concerns over the Chinese foreign policy style of always trying to relate to the other side, as if relation is the foundation of security (Qin 2011: 139–143) without which the self will suffer the loss of meaning and be unable to sustain itself. Qin stressed the "emotional convergence" (Qin 2009: 12–13) that parallels Hwang's reference to positive affect. Both Qin and Hwang tackle the process of improvising relationships to reconfirm a hypothetical greater self and not one of (re)negotiating ongoing relations as in Jackson and Nexon's formulation. Another difference with Jackson and Nexon lies in the examples of relation, which are dyadic rather than multilateral.

Positive vs. negative affect

The social psychological literature has not confirmed the designation of positive affect to a relationship constituted by a greater self. The greater self is literally a Confucian notion of prior resemblance, the contents of which are usually thin and varies in accordance with the encountered social context (Ho & Chiu 1998, Hwang 2012; Hwang, Francesco & Kesslear 2003).

The social psychological translation of the greater self points to the im-provisation of the relational self, such that roles adopted by one comes to constitute their self-identity (Barbalet 2014, Qi 2011). The greater self is a sociological necessity, although it is Confucian culture that injects a distinc-tive moral significance into the conscious celebration of its prevalence (Hsu 1971, Yang 1995). Nevertheless, social identity theory consistently demon-strates that merely belonging to an artificially constructed group is sufficient to incur favoring behavior toward the in-group and discrimination against the out-group (Oldmeadow & Fiske 2010, Stephan & Stephan 1985). This partially explains the rationality of constructing a greater self and securing one's membership regardless of the context. The greater self-consciousness is thus not uniquely Chinese, although the Chinese culture of the greater self is arguably more sophisticated than its Western counterpart.

Under the condition of the relational self, the emotional aspect of role identity is easily registered through anxiety or stress (Burke 1991, Simon 1992). The self-discrepancy in one's performance of a role, as evaluated by the counterpart, is a major source of anxiety (Higgins 1987, Roseman 1984). In addition, symbolic interactionism and dramaturgical sociology concur with the observation that 'important others' can influence one's level of stress (Turner & Stets 2006: 26–32). The relational turn in psychoanalysis similarly points to the subject of separation anxiety (Dimen 2012: 396, Renolds 2007), implying the dreaded loss of a role partner. Moreover, studies on Chinese psychology note the critical function of relationships in the maintenance of mental health (Hwang & Chang 2009, Lin, Tseng & Yeh 1995). A role, in both multilateral and bilateral settings, is constantly examined externally to cause stress (Hsu 1983, 1985: 100). A stable relationship can generate the positive affect, but a national actor rarely encounters this situation. Rather, relationship as a process of constant adaptation is the recurring condition of national role identity within the international realm.

Feeling for others is unnecessary to the enactment of role identities. Rather, it is the sentiments concerned with how others regard the fulfillment of said role identity that maintains social harmony and order (Barbalet 2001: 108). The incurred emotional stress renders the relevance of a small state in international relations, because small states, with their large number, com-pose of an imagined audience. Major powers, such as Moscow, Washing-ton, and Beijing, do not easily acquire support or consent from one another. Given the widespread status anxiety (Onea 2014, Renshon 2015), their status as major powers, their national role conceptions, and their aspirations in world politics can be confirmed only through their interactions with cer-tain smaller states. They do this by either dominating multilateral agendas where small states are acquiescent, or by reciprocating bilateral agendas where small states are articulate. In the face of small states, a major power usually benefits more from bilateralism than multilateralism (Cha 2012). This does not necessarily mean that a major power will procure specific in-terests by forcing a concession out of a smaller state. Rather, a major power can relatively enlist a small state's support more easily via both positive and negative incentives through a bilateral relationship. In such a way, the major power can secure a conception of a greater self and set up a role model for other bilateral relationships. In this sense, bilateralism that reproduces the image of status can be less stressful to major powers.

Singapore–Taiwan relations presents a puzzle to the extent that the emotional aspect of the bilateral relationship has appeared positive. This aspect is an exception to the general feeling of anxiety ingrained in relationality. The emotional literature repeatedly confirms that satisfied pursuit of self-esteem motivates relational behavior and brings forth the positive affect (Ervin & Stryker 2001, Marcussen 2006, Rosenburg et al. 1995). As will be discussed in the latter part of this chapter, emotional convergence that existed between the two nations was possible due to the personalization of relation. This case suggests that bilateral relationality embedded in a non-competitive relationship produces an emotional state that is qualitatively different from a competitive relationship that is predicated on concerns over security, status, or norms. The non-competitive relationship allows the positive affect to trickle down from the state to that of the individual level (Kleinman 1986), with the latter potentially serving to enhance leaders' self-esteem through mutually-reinforcing recognition (Hsu 1985). The case also demonstrates that emotional convergence produced by personalization is not a necessary condition for the formation or continuation of relationship as claimed by Chinese IR.

Multilateral vs. bilateral

In principle, an unsynchronized world cannot possibly subscribe to the same rules without there being considerable revision to the rules within each country. Advocacy for any universal rule, however liberal, cannot but involve some degree of intervention. By contrast, the discussion of change in Chinese literature refers primarily to the improvisation of alternative propriety that requires no ontological adaptation. Presumably, each relational self acquires the skill to adapt, thus ensuring their continuous belonging to the same and known greater self, whose boundary and scope are usually unclear. The reproduction of the greater self relies on improvised relations between members who develop in accordance with their own styles and pathways. Therefore, the greater self, represented in IRT by imagined common interests, is necessarily fluid and thin. Empirically, China's position within multilateral settings has been consistently passive. Sheer abstention characterizes the Chinese voting style on those issues where China, the 'Third World', and its other partners cannot reach a consensus. Together, active relations embedded in non-intervention, non-substantialism, and the greater self-consciousness must be bilateral. Such bilateral sensibilities incorporate the reciprocal relationship emphasized in Confucian culture, substituting the prevalent dyadic relationship for uniqueness claims regarding the greater self. Chinese IR is practically composed of a 'multilateral self', one meant to passively satisfy the ritual function required of the little self, as well as a 'bilateral self' that actively practices negotiation to secure relationality.

Both Qin and Hwang perceived relationship as an epistemological critique on synchronization. Qin criticizes Western relationalism for falling back to substantialism because reproducing relations assumes the self-other binary, albeit under the influence of prior relations. For Qin, the thesis and antithesis in Chinese epistemology do not conflict; rather, they interpret, define, and complement each other to constitute a harmonious whole (Qin 2010: 143–145). Contrary to relationalism, Qin's self-actualization relies on reproducing the greater-self-identity that circumvents the self-identity as well as the self-other binary. This indicates a kind of relationship in which everyone remains intrinsically related yet unsynchronized. Qin deemed the changes as methodological and views relationality as ontologically binding. Changes that synchronize nations simultaneously destroy relationality, such that synchronization and intervention become anti-ontological. The purpose of change for Qin is to ascertain that each accepts the other as a legitimate dyadic partner so as to continue their relationship.

Based on these views, prior relation envisages practices of synchronization, whereas improvised relation, through gift giving, envisages practices of staying unsynchronized. Arranging a bilateral relationship is a process of guaranteeing each other's place in the multiple dyadic selves, qua the greater self, which consists of these two "elements." Therefore, nations are defined collectively by their multiple dyadic selves, not by what they are themselves. In this sense, improvised relation is an emotionally reassuring process, in which differences pose no barrier to one's inclusion in the dyadic self, as long as the roles required by the relationship are faithfully enacted. Nevertheless, improvised relation is by no means peaceful because it requires a destructive policy in the face of a perceived aborted enactment. This improvised relation in diplomatic interaction initially prompted us to construct BoR theory to transcend the alleged Chinese uniqueness (Huang & Shih 2014).

Affirmative BoR

The thrust of BoR theory is that nations oblige each other to stay engaged. They balance the loss of relationship either by improvising more in the amendable relationship or by removing the eclipsed one judged to be unsalvageable. The technique chooses between exerting or renouncing self-restraint as a way to restore or destroy the greater self, respectively. The culturally neutral notion of BoR theory moves Qin's and Hwang's reference to relation away from cultural specification. Although Confucianism provides a distinctive access to relation in the Chinese context, other countries each have their own stylistic access to BoR.

The seeming contrast between Chinese and Western relations is a contrast between improvised relation, which must be bilateral, and prior relation, which can be either bilateral or multilateral. Both improvisation and bilaterality are culturally neutral notions. Culture directs one's proclivity toward a particular kind of relation over the other. The management of Chinese relation is more likely to take place within the bilateral context. Harmonizing a series of bilateral relationships independently is much less complicated or confrontational than synchronizing a multilateral relationship involving many parties. Multilateral relation calls for the nation's self-restraint to practically abide by the community's security rules at the expense of its immediate interest (Adler 2008), which implies an adamant attitude toward other deviant behaviors. By contrast, self-restraint in bilateral relation refers to the patience and concession at one's immediate expense to oblige the other to restore propriety, which appears recalcitrant (Shih 2014).

Notions of compromise, confrontation, and self-sacrifice within the BoR practices, as described in Chapter 1, may fail to convey any positive affect or emotional convergence expected by either Qin or Hwang. Instead, the emotional tendency is more inclined toward anxiety than enthusiasm when it comes to monitoring one's acceptance by the other side after one's improvisation of a self-perceived restraint. In comparison, anxiety can be comparatively less important in a multilateral situation than a bilateral one because one can always find justification in enforcing a multilateral rule. In addition, the degree of anxiety can be less under the multilateral circumstance where a nation remains in control over how much to adapt and integrate into a group. The other side holds the key to the fate of the greater self in the quest for bilateral relation, without which one is left completely without relationality.

The analyses presented by Qin, Jackson, and Nexon recognize the "unowned" nature of relational politics (Jackson & Nexon 1999, Qin 2009). The degree of an unowned process is important in a bilateral process, given how the purpose of enlisting long-term bilateral relation is to bypass multilateral principles and stay uncompliant. This formulation of relational security reflects an important feature of bilateral relation, that is its exemption from the multilateral rule. Anxiety in multilateral relation pertains to the recognition of one's amenability to the group they belong to, whereas bilateral relation is about the acceptance of one's unsynchronized values and identities by the other side. The level of anxiety is presumably higher for greater powers at the multilateral level where they compete for support to make rules. Where there is usually no such competition between small powers, anxiety is also higher when it comes to revising role identities that impinge on the bilateral relationship.

Emotional contrast does not exist between Western and Chinese relationalities. Both are characterized by anxiety. A higher level of anxiety exists in the bilateral than the multilateral relationalities and more so for the greater power than the smaller power within the multilateral relationality framework. Anxiety is prevalent as relation involves security considerations and constant group scrutiny as a result. Enthusiasm, rather than anxiety, is likely to characterize the affective perspective for occasions where a greater power is to achieve a new rule or sanction violation. This tendency is also not about the difference between Chinese and Western relationalities. The relational turn reproduces structural analyses of international politics in the sense that the discipline continues to be preoccupied with the pressures of threat, competition, and survival under conditions of anarchy. Everyday acts of IR, which are usually uncompetitive or unsynchronized as evident in the example of Singapore–Taiwan relations, require more attention so that the next stage of relational studies can be undertaken.

The ease of witnessing the delicate process of relationalism compared with substantialism in non-competitive, unsynchronized interaction is due to the irrelevance of substantialism wherever synchronization is not valued. The construction of countries' continuously improvised roles may result from non-competitive, bilateral relations as opposed to their reproduction of prior multilateral relations. The case of the Singapore–Taiwan relationship contributes insights on relationality in three ways. First, it bridges Western and Chinese relationality by bringing forth the bilateral (i.e. non-cultural) relationship through BoR theory. The case demonstrates how bilateral relationships require a broader understanding of relationality based on acceptance, as opposed to conversion, which is accessible to all.

Second, this case enlists and extends BoR theory, as outlined in Chapter 1, by proposing two rules of common-sense gift giving to explain the evolution of non-competitive relationality. This upgraded BoR is affirmative as opposed to being defensive in the sense of balancing aborted relationships. This relationship aims to generate a reciprocal relationship under circumstances of no threat through goodwill and benevolence. This process assists one party to sympathize with the other and encourages it to engage in reciprocity at a future time of need. A long-term affirmative BoR includes the following two characteristics: (1) it offers unexpected benevolence to enable the imagination of an emerging dyadic-self; and (2) it continues the practice of benevolence, despite the lack thereof shown by the other party, in order to preserve the existing dyadic-self (Hattori 2003, Klotz 1995: 13).

Third, the case brings in personal interaction between the top leaders of the two countries to explain how passion, not anxiety, can grow to reinforce such a bilateral relationship. Although personalization is not typical of BoR, the exception often reveals the rule. The rise and fall of personalization indicate that Chinese IR relationality is not about emotional convergence, which Qin and Hwang claimed. Affirmative BoR at the state level can trickle down to the personal level, which can cause BoR to become emotionally positive and, in turn, motivate improvisation. The case illustrates that the Chinese convention of treating foreign leaders with intense courtesy is only a diplomatic technique to reinforce reciprocity at the state level. Nonetheless, once personalization fades, BoR continues. This alludes to a

Table 2.1 International Relationality from a Comparative Perspective

	Western IR Relationality	Chinese IR Relationality	BoR
Scope	Multilateral	Multilateral	Bilateral
Actors	Major powers	Major powers	All nations
Identity	Rule-constituted self	Greater self	Dyadic selves
Practice	Self-restraint to honor the rule	Self-restraint to avoid enforcement	Self-restraint to bypass the rule
Emotion	Anxiety and passion	Alleged passion but anxiety	Anxiety or passion
Self-image	Self-determined	Other-determined	Other-determined
Personalization	Unlikely	Unlikely	Likely
Issue area	Security and governance	Security and interest	Interest
Ideal state	Synchronicity	Harmony	Reciprocity
Policy orientation	Competitive or interventionary	Defensive	Concessionary or affirmative

Source: Author.

generalizable rule of bilateral relationships between all nations regardless of their relative levels of power, indicating that, after all, BoR does not rely on the attitudes of national leaders toward each other. The Singapore–Taiwan relationship demonstrates that state relationality is surely processual but not necessarily personal (Table 2.1).

From rational IR to processual relationality

Singapore–Taiwan relations have developed rapidly beyond simply being an exchange of interests since their first secret contact in 1973. In 1993, Singapore not only offered the venue for a Taiwan-China meeting for an entire week for free, but its Ministry of Foreign Affairs also laboriously coordinated all of the logistics. The Singapore team made sure that every detail was arranged to fully take care of Taipei's primary concern of being equal to Beijing. Even the Singaporean media ensured that all reports and photos of the two sides were in the same length and size to relieve Taipei's extreme anxiety as a consequence of its quest for equal status. Indeed, Singapore "tried every possible action" to accomplish the task of diplomatically protecting Taipei's sense of inferiority without intervening in the negotiation process. Most importantly, Singapore expected no return for its faithful service to both sides, especially from Taipei (Chiu 2013).

However, Singapore–Taiwan relations underwent an intense crisis after the 1993 meeting. Taiwan's pro-independence leader, Lee Teng-hui, launched the first attack on LKY in his remarks on Singapore's undemocratic political system (Chen 2002: 141). LKY later recalled his goodwill to Lee Teng-hui, but the latter's attack had his "ears burned" (Ruan 2000: 186). Lee Teng-hui even invited Samuel Huntington to Taiwan to render his judgment that "[t]he freedom and creativity that President Lee [Teng Hui] has introduced in Taiwan will survive him. The honesty and efficiency that Senior Minister LKY has brought to Singapore are likely to follow him to his grave" (Huntington 1997: 13). The pro-Lee Teng Hui's *Ziyou Shibao* (*Liberty Times*) carried a series of discreditations on behalf of Lee Teng-hui about LKY's cashing in on his relationship with Taiwan for his own business profit (Tzou 2001: 360–363). Nevertheless, LKY returned to Taiwan during the term of the succeeding pro-independence President Chen Shui-bian, despite the disgraceful statement of the then Minister of Foreign Affairs that Singapore is "a state the size of nose shit" that "pampers China's balls" (Chang & Chen 2012: 56–57). Before LKY passed away in March 2015, he visited Taiwan 25 times. This level of commitment exceeded anything required by Singapore's national interests embedded in anti-Chinese Communism and economic exchange with China.

"Chineseness" has bothered Singapore since the country's independence. LKY led Singapore's independence from Malaysia as a result of the dispute over the equal rights of non-indigenous residents. Prior to independence, Singapore executed a few Indonesian mariners involved in an explosion, who became Indonesia's national heroes. (Chua 2015). The anti-Communist coup in Jakarta, right after Singapore declared independence, further resulted in an anti-Chinese massacre. Thus, Singapore was faced with a dire situation in which the Chineseness of Singapore could lead to a highly dangerous situation (Josey 1974). The potential for such an outcome was attributable to the hostility of its neighbors to the potentially pro-Communist Chinese population (Barr 1999), as witnessed in Thailand, Malaysia, and Indonesia where Chinese-language education had been terminated. Therefore, Taipei's determined pursuit of authentic Chineseness was a matter that LKY would have found problematic.

The adjustment of the lukewarm relationship only emerged upon Nixon's surprise visit to China in February 1972, where the anti-Communist allies in East and Southeast Asia anxiously watched the visit, which resulted in the Shanghai Communiqué. In response, the exodus of Taiwanese migrants to the Western world in the early 1970s reflected the anxiety of the Taiwanese population toward the uncertain future of Taiwan. Earlier in 1971, Beijing replaced the Kuomintang's seat in the United Nations. Over 30 nations switched their recognition from Taipei to Beijing, three years after Taipei lost its seat in the United Nations. The stance of anti-Communist Singapore, which did not join the trend of recognizing Beijing, suddenly appeared important. Together, Taipei and Singapore planned LKY's secret visit in 1973.

For both sides, the need to expand the anti-Communist network was the drive and, hence, the main social capital consideration. According to Peter

Pi-teh Chang's secret memo to Minister Shen Chang-huan,[1] Taipei's representative to Singapore, the U.S. ambassador in Singapore immediately followed up on LKYs trip and asked Chang about it. Chang then reported to Shen his exchange with his US counterpart. His account of LKY's trip emphasized LKY's strategic judgment on Taiwan's indirect yet significant role in diverting Beijing from any substantial ambition in Southeast Asia. Ignoring Washington during LKY's trip indicates that strategic interests of smaller states can make a sufficiently strong base of agency for change in policy orientation, without any hint from their common leader seated in Washington.

Several messages carrying important theoretical implications stood out in the same memo and the exchanges that followed. In the memo, LKY's reflections after returning from Taipei were actually first disclosed to Shen by Chang. Chang reportedly gathered the information from a "reliable source," which confirmed LKY's extremely favorable impression of his host. After all, Taiwan posed a model of being simultaneously Chinese and anti-Communist. LKY also told Chang's source that Taiwan must remain strong and prosperous so that Southeast Asia can stay away from the Chinese threat. LKY allegedly expressed his determination to help Taiwan with its international trade wherever Beijing's pressure was intense. He also planned for Singapore to be a transit for Taiwan to export goods and import strategic materials wherever Taipei needed to bypass the boycott by Beijing. (Later, Taiwan's purchase of light arms from Tel Aviv went through Singapore's mediation).

Chang's report proceeded with a key conversation with the parliamentary secretary to the Ministry of Foreign Affairs, Ong Soo Chuan, who insinuated that Singapore would not have diplomatic relationships with Beijing in the quoted statement: "...as long as the US maintains her influence in Thailand and Indonesia, Singapore will remain [the] statu[s] quo" (dated June 11, 1973). Finally, Chang noticed a qualitative change in Singapore's attitude toward Taiwan as Taiwan's Minister of Finance KT Lee's visit and request to meet with LKY was instantly approved. This change was "a dramatically improved" development compared with how past similar requests were handled.

The above-mentioned exchanges provide a few theoretical implications. First, the consideration of national interest in LKY's first visit prevailed over the value difference. However, once policy reification of such a consideration starts, the momentum that follows may become more relational than rational. The reorientation toward Taiwan attests to the volatile nature of political value in shaping foreign policy. LKY was a known supporter of constitutional democracy in his early career, which is embedded in his British intellectual upbringing (Lee 1998, 131). He was even antagonistic to Confucianism, which he considered unsuitable for the modern times.[2] Nevertheless, the anxiety toward the Nixon shock emerged in a proposal to help the non-democratic and, yet, Confucian Taiwan, which was improvised by Singapore's Minister of Finance, Hon Sui Sen. According to the proposal:

> Under certain circumstances where direct trade contacts are not possible, Singapore will provide [the] Republic of China with the facilities of transshipment so that the Republic of China can secure the supplies from certain countries indirectly. The Central Trust of China and the Intraco Limited will be designated to work together for this purpose.
>
> (Ministry of Finance 1973)

Hon promised to help Taiwan with the knowledge to "establish a Development Fund similar to what is operated by the government of Singapore and its budgetary procedures" (Ministry of Finance 1973). A Taiwanese team would also go to Singapore to learn "Singapore's Central Provident Fund, Housing Program, and Urban Renewal Project." (Ministry of Finance 1973).

Taiwan improvised something for its new friend as well. Taiwan would "provide [the] PUB [Public Utilities Board] of Singapore with engineering services and experiences in the establishment of a nuclear power plant, which include the selection of specifications, personnel training, and wherever possible loan of personnel, etc." (Ministry of Finance 1973). None of the abovementioned goodwill was expected to yield concrete and calculable benefits for either side. They were not exchanges in the business sense; instead, they resembled an exchange of "gifts". Ultimately, such expressions of goodwill apparently led to the growth of a reciprocal relationship.

Second, a well-developed relationship may further reconstitute initial identities. LKY's own perspective on Confucianism changed dramatically since 1970. Initially, he was alienated from the cultural tradition of his family. This alienation could be intellectually based since he was well-trained in Western pedagogy. His identity could also be strategic because he knew how Chineseness had been a threat to his neighbors and former nationals in Malaysia, which could lead to suspicion. Pragmatically, he also knew how Chineseness was subject to Communist China's infiltration and could lead to the disruption of his own society (Preston 2007: 130). This negative view of Confucianism stands in stark contrast to Lee's attitude since the 1990s. By then, LKY had already revitalized Chinese cultural awareness in full gear and rehabilitated Chinese language education.

A period of reconstitution had to exist in between. He listened to Mahathir Mohamad in 1980 as the latter tried to promote so-called "Asian values." Since then, liberal democracy was no longer a favorable reference for LKY. In 1983, Singapore established the Institute of East Asian Philosophies (IEAP) precisely to study Confucianism. The IEAP later evolved into the Institute of East Asian Political Economy and finally settled as the East Asian Institute. Upon observing underdevelopment during his first visit to China in 1976, he felt so confident that he decided to allow open access to China for his countrymen so that they would give up on any lingering loyalty to the imagined Motherland (Lee 2000: 573–594). His determined cultural reversal, together with his disdain toward China, pointed to Singapore's newly acquainted anti-Communist yet Confucian leadership in Taipei. The Taipei authorities were able to convert a rational exchange of national interest into a mutually constituted identity.

From Taipei's perspective, countries in the region hastened to exchange diplomatic recognition with Beijing and to sever their ties with Taipei. Singapore was the exception. However, the major nations in the Arab World remained on Taipei's side. In a conversation at a family dinner on April 7, 1978, LKY mentioned the lack of channels with Saudi Arabia. Shen took up the issue immediately, and in just three weeks, he received a message from his ambassador in Jeddah, who heard positive feedback from the Saudi Foreign Ministry. On May 9, Shen confidentially wrote to LKY to inform him of the situation. Shen also reminded him that the Kingdom's readiness to establish diplomatic relations with Singapore and to exchange envoys at the ambassadorial level could be delayed due to the shortage of personnel, staffed only by a *Chargè d'Affaires*, in the early stage.[3] LKY expressed his gratitude to Shen in his confidential reply on May 17 for "mov[ing] so quickly."[4] While one-third of the confidential message was business, two-thirds was to refresh the former's unforgettable encounter of the evening with Wego, the younger brother of President Chiang Ching-kuo. Personalization had already taken place (this will be discussed later).

Lastly, once a conceptualized relation of the greater self constituted Singapore's role identity, Singapore's concern for Taiwan's future never faded. This fact has remained despite the change in direction of Singapore's China policy. In 1978, Deng Xiaoping visited Singapore. The following year, Singapore and Beijing signed a trade agreement providing mutually preferential treatment. In 1980, the two countries established a trade office in each other's capital. Singapore's investment in China began to pick up in the early 1980s. Eventually, the relationship became so intertwined that Singapore's Minister of Finance Goh Keng Swee formally served as an advisor to a special economic zone in China's coastal area in 1985.

From anxious relationality to passionate relationality

Despite offering benevolence, the decision to form a greater self lies in the judgment of the other side. The uncertainty generated anxiety, as demonstrated in Peter Chang's intelligence work following LKY's impression of his secret trip. That both parties continuously improvised benevolence and showed goodwill proves that they are both willing to invest in the formation of a long-term bilateral relationship. No immediate national interest gains could be obtained from these investments in terms of knowledge sharing, information exchange, or military cooperation. Yet, the noteworthy development of inter-personal friendship transformed the emerging, yet uncertain, greater self into an enjoyable and caring relationship. The personalization of inter-state reciprocity could exempt both sides from spending too much in an attempt to display continued benevolence while remaining confident in the health of the greater self. The following discussion illustrates what "emotional convergence" means in practice.

Chiang Kai-shek passed away on April 5, 1975, which was the year when Singaporean troops began their training in Taiwan. LKY sent personal condolences to Madame Chiang and Ching-kuo on April 22.[5] His letter to Ching-kuo revealed a personal compassion for the loss of an important friend, beginning with a line on relationships: "My wife, children, and I send you and your family our deepest condolence on the death of your father."[6] It touched on the betrayal of US: "Taiwan has been able to ride through the very turbulent changes caused by the change of America's policy on China."[7] LKY was on a trip to New Zealand and could only arrange for Pang Tee Pow, permanent secretary of the Ministry of Defense, to attend the funeral from nearby. However, he flew to Taiwan on May 23 from Tokyo on another secret trip. The primary purpose of LKY's side trip was most likely not about military training, as Taiwan's Ministry of Defense was not given access to this memo.

From a very early stage, LKY's visits to Taiwan involved enjoying gatherings with the Shen couple and even the Chiang couple, such as the aforementioned family dinner on April 7, 1978 in which Wego participated. This example was already the second time LKY met him, and Wego so greatly impressed LKY that he wrote that it had been "an unexpected bonus" to learn from him "the philosophical basis on which one tackles the problems of life."[8]

LKY wrote his letter at the same time a message was written acknowledging the coming diplomatic breakthrough with Saudi Arabia. The obscure line between official and private interaction indicated that the personal relationship must have improved quickly and steadily in the past three years. LKY later wished to invite Wego to visit Singapore so that the former could learn more about Chinese *ch'i kung*.

One time in 1982, Chiang sent Vice Minister of Foreign Affairs Frederic Chien to Singapore to inform Lee of Chiang's eye operation, which would keep him from receiving LKY at the airport in person as he had always done. Considering that Chiang never received any other foreign leader in the capacity of president at the airport, his sending of Chien deeply touched Lee "by the enormous demonstration of courtesy and friendship," which had no apparent purpose for the national interest.[9] Over three decades later, Chien still recalled having seen tears in LKY's eyes at the very moment.[10] In the same exchange dated February 22, 1982, LKY attended to the issue of aborted arms sales to Taiwan and conveyed his worry that Ronald Reagan could be under "more pressure" to downgrade Taiwan's importance.

On 15 February 1982, LKY called on Chiang after his eye operation, during which they sent greetings to each other on behalf of their wives. Shen also passed gifts from Madame Chiang to LKY's and Shen's respective wives. As an appropriate practice between friends, they often exchanged small gifts, such as special flavored curry that LKY's wife once prepared for the Shens.[11] Upon returning, LKY wrote to Chiang that "[I]t cheered me greatly to find you in such good spirits.... There was no flagging in vitality or vigour despite the operation. Your voice was spritely and clear, and your mind sharp and crisp."[12] They had known each other so well by then that LKY encouraged his friend at the end of the letter: "...the Republic of China requires a leader who is well known for his steadfastness, and will be respected for being an upright and just ruler."[13]

Shen discussed Chinese culture with LKY every time he escorted him to different sites in Taiwan, either for official or leisure purposes, during LKY's numerous visits. Over the years, tourism in Taiwan had encountered extensive exposure to traditional Chinese religions and cultures, filled with historically and philosophically challenging topics, which provided the two thinkers with food for thought and subjects of comparison between the Taiwanese and Singaporeans. Shen arranged all the trips up to the smallest details to the comfort of his guest, especially when Lee's wife came along. A letter by Lee dated March 31, 1984 indicates such considerate caring.[14]

LKY's visits to Taiwan, especially those with Shen, were immersed in intensive acculturation. Their correspondences often cited Chinese aphorisms. In his letter on March 31, LKY complimented the "redeeming advantage" of his trip, that is,

> by travelling together in a car I had the opportunity to hear you speak candidly.... You taught me another Chinese aphorism — 'sit in a command tent and devise strategies that will assure victory a thousand li away'. It is apposite of President Chiang....[15]

LKY actually hand-wrote the newly acquired aphorism in Chinese characters in a parenthesis behind the citation, albeit an error in one of the words. He was not worried if his writing appeared legible. In Shen's reply typed on April 13 by his secretary Ma Ying-jeou (Taiwan's president between 2008 and 2016), another Chinese aphorism was cited to compliment LKY: "I myself learn a great deal from you every time we are together. This can best be described by another Chinese aphorism—'one talk with you gives me more than what I can learn in ten years of study,'" followed by Shen's hand-written Chinese characters.[16] Although Shen assured LKY that "there was absolutely no intrusion of my time," he apologized for his belated reply, dated May 7, because of "the busy political season... in this country."[17] Shen signed his letter in hand-written Chinese.

In 1985, LKY received Chiang's son Hsiao-wu as Taiwan's Representative to Singapore so that the latter could stay away from the political storm caused by a scandalous political assassination involving Hsiao-wu.

Role identity beyond personalization

Contemporary diplomatic history has witnessed other examples of emotionally rewarding personalization, e.g., Reagan–Thatcher (US–UK), Schmitt–Mitterrand (Germany–France), and Mao–Ho (Chi Minh) (China–Vietnam). Although personalization contributes to diplomacy, neither BoP theory nor BoR theory considers it essential to an international relationship. A complete turn of a personal relationship between Singapore and Taiwan in the 1990s demonstrates the tenacity of relation independent of positive emotions.

LKY's frequent visits to Taiwan did not end after 1990, which was the year Singapore and Beijing established their diplomatic relationship. In the same year, Lee Teng-hui began his own presidential term after two years of acting the presidential role at the death of Chiang Ching-kuo. LKY provided Lee Teng-hui the best the former could—to undertake an international trip in March 1988 to Singapore in the capacity of the president, although Lee Teng-hui did not arrive in the official title of the Republic of China'; he instead agreed to use the title "President from Taiwan". This event was considered a diplomatic breakthrough for Lee Teng-hui. LKY was also the first world leader who visited Taiwan after Chen Shui-bian became president in 2000, despite Chen's apparent pro-Taiwan independence. LKY's acquaintance with Ma lasted over two decades. Ma noted LKY's consistent concerns over Taiwan that one would not see in any other national leader in the world. Ma was the first president of Taiwan who could visit a country that recognized the PRC without Washington's facilitation, in order to pay respect to the Lees after LJY's death.

The period of the personalization of the bilateral relationship was an exception. It was self-restraint for the sake of an affirmative relationship that enabled LKY and his son-successor to continue to care about Taiwan's future with China even after Chiang and Shen passed away successively. His pragmatic judgment that unification is inevitable did not change his initial suggestion that Taiwan should be a strategic point to confront China. His willingness to mediate between Taipei and Beijing was voluntary. It was typically self-restraint because both Lee Teng-hui and Chen intended to be destructive in the bilateral relationship. By then, LKY's adherence to self-restraint and his show of goodwill were no longer vital to the national interest of Singapore because China was no longer a revolutionary threat. LKY was able to care for Taiwan's future despite the irrelevant passion toward Chiang. LKY received both Ma and his pro-independence competitor in Singapore before the presidential elections in 2008 (Er 2007: 45) to continue affirmative BoR.

Personal preference brings passion into inter-state relationships. Its disruption contrarily testifies to greater self-role identity that transcends personalization. President Ma, once Chiang's secretary, was able to facilitate, together with Chinese President Xi Jinping, their 2015 summit in Singapore, the first summit between the two rivals since 1949. Beijing must have trusted Singapore so immensely that the former's insistence for the two sides never to meet officially at an international site was diminished. Singapore's relationality policy, which binds Singapore with Taiwan and China respectively, successfully expounds/explains the internationality of its site being outside sovereign China. The greater selfhood is sufficiently convincing that Singapore does not represent internationality to China. In 2015, President Lee of Singapore arranged a meeting with Ma in the aftermath for Ma to claim, for the domestic audience in Taiwan that abhorred unification, that he was in an international, as opposed to a Chinese internal, occasion. Lee's considerate improvisation is the continuation of affirmative BoR.

Conclusion: the bilateral and affirmative relational turn

This chapter bridges the Western and Chinese relational turns by explaining how Singapore and Taiwan successfully developed a long-lasting reciprocal relationship. Their relations did not evolve from practicing a prior collective norm that eventually reconstituted the national identity of the two states. Rather, it was the result of care and consideration exerted by both sides, which enabled the transcendence over the initially strategic calculus. The processual analysis of the case further shows that the two countries did not form their emotional alliance through a give-and-take negotiation. Both of them unilaterally improvised needed "gifts" for the other. To that extent, it was more a BoR than BoP or balance of interest. This is in line with Chinese IR that highlights the importance of the greater self, which is embedded in role-playing and does not request the reconstitution of an individual state's national identity. Such relationality is different from the one described by the relational literature that emphasizes the self-restraining practice of collective norms and the ensuing change in self-identity.

This chapter qualifies the uniqueness claim made by the Chinese relational turn by indicating its bilateral sensibilities. The affirmative BoR demonstrated by Singapore and Taiwan reproduced the Cold War at the systemic level. Theoretically, the case illustrates how bilateral relationality, even between small states, can constitute IR in general, without which the relational turn is at best incomplete. Both nations failed to adapt to the emerging norm of détente due to strong domestic anti-communism and made up for the loss of multilateral relation through their bilateral relation. The Western and Chinese relational turns are thus simultaneously complementary and contradictory. They are complementary to the extent that the nascent dyadic greater self provided relational security when the Cold War alliance weakened. However, they are also contradictory in the sense that bilateral relations transcend multilateral rules and norms.

Finally, the bilateral sensibilities of Chinese IR offer a methodological vehicle for the study of relationality. The relational turn emphasizes the constitution of the state more than that of relationality itself. Indeed, the formation and change of relations are visible when the interactions between two states evolve and converge to form a shared resemblance that can constrain and motivate their policy choices. Such a bilateralism seeks to attend to the other state's specific policy, leadership, and emotional attributes so as to enable a more nuanced analysis of the dynamics of the relation. Methodologically, this encourages processual analysis which, while retaining some lack of clarity regarding the focus on national self-identity as constituted by existing relations, remains essential to understanding how relations evolve out of the differing practices of states.

Notes

1 The hand-written confidential memo, numbered 29, dated June 11, 1973, read by Shen on June 16, and forwarded to Deputy Minister on June 18.
2 Lee Kuan Yew to Australian Prime Minister Robert Menzies, April 20, 1965 (quoted in Footnotes 27–35 in Barr 1999).
3 Shen Chang-huan "strictly confidential" letter to Prime Minister Lee, May 9, 1978, mimeograph.
4 Lee Kuan Yew "confidential" letter to Shen Chang-huan, May 17, 1978, (67) 興邦字N. 2461, File No. 09111, mimeograph.
5 Lee Kuan Yew to "Dear Madame Chiang Kai Shek," April 22, 1975, delivered through Peter Chang on April 24 in a confidential envelope.
6 LKY to "Madame Chiang," April 22, 1975.
7 LKY to "Madame Chiang," April 22, 1975.
8 LKY to Shen, May 17, 1978.
9 Lee Kuan Yew to Chiang, February 22, 1982. In this letter, which was dated on February 22, 1982, Lee handwrote the title of "My dear President Chiang" and signed "Yours ever Kuanyew."
10 Lee said to Chien, "I was overwhelmed." (Yi and Wang 2000).
11 Lee Kuan Yew to Chiang, February 22, 1984. Shen to Lee, May 15, 1984, which was delivered in person by Taiwan's representative in Singapore, Hu Shin.
12 Kuan Yew to Chiang, February 22, 1982.
13 Lee Kuan Yew to Chiang, February 22, 1982.
14 Lee Kuan Yew to Shen, March 31, 1984. Lee already hand-wrote Shen's title in his letter.
15 Lee Kuan Yew to Shen, March 31, 1984. The aphorism presumably engrosses the speaker in the imagined massive geography of China's ancient battlefield where only rationality and determination count.
16 Shen to Lee, May 15, 1984. Contrast to the previous aphorism, this one is filled with Chinese humanism pointing to the importance of philosophical depth in human lives, in comparison with dicta in the books.
17 Shen to Lee, May 15, 1984.

3 Relational policy
of major powers

Chapters 1 and 2 illustrated the difference of a relationship-oriented foreign policy from the principle/rule-based IR. Chapter 3 demonstrates how these two types of IR each reflect a sociological and psychological necessity. The former holds that relation mainly manifests in social relationships, which compromise and even discourage the construction of essential identities. The contrasting latter notes particularly the prior constitution of state identity, so a national self-conception already sufficiently reveals its relations to all. Studying the psychological identities of a state is necessary in exploring its sense of resemblance/difference to all other states. Between the two, an epistemological divide exists in the degree of influence allowed for others to have in making one's immediate identities and relationships. The relational literature presents different predictions. One attends to how psychological identities reproduce and reconstruct imagined prior resemblance, whereas another examines how improvisation of resemblance requires evasion of identities.

Role theory is particularly suitable for connecting two relational agendas because they fit two distinctive categories of role source according to the role theory literature. This chapter compares China with the US because they are major powers capable of enforcing grand strategies of a broader scale. Such a comparison can also more clearly reveal the representative styles of the two countries because they can represent sociological and psychological relationality. We use them to illustrate two different role-styles of how a national actor may belong to IR—either role-making or role-taking. The purpose is not to assert that China does not need rule-based governance or that the US, mutual relations. Considering each as taking a role to fulfill one of the two necessities is appropriate.

Role and relationship in the study on grand strategy

In this chapter, grand strategy refers to an integral set of goal-oriented strategies informed by the self-role that a state assumes. IR requires super powers to adopt grand strategies. The grand strategy of China has become a crucial issue for IRT worldwide since the rise of China at the end of the Cold War era (Wang 2005: 68–79). Nevertheless, this grand strategy is difficult to identify. The goal and logic of the Chinese grand strategy can only be comprehended when a broad time frame is applied (Goldstein 2005: 19). By combining the characteristics of both strong and weak states at the present time, China's ambiguous grand strategy is assumed to become clear/ clearer in the future (Swaine & Tellis 2000). However, we argue that China, on the contrary, possesses a grand strategy whose style is precisely to evade any consistent self-role conception so that China can craft a sense of resemblance to different others.

A grand strategy that enforces a self-centric and often universally applied order and its role expectations of nations upon others is not the typical foreign policy style of China. Chinese role playing is mainly embedded in ritual, face culture, and group orientation (Evans 2010: 42–57, Tu 1994, Wills 2009: 23–39), as well as gift giving. The style of role-taking and the resultant Chinese grand strategy consciously make the role of China and the role of the interacting party mutually constituted. China's self-role that emerged in the 21st century was ingrained in the dictum of a "responsible major power" and the "community with a shared future for mankind" that promotes a "harmonious world" through mutual accommodation for each other's "core national interest[s]."

Given that strategy conceptualization requires a nation to be unequivocal in its perceived role in the world, a self-centric reference is necessary to prescribe norms both consistently and unilaterally and assign responsibilities to other nations. The question lies in the capability of a consciously role-taking state to possess a grand strategy. Using role theory, which breaks down the style of role into identity-based and relationship-based formulations, we discuss the Chinese grand strategy style. China's approach to negotiating constantly with specific parties to accept the country's relational role divides its grand strategy among various simultaneous sets of bilateral role relationships. The usual disinterest of the bilateral style in any multilateral order or general rules of IR can even undermine the formation of stable national interest conceptions. We use China's wavering on the issue of US arms sales to Taiwan to illustrate the volatility of Chinese core national interests in practice. We believe that the undecidability of Chinese foreign policy between relationship and national interests explains the obscuring of Chinese grand strategy better than the fact that China is caught in the transition of becoming a greater power.

By examining China's policy toward US arms sales to Taiwan, we show how China has tried to coach the incumbent hegemonic power to acknowledge the country's rise to the status of an equal power. To ensure a mutually agreeable role for China, Chinese foreign policy has the double mission of presenting China as an accepted and respected equal power and of assuring the incumbent hegemonic power that China is a role player, rather than a revisionist or an agitator. The Chinese grand strategy pertaining to the China–US relationship is not to promote any alternative rule of international relations but to convince the US of China's trustworthy partnership.

Accordingly, China shows its determination to protect its rising power status on the arms sales issue, as a core national interest, through certain acts of retaliation and the willingness to compromise by renouncing its retaliation. The repeated cycle of probable inconsistency reflects that the style of the Chinese grand strategy is not about rule making.

Identity-based role vs. relationship-based role

Based on the tradition of symbolic interactionism, we begin with the distinction between the two sources of social behavior, namely I and me, role making and taking, and interaction within and between individuals (Charon 2004, Mead 1934). Role sources in role theory can be either psychological or sociological. This division of role sources is particularly useful in comparing the styles of American and Chinese grand strategy, as the American grand strategy historically conceptualizes national roles based on an isolationist tradition, whereas the Chinese grand strategy derives roles from the reciprocal convention of the tribute system. Nevertheless, the American grand strategy can accommodate sociological sources. For example, the US has been suggested to have instituted a tributary system that commits the hegemonic power to benevolence and civilizational diffusion (Khong 2013: 27–28). By contrast, the Chinese grand strategy can contain psychological sources. This observation was apparent during the Cultural Revolution, when China endorsed national liberation elsewhere "to win adherents to the Chinese program for radical change in the international system" that China had desired (Van Ness 1970: 189).

The psychological sources of role refer to its cognitive construction, whereas sociological sources primarily comprise interactions. Psychological role conceptions emerge from the prior embedding of the actor and their self-identity that provides universally applicable self-references. A psychological role conception is context free and can aid the actor in evaluating others. This conception includes whether or not other actors are capable, cooperative, or equal and how they deal with other actors consistently (Cottam 1994). Such a self-identity-based role exists in the perceived resemblances/ differences between self-conception and other-conception. This role is therefore sensitive to the relative power necessary to defend self-difference.

Sociological role conceptions adapt to the context and remain negotiable to acquire the recognition of the other. The rationality behind allowing the other, even weaker, side to determine the outcome of an interaction rests on the long-term concerns, with regards to a nation's reputation as a relational player. Bound to the specific conditions of interaction, a nation subscribing to the sociological role conception must always flexibly adapt to such conditions. Conversion according to the role expectation of others is the goal of psychological role conception, whereas adaptation is the goal of sociological conception. The former seeks to transform the rest of the world from a potentially threatening one to an accepting one, whereas the latter seeks to convince the other side that the nation is not a threat to others.

Sociological role conceptions that avoid rigidity in mutable conditions can be consciously compromising and contingent at one time but punitive and confrontational at another, hence making it a BoR practice. The credibility of a role player, without which no grand strategy can be deemed convincing, is of paramount importance. Compromise coming from a strong position is a deliberate act of benevolence, whereas confrontation coming from a weak position destroys the reputation of the other side as a credible role player. For psychological role conceptions, however, compromise is only sensible coming from a weak position, and discussing the grand strategy for a weak nation is pointless.

These sociological conceptions comprise relationship-based roles born out of interactions. (Coser 1995) This other-oriented formulation of role is more likely bilateral than multilateral as a general rule, universal principle, or strong common interest is almost indispensable in a prior multilateral order (Ruggie 1993: 11). Thus, multilateralism is a challenge to countries that adhere to the sociological conceptualization of roles. By contrast, bilateralism embedded in relationship tolerates deviance from universal rules, encourages patience, and appeals to idiosyncratic symbols or specially crafted gifts. Under the bilateral condition, judgment of relative strength is not the dominant factor when designing the grand strategy.

From time to time, China must craft resemblance over differences in race, value, religion, or institution, etc., given the volatility of identity politics everywhere. Whenever signs indicate that a relationship is under threat, China consistently interrogates whether or not national differences are still respected. China's improvised reward or punishment system often fails to fully convey its message or, if it does, the other is not able to reciprocate due to its own internal conditions, thus defeating the purpose of sociological role playing. We will discuss this further in Chapter 9. This type of miscommunication can even lead to war, as was the case during the Sino–Indian border clashes in 1962 and the Sino–Soviet clashes in 1969 (Fang 2014, Wich 1980).

By conveying and imposing one's role to the rest of the world, a nation automatically generates pressure of altercasting on other states. (Harnisch 2012: 47–71) Altercasting is enacting one's role conception either to assert one's national interests or to highlight one's social value, while expecting other nations to understand and positively interact. Altercasting of the identity-based role tends to impose the same norms on all alters, as "others," to comply with them, in contrast with specific and different duties that the relationship-based role demands from specific alters, as members of "a greater self," to restrain self-interests. The characteristics of the alters indicate how China can best entice or coerce them to a reciprocal pattern of interaction.

Practically, as well as culturally, several nations rely more on psychological conception whereas others rely on sociological conception. However, no nation can rely on only one type of role conception without the supplemental contribution of the other. Although comparing two societies, or their foreign policy making, strictly according to the dichotomy of psychological and sociological roles is an exaggeration, we detect the contrast between the US and China in the formulation of their grand strategy. The American grand strategy is more used to promoting a specific set of principles or rules, where the presentation of different norms is deemed a threat, or potential threat, that should be ultimately converted. Liberalism in the US is at the core of these norms. By contrast, the Chinese grand strategy does not promote a substantive norm but is preoccupied with achieving an image of harmony.

The ultimate goal of the American grand strategy will hold even without a second player, consenting or dissenting, but this does not mean that Americanness pays no attention to relationship or social recognition. (e.g. Lake 2009: 331–353, Slaughter 2009: 94–113, Thie 2013) Rather, US foreign policy concerns about relationship are assessed and maneuvered to suit the purpose of certain general principles embedded in either liberalism or hegemonic stability. By contrast, Chineseness depends on social recognition. It too does not mean that Chineseness contains no universal inspiration. Nevertheless, from a sociological role conception, China's universal inspiration is in a more abstract nostalgia for the status of Middle Kingdom than in a concrete world order. Contrary to realist assessment, (Dreyer 2004: 85–104, Kissinger 2011: 10, White 2012) it is no more than a thin belief that all are bound to relate in an indefinite common origin and destiny. For example, even the seemingly universal conformist roles expected of Taiwan, Hong Kong, and/or Tibet present divergent unification models.

The difference in role sources further divides the purpose of the grand strategy with regards to altercasting associated with role conceptions. The power to impose sanctions according to psychological role conception is essential to American strategists, whereas the power to improvise togetherness according to sociological role conception is the key to understanding the behavior of the Chinese grand strategy. The relational orientation in the Chinese grand strategy does not contradict most studies on the Chinese grand strategy or claims that a more assertive China will or is already emerging (Jacques 2012, Swaine & Tellis 2000), as its national capacity continues to grow. Rather, our prediction is that an assertive China will continue to seek bilateral relationships, each in its peculiar way to recognize the return of the benevolent Middle Kingdom, but bypass any serious quest for general rules of IR. The relational style of the Chinese grand strategy is independent of the rise of its power. That said, altercasting based on sociological role conceptions does not necessarily guarantee smoother reception than with psychological role conceptions, as intended mutuality under the sociological circumstance can be biased and therefore unwelcome, not to mention that at least one aspect of relational policy concerns punishment.

Chinese grand strategy

In this section, we will not elaborate on the American grand strategy except noting the apparent proclivity toward identity-based role conception as conceived by the literature (Bastiaan & Graaff 2012, Brooks, Ikenberry & Wohlforth 2012, 2013, Caldwell 2009, Cottam 1986, Ikenberry 2000, Nye 1995, Thies 2010, 2013, Trachtenberg 1999, Van Ness 1985). The conceptualization of the American grand strategy is consistent with Christian doctrine, which emphasizes certain standards of truth and universal morality and focuses on the binary values of good and evil. Based on the judgment of its relative power, Washington designed its grand strategy and manipulated it with initiative and assertion. When designing the grand strategy, the US has a precise definition of exactly who its enemies or rivals are. This identity-based role conception ensures that the American grand strategy always focuses on picking an enemy from outside the boundary of democratic states and the market system.

Perspectives of the literature

Based on the literature on Chinese social relationships and roles (Gold, Guthrie & Wank 2002, Hwang 2011), we suggest that the conceptualization of the Chinese grand strategy emerges from a relationship-based role conception. Relationality is an ontological component of IR and therefore a systemic necessity, according to advocates of the Chinese school of IR (Qin 2009: 5–20). We adopt a minimal approach in the following discussion by treating relationality as conditions of being related. Relationality prompts Chinese leaders to improvise stronger connections with the other party and oblige it to reciprocate. A relationship-based role primarily involves bilateral relationships, which constrains China's performance in the multilateral setting, as indicated in Chapters 1 and 2.

From Qin's perspective, China adapts to each context, thus reiterating the principle that differences in national conditions never lead to problems in its existing relationships with other nations. Particular bilateral relationships should evolve into a distinct pattern over time, and bilateral relationships on different sites require varied arrangements. According to Chinese relational IR, the Chinese grand strategy has no consistent values or universal order other than stabilizing the relationship with each specific other. China does not expect another nation to promote any universal form of morality. Confrontation usually arises from Chinese foreign policy under the premise of being betrayed rather than of violation of a just order or universal value.

No prior values complement Chinese rhetoric on a harmonious world. Chinese scholars acquainted with the grand strategy logic are perplexed at China's reluctance to develop a grand strategy that involves an effort to modify the environment rather than just adapting to it (Hao 2010, Xin 2013).

In practice, China has rarely adopted a self-identity with respect to the rest of the world, unless its goal is to achieve a lofty image in a multilateral setting. The American grand strategy compels China to examine other states, such as North Korea, Myanmar, or Syria, and abide by a certain fixed principle, which is tantamount to ruining the reciprocity between China and those of opposing values. Singh pointed out this focus in Chinese foreign policy on bilateral relationships,[1] which is a style that has made the Chinese grand strategy appear inconsistent and transitional. (Goldstein 2005: 19–20, 30, Tang & Zhang 2005: 54–74).

Avery Goldstein (2005: 30) asserted that China understands grand strategy. However, he also suggested that the trends and themes of the Chinese grand strategy can only be understood through long-term observation of Chinese leaders' policy making. In particular, how policy makers make decisions about foreign policy and how these decisions reflect China's logic with regard to the distribution of military, political, and economic resources should be considered. Goldstein (2005: 38) further affirmed that China does not follow the pattern of revisionist rising powers such as Nazi Germany or post-Meiji militarist Japan. After the Cold War, the Chinese grand strategy design shifted toward building national power and cultivating international partners. Goldstein's observation revealed the responsive and defensive nature of the Chinese grand strategy style. David Lampton indirectly restated/reaffirmed Goldstein by cautioning against any expedient analysis based purely on China's capacity, which ignores the intentions of Chinese foreign policy (Lampton 1997: 120–40, Liberthal 2007: 29–31, Swaine & Tellis 2000).

Critical Chinese scholars often consider the Chinese grand strategy as problematic, if not awkward. The current debate about the Chinese grand strategy originates from the frustration and difficulties China has encountered throughout its development. China's involvement in territorial disputes with its neighboring countries has exacerbated the debate. Several Chinese scholars criticized Beijing's absence of an efficient approach and resolute attitude in confronting other states. China can consequently become a super power that has no substantial influence or voice in important global issues. Lin (2012: 14–16), for example, argued that the absence of efficient, effective methods to resolve sovereignty disputes over certain islets has been a chronic problem for China. Moreover, China has never developed a productive mode of maritime governance due to long-term negligence by the Chinese government. Furthermore, Lin opined that China can only assume an actual grand strategy by strengthening marine power and constructing a sound method of governing the oceans.

Chinese scholars called for a more assertive grand strategy. They maintained that China's relatively weak and inefficient reaction to crises in both the South China Sea and over the Senkaku/Diaoyu Islands resulted from having no grand strategy.[2] Most scholars believed that China should learn from the Western great powers and develop a defense-oriented grand strategy to strengthen its marine force. They emphasized that strengthening China's marine force is not aimed at domination over the ocean but rather at establishing a grand strategy through a focus on their naval fleet. This emphasis intends to protect China's national interests by defending its sovereign rights over disputable seas and exploiting the marine resources that can significantly further support China's economic development (Cao 2011: 92–95, Lin 2012: 41–42).

The criticism from Chinese scholars essentially focuses on the fact that the rise of China does not conceptually change the defensive tone of Chinese foreign policy. Recent literature on status recognition describes the range of bilateral relationships with the US that are open to China. In the literature, China has three options, namely, improving performance on US-guided values, competing with the US, and raising substitute values for liberalism (Larson & Sevchenko 2011: 70–76). China has virtually attempted all three options, by joining the WTO, confronting the US in East Asian and international trade, and stressing national differences. However, the national difference to which China consistently and adamantly adheres is, at best, a peculiar value that provides no substantive rule of international society other than a soft attitude based toward defiant nations. This attitude has been referred to as the value of a harmonious world, which is embedded in the Middle Kingdom complex.

Perspectives of policymaking

The notion of the Middle Kingdom has emerged along with the rise of China. Despite the rhetorical denial that China is pursuing Middle Kingdom status, both government propaganda and policy statements consistently suggest the re-emergence of such an identity (Yoon 2014). In addition, the defensive nature of Chinese foreign policy may also change. President Xi (2013a) raised the ideal of the Chinese Dream and declared, "We are closer than in any other period of history to the goal of the great revival of the Chinese nation." (Xi 2013a, 2013b, 2013c) The idea of China being at the center of the world is apparent in his statement that "Not only should we understand China's history and culture, but also open our eyes to observe the world. We want to understand different nations' history and culture, remove unwanted elements in them, and take the top off their cream" (Xi 2013a). President Xi then announced, "Those who know us are within the seas, and the brink of heaven feels like a next-door neighbourhood" (Xi 2013a). This statement also led President Xi to express hope that, "We turn the opportunities of the world into China's opportunities and China's opportunities to those of the world." The Central Party School explained, "The Chinese traditional culture praises perpetual self-strengthening and deep virtue to accommodate varieties. It simultaneously advocates everyone owning all under-heaven in order for all under-heaven to reach great harmony" (Central Party School Research Centre for Socialist Theory with Chinese Characteristics 2014).

Despite the implicit Middle Kingdom and the explicit Harmonious World speeches of Xi's national identity and of China's relational role in the world, the policy implications are consistently relational and devoid of universal rules; hence, the continuation of the defensive stance. No development of institutional values or policy programs has been initiated for the rest of the world to follow. On the contrary, self-consciousness does not attempt any universal guidance. When expounding the foreign policy implications of the Chinese Dream, Foreign Minister Wang Yi (2013: 16) reminded that, "China has never been as close to the center of the world stage as it is today" and that China's relationships with surrounding nations rely on "tens of thousands of differing connections in humanity and a spontaneous feeling of affinity," of which he specifically mentioned Confucianism in East Asia and Buddhism in South Asia. Wang Yi also mindfully referred to the special privileges that China has willingly arranged for ASEAN countries. National Minister and former Foreign Minister and Chinese Ambassador to the US Yang Jiechi (2013) further explained the Chinese Dream by specifically referring to equal and mutually respectful bilateralism as an instrument through which to undertake conflict resolution, be it a territorial dispute (with a weaker party) or a discussion on human rights (with the stronger US).

In a multilateral context, relational role-playing requires China to exclusively address the contributions of the so-called "Chinese Dream," as former Foreign Minister Wu Jianmin (2013) maintained. According to Wu, only by sharing China's economic development internationally will the rest of the world willingly cooperate with China. The goal of alternative relational role playing under the multilateral frame is to protect national differences while considering global rules. Relational role playing presumes national differences; hence, China must not commit to any policy that intends to synchronize its institutions or convert a locally held national interest conception into a global value. Presumably, such relational role playing justifies China's defensive attitude toward the intervention of global rules in Chinese affairs.

One noticeable example is China's boycott of the major power consensus at the Copenhagen Summit on Climate Change 2009 on the distribution of responsibility to control and reduce carbon emissions. The Chinese delegates were generally absent during the plenary sessions but were intensively involved in bilateral talks. China particularly stressed that the leeway in which developed countries accorded developing countries allowed the latter to voluntarily decide on their own levels of reduction, but at the same time emphasized the historical climate damage that the developed countries had committed (Watts 2009). Another example is that of China's consistent reservations about UN interventions, on the basis of humanitarianism, in failing states, on occasions when the consent of the local regime had not been acquired first.

Perspectives of core national interests

The defensive characteristics of the Chinese grand strategy can be traced back to the imperial China era. For example, a historical lens assumes that the classic Chinese grand strategy prefers a "low violence" approach. Although China conquered other nations through force,[3] the ancient Chinese grand strategy of developing and maintaining military power may be restrained from excessive use of force (Zhu 2011: 5). The construction of an amicable international environment beneficial to China's progress has always been the main theme of discourses about Beijing's grand strategy (Goldstein 2005: 20–26, 177–80, Wang 2005: 68–79). Hence, modern China follows a grand strategy culture, which is responsive and defense-oriented but not always peaceful. This responsive characteristic is supported by the emergent refocusing of Chinese foreign policy on the protection of core national interests (Nathan & Scobell 2012, Wang 2005: 68–79). However, aforementioned critics argued that these adjustments are insufficient in regards to the challenges facing China on the rise (Ma 2013: 155–168).

A defensive grand strategy focused on core national interests is a step ahead of the relationship-based role, which implies that relationship becomes merely a functional concern. The popularity of the discussion on core national interests in the current century enhances the instrumentality of the harmonious world ideal. The appeal to core national interests can reflect a new style of role conception, namely, one that is identity-based. China is intrinsically a distinctive national entity in this regard, with a quality that is not shareable with others. By contrast, relationship-based identity, as Qin (2009) argued, involves an ontological statement. According to this ontological sensibility, China's self-fulfillment is complete only when comprehensive reciprocal mutuality is achieved with all different others. Emphasizing core national interests, therefore, estranges China from mutuality. However, we show, in the following discussion, that core national interests are pretentious and that the purpose of listing core national interests remains part of the grand strategy embedded in relationship. We argue that references to core national interests, as well as their cancellation, are examples of improvised self-restraint in accordance with each situation. Shelving a core-national-interest issue enhances the felt level of resemblance to the other party, which may be very thin in reality. Raising the issue contrarily shames the other side for losing the status of being a friend.

Core national interests that are not core

China's determination to grasp the "period of strategic opportunities" (*zhanlue jiyu qi*) has been the official party line since the 16th Party Congress in 2002 (Ye 2011: 69). These opportunities, as provided by the decline of the US, also include globalization, the return of Hong Kong, and the smooth power transition to the fourth-generation leadership. The new rhetoric wishes China to develop peacefully into a great, or the greatest, power in the world (Wang 2006: 16–17). This pursuit of strength and wealth was featured a decade later in the Chinese Dream that President Xi announced in 2012, in terms of "national wealth and strength."[4] Given that the dream is not an idea of global order, China still does not have a prepared plan to convert the world into any ideal type. Rather, the country is compelled to cope with each nation, given the imperative to harmonize many a relationship that will be greatly affected by China's rise. In hoping to form "communities of shared future" (*mingyun gongtong ti*) with each of its neighbors, China can either lure other nations into its grand development through China's contributions or persuade them not to hinder such development.[5]

Thus, bilateral diplomacy is the proper focus for China in its attempt to become allies with a world divided by national interests, due to the exemption of bilateralism from linear historiography or duties of global governance. China's official white papers on peace and development do not adopt the term "all countries" when referring to the world at large. Instead, they always refer to "each country" (*ge guo*) when explaining them in China's foreign policy,[6] because each country is different in various ways. The emphasis pertains specifically to China's undeclared preference for bilateralism. While the notion of strategic opportunities in China is similar to the American grand strategy thinking, China's purpose is to demonstrate a self-restraining role in exchange for other countries' acceptance of its progress. Presumably, no country is required to adapt to China's rise. The Chinese terminology for its national role is specifically "a responsible major power" (*yige fuzeren de da guo*) (Xia 2013: 70–77), with the official Chinese interpretation of being responsible as "handling our own affairs well" (*ba ziji shiqing zuo hao*). Other countries are also expected to assimilate this perspective with regard to handling their own affairs well (Shih & Huang 2013: 351–365).

Two strategic options are available to other nations in the eyes of China. They can change their values or institutions to improve their suitability in compliance with China's national role conceptions. This kind of altercasting is called "change perspective." Or, they can be flexible in determining their specific values or institutions when coping with China's rise, as long as a sense of resemblance to China obtains confidence on both sides. This option is called the "leeway perspective." The former reflects an interventionary self-identity that requests others to comply,[7] whereas the latter originates in a restrained self-identity that highlights how China adapts to the conditions of the interacting party.[8] The leeway perspective adopts a kind of soft altercasting in comparison with the change perspective. In the leeway perspective, China continues to have high expectations of the other side's transcendence of differences in values, institutions, ethnicity, ideology, alliances, and other national traits, thus allowing China to feel secure in and certain of stable reciprocity. In allowing leeway to accommodate their otherwise estranging differences, peculiarity usually exists in the bilateral arrangements improvised for the establishment of confidence between both sides. However, China is prepared to resort to confrontation if such differences threaten to compromise the contrived resemblance between them. Considering that the change perspective typically targets political, ideological, and institutional reforms, the leeway perspective is satisfied in ritual and cultural exchanges and in symbolic concessions or sanctions.

Adopting the "change perspective" involves the power to enforce adaptations and the direction they should take. Even a hegemonic power that guards the *status quo* may request a change in the other's values or institutions, in order to reinforce its reign or contain potential challenges. China is on the alert for any such interventionary hegemony to prevent the spontaneity of other nations from appealing to their particular identity-based roles or promoting their differences.

China needs to examine the other side when signs indicate that relational reciprocity is under threat. To assure whether such a threat is imminent, China consistently observes how national differences are respected when dealing with the US or international organizations. When facing a weaker power along its borders, China resorts to testing and warnings. In any event, the relational role concept should not affirm the contents of China's differing core national interest. All nations are different to some extent in their ideologies; thus, China's long-held pledge of peaceful coexistence evolves primarily upon how nations improvise resemblance through creative gift giving to deal with differences rather than how different they are from one another. The Chinese grand strategy proceeds from the choice between the use and non-use of coercion rather than from the enforced value of coercion. For example, official white papers include territorial security, sovereignty, economic development, political stability, and socialist values as core national interests, which are not unusual, even though other nations may dislike socialism. However, China and the US are faulted for being civilizing nations that inadvertently look down upon other nations and seek to rectify them according to their own identity-based roles. This civilizing style of practices seriously affects IR more than whether or not they represent socialism or liberalism.

China's style of self-role conception on how to interact with others is intrinsic to its expectation of others to adopt either the change or the leeway approach. This makes considering the level of power, which is the judgment of a country's relative power that affects how the two options function in the target country, less relevant. Given that the self-role of China is relational, silence or neutrality between local factions can be observed toward remote conflicts, regardless of their apparent risks to humanity. Non-intervention can be anticipated although China may possess power leverage. This observation is apparent in Beijing's response to various noticeable instances in Africa and the Middle East. However, symbolic infringements on reciprocal respect may ironically cause disproportionate retaliation. This phenomenon reflects China's approach to its maritime disputes in the South China

Sea, where China intermittently demands a change in policy from the Philippines and Vietnam but not in their values or institutions. China's retaliation is often resolute but symbolic, in order for the bilateral talk to resume and the sovereignty issue to be deferred (Swaine & Fravel 2011: 1–29). In fact, unilateral withdrawal has been a noticeable trait in the Chinese style of conflict and conflict resolution (Chan 1978). China's resentment rarely lasts long as the aversion is more a ritual than a value.

On the contrary, China's relational sensibility allows its weaker opponent to resort to resistance. North Korea and Taiwan used to act tenaciously in anticipation of reconciliation from China.[9] Thus, whether China achieves a reciprocal relationship over time depends on Chinese leaders' judgment on the country's manipulation of the other side. Similarly, China can resort to resistance against its stronger opponents while never really demanding a change in the latter's values or institutions. The evaluation of power difference or value difference is not the cause of Chinese leaders' adoption of confrontation and counter-confrontation. Policy makers design the means to confront only after deciding to do so, according to the disparity of power between China and its opponent.

The leeway approach does not consider any serious threat from a target rising in power, but still practices opposite values. The threat can be greater proportionally than another nation, even if both comply with the same value system and deny reciprocal responsibility. Vietnam and China, for example, have had disputes over many an issue for over 2,000 years, regardless of their power asymmetry or similar political economic conditions (Womack 2006). The adoption by the other party of the leeway approach that disregards differences in values and ideologies implies China's adherence to relational role playing. China hopes that other nations do not interpret China's assertion of core interests as a threat to these nations' values. Such disregard for the formation of global values can discomfit identity-based thinkers, who convert wrong to right in the name of global value. These identity-based thinkers also ambiguously perceive China's hidden realist's intent to establish alliances with offenders. However, Chinese foreign policy is consistent in its negligence of ideological differences, showing lukewarm interest in strategic alliances to protect socialist values.[10] On the contrary, Chinese national leaders are constantly out to secure each discrete bilateral relationship, especially in Africa and Southeast Asia, where no other nations visit as frequently and systematically. For example, it has become traditional since 1991 for Chinese Foreign Ministers to visit Africa every year. Another example is that every Chinese Foreign Ministers goes to Sri Lanka.

Despite citing core interests in familiar realist terms and with an implicitly nationalist tone, official white papers have a strong non-identity-based context that implies China's unfailing preference for the leeway perspective. Including the Mao era, China has rarely taken sides in global politics beyond the superficial denouncement issued by the Red Guards during the Cultural Revolution. The Ninth Party Congress of April 1969 actually praised China for its non-alliance, while simultaneously confronting both superpowers (Author n.a. 1969: 187–189). Mao's characterization of the world on the eve of the establishment of the PRC, as divided by the two camps and the intermediate zone, was most characteristic of the Chinese grand strategy style. China's active participation in the non-alignment movement of the 1950s, which later extended through to the three-world policy of the 1970s and its equidistant diplomacy in the 1980s, demonstrates a conscious preference for contextualized, though inconsistent, reciprocal relationship.

Unconventional China has no route map should all the rising powers raise a grand strategy to rectify world order. Deng Xiaoping's witty "cover light and nurture in the dark" (*tao guang yang hui*, also translated as "keeping a low profile") advice in the 1990s reflects the similar wisdom that China should not mire itself in troubled areas. Deng's legacy has repeatedly inspired contemporary leaders. The climax was Hu Jintao's establishment of the "harmonious world" as China's ideal world that combines Confucianism and Socialism in one slogan. In this concept of the world, values, institutions, and ideologies are secondary to reciprocal relationships among nations. On the eve of the handover to the fifth-generation leaders in 2012, China denounced the rise of new interventionism in the world,[11] deeming intervention as an abomination to its support of the leeway approach. China unfailingly holds that such incidents are vehicles for other major powers' misuse of their advantage. Xi Jinping, upon succeeding Hu's leadership, raised the idea of "communities of common destiny" to cope with neighboring relationships. (Xi 2013a).

The image of compliance is important to the protection of China's self-perceived differences of values and institutions. The foremost challenge to China's relational-based role playing is the image of the so-called China threat and its competition with the US for hegemonic leadership. The Chinese grand strategy does not include converting the US into acceptance of Communist party rule, but rather focuses on demonstrating China and US as not confronting each other—a modest goal for any grand strategy. The overall idea of listing core national interests is to help the US maintain a reciprocal relationship with China. Nevertheless, these interests are negotiable, to the extent that the image of reciprocal role-playing can be secured, as it is perceived by the world. In order to forge a reciprocal relationship with the US, China's core national interests are composed in Chinese terms, i.e., "the new type of major power relationship" (Xi 2013b). A bilateral relationship with the US has thus become one of the major themes of the current Chinese grand strategy.

There are numerous examples of China's concessions on core national interests. The purpose of expanding the list of core national interests is to make subsequent concessions dramatic enough to oblige others to stabilize reciprocal relationships for at least a period, hence the Chinese style of altercasting. However, even in cases where China is on the powerful side and unilaterally imposes concessions, relational security still relies on the weaker side to reciprocate. China has accordingly tolerated ambiguities along its disputed borders, and even granted land to smaller neighbors, such as North Korea, Myanmar, and others. Official white papers speak triumphantly of discretely resolving territorial disputes with 12 neighboring countries, which is a clear indicator of a harmonious world where no one's core interests are under threat. Ironically, promoting the image of the harmonious world can, paradoxically, override the core interests of territorial integrity. No other case is more peculiar or apparent than the issue of US arms sales to Taiwan. Thus, the identity-based role that undergirds the core national interest discourse is no more than a vehicle for achieving the aspiration for a relationship-based role wherein China would never be treated as a threat.

Case of US arms sales to Taiwan

The improvement, preservation, and restoration of bilateral relationships comprise the practical theme of the Chinese grand strategy. The theme is a product of the enactment of China's role as a partner. To prove this partnership, China would shelve its core national interests in certain circumstances to craft resemblance of a common commitment to friendship. For example, China–US relations show that the term "core national interests" has been fraught with controversies and ironies. China would peculiarly highlight its core national interests to inform Washington of its bottom line and, so, save the bilateral relationship from damage. China could acquiesce on core national interests and put aside contradictions between words and deeds to compromise. This would reproduce friendship and oblige the US for reciprocity.

We argue that the importance of maintaining a stable relationship with the US has trumped China's core national interest of unification, pertaining to the US arms sales to Taiwan. Arms sales not only threaten China's security, but infringe upon its claimed sovereignty. Sovereignty has been the sole prior principle China has invoked to defend national differences everywhere in the world. In fact, the Taiwan issue is on top of the list of China's core national interests. With the rise of China, status recognition is becoming a salient issue. Arms sales infringing upon its sovereignty compounds China's poor bilateral relationship with the US. This is the main reason China's improvised cycles on the issue of arms sales merits further attention.

In practice, China considers arms sales a bilateral issue. China could simply have raised the universal rule that arms sales to citizens of other countries should, by any reckoning, be a violation of sovereign rights. However, it has never taken such an action. Instead, China has painstakingly and repeatedly pressured each US president on the same issue while simultaneously compromising its position each time. China would rather appeal to sociological role expectation through a bilateral convention than through any general value. By contrast, the US, despite its willingness to cope with

China in an exclusively bilateral format, has always tried to push China to accept universal rules at the expense of the alleged national differences between the two countries, thereby confounding the sociological role expectation. Although President Xi has imposed the sociological notion of a "new model of major power relationship" on the US, the US undermines the model by treating it as the mechanism through which to condition a newcomer into becoming a responsible follower of the existing rules of international relations, which are principally led by the US.

The US arms sales to Taiwan, which China claims as part of its territory, is indeed a major irony in China–US relations. The US partially consents to China's position. Nevertheless, continuation of US arms sales to Taiwan poses a grand strategic threat to China in at least two aspects—the sales are premised upon the theme/concept of China as a threat that defies the image of peaceful rise, and they are indicative of China's inability to protect a piece of claimed territory. Taiwan used to be a US partner in the latter's containment of China. In this context, US arm sales to Taiwan have been an issue since the beginning of the Sino–US normalization in 1979. To normalize this bilateral relationship, China insisted on the one-China principle. Normalization did not occur in the heyday of the Sino–Soviet rift but on the eve of reform, which called for rectification of the relationship with the capitalist world. However, China tolerated the continuation of arms sales upon the termination of the Mutual Defense Treaty between the US and Taiwan in 1980. Moreover, the country immediately ended the symbolic bombardment of the offshore islands that had been a practice throughout the previous two decades to dramatize the sovereign relationship with Taiwan despite the US containment policy. China undertook such a decision to honor its pledge of peaceful unification, which has prevailed since normalization. The continued sales might imply China's seemingly compromising attitude toward the issue. In 1982, the country engaged in a joint communiqué, in which the US promised to gradually reduce its arms sales to Taiwan. The US, however, was not ready to implement the communiqué, considering that the Taiwan Relations Act demands the US to supply Taiwan with arms sufficient to meet its security needs, which have intensified over time.

The grand strategy of becoming an acknowledged and respected role taker corresponding to the US makes the bilateral relationship with the US a particularly significant concern. However, China's progress in the 21st century has faced the unwanted image of the so-called China threat, which China's claim on Taiwan ironically reinforces. China's first major attempt was to formulate a bilateral relationship as one of the measures for a "strategic partnership," whereas the emerging conceptualization is to develop a "new model of major power relationship." During Xi Jinping's first visit to the US as president, he encountered and was introduced to different issues concerning global governance. On Xi's list, however, were the long-standing issue of arms sales to Taiwan and problems concerning Tibet and Xinjiang, which also required mutual attention. No bilateral discussion is available in the discursive repertoire of the US. The understanding in the US on the arms sales has been either self-centric, which means that it abides by the domestic Taiwan Relations Act, or multilateral, which means that it is balanced between China and Taiwan. Neither answers the concerns of the Chinese grand strategy for a trustworthy bilateral relationship. The perception of the US is that China deliberately uses the issue for symbolic and harassment purposes (Paal 2010). This perception explains why the US offers no more than lip service to the arms sale issue, merely to let China off the hook.

Given the US's underestimation of the arms sales issue, China's protest halted scheduled military exchanges. This show of disapproval was the minimal execution of the Chinese grand strategy to restore a vulnerable bilateral relationship. However, this type of impediment rarely lasts for more than a few months. The first such protest in response to the arms sales to Taiwan was on the eve of the first visit of the highest official of Taiwan Affairs from China to Taiwan in October 2008. The scheduled visit was subsequently cancelled. Notwithstanding, military exchanges were resumed in February 2009. The message on the resumption first appeared in December 2008. The second suspension was in response to another arms sale to Taiwan in January 2010, though by September the message of resumption had already been reported to the media. The actual exchange heightened during the visit by the Secretary of Defense to China in January 2011. However, the third suspension took the form of a relatively low-key cancellation of a few scheduled exchanges in September 2011, as the sales arrived at the onset of the transition in China's leadership. At present, no one in the US has seemed to take Chinese protests over the arms sales seriously. Neither China nor the US can afford to continue to exacerbate this issue.

However, in line with the grand strategic goal of winning the US's acceptance of China's peaceful rise, the angle China has taken is unambiguously bilateral and relational. Thus, evaluating it from an identity-based grand strategic perspective is implausible. No reference exists concerning the universalistic value of peace in China's criticism of arms sales. Global governance, justice, or even the notion of balance does not exist in this perception of the world. Instead, the available references discuss the damage done to the relationship by the US when it aborted its alleged role obligations to China. In 2008, the Chinese military was quoted as accusing the US of causing "four serious harms," (*sige yanzhong*) which predominantly referred to bilateral role expectations:

> ...seriously violate the solemn promise on the Taiwan issue; seriously betray the consensus reached between the national leaders of the two sides on China–US relations; seriously contradict the expressed support of the US for the peaceful development of the cross-Straits relations; seriously disturb the military relationship between China and the United States.
>
> (Ni 2008)

As the Chinese grand strategy stresses relational security, these criticisms were referred specifically to the US' violation of role obligation. In 2010, the concrete version of *sige yanzhong*, typically from a bilateral rather than multilateral perspective, was likewise given by the Ministry of Foreign Affairs, which stated:

> ...seriously harm China's core national interests; seriously harm China-US relations; seriously violate the three communiqués between China and the United States; seriously endanger China's national security.

> (Author n. a. 2011)

The timing of Chinese resumption was equally revealing because it followed the grand strategic goal of restoring relational security. It improvised the earliest possibility to signal China's sincerity toward an improved relationship. In the first incident, the message regarding resumption was delivered after President Obama was elected in 2008, although the actual resumption happened after his inauguration, which signaled hope for a brand-new relationship that could transcend the problematic record of the previous administration. In September 2009, the resumption coincided with the initiation of negotiations that later paved the way for Hu Jintao's state visit to the US. In January 2010, Secretary of Defense Robert Gates' call to China was immediately done before Hu's actual visit. These timings reflected China's exact compliance with the bilateral frame. China consistently expressed its disappointment and accused the United States of harming the relationship. The notion of offense should distinguish and purportedly highlight China's desire to restore the correct relationship at the point of resumption. The rise to power of the Obama Administration was one evident occasion, which was followed by Hu Jintao's state visit.

Notably, Hu's symbolic state visit could never be an item on the list of core national interests. Thus, the grand strategy of restoring the relationship transcended the protection of core national interests. The theoretical implication is that the core national interests of China are neither universal nor core. Rather, the improvised cycles of suspension mainly serve to retain the seriousness of the relationship that is harmed, but the temporary compromise, together with its timing, is intended as a display of China's self-restraint and yearning for restoration. Both arms sales and Hu's visit are regarded as relational issues and the latter was considered more salient than the former in 2011. This is the leeway approach that China wishes for the US to take and to reciprocate so that no side would require face interference from the other in its particular values or institutions. The core national interests, if based on China's own identity, should rely more on the practice of change perspective by the US. However, as reflected in the practices concerning the arms sales issue, they are never taken consistently.

Conclusion

The differences between the types of role conception, namely identity-versus relationship-based conception, have led to the diverse logic of the US and China in designing grand strategies. The identity-based role perspective corresponds to the US worldview, particularly that of promoting liberalism. This role has a profound influence on Washington's management of foreign relations that seeks to extend the American value system. Changing the international environment toward the US model has always been the main goal of the American grand strategy. Such strategy represents the change approach, which is contrary to that of leeway. Actors who hold a relationship-based role perception usually expect the leeway approach.

Therefore, with regard to the issue of the arms sales from the US to Taiwan, the preservation of Taipei's vital position involves altercasting, in which Taiwan is a liberal base to be protected against China, who acts a threat to liberalism. Such altercasting synchronizes the situation to benefit Washington's national interests and encourages the other side to accept and adopt the US value system.

Rather than denying China's lack of a grand strategy, we argue that the Chinese grand strategy uses a different style of altercasting, one that expects the other side to stick to a bilateral role to reciprocate respect for national differences on China's terms. The analysis of role style can explain why a rising power deliberately avoids focusing on employing an interventionary grand strategy. To rectify the world according to one's own identity is incompatible with concerns about relational security that seeks to stabilize international relations. The self-role expectation of being a responsible state rejects a scheme of grand strategy that would require China to challenge other rising powers, failing states, or transnational fundamentalists in accordance with any general rule. For the self-centric hegemonic power, all general rules involve a kind of imagined prior resemblance to the rest of the world. A self-role expectation in the ideal state would be reflected in China as neither causing problems nor increasing the burden of other states. Positioning on behalf of a principle that emerges as one's identity goes against relational security.

China possesses a different style of grand strategy. Its goal is to preserve national differences in IR in the short run and keep the identity-based grand strategy of the US from intervening in the values and institutions of China and other countries. This requires the sacrifice of core national interests, and confrontation to rectify perceived betrayal. Chinese scholars specializing in IRT are concerned that China does not seem to have an identity-based style of role conception. However, the schemes that typically interest them are more responsive than assertive. Even those who assert a stronger position on the maritime disputes with smaller neighbors have no plans to change their internal arrangement. Therefore, the relational-based role conception will continue to prevail in shaping the thinking of the Chinese grand strategy for an extended period of time, regardless of China's rise or the risk of war that may be incurred. Ultimately, China can be the greatest nation, but the current Chinese grand strategy is to ensure that all other nations can distinctly benefit from China's greatness.

Notes

1 Swaran Singh interviewed by Tang Lu, "*Zhongguo waijiao dazhanglue: jianchi duobian xuanze bu ba jidan quan fangjin yige lanzi*" ("The Chinese Grand Strategy: Insisting Multiple Choices and Not Putting All Eggs in One Basket"), December 28, 2013, http://mil.eastday.com/eastday/mil/node3510/userobject1ai757527.html.
2 Yan Xuetong, in a lecture he gave at National Chengchi University (Taipei) in March 2013.
3 For a detailed account of China's realist calculus, see Johnston (1998).
4 "Xi Jinping zong shuji shenqing chanshu Zhongguo meng" ("General Secretary Xi Jinping Elaborated 'Chinese Dream' Affectionately"), November 30, 2012, http://news.xinhuanet.com/politics/2012-11/30/c_124026690.htm.
5 To connect China's dream to the dream of each country in the world is the message conveyed by Chinese official channels. For example, see Wang (2014).
6 "Zhongguo de heping fazhan baipishu" ("White Paper of China's Peaceful Development"), September 6, 2011, http://news.xinhuanet.com/politics/2011–09/06/c_121982103.htm.
7 For example, the perception that the rise of China will force the US out of Asia is a typical practice of altercasting. See Freiberg (2012).
8 One representative view is that of Zhao (2009: 5–18).
9 For case studies embedded in historical sensibilities, see Chung and Choi (2013: 243–264) and Bush (2013).
10 Representatives of such value alliance include Freedom Alliance, WARSAW Pact, and the NATO.
11 "Report of Hu Jintao to the 18th CPC National Congress," November 16, 2012, www.china.org.cn/china/18th_cpc_congress/2012-11/16/content_27137540_11.htm.

Part 2
Philosophical resources

4 Relational ontology

Introduction

Both BoP and BoR are universal because they are epistemologically accessible to every national actor rather than when they continually monopolize the practices of all national actors. In Chapter 1, we argued that BoP and BoR prevail in different policy-making processes and form a plausible alternative for each other. Anarchy prompts self-help, and relationality produces self-restraint. A threat of failure or an opportunity of success can trigger a shift. In Chapter 2, we showed how Singapore's Taiwan policy shifted from an initial BoP calculus to a concern for a bilateral relationship as the threat of the realignment between Washington and Beijing pressed strongly while the opportunities for long-term reciprocity with Taipei arose. Chapter 3 further demonstrates how China's relationship-based role and the US's self-based roles coexist. They rely on different social psychologies and thus potentially pose to each other a threat of entirely different nature. Chapter 4 calls upon the Kyoto School of Philosophy (KSP) or its Philosophy of Place to tackle the issue of paralleling ontologies that have implications for IR theorization, as well as policymaking.

The coexistence of BoP and BoR does not echo Alexander Wendt's (1999) portrayal of the three paralleling anarchical orders, namely, Hobbesian, Lockean, and Kantian orders, which follow a linear arrangement with the Kantian order at the highest level. IR used not to bother with the metaphysical or methodological issue of how culturally bred ontologies complement rather than mutually substitute each other. The introduction of BoR, however, leads to the realization that all mundane affairs create ontological contingencies. A policy cannot help but reproduce, jettison, or revise the previously held ontology. We provide in this chapter a philosophical scheme to understand the coexistence of different ontologies and their mundane agendas in the practical world. The philosophical resources that are specifically available for China to undergird BoR are the subjects of Chapters 5 and 6.

Nishida Kitaro, philosopher and founding father of the KSP, stimulated curiosity on the new possibilities of arranging alternative IR for the 21st century primarily through his so-called the Philosophy of Place. Nishida sought to overcome the Europeanization and Americanization of the world prior to World War II (WWII) through developing cultural sensitivity and anti-hegemonic thought. Most revisits to Nishida exclusively perceive the Philosophy of Place as a normative theory on improving world politics (Davis, Schroeder & Worth 2011, Goto-Jones 2007, Wilkinson 2009). However, Nishida was explicit about his ontological appeal to pure experience. Together with his epistemological quest for universality, the KSP indicates a potential for scientific inquiry.

Other theoretical attempts to counter the perceived hegemony of Anglo-Saxon IRT are simultaneously scientific and normative, for example, the emerging trend of re-worlding subaltern subjectivities. This trend takes place through demonstrating that the actual world politics differs from the understanding presented in mainstream IR literature (Tickner & Blaney 2012). Chapter 10 on worlding thus explores normative versus actual practices. Reflecting on the widely shared perception of China as a rising country, an additional nascent struggle against the mainstream arises from the anxious efforts to establish a Chinese School of IR (Noesselt 2012, Wang 2013). IR scholars that propagate the Chinese School draw from Chinese cultural resources to present a different ideal view of world politics (Zhang & Chang 2016, Zhao 2009). Scientific endeavors to explain the different manners of the interaction of nation states in comparison with those explained in mainstream IRT, such as the practices of relationships, can potentially lead to a Chinese perspective with universal implications (Kalvaski 2018, Qin 2018, Yan 2011). The current normative challenges to mainstream IRT typically offer the scientific explanations of world politics, which render the revisit to Nishida incomplete without the simultaneous exploration of the scientific implications of the Philosophy of Place.

Three anti-hegemonic attempts

The concept of "hegemonic IR" is used to refer to the nature of world politics as explained by a dominant single discourse favoring the reproduction of one hegemonic power. The current hegemonic view of the nature of world politics is that it is essentially state-centric and undergirded by one superpower and other major powers, mainly the US and western European countries, and that the interaction in between the states consists of peace or war. The current hegemonic IR contradicts with and transforms non-western world orders elsewhere, as well as the relevant cases of Japan, Taiwan, and China in this chapter, which result in ambivalence toward their pasts. The Philosophy of Place clarifies the identity puzzle of Japan and other nations with a similar problem by providing the possibility of a nation to represent East and West at the same time, which leads to a non-western, non-territorial, or non-centrist position. The puzzle emphasizes the aim of Japan for the normalcy of in-betweenness, (Shimizu 2014) which is a statement of alienation from hegemonic IR.

In contrast with hegemonic IR but in line with relations that exist in imagined resemblance, Nishida perceived universalism as the idea of becoming others. This idea is constantly enhanced through accommodating or mimicking additional thoughts and identities into one's own self-imagination. It sees conversion and synthesis as a bridge between civilizations as redundant, if not harmful (Shimizu 2009). Western modernity demonstrates a strong need to convert others from a differing trajectory to a common and universal destiny, and KSP exhibits a strong need for self-conversion. Self-conversion is to ensure for Japan that Western modernity is adopted while the process of Japan's universalism can be increased. Japan remains as the sole nation that is capable of constantly becoming others to eventually encompass all. The Pacific War that the Japanese military launched against the US proceeded in the name of the universalist "World History Standpoint (WHS)" to expose the partial nature of Western modernity. WHS' mission was "to overcome modernity." This mission did not deny modernity in its entirety but transcended the provinciality of western modernity. It also aimed to modernize the rest of "the Greater East Asia Sphere," which the Japanese military considered as the entirety of the Japanese self. Therefore, the double missions were to defeat the partial West and convert the backward portions of East Asia.

Japan's in-between place is presumably a place of nothingness or a non-place where Nishida wished that differing nations could meet without mutual naming or judgment. Japan exemplifies a civilizational origin and bridge that enables the East to meet the West and vice versa. The assumption of the Philosophy of Place is that neither the East nor the West should expand or conquer the other. Their commonality must not lie in teleological historiography because the preservation of their difference is the spirit that guarantees their inclusion in a universal world, which results in the multi-directionality of the WHS. Multi-directionality implies the coexistence of the East and the West while they each flourish on their own conditions. Moving between the two requires one to move deeper than merely being conscious of their differences. This leads one to a place of nothingness. Therefore, the Philosophy of Place does not propagate the same self-other concept as the one mentioned in the literature on identity. The Philosophy of Place states that the self and others are non-synthesized identities gathered in an ultimate being in nothingness. Thus, the formulation of the Philosophy of Place can easily be connected with the imagined origin of the universe and is coupled with Japanese Shinto, which provides a metaphor of the origin of Japan.

The difficulty that Japan encountered with the "backward" East Asia, particularly China, was its perceived incapacity for effective learning. From the past dynastic China and Communist China to the rise of capitalist China, the Chinese have practically accepted the coexistence of Western values, identities, and institutions in their political life. However, China has suffered (or perhaps enjoyed) false, insincere, and incompatible learning.

The KSP perceives this as China's incapacity for true learning. In the classic Japanese explanation, which remains popular with the ongoing reforms in China, China's over-reliance on rituals to harmonize relationships with superior invaders has hindered the country from achieving authentic modernity. (Tanaka 1993) China has the capability to accommodate differing values and identities by ritually relating them but does not learn at a level deeper than the instrumental use of the alien civilization. Therefore, the classic Japanese explanation states that the Chinese's claim to universality is nominal, spurious, and lacks curiosity despite China's similar capability to facilitate the coexistence of Western modernity and Chinese culture. Thus, Chinese learning is at best partial and eventually reduced to the harmonizing and stabilization of a relationship, which makes China, in the WHS perspective, unable to resist the West or engage in serious reform by itself.

Japan executes entry into and withdrawal from any provincial identities that are not to be synthesized to become genuinely universal. Japan can exemplify for the West and East Asia the process of withdrawing from the site of their existential experiences to exercise re-entry elsewhere. A "place" must be considered as a metaphor of identity, along with the notion of "site" that is adopted in the post-Western literature. For the KSP, the exercise of withdrawing from a specific "place" to a "no place" allows the imagination of freedom from either one's own past or Western modernity. This withdrawal, called self-denial, also allows the further imagination of re-entry from nothingness into many potentially differing sites, which includes that of the intruder. Therefore, the metaphor of nothingness exclusively provides Japan with the capability to see the limitation of all sites, which includes the alleged hegemony and all the strings of universalism, to achieve the emergence of a world history that accommodates and transcends instead of converting any site.

The Philosophy of Place can frame Western modernity, East Asian resistance, and the Chinese management of relationships, along with Japan's WHS, and categorizes a "place" into four different types (Ng 2011). First, a place of absolute being/identity is an absolute place trapped in false rationalism and universalism, such as Western modernity. The place constitutes contemporary hegemonic thought. Second, a place of relative being/identity is a relative place that resists hegemony, where post-Western re-worlding belongs, for example, the East Asian quests for indigenous identities in Taiwan, Korea, and Vietnam. A typical formulation of relative being/identity is postcolonial hybridity. Imagined nationalities and aboriginality are strong versions of a relative identity. Third, a place of relative nothingness is a transcendental place that connects or permeates absolute and relative places, such as the Chinese scheme of relating to each other in specific contexts, which include BoR. Another example can be the non-alignment thought by Jawaharlal Nehru. Finally, a place of absolute nothingness is where time and space meet to render the other three places thinkable and seeable. The WHS cultivates archetypal subjectivity to transcend any mundane condition and demonstrates this perspective. The second, third, and last places are explained in more detail as follows.

Relative identity

The place of relative identity uses the non-Western or post-Western IR concept of "worldliness." Creating worldliness in a site is done by essentially "worlding" it. Worlding was a geo-cultural project of global capitalism/ hegemony to monopolize meanings. (Spivak 1985) Resisting this project is known as re-worlding, a form of self-worlding that emerges from a supposedly subaltern site for and by the self. Re-worlding is a discursive reclaim of the lost soul by excavating, retrieving, reviving, and rejuvenating a narrative of the past. Sited worlding results in a declaration that hegemonic power cannot monopolize either ontological or epistemological resources and critically assesses any hegemonic attempt to reproduce dominance over subalterns. Sited worlding resists, undermines, or revises a hegemonic division of work through uncontrollable fluidity caused by the incongruent schemata of the subalterns, their ideological inconsistency, opportunism, self-denial, and self-assertion (Paolini, Elliott & Moran 1996).

The methods of re-worlding must be multiplied and improvised as they recast memories of various forms. Re-worlding testimonies to differences are achieved, which are aimed at recalling the hegemonic arrangements of lives at subaltern sites and writing back to provincialize hegemonic order. Worlding incurs site-centric methodology and aims at cultivating a counter perspective in the face of an overwhelming hegemony. Worlding seeks to identify alternatives for thinking about the "international" factors that are more in tune with local concerns and traditions outside the West (Tickner & Waever 2009,, Ling 2014). Victimized people can revive by looking back through an imagined subjectivity that belong exclusively to a particular site, which is not subject to false universalism.

Relative nothingness

The place of relative nothingness has a parallel place in the nascent IR literature, that is, in the Chinese School. Several Chinese schools invest in Chinese cultural resources that formulate general theories of IR; hence, Daoism, Confucianism, and Legalism are employed to examine the coexistence of differences (Zhao 2009), relational reciprocity (Qin 2018), and hierarchical stability (Yan 2011). They indicate a shared longing for an order that can transcend the self-centrism of individual nations. As a result, the quest for a relational order subscribes to no specific institution or value. Examples can be found in the arrangements between the Chinese dynastic court and its neighbors or between the late Qing court and various imperial powers, which were flexibly designed to meet the differing conditions of each tributary state or imperialist power. Aside from the distinctiveness of each bilateral relationship, the rules that have governed China over generations are hardly ever the same. Thus, the Chinese consider an imagined cycle of "governability" (*zhi*) and "chaos" (*luan*) as typical (For more details, see Chapter 6).

The Japanese criticism of the Chinese over-reliance on ritual and relationship implied that Chinese intellectual history is not keen on the adoption of Western institutions or values. Therefore, Chinese international relations are highly independent from values or institutional considerations. Chinese international relations are likewise not strong in ensuring defense against invaders. Local gentries and the dynastic courts look for ways to coexist with invading powers. Achieving a balanced relationship is the quintessential philosophy of life that seeks to transcend the power difference by constantly improvising reciprocity.

If IR can be reduced to a combination of improvised relationships, then other universal learning is no longer necessary because the order is already existent and the source of good governance introduced at present may become the source of chaos in the next cycle and vice versa. What would be the excitement of forcing a conversion in a subaltern site when one knows that nothing will remain the same in the long run? Anything that fades at present can return to consciousness given the right cue, which leads to a situation where only reciprocal improvisations are practical and stable (Hwang 2012). Patience, instead of forced transformation, is the main characteristic of BoR in Chinese IRT and is known as the "Great Way" in Chinese discourse, upon which all strangers walk alongside a self-cultivating prince.

Absolute nothingness

A KSP scholar stated that transcendence replaces resistance under the condition of nothingness (Nishitani 1983). Nishida mentioned that the place of absolute nothingness is composed of pure experience prior to any acquisition of meaning. All past and future encounters co-exist in nothingness where one transcends one's sited limitations. The place of absolute nothingness calms all conflicts with or without justice. It contains all possibilities before these possibilities acquire any meaning, but they guarantee no single result or success. The lack of duty is even greater than in the place of relative nothingness because one can do without the sense of duty toward one's own life or that of others in insensible and insensitive nothingness while relative nothingness cultivates a sense of duty toward a related other (Heisig & Maraldo 1995, Hubbard & Swanson 1997).

The freedom to act beyond the physical limit testifies the fearless spirit that is expected of Japan that possesses WHS. This fearlessness manifests in self-becoming and self-disciplining and in overcoming the physical restraint imposed by the materialistic civilization of the West. The constant self-becoming indicates the spirit of continuous self-denial required of Japan and East Asia to exercise withdrawal from one's own limited place of

Table 4.1 Philosophy of Place, Conditions of Identity

Multi-sited	*Synchronic* *Yes*	*No*
Yes	Philosophy of Place as Absolute Nothingness	Worlding as Relative Identity
No	Hegemonic order as Absolute Identity	BoR as Relative Nothingness

Source: Author.

relative identity. The place of absolute nothingness is properly represented by the arrival of an international society that centers on the principle of in-betweenness. Self-denial is the essential characteristic to achieve this kind of international society because Japan must display to the rest of the world its transcendent capacity for being anyone else. Japan can be as good as or even better than other civilizations by the standard of the latter with thorough self-denial from its East-Asian qualities. Worldly Japan must strive for being the best in all standards, albeit mutually incompatible.

Each entry is extreme in that Japan endeavors to become more modern than the West or practiced in Sinology than China. Becoming Western or Chinese first requires withdrawal to nothingness. Learning after entering a place does not stop until one is physically or socially exhausted and unable to reach further perfection. This quality is unavailable in a place of relative nothingness where learning is insincere and relational coupling is more important than learning. Pre-WWII Japan considered itself as the best pupil of Sinology and the genuine successor of the Chinese culture to sustain and improve its modern fate (Tanaka 1993). Given the country's Sinological spirit, Japan's acquisition of modernity proceeded at a level much deeper than the materialistic civilization of the West and provided the identity of in-betweenness that fully describes the international society.

Table 4.1 lists the categories of places of the Philosophy of Place, which are as follows: (1) the place of absolute identity, (2) the place of relative identity, (3) the place of relative nothingness, and (4) the place of absolute nothingness. Synchronization should be an enactment of the place of absolute identity and is a process in which unrelated national actors conjunctionally fulfill their self-assigned functions to interact rationally. Synchronization ironically echoes absolute nothingness to the extent that all exist in meaningless pure experience in nothingness.

From normative failures to scientific inquiries

Normative failures

Spatial sensibility runs through the conditions of relative identity and absolute nothingness and keeps the danger of being conquered and conquering alive. Regarding the conditions of relative identity, spatial multi-sitedness, worlding, place, sovereignty, agency, subjectivity, Asia, and China-centrism are popular yet estranging concepts that celebrate their sited subjectivities. These concepts defeated the WHS's quest for nothingness before WWII, which treat the role of local/national differences seriously that their subscribers engage in expansion and colonialism (Williams 2004) (See Chapter 10).

Re-worlding is a path for the self-perceived subaltern to reclaim subjectivity. Nothingness uses self-perceived in-betweenness to transcend the false universalism of hegemony and reach allegedly true universalism. The epistemological caveat lies in the shared spatial anxiety of the loss of sitedness under the sensed hegemonic intrusion. The notions of "post-White" order of the WHS and the "post-Western" claim of many post-western projects coincide with the identification of an imagined self-site. WHS disciples attempt to thaw sensibilities toward space by claiming themselves to be all-encompassing. Sun Ge (2003), a Chinese admirer of Japanese modern thoughts, traces a string of obsessive adherence to a certain inexpressible but invincible sense of space that is similar to a shelter or an identity. This spatial sensibility reproduces the imagined and re-imagined possibility of being controlled, monopolized, brainwashed, invaded, intruded, suppressed, and exploited. The claim of difference in an exclusive self-ontological site would lead to the desire to overtake and transform it (Ling 2002). Only those who possess a different site can be the target of intervention.

If sitedness and identity are two sides of the same coin, then the thorough invasion of the site can only take place by annihilating the identity of the people. Each invasion at these hegemonic moments symbolizes the collection of another fresh trophy of universalism. Thus, the effort to construct sitedness embedded in its own historical, religious, and cultural trajectory may dangerously incur the label of fundamentalism. The worst case is multi-sitedness that challenges the hegemonic instinct to conquer as many sites as possible but discourages united resistance because of consciously cherished differences. Therefore, the normative appeal of the worlding project may practically backfire. A late veteran Sinologist called for a methodology in Sinology that stops the treatment of China as Japan's other. Sinology "should be" the method for Japan to withdraw from the Japanese condition and become universal (Mizoguchi 1999). Could nothingness, as a substitute, have any empirical relevance except its normative claim of transcendence?

Scientific inquiries

Normative failures of re-worlding can be proven or disproven by empirical research, which may contribute to the improvement of the worlding project. Worlding and BoR have scientific potential. Worlding is a method of tracing how the empirical learning and practice of hegemonic role assignments in the world political economy proceed at a particular site. Describing the enactment of the roles and their meaning to the subaltern site is a normative challenge to the hegemonic discourse. The sited understanding, which is rooted in sited knowledge, suggests how hegemonic order suffers revision and subversion despite the absence of a conscious attempt or capacity to resist. The literature has noted abundant examples of this kind of resistance (Tickner & Blaney 2013). BoR can enlighten the scientific research of IR by explaining how nations transcend power politics and maintain long-term, reciprocal stability. The literature on China's relationships with Southeast Asian countries provides ample examples (Huang 2015, Kang 2007, Womack 2006).

We contend that the Philosophy of Place can be scientific, similar to worlding and BoR, but a scientific mode of the Philosophy of Place is rarely attempted. The Philosophy of Place explains the capacity of a society to store suppressed or unwanted identities in a subconscious state of nothingness by generating scientifically hypothesized processes of transcendence. Such identities are awakened by the conditions that ripened for their revival. This process also includes the capacity to acquire new perspectives in the future. The place of absolute nothingness is a site where all alternatives are temporarily stored in oblivion. Amnesia is a plausible contingency in the aftermath of ideological, institutional, and identity conflicts. It transforms societies of in-between civilizations into practiced adaptors to conditions: a threat of failure or an opportunity of success. Thus, no value, ideology, institution, or identity can be permanent. Cyclical and inconsistent self-understandings are the archetypical pattern in the long run in worlding and BoR research. They are able to partially predict cycles scientifically on the basis of the following three propositions.

1   Nothingness Proposition. Aborted identities are highly likely to return in the future, and no identity can be permanent. IR based on existing identities between nations are inherently unstable. This proposition is derived from the Philosophy of Place ontology that disregards space and temporality to accommodate various possibilities and formulate a repertoire of identity strategies. Identities co-exist instead of undergoing synthesis. Identities can be aborted if further improvements are not consciously accessible, while the thorough dominance of the current identity will eventually always exhaust the country. Reaching the limit of the pursuit on the current track triggers the emergence of an alternative principle of IR. However, the systemic level does not determine exactly which one returns. This is determined by idiosyncratic factors, such as family traditions, political correctness, and economic declines. This proposition makes possible drastic turns to different IR principles by nations torn between incongruent identities. Their incapacity to establish a compromise is in line with their readiness for a drastic turn. The cooperation of the domestic constituency in support of such turns indirectly testifies the inexpressibility of absolute nothingness.

2   Worlding Proposition. Identities that can provide evaluative perspectives on dominant identities are likely to stay or return over time. IR cannot proceed with one dominant identity in the long run. Derived from the worlding epistemology, the worlding proposition suggests that the recollection of an identity from the subconscious condition has a good chance as long as the present hegemonic circumstance can be critically assessed. This proposition is particularly germane to weak nations engrossed in an encountered hegemonic influence. Such nations reify the condition of relative identity by excavating and appropriating cultural resources not currently in use. The Philosophy of Place epistemologically anticipates these nations to resort to memories or utopias that are not shared by the encountered hegemony.

3   BoR Proposition. To the extent that role-identity is contingent upon the context, identity switching becomes easy, and the synchronic rules of international society become difficult to prevail. This proposition is derived from the BoR epistemology, which argues that nations live together easily if they can improvise a sense of resemblance to disregard their differences otherwise. Therefore, all cultural resources should be always ready to comfort a particular target. Conscious transcendence over encountered differences reifies the condition of relative nothingness. Relative nothingness is particularly germane to nations that face an extensive and expanding scope of encounter that disallows the enforcement of any synchronized value or institution. A declining hegemony may as well engage in relative nothingness by jettisoning the extant synchronic values to appease allies. The condition of relative nothingness is illustrated by countries that consciously avoid specific positions in a multilateral setting or rely on different identity strategies in a variety of bilateral settings.

Empirical philosophy of place

Three cases and three propositions

All anti-hegemonic schemes in East Asia in the 21st century compete over the Senkaku/Diaoyu/Diaoyutai Islands. Japan derived the WHS from the Philosophy of Place. Taiwan applied the double-worlding scheme. China adopted the balance of relationships. These schemes were performed in cycles. None of the three schemes is a direct respondent to power politics nor to immediate or apparent national interest considerations. Each scheme involves a cyclical drive to obtain the in-betweenness caused by co-existing yet non-synthesized identities. Japan's return to the WHS Asianism, after experiencing exhaustion at having been the pupil of the West since 1950, shows the country's indifference toward Chinese values or feelings and cultivates future readiness to move beyond the US occupation. Taiwan's return to postcolonial aversion to China tolerates Japan's nationalization of the Diaoyutai and achieves Taiwan's independence from China, with the support of the postcolonial identity left by its former colonizer, Japan. China's return to an ambiguous, pre-modern condition of sovereignty that relies on the ritual of joint venture or on a deliberately ambiguous rhetoric stabilizes bilateral relationships in a preferable state of no solution. According to the three aforementioned propositions, Japan's return is irrevocable until it is completely exhausted. Taiwan's return is bifurcated into anti- and pro-China. China's return is to deliberately avoid positioning.

Japan

The place of absolute nothingness is expected to provide endless retrieval, recombination, and creativity that ensure the unstable nature of IR for any self-searching country caught between incongruent identities, such as Japan. Being positioned on the territorial dispute reveals the impossibility of being simultaneously Western, Asian, and Japanese. Once submerged in a particular identity, the nothingness proposition predicts that Japan does not yield until the continuation is no longer feasible physically (i.e., economically or militarily) and then yield quickly and thoroughly.

Taiwan

The place of relative identity remains based on the epistemological necessity of re-worlding by a self-perceived subaltern nation in a rediscovered site, such as Taiwan. The desire for re-worlding, versus the hegemonic conquest, exposes Taiwan's multiple subaltern positions regarding China, the US, and Japan to bring forth the impossibility of self-becoming. In contrast to seeking independence from China, Taiwan cannot refuse any form of coalition with the hegemonic US. This coalition further leads to the inevitability of to allow Japan's unilateral nationalization of the disputed island. The worlding proposition predicts that Taiwan alternates between the three candidates of hegemony that exist in its layered history as the target of resistance.

China

The place of relative nothingness mediates relative identity and absolute nothingness for a country that experiences a decline, such as the late 19th century Qing court, or a rise, such as the early 21st century China. The resulting undecidable roles for China to play pragmatically dissuade, accommodate, or urge its emerging identity to improvise various kinds of relationships. Territorial interests are presumably inessential for China in improvising self-restraint and common destiny to stabilize bilateral relationships. However, sovereign status symbolizes China's being accepted as a normal state and has to be an important issue. Ironically, insistence on sovereign integrity would ruin the sense of resemblance to Japan in terms of the greater East Asian or Confucian identity. Thus, the BoR proposition predicts that the Chinese pursuit of harmony and peaceful coexistence would not be satisfied by Chinese exclusive ownership of the disputed island. Rather, ambiguity and patience are preferred to clarity in this case where a mutually agreed proper relationship is unlikely.

Japan and nothingness principle

The Japanese modern history has been full of cycles. Each cycle has appeared irrevocable in the beginning. The cycles were aborted upon the forced realization of exhaustion but replaced with another seemingly irrevocable agenda. The key question is in the manner of coping with Japan's Asian identity. Asia has alternatively exhibited its backward otherness under modernity, the base of world revolution under socialism, its backward self under the WHS, and a method of self-becoming under the pressure of modernity. The disciples of each prior theme always appear uncompromising, but their causes vary relative to whether the physical conditions of their continuous pursuit are obtainable or expiring. The complete involvement in a particular version of Asianism and the sudden subsequent switch strike the prototype of the nothingness proposition.

The aborted prior ideas of Asianism have returned to contemporary Japanese IR thinking in various versions. East Asia once had a crystal notion in support of Japan's quest for worldliness before the war. Asia, as a place of absolute nothingness, inspired a philosophy to overcome the compulsive Western modernity or the inevitable Asian backwardness. This perceived superior Western modernity returned after WWII with the arrival of American occupation forces in Japan. Moreover, the image of a backward Asia lingered on in China's estranging socialist identity. The Fukuzawa solution of "Leaving Asia, Joining Europe," rendered politically incorrect by the Pacific War, reappeared and overshadowed Asianism. The literature has noted other interpretations of Japan's proper identity, such as liberal democracy, peacemaker, profitmaker, and development aider, which have arisen alongside nascent Asianism. In the aftermath of the Maoist Cultural Revolution in China, the socialist and left-wing perspectives that evolved after the war lost their appeal, despite being revived in academic circles. Each politically incorrect view had its turn in history and waited for another opportunity after being silenced by conditions. The cycles of political (in)correctness, which are frequent in subaltern societies, attest to the place of absolute nothingness as a depot of subconscious identities. The message for any hegemonic discourse of the time is that non-synthetic identities can never be quelled at the subconscious level.

The left wing yielded to suppressive authorities during the early Showa period. A significant portion of the left-wing supporters left Japan but their spirit remained in the remote land of Manchukuo, the origin of civilization for Shiratori Kurakichi (1865–1942), a Shinto absolutist who founded the Tokyo School of Sinology. Manchukuo was considered the common root of all civilizations and designed as the princely land of all nationalities. Therefore, Manchukuo is a reification of the place of absolute nothingness (Shih 2012). Socialist intellectuals surrendered their political correctness to Shinto under the fascist condition, gathered at the Research Department of the Southern Manchurian Railway Company, and, nevertheless, embedded a left discourse in their class-related research on land property and the conventions of village life in Northern China. Their anti-imperialist activism resumed atavistically after the American occupying troops liberated them from political incorrectness, which culminated in the 1960 mass demonstration against Japan's signing of the Security Pact with the US. The views of these intellectuals on Socialist China were sanguine and hopeful, but the end of the Cultural Revolution silenced them again. While their place has always been opposite of that of the right wing, left- and right-wing supporters share a career style of vicissitudes.

The same career style has a wider scope of practice than Japan. A parallel vicissitude submerges Euro-Asianism in Russia, which first appeared in the 1920s and acquiesced under the Communist Party rule for 70 years before finally re-emerging in the 1990s to assist in the pursuit of an integrated statehood of Russia (Laruelle 2008). The pursuit of statehood in the 21st century Japan by the right wing, supported by Premier Abe (2013), was an attempt to move Japan beyond being an occupied territory of the US or the West. To embark on a journey toward statehood, Japan cannot directly challenge US leadership but must demonstrate its ability to face and overcome the rising China that disturbed the hegemonic order under the leadership of the US. A normalized Japan that is no longer under the US protective umbrella would make a contemporary pledge to the WHS while the US fails to provide a civilizational model for neighboring China to emulate. This is a destiny that Japan has not taken but can take anytime.

The nationalization of the Senkaku Islands of Japan in 2012 and the demonstration of Japanese military strength against China from 2013 onward won the support of the Japanese general public, particularly the right-wing supporters. The pursuit of statehood, justified by the need to protect Japan's claimed territory of the Senkaku Islands, paralleled prior attempts to overcome modernity, which was prescribed for Japan by the lessons obtained from Europe since the Meiji Restoration. The Hegelian designation of the Orient as backward must be addressed. Japan believed that it could transcend its own Oriental backwardness by confronting China, and the return of the Senkaku Islands dispute has been the single and most significant confrontation between China and Japan in the 21st century.

The struggle began in 1876 when Japan kidnapped the king of Ryukyu, a Chinese protectorate that owned Senkaku. This incident is similar to the nationalization of the Senkaku Islands by Japan in 2012. In the first initiative, former US President Ulysses Grant served as a mediator between Japan and China to ensure peace. However, Japan was reluctant and did not accept the compromise indicated in Grant's proposal to preserve Ryukyu as a Chinese protectorate. Japan defeated China 20 years later in 1895 and Russia 30 years in 1905, which resulted in a successful Westernization of Japan that placed Japan on the world's radar. Japan's dilemma of being indebted to China and the West in its quest for national identity occurred in the Meiji period and the 21st century. Modern statehood means that a state does not live under the protection or shadow of any Western country. This independence to any Western country in the 1920s led to the refusal of Japan to succumb to the Washington Treaty system, which downgraded Japan's status to a secondary power in East Asia. Japan decided to exercise the WHS by grouping the entire East Asia together as a bloc to challenge the West. Thus, Japan should also display dissatisfaction as an occupied nation where US troops are stationed in the 21st century.

With the demonstration of Japan as the only actor capable of modernizing Asia in the mid-20th century, the transcendence of Western civilization was first enacted. Japan is similarly exhibiting its exclusive capability to curb and transform China in the 21st century. Japan is confident it can transform China into a civilized nation. Thus, Japan must represent both the West and China. This statement is true for Japan in the 2010s and the 1920s and embodies the spirit of the WHS rooted in the Philosophy of Place and emerging from the KSP (Goto-Jones 2005a). Absolute nothingness is sufficiently embracive to the extent that other similar forms of Asianism in stock cannot remain idle in the long term. They return to service after a long interlude. The metaphor of Manchukuo inspires the different versions of Asianism to become a single method of self-denial (Takeuchi 1967) and a method to transcend sovereign order (Hirano Kenichiro 1982, a student of John K. Fairbank). China also inspires a different form of Asianism in the Japanese intellectual circle, which is an Asianism that advocates peace, as exemplified by the liberal Asianist Akira Iriye (another disciple of Fairbank).

Once into the cycle, the then incumbent Abe administration submerged completely into the revival of the same WHS spirit. It has the goal of becoming a normal state. The Senkaku Islands policy exemplifies Japan's need and capacity to determine the use of a piece of Asian land. This policy does not reflect useful power politics because it ironically exposes Japan's vulnerability, nor is it a calculated national interest because China already provided consent to the joint access to natural gas. Politically inadvertent, the escalation of the issue requires the resolve to discipline China and the promise of US support. Ironically, the US is the last hurdle before Japan can normalize its statehood. Rising above China and the West was the goal of Abe's grandfather Nobusuke Kishi (1896–1987) during the war. Nobusuke and Abe's grand uncle Sato Eisaka (1901–1975) were right-wing prime ministers. The atavism of the Great East Asian Sphere reveals the aversion to China's anti-Japan sentiment, parallel to the situation 150 years ago, as well as the present disapproval of Japan on Chinese nationalism. The rise of Japan in the early period was launched by a dispute over Korea's jurisdiction. This dispute was greater and more significant than that over Senkaku, which the US restricted. Nevertheless, Senkaku symbolizes revival and hope for success in the 21st century.

The ideal state that Japan pursues for itself through the Senkaku Islands dispute is a Japan that possesses its own national defense troops. This militarily independent Japan would then deprive the American troops of any legitimacy to stay and Japan's sovereign right to engage in war would then be legalized. The Senkaku Islands dispute thus registers a thrilling agenda and a renewal of the WHS. Thus, the agenda Japan pursues through the Senkaku Islands is neither Chinese nor Western. The pursuit does not end until it succeeds or fails. This determination is illustrated by the fact that right-wing politicians have visited the Yasukuni Shrine where war criminals are honored. These and other incessant series of morale boosting campaigns constrained the Abe government from any sign of retreat. A revoking move would require strong pressure from the US or China. However, such pressure, especially from China, is what constitutes the origin of Japan's desire to restore its national defense. The opposite versions of Asianism would emerge in due time if either the current rise of China or the lingering US dominance could defeat the recollection of the metaphor of the initial rise of Japan in the beginning of the 20th century over the Korean issue to inspire the Senkaku Islands dispute.

Taiwan and the adoption of a double-worlding strategy

Taiwan is an exceptional place to practice the philosophy of nothingness because of the country's uncertain and layered political history. Taiwan's political regimes have constantly changed along with a population composed of generations of immigrants. Each regime has built upon the basis of another high-performing regime established originally outside of the island. Historical Japan consciously drifts between having European and Chinese characteristics. Contemporary Taiwan intentionally floats between having Chinese, Japanese, and, after WWII, American characteristics. Early suspicions that Taiwan was in a position of in-betweenness arose during the conflict between China and Japan in the 1930s and the 1940s. Confucian and colonial Taiwanese intellectual Tsai Peihuo adopted the notion of East Asia from Japan's imperialism to resolve such an inner confrontation. Taiwan in those days was a more devout and sincerer practitioner of KSP than Japan. Proclaimed as the "son of East Asia" and loyal to the Japanese Emperor, Tsai imagined Taiwan belonging to neither just Japan nor just China. Tsai's East Asian stance was mimicry of the WHS (Shih 2011).

Tsai was imprisoned by the Japanese authorities due to his thoughts of self-surrender to an identity of a nobody. The political powerlessness of Tsai during WWII and the shaky regime in Taiwan that followed the war ironically confirmed the principles that a faithful following of the KSP is possible for the subaltern only. Subaltern people usually suffer from the incapacity to change the world around them. This incapacity can also stimulate deeper reflections that motivate learning. The motivation first requires withdrawal from one's own condition and entry into another condition to acquire different experiences or self-knowledge.

Developing a strong power, such as Japan, which practices the WHS, is similar to constructing a civilizational bridge to preach and urge mutual learning. These disciples—the partial West and backward China—may become a burden of nothingness. Japan undertook this burden during the war but did not realize success having already emerged in subaltern Taiwan, which first became a Japanese colony and later an asylum for the defeated Chinese Civil War regime of the Kuomintang. Nevertheless, the intellectual capacity to deposit the inexpressible feeling of in-betweenness in the subconscious condition for the time being and launch atavistic revival decades later validates the power of nothingness as a mode of self-identification.

The unavailing appeal to the ontological equality of Tsai's East Asian childhood continued during the Kuomintang takeover after WWII and was furthered by American intervention in East Asia, where the containment of a Communist China imposed a strategic and ideological role for the Kuomintang regime. However, the Kuomintang had its own civil war agenda/legacy. Thus, Taiwan did not become another Vietnam or another base of containment. Chiang Ching-kuo, the last Civil War leader, struggled to establish his own platform on which the Cold War mentality and the preparation for a post-Civil War Taiwan could coexist. The Cold War mentality had the idea of containing China under US leadership while the preparation for a post-Civil War Taiwan existed by the reconnection with China against US interests.

Post-colonial Taiwan had its own independent agenda that was different from the one of the ruling Kuomintang. The colonial worldview may have been suppressed under Kuomintang rule, but Lee Tenghui capitalized on the aging of the Kuomintang in accordance with a retrieved colonial platform. Lee's alienation from China awaited its turn to replace his Chinese qualities influenced by the Kuomintang. The first hidden agenda was the attempt by Chiang Ching-kuo to bypass the hegemonic Cold War. The second agenda that carried post-colonial alienation from the Kuomintang was hidden from the ruling Kuomintang. The second agenda was self-suppressed by Lee for four decades because of the strategic silencing of the anti-Chinese identity, which was powerfully bred by Japanese colonialism.

The unique double hidden agenda displayed compromises of hiding between the Kuomintang's post-Civil War and the US Cold War and between the post-colonials of Taiwan and Kuomintang's Civil War. These double hidden agendas empirically demonstrated the philosophy of nothingness. Worlding is the proper method to excavate these hidden agendas to recognize the agency that resisted the consecutive rising powers of the ruling regimes that had arrived in Taiwan. The first hidden agenda utilized US Cold War resources for the purposes of Chiang Ching-kuo to reconnect with China, in addition to the role assigned by the US to contain China. The second hidden agenda was an affective memory, completely unattended and without utterance, which ensures no indication of alienation from China. Therefore, becoming related to the incumbent power in post-colonial Taiwan is always more imminent than any platform of rationalism. Each hidden agenda empowers the subaltern in question with a ready subjectivity to act incompatibly with the hegemonic expectation, regardless of a positive judgment toward their hegemonic leader, such as in the case of the Kuomintang toward the US, or a negative judgment, such as in the case of post-colonial Taiwan toward the Kuomintang. The hidden agenda ultimately impacts the world agenda by critically reflecting on the hegemonic discourse and leads to worldliness.

Taiwan's uncertain and layered political history prepares its residents efficiently to accept incoming regimes. Thus, the society does not intend to recollect politically incorrect history for its present time. Double-worlding serves two different generations of the Philosophy of Place, namely, one generation that arrived before the Japanese colonial rule and the following generation. The self-suppressed conditions of the two generations usually persevere in the sub-consciousness and the Philosophy of Place articulates the condition of layered sub-consciousness in a consistent rationality of hidden resistance. Taiwan's condition of double worlding also provides a more sophisticated case of worlding. The post-colonial agenda, which came to power upon the demise of the Civil War generation, thrives on a pro-Taiwan independence discourse. Worlding is no longer a mere resistance to hegemony but comprises cycles of hidden agendas, recalled to service from a long-term, albeit subconscious, memory to resist a substituting, albeit imagined, hegemony. Taiwan's bifurcated populations each in support of a particular scheme of worlding are conscious of the existence of each other. The decision is about whether or not China is the hegemony to resist. The double worlding strategy is contingent upon the identity that is more functional in providing Taiwan's global representation. This case is different from Japan, where the population is not constantly divided by successively arriving regimes.

The coexistence of contradicting positions toward the Diaoyutai Islands should not be surprising under this layered circumstance. The Kuomintang changed its position from being the true representative of China that would regain the islands to a non-Chinese nation that only cares for a peaceful resolution. The pro-independence force supports Japan's claim of sovereignty. Partially plagued by the Chinese image of Chiang Ching-kuo, the US is continuously worried that a pro-independent Taiwan would desire cooperation with China. With China's expectations to support Taiwan's position on the Diaoyutai Islands, Taiwan's quiet attitude toward the nationalization issue is apparently most serviceable to the acquisition of negative evaluation on China. As Sino–Japanese relations become extremely weak, Taiwan's post-colonial link with Japan contributes best to the representation of a non-Chinese Taiwan. This worlding strategy is effectively revealed in Taiwan's agenda, which focuses exclusively on fishing rights. The agenda dissolved the political demand for action to confront Japan's unilateral nationalization of the Diaoyutai Islands and removed any lingering speculation of Taiwan-China cooperation for the time being.

China and BoR proposition: relationship as a conscious place

The self-perception of China was at the center of the world during the dynastic period, and the application of its tributary system was hardly synchronic. The Qing court arranged tributary relationships with its neighbors according to their own conditions. The Qing court followed no single formula, and exemption from a rigid model was the only formula that was applicable in all cases. This arrangement explained why the kidnapping of the king of Ryukyu did not immediately incur a military reaction from a presumably strong China at that time (For more details, see Chapter 7). Such inaction avoided the embarrassment of the Chinese fighting with a small neighbor over a small land and camouflaged the embarrassment that China was completely uninterested in its own suzerainty.

The relative negligence of BoR toward principles or values is in contrast with worlding in the sense that the worlding philosophy seeks to overcome the heavy dependence of the subaltern on the hegemonic sanctioning of economic, political, and ideological partnerships. A worlding method for Taiwan brings out the subaltern's agency hidden in its mimicry of hegemonic discourse by presenting Taiwan's maneuvering of the US partnership in its own battle with China. Worlding is not in China's favor. BoR is the rationality for China to bypass the containment of a rising China contrived by the hegemonic forces. China can offset the challenge of containment by improvising reciprocal relationships on a bilateral basis with as many neighboring countries as possible. Therefore, China must disregard the domestic institutional, ideological, and religious characteristics of its neighboring countries. BoR is valuable for any newly emerging nation, any rising power in the face of an increasingly expanding and complicated encounter of the world, and any declining hegemony with a relaxed synchronizing imposition to appease allies. The declining hegemonies can include the late 19th century Chinese dynasty and the 21st century US. All of the declining or rising powers face an IR full of contradictions. The nation should manage its uncertain environment to survive or proceed by avoiding synchronizing relationships that proliferate in the expanding or shrinking scope of negotiation.

China rises and faces the challenge of proliferated relationships. The influence of these relationships expands to exert an improvised presence in all its neighbors and reaches far into Africa and Latin America. Thus, the existing hegemonic US and its allies sense the threat of the newcomer in transcending boundaries that previously restrained the sphere of influence. Defending the rise in world politics from the rebalance of power by the hegemonic US and soothing anxious neighbors are different tasks. Moreover, a watching Europe that is composed of the self-regarded moral superpower in West Europe, a post- but anti-communist East Europe, and a competitive yet occasionally and conveniently allied Russia require soothing as well. These tasks are not the most complicated, except when compared with those in anti-unification Taiwan, recalcitrant North Korea, and assertive right-wing Japan, not to mention the potentially rebellious Hong Kong.

Exemplifying relative nothingness, China's difficulty in handing complicated relationships does not arise from its confused identity but from the various incongruent roles expected by countries worldwide to be performed by China. Japan's international environment has not undergone significant change except during the rise of China, which resulted in an identity puzzle that forces Japan to align either to the West or the East. This idiosyncratic, internal puzzle compels the Abe government into the conservative side that may send the less conservative sides of national identity into acquiescence and repeat a familiar cycle. However, the rise of China proceeds with the art of relationship. Relationship management in East Asia means that China has to cope simultaneously with Taiwan, which intensively asserts its worldliness, the US, which anxiously applies some synchronic values/institutions to co-opt China, and Japan, which ambivalently switches from being a member of Asia to a junior ally of the US and to a normal state in the world.

The cycles of right-wing identity in Japan are drawn from the depot of all historical identities. The cycles likewise come from the worlding strategy of Taiwan to distance itself from Chinese identification and answer to the call for a clear self-identity under globalization that is embedded in the hegemonic order and has multicultural sensibilities. This quest for difference brings Taiwan and Japan close in portraying an estranging China that rises on illiberal politics, which the two countries oppose. Taiwan's quest for independence requires a statement of difference while Japan's adherence to Western synchronic values imposes a duty to transform China. In line with its relational sensibilities, China must concede to Taiwan's liberal arrangement, which demonstrates that Taiwan's return to China would not cause any serious adaptive problems. However, China would resist any liberalization proposed by either Japan or the US. BoR is alienated from such an interventionary policy. Therefore, BoR requires China to treat liberalism depending on who promotes it.

BoR serves as a bridge between the Philosophy of Place and worlding because the purpose of BoR strives to bypass sited identities and pushes for alternative sited identities to be recollected from memory. Taiwan confronts China's BoR and recollects a dormant colonial identity to support the re-worlding of an exclusively non-Chinese Taiwan. Nevertheless, China's BoR can also support a pro-China identity in Taiwan. For example, China can concur to the sovereignty of the Diaoyutai Islands with Taiwan's pledge given that Taiwan willingly continues to represent China and bypass the colonial identity.

To distinguish China's intended, albeit unsuccessful, compromise to Taiwan and Japan, China must avoid providing the impression to the US or other potential parties of territorial conflict, such as Vietnam, the Philippines, and India, that it is ready to yield in the latter cases. China resorts to relationship improvisation. China proposes joint ventures over disputed territorial seas or islands with other parties of conflict being able to make their own claim internally. The claim should not cause concerns from other parties as long as the internal claim is not brought to the bilateral relationship. China resorts to symbolic and mixed sanctions before any consensus can be achieved to simultaneously show the country's determination to defend sovereign rights and its willingness to compromise. In the case of the Diaoyu Islands, China has engaged Japan's nationalization by patrolling the air and the sea around the islands, announcing an air defense zone, and occasionally approaching without landing on the islands as if the dispute requires no immediate resolution. China actually demands a statement from Japan that nationalization does not affect the disputed status of the island. The rationale behind the mix of unilateral compromise and the subsequent demand of the other side to yield is to cut cross-positions. Along with China's proposal of conflict resolution is the unfailing reiteration that the dispute is bilateral. Thus, any hegemonic intervention can be considered as ill intended and counterproductive.

Conclusion: systemic transcendence over interest and power

The Senkaku/Diaoyutai/Diaoyu Islands have limited national interest implications regarding natural gas, which no one has actualized yet. Joint ventures have been attempted and agreed upon to avoid the reoccurrence of disputes. Therefore, no significant national interests are involved in the dispute. China has not shown any interest in obtaining the islands from the current occupier Japan. Maneuvering for more power on the islands can be considered disadvantageous to Japan. No one is ready strategically or can force a solution. Japan's nationalization is apparently premature from the BoP perspective. However, Japan's nationalization reflects the desire to recount the rise of the country at the turn of the 20th century. The ability to determine the fate of the islands is critical to the transcendence of IR, which is dominated by China and the US. Taiwan's acquiescence over the process of nationalization reflects the quest for the independent representation of an anti-China identity, which was initially planted by Japanese colonialism. Finally, China's improvised ambiguity reflects the substitution of relationship for territorial sovereignty.

The Philosophy of Place propositions do not predict the actual foreign policy or the necessity of nations to behave in certain patterns, given the context of the international structure. The Philosophy of Place propositions do not formulate predictions on how nations generally behave. However, all three Philosophy of Place propositions make predictions about how the system behaves in the long run and how asymmetric relationships proceed. First, Philosophy of Place theorization is not a study on how the order between major powers can be established or explained. The study cares about how nations adapt to major power politics by joining, resisting, appropriating, reconciling, avoiding, transcending, or even defeating them. The Philosophy of Place theorization predicts that the order is never orderly. Second, the Philosophy of Place theorization specifically allows nations to make judgments that affect systemic behavior. Unlike the majority of IRTs with a structural argument, the Philosophy of Place theorization demonstrates how the structural explanation can accommodate judgmental factors and how nations are capable of thinking and choosing under undecidable circumstances. Third, the Philosophy of Place theorization confronts purposes and their systemic consequences for all varied nations while other theories focus primarily on major powers.

IR theorization, in accordance with the Philosophy of Place, relativizes major power politics and their quest for an order that is composed of synchronic values or institutions. However, the Philosophy of Place is premised on non-synthetic identities in layered or multilayered histories. No pretension of either a destiny or a destined fate exists. The Philosophy of Place IRT explains how nations under the influence of major power politics judge their conditions and rely on combined existing cultural resources to determine their place in world politics. The Philosophy of Place predicts that IR's systemic stability cannot be maintained over a set of congruent identities because history's longevity allows for previous politically incorrect identities to either return in due time with proper clues or emerge from the creative recombinations of old and extant cultural resources. The Philosophy of Place specifically predicts that nations caught between different identities experience cycles in their IR, whereas those with an expansive scope of IR or experiencing a decline from the hegemonic status adopt BoR. Less influential nations practically reinterpret hegemonic order to meet their otherwise inexpressible motivations.

5   Buddhist state of nature

Buddhism, especially Zen Buddhism, inspires Nishida Kitaro and later informs the reference to nothingness espoused by his Kyoto School of Philosophy (KSP), according to which the Confucian relationship fits well in the relative place of nothingness where actors adapt to the present conditions and take appropriate roles. However, Confucianism does not teach relationships outside of one's close circles, other than anticipating that those in an alien land far away also salutes to a selfless prince. In the time of Confucius, the place far away was nonetheless within the reachable territories of the princes that subscribe to his advice. In modern times, the interaction with forces far away to which Confucianism has not provided any clue has come true. These forces can arrive from the remote West, or they can stay in Africa or Latin America. Gift giving and ritual interaction were the only mechanisms to improvise relations. Dealing with those whom a Confucian pupil lacks imagined resemblance creates a puzzle, especially wherever it causes interference with Chinese affairs or demands China's involvement in its affairs. This is the challenge brought forth by modern international relations. Zen Buddhism that has inspired the KSP similarly inspires modern neo-Confucianism to cope with the challenge.

This chapter argues that Confucianism relied on Buddhism to approach the encounter where no prior resemblance is retrievable in one's cultural memory. Buddhism offers an epistemological vehicle for the incurious, self-restraining Confucian thinkers to diligently acquire alien means. The Buddhist touch causes Confucianism to willingly acquire alien components for the sake of engendering a greater-self relation that can encompass the alien actors. This selective epistemological shifting echoes the exercise of retreat and reentry expounded by the KSP. The Buddhist conviction of nothingness releases Confucianism from its rigid role conceptions and allows for the adoption of an alien institution or technology forced upon China to be conceived of as a way to improvise respectable resemblance. The involvement in unrelated others' affairs on China's own initiative remains unnecessary and sometimes unintelligible. Thus, the criteria that China uses to judge the kind of actions called for in its and others' internal affairs are necessarily inconsistent.

Inconsistency puzzle

Contradictions between theory and practice are noticeable in the foreign policy of any government, whether a hegemonic government, such as the United States, or the government of a rising power, such as China. In the following discussion, the foundations in the political thought of one particular contradiction in US intervention policy and Chinese nonintervention policy are compared. Examining differences in relational practice helps explain why the Chinese understanding of intervention, which is influenced by Confucian, Buddhist, and Daoist traditions, usually appears apologist from the perspective of the Western thought. We argue that American interventionism, whose sense of duty reflects a prior commitment to natural rights, is *Lockean* in the selection of targets and *Hobbesian* when enforced. However, Chinese noninterventionism in others' internal affairs is aligned with bilateral sensibilities embedded in sovereign propriety that justify self-restraint from action elsewhere and materialist self-strengthening in China's own internal affairs.

A contradiction between theory and practice is manifested in intervention policies. We focus on the internal contradiction between the principles based on which Washington and Beijing evaluate whether a state should be subjected to intervention. Such principles include a different set of principles that guide actions toward such states and the principles that guide how states rule themselves. A realistic view of this kind of contradiction would accept such hypocrisy as easily explained by national interest calculus (Acharya 2007, Krasner 1999, Lipson 2007). However, a highly complex approach seems justified as foreign policy leaders typically act with a decent reason and argue for public support. In cases where the theory–practice contradiction bothers neither policy makers nor their constituency, a concept that is deeper than functional hypocrisy must be the premise of this apparent desensitization.

A loss of sensitivity occurs when individual military interventions mandated by Washington do not comply with human rights norms that the United States uses to identify failed states that require intervention. US interventions have resulted in massive civilian casualties and jeopardized the treasures of civilization. However, this irony does not incur serious self-criticism as if the duty to protect and the instinct of self-help constitute the United States' self-identity without incongruity. China's insistence on nonintervention in failed states in that spontaneity may take over the course of events contradicts Beijing's constant appeal for self-strengthening in domestic governance.[1] The Chinese government and people's disregard for failing governance in other countries are in contrast with the portrayal of good governance as a triumph of the Chinese Communist Party. We rely specifically on the Buddhist notion of suffering as the nature of "this world" as opposed to that of "the afterworld" to understand the apparent apathy toward the failed state. Thus, China has the duty to restrain the national self from becoming a problem of others, and others have the duty from becoming a problem in China. China's self-disciplining and failed states' loss of governance can testify to the ubiquity of suffering.

If this basic contradiction does not distress those who sustain it politically or their domestic audience, then the contradiction must be perceived as "natural" or required by the state of nature. The subject of humanitarian intervention presents an excellent opportunity to discuss what the state of nature is or should be, that is, intervention appears easily justifiable in cases where intervention restores or improves the state of nature depending on the theory. The imagined states of nature that desensitize the contradiction in the US intervention policy are Lockean and Hobbesian (Buchanan 1999, Burgess 2002, Hehir 1979, Ward 2006). China can find means to desensitize the contradictions in its noninterventionism through the dialectical relationship between transcendental cosmology/ontology that favors inaction in unrelated countries and transcendental epistemology that favors self-strengthening, as required by the need to restore a proper relationship with Western countries. Buddhism has inspired such dialectics to enable neo-Confucian ideology to relate China and the outside world since the early 20th century. This last statement is the topic of this chapter.

Contradiction and state of nature

One significant contradiction in the US humanitarian intervention policy is its militarist tendency. Militarism has driven the fabrication of evidence, the torture of prisoners of war, and the looting of treasures in addition to unilateral withdrawal before the full restoration of order. The existence of separate principles for the rule of the other and the self detaches militarist intervention from humanitarianism that prompts interventions. We argue that the treatment of other states echoes the idea of Locke, who attributes the failure of the state to its incapacity for democracy and human rights; people should be free, equal, and independent in the Lockean state of nature (Eriksen 2011, Jahn 2007, Lucinescu 2010). Failure to conform to this state merits outside intervention. However, the norms the United States that carry out intervention echoes Hobbes' idea because intervention occurs through international relations, and international relation theorists generally adopt Hobbesian anarchy.[2] The double states of nature within and between states as prescribed by Locke and Hobbes are the plausible mechanisms of thought that are required to desensitize the contradiction between humanitarianism and militarism. We leave further exploration on this subject elsewhere given that our primary concern is China and the international theory.

Political thought pertaining to the state of nature exists in the Chinese classics and in its modern derivatives. Perhaps, the most widely noted version is the symbiosis of *yin* and *yang*, which refer to the opposite and yet combined characteristics of matter that give rise to each other and evolve dialectically (Fang 2012, Li 2012, Yolles, Frieden & Kemp 2008). This model supports the cyclical view of harmony and chaos taking turns in the philosophy of history. Cycles are intrinsic to the Buddhist belief. Classic Confucian and Daoist thoughts similarly connect mundane affairs and chaotic conditions to an amorphous being, who/which is pervasive, inexpressible, and retrievable through learning. For Daoism and Buddhism, the ultimate being is Dao (or the Way), which equalizes all, and emptiness/nothingness, which transcends all meanings. For Confucianism, the ultimate being is the kingly way that transcends space and connects all-under-heaven in a metaphor of kinship through natural benevolence. One shared tenet of all three schools of thought is a combination of self-cultivation and "non-action" (*wuwei*), which allow matters to settle into their harmonious nature (Ames 1985, Goulding 2002). Harmony ultimately depends on the presentation of an example of the greater self for the rest to imagine resemblance.

However, transcendence may sometimes require actions as opposed to meditation to stop the expansion of the power of chaos and restore one's place in harmonious relationships (Pittman 2001). For Confucianism, this is the moment when the civilized world encounters the danger of extinction during the barbarian invasion. For Buddhism, an initial stage of transcendence is the sympathy for the majority of people that suffer hardship. Neo-Confucianism is particularly keen for a thinking mechanism that enables a believer of harmony to learn science that exploits, rather than respects nature. Neo-Confucianism relies heavily first on Buddhism to construct a formless and nameless subjectivity that encompasses everything through nonaction and second on the enlightened self-understanding that is no longer subject to the material world. This self-understanding includes acting with great compassion (*da bei*) through reform and self-strengthening in a mundane world to ultimately enlighten the unaware commoners and enhance one's own spiritual life (Kuah-Pearce 2014).

Neo-Confucianism thus adopts modernity as an intellectual challenge required by the occasion. The challenge of modernity is reduced to adopting a tentative mode of reform that accommodates contemporariness. Western values (e.g., nationalism, liberalism, and socialism) imply that institutions and technologies constitute modern self-strengthening. Learning is essential to the understanding, engagement, and reform of this world. Consequently, the symbiosis of yin and yang continues to guide the view of the world (Dellios 2011) and subsequently leads to an apparent contradiction between the ontological acceptance of the world as being overly transient to be worthy of care and the simultaneous epistemological endeavor to enlighten commoners through self-strengthening. The former sees no need for intervention because everything is of the same characteristics in their ultimate formless existence. The latter views the mundane world as in need of transcendence and learning for the purpose of enlightenment. Transcendental enlightenment presumably exempts the population from indulgence in materiality when learning from the West. Leaders set examples for the population, and China sets an example for international relations.

Traditional Chinese attitudes bifurcate into two strands; one strand stresses patience and nonaction for chaos to settle down naturally, and the other strand emphasizes self-strengthening to enlighten commoners that are related in the metaphor of kinship. Either tendency is familiar to the Chinese. These two strands desensitize the contradiction caused by the shift between them. Belief in the inevitability of the cycle of harmony and chaos reduces anxiety about the suffering of people elsewhere. The coexistence of the ontology of formless subjectivity and the epistemology of learning desensitizes the contradiction caused by a policy of nonintervention that considers the failure of others and China's own improvement as necessitated by the states of nature.

The most important contradiction in China's nonintervention policy is between the belief that China must strive for good governance and success by means of heavy intervention by the state in society and the perception that China should not be involved in failed states and societies elsewhere. Official Chinese sources state that local people in their own metaphor of kinship must determine local values and institutions (Hu 2005, 2012). External intervention weakens and impairs the local mechanisms required to restore order. Such official indifference reflects the long-held philosophy that harmony and chaos are destined to take turns. Thus, any intervention would be in vain despite its being well intended or heavily invested. Nevertheless, secular engagement is adopted in the Chinese case to reform the mundane world and improve the learning of the suffering population (Tan 2008, Tu 1993). By setting the example of self-reform, which enables the people to see the nature of suffering and injustice, the unenlightened population can transcend the forms to achieve actual universal being. The task for contemporary neo-Confucians is to think of what they should and could do for China in the face of the suffering of the Chinese population.

Two discourses on Buddhist transcendence

The role of Buddhism in contemporary Chinese foreign policy has been rarely acknowledged because Buddhism has never provided a clear principle of international relations and because the influences of Buddhism on Chinese modernity had been incorporated into the historical trajectory before the establishment of the People's Republic of China (PRC; Hammerstorm 2012, Tao 2002).[3] Buddhism has contributed to the understanding and appropriation of modernity in China in ways similar to how it integrated Confucianism and Daoism in Vietnam in the latter's encounter with Christianity and modernity (DeVido 2009, Do 1999, McHale 2004). Confucianism and Daoism are conservative with regard to the use of industrial power in the exploitation of nature. Confucianism and Daoism are uncomfortable with the ideas of individualism, rationality, or competition that come with liberal democracy and market capitalism. Modern thinkers in Vietnam and China intensively consulted Buddhism to reorient the local intellectuals toward modern technology and institutions. By contrast, Buddhist intervention in Japan's coping with modernity and the West was extreme in thought because it undergirded the country's adoption of imperialism in the 1930s (Hesig & Maraldo 1995, Sharf 1993).

Indigenous access to modernity via Buddhism in East Asia comprises two aspects. The classic aspect is the shared pursuit of transcendence among Confucianism, Daoism, and Buddhism over individual mundane concerns for immediate interests. Confucian teachings urge the self-rectification of the learned class to serve as a model for people all-under-heaven to emulate and harmonize the latter into an orderly relationship. Daoist teachings deconstructed all immediate interests into meaningless eventuality, with the highest respect for nature already in harmony. Buddhist teachings provide an imagined cycle of life that makes everyday suffering tolerable and the afterworld a place of emancipation. The three teachings are characteristic of the worldview and philosophy of life. The three teachings were all conceived with individuality as a questionable basis of ontological imagination that requires transcendence (Brook 1994, Fu 1973). The other traits of Buddhism, namely, reformist and critical, fit its believers into the mundane world whose incessant evolution into varieties is a useful reminder of their actually transient state. This last aspect smoothly connected the believers to modernity and its various progressive claims ideologically, institutionally, and technologically.

Modernity changed the way of life and rules of political economy. Transcending the dazzling changes in the individual and national life requires the establishment of an understanding of the principles of modernity. At least two Buddhist approaches are available for the suffering population to rely on and make sense of their suffering: the meditation of experiences and letting go through learning (Epstein 1989, Rinpocije 1986, Watson 2001). The first approach considers suffering as the result of false feelings or images induced by materialism. This approach is in line, albeit slightly similar, with the Daoist solution to look beyond or the Confucian solution to retire from the public life until the return of order. The second approach seeks the reason behind modernity, grasps its essence, and practices its rules in that modernity would no longer be superior, destined, universal, teleological, rational, or Christian. If modernity could be reduced to the knowledge of this world, the limit of its power would breed the desire for further transcendence. The belief in the afterworld at this transcendent moment becomes appealing. Therefore, Buddhism can encourage learning about modernity in a way that Confucianism and Daoism cannot. However, no consensus has been reached among Buddhist thinkers with regard to this approach. The debate of such thinkers reflected the two different states of nature that could have sneaked into the noninterventionary policy of contemporary China.

The debate centered on the state of nature. Chinese Buddhist thinkers believed that the human world is full of sufferings, but whether these sufferings are composed of a violation of the state of nature is debatable.

On one hand, the state of nature is nothingness. People of this world should transcend fast-passing attractions to the senses to retrieve and return to the enlightened state of nothingness (Kieschnick 2003). On the other hand, the state of nothingness is not the nature of this world. Nothingness is a transcendent place that is accessible only to those who undergo proper preparation. Nothingness can only be reached through hard learning and reform. The latter approach is, therefore, in need of epistemological rigor (Wallace 2013). A parallel debate ensued in Japan and China. The Chinese debate began much earlier because of China's failure to adopt modernity during its encounter with the West. Neo-Confucianism was desperate for a solution to the inability of Confucianism to acquire modernity without jeopardizing the Confucian sensibility toward kinship, self-rectification, and its concomitant aversion to materialism, which modernity seemed to represent compellingly. In this regard, the Buddhist debate on the attitude toward this world is informative (Ritzinger 2014). The sufferings of the failed state in the 21st century appear typical rather than alarming. The Japanese debate emerged recently (Hubbard & Swanson 1997). This recent emergence was probably caused by the fact that the success of Japan's modernization project before World War II (WWII) generated insufficient alerts for engaging in critical reflection. However, the project was also imperialist. Finally, Japan's modernization project incurred criticism from critical Buddhism in the 1980s because the philosophy of nothingness was believed to have caused disaster to Japan and its Asian neighbors during WWII.

The philosophy of nothingness, which legitimized Japan's imperialist pursuit of the World History Standpoint during WWII, argues forcefully that the subjectivity of Japan was nothingness, where all, namely the West and the East, should have coexisted (see Chapter 4). Although the World History Standpoint dissolved the hierarchy of the West over the East, according to critical Buddhism (Stone 1999a), it also privileged the imagined non-place of Japan as claimed by the philosophy of nothingness in that the West and the East could be sacrificed mercilessly in this philosophical annihilation. Moreover, critical Buddhism detects that this privileged place coincides with Japanese Shinto's worship for Amaterasu in that Shinto and the philosophy of nothingness are about the origin and premise of world history. These principles do not rely on knowledge, experience, or facts and establish an exclusive claim on Japan's superiority. The philosophy of nothingness formulated by Nishida Kitaro is significantly indebted to the Buddhist concept of Zen (Hesig & Maraldo 1995). Clothed with Buddhist thought, the soldiers of the imperialist government lost worldly feelings toward the victims of their violence. The sense of responsibility is particularly weak in the Zen philosophy. The rules for entering, taking, destroying a mundane place, and disposing of it are obscure or arguably unnecessary. Consequently, the will to annihilate and transcend has become indistinguishable.

Original enlightenment and silence in the Chinese debate

The Chinese debate is of a different nature because the Chinese authorities during the late Qing and Republican periods had never been fully able to group their society and people into any coherent modernization project as Japan did.[4] The responses were uncoordinated, slow, and insincere. The suspicion toward a perceived materialist (i.e., inferior, Western civilization) continued to support the imagined self-respect preserved for the thoroughly demoralized China's multiethnic greater self. Nevertheless, the consensus was that something had to be done to rescue the nation from perishing completely. The typical formulation, which was first indoctrinated in Zhang Zhidong's "Chinese Essence, Western Practice" (Bays 1978), lingered on through the 21st century in the notion of "the China model."[5] However, why would a materialist build something that is initially necessary but would eventually be useless if these efforts would ultimately be transcended in a state of grand harmony? This concept is especially confusing if "essence" remains in a harmonious world and if "practice" involves struggle. This confusion led to the debate on whether essence and practice comprise one thing. Alternatively, essence and practice should be regarded as separate formulations.

The basic difference between essence and practice is the route through which one could reach the state of transcendence. One route is through enlightenment given that the state of transcendence is the state of nature cloaked by all kinds of distractions. Relying on one's own effort is critical to retrieve the mind to trace one's origin. Confucianism and Buddhism could appear to be in a state of loss once away from the imagined origin because learning appears irresistible in the modern world. Accordingly, the School of Enlightenment mentioned that the real seed of transcendence is concealed internally. One's learning in the external world could only lead to the loss of direction or rampant materialism without being conscious of one's internal source of transcendence (Leung 2008). Therefore, the state of enlightenment is not related to the external artificial world. It is ultimately about withdrawal from the external world or from epistemology. Nothingness is the assumed and normatively targeted state of nature. Enlightenment can consciously overcome loss in this world as the targeted state of nature. Nothingness as the assumed state of nature enables learning and practice to have a basis to avoid drifting away from the origin (Johnson 2002).

The School of Enlightenment believes that essence and practice come from the same mind. The mind is where all reasons and phenomena are generated. Essence and practice are absolutely equal in the context of an individual's learning. However, the mind is inexpressible, formless, and pervasive. Such origin is rather similar to the formulation of nothingness based on the KSP. The mind has no beginning or end and is perpetual for both schools of thought. Its original state is of grand harmony that encompasses all that is transient and permanent. The unity of seeming opposites in the original mind ensures one's capacity to possess all possible knowledge and necessary functions; this condition makes Buddhism and science intrinsically compatible (Lopez 2008). Enlightenment allows one to see through the bewildering world and is exempt from being reduced into materialism when learning science. Without enlightenment, learning and practice would lead to anxiety because the population would only see the varieties and differences in passing phenomena and would desire to pursue more phenomena aimlessly. The population would eventually drift away from the original mind.

Enlightenment can provide the type of creativity that would enrich this world and still contribute to transcendence through the presentation of nonmaterialist modernity. Science in itself can never be the route to reach the transcendent mind. Therefore, the phenomenon and cosmology belong to two distinct levels. Self-rectification is essential to moving an individual from pre-enlightenment to enlightenment. However, sheer learning cannot because it would confuse the mind. The subjectivity of China as a nation would be saved as the sage acquires scientific learning. At this important moment of revival, commoners would see how China, which now possesses the power of science and technology, can use such knowledge in a nonviolent, nonexploitative, and non-expansionist manner (Jacques 2009). The demonstration of transcendent modernity should further enlighten the West and makes neo-Confucianism a categorically different norm from the Buddhism-informed world history standpoint of imperialist Japan. Nevertheless, this neo-Confucian philosophy, which became popular again in the 21st century, is heavily indebted to Buddhist engagement with modernity.

Practice and essence are not two separate processes, but creativity and retrieval are two sides of one coin. Therefore, the same mind has two doors: one open to the transient world and the other open to the transcendent world (Billoud 2011, Chan 2011). The latter door is accessible only to the sage. It is the first door that paves the way for neo-Confucianism to acquire the enlightening message on the importance of improving one's standing in this world, where Chinese and Western knowledge is similar in terms of their common belonging to the transient world. Something significant in the transient world emerges in this formulation. Confucian sages must rely on self-subduing (ziwo kanxian) to the transient world to speak to and save the suffering commoners and the world.[6] They must learn scientific knowledge to breed the seed of enlightenment in the consciousness of the masses related to them. The Buddhist notion of Great Sympathy inspired neo-Confucianism into the long route of scientific learning to retrieve the origin despite the exclusion of science from the transcendent world.

Buddhist thoughts inspired neo-Confucianism in at least four different ways regarding the latter's adaption to modernity. First, Buddhism provided Confucian sages with an imagined link to a pervasive universe where self-rectification required by Confucianism acquired a broad scope of influence, such that constantly self-rectified sages are a model to be emulated by others and the mind of the universe to claim an all-encompassing spirit. This condition means that the sages can actively engage this world and present themselves in science and democracy. Second, Buddhism provided the notion of "transcendent origin" and that of "this world" in that accessing this world through learning science does not affect the capacity for transcendence but may even enhance such capacity if the sages decide to engage this world. Third, the great sympathy that Buddhism exhibits to commoners transformed the society into a modern state, which is a legitimate goal in Confucianism. Nevertheless, the paramount duty of the sages is the retrieval of the mind to transcend the limit of the self and its materialist pursuit. Learning would be useless if not harmful without a constantly rectified self. Finally, the achievement of Buddhist enlightenment ultimately lies in everyone's own mind, where the hierarchical value in Confucianism is reconciled with egalitarianism sanctioned by modernity.

In contrast to the School of Enlightenment, the School of Silence in China adopts a similar strategy that was later used by critical Buddhism to deconstruct the philosophy of nothingness (Heine 2001, Hubbard & Swanson 1997, Stone 1999a). Silence thinkers emphasize authentic Indian Buddhism (Yuan 1989) and contend that it used to be reform-oriented given that commoners constituted a significant portion of the believers. However, Buddhism exported to China was primarily the religion of the well-to-do stratum, whose interpretation turned it into a conservative thought. Despite the evolution of neo-Confucianism toward self-strengthening, the learning of the enlightenment thinkers eventually corrupted the mind and extinguished the seed of transcendence in the self-involving elite. The School of Silence worries that practice would corrupt the mind if essence and practice were connected as alleged by enlightenment scholars. The School of Silence argues that no nature in the original state is enlightened because the duty of transcendence is only possible after knowledge of this world is learned. The pursuit of knowledge in this world breaks and makes silence thinkable. Essence and practice must be separate to preserve the incorruptibility of essence for transcendence. Reaching such essence is the next step that follows learning rather than the first step before learning. Learning is perceived as a necessary evil for enlightenment and a necessary good for silence.

The incorporation of modernity into one's life should not be the end of learning. Modernity is a means to achieve transcendence albeit in different sequences depending on the school of thought adopted. Transcendence is the original and ontological state to be restored for the School of Enlightenment, whereas transcendence is a desired ontology to be accessed by crossing the divide between essence and practice for the School of Silence. Therefore, the epistemological function of learning is necessary for the School of Silence but not for the School of Enlightenment. However, enlightenment attracts President Xi Jinping, who is likewise from the privileged echelon. It is regarded as the guarantee for neo-Confucianism to save the greater self. Neo-Confucianism seeks to attain a respectful place for

China in the modern world via learning and further transcends materialism to supersede the modern world.

Enlightened noninterventionism and transcendent modernity

Understanding China's reservation toward the restoration of order in failed states and the aggressive concern for China's own state of governance requires a level of appreciation deeper than that provided by the usual interpretation embedded in the mainstream IRT. China would not have adhered to any rigid principle pertaining to the suffering of the failed state's population if it were a realist state that practiced self-help under anarchy (Pang 2009). However, China's noninterventionism is almost rigid. Thus, Buddhism can provide insight. Buddhism considers suffering to be a characteristic of this world that reduces failed states to normalcy. The School of Enlightenment views that transcendence cannot be achieved by merely engaging this world. The neo-Confucianism reappropriation of enlightenment to make sense of learning acknowledges the possibility and rationale of learning. However, learning would be futile if the mind is not consciously prepared to be in transcendental unity with heaven (Tu 2001, Yu 2002). Confucian sages could decide to reach commoners, who are composed of the greater self, out of his Great Sympathy for their suffering by displaying his scientific learning and engagement with modernity. However, neo-Confucianism's predilection toward learning has not prescribed any mode of a scientific method for commoners (Chan 1957, Needham 1991). The return to the original mind is ultimately the duty of commoners. This thought could have been the political barrier to a Confucian's adoption of interventionism to save the unrelated suffering population. Great sympathy provided no method, and the local mind of the failed state's leadership could not be made ready by an outsider for the transcendental purpose.

However, the thinking of the original silence that urged scientific learning alienated neo-Confucianism. The School of Silence did not contribute to the contemporary interventionary tendency of the global governance regime, either because it was critical of the unjust or lack of equality in its spirit. This spirit of reform fell outside the scope of global governance that sought the top-down synchronization of order. The silence thinkers were critical of the indiscriminate application of rules that ignored reality. The knowledge of local conditions was presumed to be more important than liberalistic values that dominate most of the global governance regimes. The silence thinking fell on the deaf ears of neo-Confucianism despite its rational pursuit of knowledge of this world. The neo-Confucianism dreads the assumption that no transcendence exists in the original state and frowns at the belief that transcendence could be reached through reform and reordering informed by a correct grasp of the materialist world.

China's attainment of respectable resemblance informed by modernity was the paramount concern of neo-Confucianism (Xue 2005). The political

thought that served as the foundation of China's self-strengthening originated from the apprehension of neo-Confucianism toward a perceived reality
constituted by the decline of the Chinese nation, the breakdown of traditional Confucian values, and the failure of the sages' teaching on harmony
and self-rectification. Neo-Confucianism lacks a link to modernity that could
make sense of the materialist pursuit that seemingly prevails under modernity. The Buddhist Enlightenment thinking inspired neo-Confucianism to
envision the route toward modernity because enlightenment thinkers believe
in the original (non-Western) state of transcendence and contend that learning could continue without losing mind control. Self-rectification is the only
correct way of life in the traditional Confucian state of nature. In the contemporary world, modernization is the method of self-rectification.

From the perspective of Chinese political thought, American interventionism does not come from enlightened self-understanding embedded in
transcendence because of its inherent and value-laden teleology that seeks
to transform anything local. The American call for intervention stems from
a mundane desire for material dominance and is a source of chaos in itself.
China invariably finds evidence to support this impression in the Hobbesian style of the unrestrained use of military force and abuse adopted by
the United States in its interventions. This situation prompts a reaction in
the form of calls for self-strengthening, which the (Communist) Confucians
have come to accept as their duty in that China may serve as a lesson to the
rest of the world. A Buddhist sense of great sympathy is essential for China
to expansively and extensively engage failed states or anyone in the quest for
modernity. Such sympathy, informed by imagined, albeit thin, resemblance
between China and the failed state in terms of shared suffering in the state
of nature, does not justify interventionism. Sympathetic assistance can proceed only in manifested transcendence. China's "Belt & Road" campaign
that presumably spreads material welfare everywhere comes close to this
understanding. However, this would remain far from interventionism. Alienation from great sympathy would contrarily incur corruption and suspicion as if materialist power subdues the mind of the Chinese authorities into
sheer self-centralizing materialism.[7]

The national implication of the return to mind at the individual level is
most obvious in China's emphasis on always finding solutions to problems
through abiding by national conditions. Intervention is a false prescription
as long as one believes that enlightenment is possible only by returning to the
mind. China's appeal for respect for national conditions to justify the rejection of external intervention in China and the avoidance of China's intervention in other countries' domestic politics has become common. For instance,
a Chinese diplomatic message from the Arabian delegation states that

> In today's world, changes are turning the heaven and the earth upside
> down. Whatever ism, system, model, or line one takes has to pass the
> test of time and practice. Tens of thousands of varieties exist between

the national conditions of each country. There is no such thing in the world as the best, omnipotent, and synchronic model of development. There is at best the road of development fittest to the national conditions of the country. (Wang 2012)

The Chinese literature consciously appeals to traditional political thoughts in viewing the world. The Daoist notions (tiptoes do not sustain long standing, big steps do not sustain long walking, self-referencing does not sustain far sight, self-righting does not sustain reasons, self-exaggerating does not sustain achievement, and self-promoting does not sustain leadership) cited by Chinese international relation watchers are on the track of neo-Confucian enlightenment (Zhang 2014). Another Daoist insight, "strong things turn old," was utilized as a disincentive for stretching over borders. All these do not preclude the possibility that a specific portion of the policy circle could conceive various mundane strategic concerns, side products, and windfall profits. However, the reasonableness of nonintervention is the long-held belief.

The rationale behind each of China's decision on nonintervention or the use of intervention in a particular manner differs according to context. The literature cites the Bible of Change (*Yi Jing*) that says "the excited dragon regrets" (for flying too high to keep on) to caution against the expansion of influence. The inconsistency of the policy of nonintervention in certain situations, such as in Somalia in 1992 and East Timor in 1999, are the two cases that China painstakingly explained as exceptional upon giving China's consent. However, China has deliberately tied its own hands by discursively ruining the legitimacy of China to become an interventionist in the future. The mainstream thought on international relations is that the entire point of becoming strong is expansion. Chinese noninterventionism and alleged self-restraint must be logically culpable. The constant return to classic wisdom conveys a longing for prior resemblance between China and the modern world in terms of their access to modernity.

Western versus Buddhist states of nature

Western critiques that usually find Chinese noninterventionism as theoretically culpable and practically laughable can be broken down into normative and scientific categories. The normative category points to China's lack of sympathy for the suffering of people in need of help under the circumstances of Civil War, suppression, and incapacity to supply basic needs. The scientific category attends to the strategic calculus of China's noninvolvement to reflect at best mundane interests pursued by everyone else. The two modes of critiques overlap on the observation that China relies on local corruption and dictatorship to promote its own interests. China's rebuttal to normative criticism is rather relaxed and conveys that intervention would eventually be useless if local conditions cannot breed a local resolution. The Chinese

Academy of Social Sciences presents the typical Chinese logic of nonintervention not as lack of concern but as one that appeals to national conditions. Thus, China should seriously consider the limit of its own experiences for the rest of the world.

> … China's support for Africa to choose its own road of development reflects the most sincere attitude. China has never pointed to Africa one direction or another as for its choice of political system. Neither has China determined its close relationship with Africa according to the ideological position. Some African countries suggest to "look to the East" or to learn the Chinese "model of development." China is willing to exchange governing experiences with them while indicating that the most important lesson of choosing the road of development should be to fit in one's own national conditions. China's modesty is seemingly incomprehensible to the Western countries, but is increasingly appreciated among the African countries. By adhering to the principle of non-interventionism, China stands on the reason. (Wang 2012)

The politics of global governance sees one state of nature as opposing another state of nature. The American vision of the state of nature emphasizes equality, freedom, and the independence of individuals. The state of nature in Chinese Confucian thought involves chaos and harmony that take turns spontaneously in accordance with the way, and the state of nature in Buddhist thought involves either enlightenment or silence, in addition to suffering. Intervention is unnecessary and would be harmful if the local mind or knowledge is not present to exercise transcendence. The Chinese approach to investing in local infrastructure and the ruling elites' well-being embodies the principle of nonintervention in that the elites' capacity to act with increasing tolerance under material improvement would restore the general order eventually. China shows its willingness to facilitate negotiation between local rivals. Considering that the philosophy of harmony opposes division, China typically receives disputing parties in succession in Beijing to create an atmosphere for a peaceful settlement.

Nonintervention in human rights violations points to a weak conception of human rights from the perspective of the Lockean state of nature. Nonintervention amounts to a convenient alliance between the nonintervening state and the target state from the perspective of the Hobbesian state of nature. Both traditions are important references in the consciousness of mainstream analysts. From their human rights perspective, China constitutes a failed state (Hodel 2008, Tull 2008). China could also associate itself with those states that, according to US intervention policy, should be treated as an enemy within an anarchical international system (Karlsson 2011). Such presumably scientific criticism contends that nonintervention is not an act that arises from any transcendent wish but is a reflection of sheer incapacity to compete with the West or the pursuit of national interest at the expense of local human rights (Chaziza & Goldman 2014, Lagerkvist 2012, Osondu 2013, Taylor 2006).

However, the impact of political thought is rarely on the immediate policy choice. It is an orientation to either motivate a certain direction or constrain the range of options. The political belief shifts the population's focus away from specific concerns and distracts them. China's self-strengthening cycles in modern and contemporary history and its leaders' reiteration that a rising China does not turn into a hegemonic power are statements of transcendence. A rising power under the firm control of the mind looks beyond the materialist world. In fact, Xi urges his advisors to prescribe for China a proper role, assuming the world is a greater self. If such a wish for transcendence of self-interests does not show consistently in China's alleged noninterventionism because of immediate urgency, complication, or the interlude of sheer opportunism, it still shows in later role-playing that renounces certain interests or power gains to reify transcendence over materialism.

China can intervene under various disguises, assist in Western intervention in a soft and harmonious manner, and remain acquiescent at selected interventions while being critical of others. The domestic policy debate in most of the situations where China decided not to intervene hears pro-intervention positions that are at least considered legitimate if not eventually accepted. The incapacity of ontological and epistemological standpoints to either directly guide ex ante policy making or provide useful ex post explanation of policy behavior is apparent despite China's effort to remain discursively consistent. This incapacity makes the mainstream IRT of power and interest particularly attractive to those who view China's noninterventionism as hypocritical and the Buddhist interpretation as an apologist. However, the power of scientific explanation should and can remain spurious where policy assessment proceeds in the aftermath to make any earlier act of intervention inconsistent and reluctant in the long run. How a particular notion of national interest is invoked, re-invoked, and revoked in policy making is not the concern of the current IRT that focuses on consistency.

For a student of the IRT, selecting nonintervention or revoking an act of intervention is usually based on the consideration of national interest even though the initiation of intervention could be simultaneously inspired by normative concerns. The Buddhist perspective explains how an act of intervention is revoked even though remaining interventionary is presumably more in line with the national interest. IRTs must explain situations where remaining interventionary and keeping out are reasonable depending on how national interests are calculated. The question of how nonintervention remains a reasonable option to Chinese foreign policy makers calls for an answer in that intervention would always demand painstaking justifications. The prevailing suspicion among Chinese commentators is almost always about the purpose of Western intervention becoming infamously reduced to the materialism of power and interest.

Inattention to the suffering of other people is natural in neo-Confucianism that no believers of natural rights understand with respect. Buddhism provides entirely opposite formulations of the state of nature, being suspicious of interventionism. Local subjectivity for enlightenment thinkers has to be the premise of any reform. US intervention that typically installs local leadership in a culturally estranged institution would easily fail such subjectivity, without which the return to mind could not proceed and materialism would follow. Buddhist thoughts on the state of nature thus make nonintervention a permanently legitimate policy position. It similarly keeps alive a critical and self-critical component to cope with any country's intervention on any pretext. Briefly, nonintervention is a naturally provided policy but does not always prevail. The point is not how it fails to constrain intervention at a particular point but how nonintervention is a constantly available and intuitively proper alternative and a critical perspective to be incurred regardless of wherever and by whomever intervention occurs.

Therefore, noninterventionism is not entirely noninterventionary. It proceeds in internal and external cycles. The cycle is composed of great sympathy, reform, and opportunism, which are all epistemological and can either be enlightenment or silence oriented. It also involves patience, withdrawal, and the restoration of local subjectivity, which reflect ontological premises embedded in the original and desired transcendence. According to the School of Enlightenment, one can learn modernity successfully only after retrieving the ontologically original state of enlightenment. The School of Silence urges learning because only breaking silence would establish a transcendent ontology of silence. Interventionism is never entirely interventionary. Thus, all acts of intervention are also cyclical. Note that militarist intervention and cold-blooded withdrawal call for the Hobbesian state of nature to make sense; these perspectives are in contrast with the Lockean state of nature that prompts intervention.

Conclusion: practicing Buddhism without being aware

Chinese President Xi Jinping gave a speech on "The Core Value of Socialism" in Peking University on May 4, 2014, the memorial day of the May Fourth Movement of 1919. The May Fourth Movement symbolizes China's quest for modernity that takes place in an anti-Confucian discourse. Later generations have found solid Confucian strings in the movement that wished for the substitution of modernity for Confucianism. Xi's reiterated the spirit of the movement, patriotism, progress, democracy, and science and cited all kinds of Confucian values from Confucian classics. He then enumerated the three Buddhist transcendental stages, namely, seeing mountains as mountains, seeing mountains as non-mountains, and seeing mountains again as mountains. The second stage is the transformational stage in which the mind is no longer affected by the outside world. The third stage refers to the transcendental stage in which the mind enjoys but is raised beyond the outside world. Xi further encouraged students to rely on the values that the Chinese population "practices without the consciousness of practicing them" (*yong er bu jue*).[8] The last remark relates to the third stage and is parallel to the enlightenment discourse, where the core values of socialism cannot lie in socialism because it is still the consciously applied slogan in the official language. The unconsciousness of naturally using values in daily life connects this world to a transcendental mind no longer entangled with materialism or socialism. The word "Buddhism" was not mentioned in Xi's remarks, which makes Buddhism a completely hidden perspective.

This chapter seeks to explain the apparent apathy in Chinese foreign policy toward the suffering of the population elsewhere while highly active in pursuing good governance in China. We discover a plausible answer in the combination of Confucian self and the Buddhist enlightenment. From the perspective of improvising relation, hope for self-transformation to achieve resemblance to the modern world and aversion to other-transformation to reproduce thin resemblance to failed states in the shared natural state of suffering can coexist among Chinese without causing anxiety. The pursuit of transcendence prepares the Chinese to hold the self-image that their self-transformation would not commit materialism and that other-transformation cannot help but be materialistic without local enlightenment. All in all, intervention could be harmful to the pursuit of transcendence over materialism, such that Chinese leaders, academicians, and the media consciously resort to enlightenment as a self-reminder against interventionism. The hidden but powerful Buddhist influence in the Chinese state of nature restricts the realist criticism of noninterventionism from receiving any sophisticated review and revision.

Notes

1 For a few examples of the familiar slogans in the 21st century, consider "the view of scientific development" (*kexue fazhan guan*), "do something" (*yousuo zuowei*), and "strive for achievement" (*fenfa youwei*).

2 The literature on intervention rarely engages Hobbes on how the use of his notion of interstate anarchy can justify or release the responsibility of false killing in the process of military intervention. The literature engages Hobbes primarily on the issue of whether sovereignty can be rightly made subject to humanitarian concerns. For a nearly exceptional engagement in the former case, see Iris Marion Young (2003). In the latter case, see Charvet (1997) and Ayoob (2002).

3 Nevertheless, Buddhist modernity in China adapts to the context. It has adopted differing forms and acquired differing meanings (Borchrt 2008).

4 Takeuchi Yoshimi (1910–1977), an influential critic of Chinese literature sympathetic to the KSP, firmly believed that China's incapacity for modernization actually reflects an amorphous subjectivity that powerfully protected China from cultural subjugation to Western civilization in ways that Japanese modern thoughts failed to (Uhl 2009: 207–237).

5 The debate on the China model has produced literature in English and China in the 21st century. For the earlier debate on essence and practice, see Fewsmith (2011).

6 Self-negation is the popular translation of the notion of *ziwo kanxian*. However, self-subduing connotes the sage's decision to momentarily sacrifice his transcendence for the sake of awaken the population (see Angle 2009; Chan 2008: 171–184).

7 This leads to the adoption of the strategy of shaming by the self-perceived victim of China, which rises during the 2014 maritime dispute, for example, Hiep (2014) analyses on behalf of Vietnam to conclude that "the most important thing Vietnam can do now is to name and shame China internationally."

8 He actually used the Buddhist dictum to express a Confucian advice because he meant to urge each to adhere to each's value without being affected by the circumstance.   http://news.xinhuanet.com/politics/2014–05/05/c_1110528066.htm, accessed May 26, 2014.

6 Cyclical view of history

How Neo-Confucianism enlisted Buddhism to rationalize 'self-strengthening' during a crisis was discussed in Chapter 5. Here, Buddhism was used to prevent self-strengthening from being reduced to mere materialization. However, self-strengthening during a crisis is neither commonly instinctive, nor culturally familiar, for all human societies. This consequently raises the question of whether it is proper for China to facilitate or initiate self-strengthening in other societies riddled by crisis or a protracted conflict? This chapter examines how a Confucian philosophy of history as cyclical advises patience toward crises elsewhere. Cycles are likewise intrinsic to capitalist markets, both theoretically and practically. In fact, 'laissez-faire' as an approach is shared between classic Confucianism and classic liberalism; however, the former adopts a relational logic, whilst the latter suggests an autonomous one. The chapter introduces the BoR logic of governability as a relational necessity that cautions against hasty intervention based on supposedly 'universal' norms. The idea of governability fundamentally challenges the rules-based global order that seeks to govern and synchronize autonomous actors, as it perceives states of order and disorder as transitory and occurring in repetitive pulsations.

To interrogate how governability thinking has influenced China's engagement with global governance, whilst acting as an alternative mode of world ordering, this chapter focuses on China's approach to non-interventionism in interstate affairs. This Confucian-inspired outlook is aptly reflected in President Xi Jinping's "5-no" pledge made during the 2018 Forum on China-Africa Cooperation (FOCAC). It speaks directly to a central tenet of BoR practice, which dictates that a return to order and prosperity is unattainable through the external imposition of values and institutions, as such imposition undermines the indigenous mechanisms required to restore a sustainable order from a 'corrupt' relationship. According to the pledge,[1] China commits to:

> no interference in African countries' pursuit of development paths that fit their national conditions; no interference in African countries' internal affairs; no imposition of China's will on African countries; no

attachment of political strings to assistance to Africa; and no seeking of selfish political gains in investment and financing cooperation with Africa.

Xi also appealed to a "similar fate" and a "common mission" to further expound the deep relationships between China and African countries. This effectively echoes Confucian thought, where a contribution to the relationship at the collective level depends on an actor's ability to first maintain internal harmony. And by the same token, the maintenance of harmony at this higher, collective level can work to enhance an actor's capacity to meet the requirements of self-governance.

BoR embraces the notion that each society and, by extension, country follows a cyclical pattern of historical change, but that each will also pursue pathways unique to their respective sociocultural context to achieve self-governance. Generations of Confucian scholars have attempted to prove their cyclical theory of history, particularly through the study of dynastic cycles. China 's modern-day appeal to self-governance not only echoes this Confucian perspective on politics and history, but also serves to challenge global governance and the synchronic institutionalism that arguably undergirds its liberal governmentality. In effect, what this chapter seeks to reveal is how the concept of Confucian governability has the potential to deepen the understanding of global governance.

Alienation from governance

For actors attuned to relational sensibilities, global governance causes anxiety because it seeks to alter relationships, as evinced by the example of 'failed' or fragile states, and fashions unwanted resemblance in the case of former colonial relations. However, altering relationships will be redundant with failing states that can resume order by themselves. The BoR style of governance is inclined to restore the capacity for self-governance in an international system that is lenient rather than interventionary. This tendency is likely the reason China has had an uneasy relationship with the extant system of global governance ever since its formal admission to the United Nations in October 1971.[2] While this remains a matter of heated debate, China has frequently been depicted as a rule-breaker or a revisionist power, and continues to be accused of not contributing enough to the global public good. This is despite Beijing's insistence that China remains committed to maintaining a peaceful international environment—a narrative that feeds directly into the country's enduring preoccupation with safeguarding orderly relations both within and without its borders.

Some observers have been inclined to dismiss such political statements of China's peaceful intentions as mere rhetoric (Chaziza & Goldman 2014); however, the Chinese fixation with sustaining order internally and externally is one that is predicated on the capacity of the regime to restore harmonious relations embedded in a cyclical view of history, which is not exclusively Chinese (Kennedy 1987, Spengler 1991). Resonating in some ways with the realist understanding of world politics as "the realm of recurrence and repetition" (Wight 1966: 26), the traditional Chinese worldview is defined by its Sinocentricism and the iterated interactions between *zhi* (order/governability) and *luan* (chaos/ungovernability), upon which the governance of the Chinese empire or "All under Heaven" (*tianxia*) is supposedly founded. Within this cosmological schema, the primary concern of the political leader is on restoring order as a patterned relationship amid the looming specter of chaos.

As previously mentioned, this Chinese worldview is best represented by the theory of dynastic cycles (Thapar 1996). Epitomized by the famous opening line of the historical novel, the *Three Kingdoms* (*San Guo Yanyi*), which states that "the empire, long divided, must unite; long united, must divide. Thus, it has ever been" (*Tianxia he jiu bi fen fen jiu bi he*) (Luo 2001: 1), classical Chinese historiography empirically documented the rise and fall of ancient dynasties, whereupon the Mandate of Heaven (*tianming*) was habitually revoked from one emperor and bestowed upon a new emperor. The quality of leadership was particularly central to this iterative dynamic: "immoral" rulers invariably lost their ruling legitimacy and would have to go through the natural processes of demise. Only those leaders who showed self-restraint in deriving resources from their people could provide strong enough incentives for the population to continue engaging in production and avoid popular discontent that could then lead to social strife.

The implications of such thinking for China's foreign engagement are arguably profound. Although debates over the extent to which traditional Chinese philosophy has an influence over China's contemporary policymaking persist, we posit that this cyclical view has since given rise to a distinctive relational mode of thinking in contemporary China about governance domestically and globally—albeit one that stands at odds with current practices and discourses of global governance. Here, the idea of "governability" is identified as being deeply rooted in Chinese political thought as well as the country's present-day foreign policy praxis.

Governability refers broadly to the condition of being governable which, in turn, relates to the capacity of a state to exert governing authority (Kohli 1991: 24). The passive state of governability—that is, when the population is controlled, regulated or monitored—is not the desired state here, however. The active state of governability, when the population also adopts a responsibility to maintain social productivity and relations of mutual acceptance, is the ideal state as order becomes predicated on a degree of localized autonomy. In some respects, this ideal resonates with the Lockean state of nature. Yet, for Confucianism, there is the added requirement for the leadership to be perceived as 'selfless', as opposed to 'extractive', by the populace in order to maintain ruling legitimacy and social order.

Applied to the Chinese experience, governability thus constitutes a useful analytical prism for making sense of China's stance toward (external) interventionism, whereby Beijing espouses a "hands off" or minimalist approach to acts of interference in the affairs of other states. This has been the case since the promulgation of the "Five Principles of Peaceful Coexistence" in 1953 and, more recently, through Xi Jinping's aforementioned "5-no" approach.

Accordingly, we advance three key propositions. First, state attitudes toward (non-)intervention within the Chinese context do not necessarily change as the sole result of shifting understandings of sovereignty and the humanitarian imperative. Rather, the decision as to whether the Chinese government decides to sanction intervention under certain circumstances rests with governability rationales that prioritize the maintenance, as opposed to imposition, of order and the capacity for "self-governance" of the state in question (Shih & Huang 2013). This accounts in part for why China has engaged in intervention in certain countries but not in others, as primary importance is placed on acquiring prior consent from the local regime or regional organizations involved. In stating this, we do not mean to take Chinese political rhetoric at face value or argue that the idea of governability is purely founded on 'moral' considerations. We acknowledge that acts of governability can likewise be informed by geopolitical concerns; however, these on their own are also insufficient for explaining the genesis and nuanced evolution of China's non-interventionist policy over time.

Second, Chinese thinking on governability presents an example of how alternative governance at the interstate level can—if not ought to—be exercised, as well as how it can go beyond the practices and techniques of global governmentality. The boundaries that separate the domestic from the international sphere puts forward a vision of "global governance" that is based not on the prior resemblance of norms that synchronize identities and practices, but on improvised resemblance that works to neutralize diversity and difference. Third, governability as a concept has deep roots in China's quest for relational security, which flows from a preoccupation with order and undergirded by reciprocity, self-restraint and a cyclical view of history, as evinced by Chinese thinking on the *zhi-luan* relationship (Huang & Shih 2014, Qin 2011).

From this perspective, the challenge posed by China as a rising power within the international system centers not much on the contention for China to assume a leading role in global governance; nor is it simply about China's supposed revisionist impulse to fashion new international norms and rules against the West. The challenge leveled by China is arguably an epistemological one. The conventional espousal of governability in China as a "standard of reference" against which international conduct is assessed and consequently legitimized creates emergent rifts in the basic structure of global governance as premised upon a liberal governmentality.[3]

Governmentality in contrast to governability

The adherence of China to the principle of non-intervention may appear peculiar considering its active involvement in global governance and its articulated commitment to the rules, norms, and values that underpin this system. Global governance and intervention are two sides of the same coin, insofar as global governance deals with issues that transcend national borders that may entail interventionary action on the international community's part to ensure state compliance with prevailing norms and rules. This prerogative is evident from the case of failed states, where interventionary acts of rule enforcement are often deemed necessary to (re)establish order.

In light of the ongoing processes of globalization, we also witness the rise of a novel cast of non-state actors involved in the management of exigent global problems whilst concomitantly contributing to the increased fragmentation of state authority. Individuals and groups of individuals have never played such a prominent role in norm diffusion and global governance before. Even so, the rise of non-localized, individualized agency in global governance remains relatively unfamiliar to a country where sovereignty remains central to its national identity. Thus, the Chinese case can shed light on why the Foucaultian notion of governmentality, which emphasizes the importance of individualized agency in governance, has further resulted in China's alienation from interventionism in global governance.

This chapter directs attention to three key concepts—governance, governmentality and governability—to make sense of Chinese non-interventionism. Engaging in governance means being involved in the processes of defining and recognizing prior relations, as well as the corollary processes of norm specification and rule enforcement to adapt these relations to global conditions. Global governance at the international level is concerned with diverse challenges, such as environmental pollution, natural disasters, nuclear proliferation, international trade, terrorism, and the freedom of maritime navigation, and calls for the establishment of an intricate system of institutions and governing mechanisms to tackle these complex problems. Since the time of the Council of Rome in 382 AD, governance was used broadly to denote "the command mechanism of a social system and its actions that endeavour to provide security, prosperity, coherence, order and continuity to the system," with the scope of governance "restricted [not] to the national and international systems but...[also] be used in relation to regional, provincial and local governments" (King & Schneider 1991: 181–182).

The Foucaultian notion of governmentality represents the "rationalization of government practice in the exercise of political sovereignty" (Foucault 2004: 4). The state itself is the product of these iterated practices, such that the government "must be studied as a process, not as an institution" (Sending & Neumann 2006: 651). Just as the state works to proliferate certain forms of knowledge, so is it likewise constituted by political knowledge which imbues the state with the power derived from the propagation of discourses, worldviews, and "styles of thought". These, in turn, work to inform and are further reinforced by the practices and strategies used by political actors to attain their specific goals (Hindess 2004, Joseph 2010). "Governance" is conceptualized here as a discourse that rationalizes the attributes, norms, and objectives of a governed reality. Stemming from a liberal conception of the state, it places emphasis on achieving a common basis for cooperation, social consensus and the harmonization of interests— that is, a liberal progression of political and social relations (Lemke 2007: 114–115). Alexander Wendt's claim that a world state is inevitable speaks to this underlying sentiment (Wendt 2003).

Transposed to the international realm, global governmentality has gained greater resonance within the IR discipline in the recent years. It remains a highly contested term, however, due to skepticism over whether governmentality can be justifiably "scaled up" to the global level or applied to the non-Western world. Sending and Neumann (2006: 6) state that global governmentality can exist in view of how:

> the meaning and role of sovereignty are largely defined by governmental rationalities that now increasingly operate on the global level. The liberal rationality of government exerts structural pressure on states to open more and more interfaces with other agents, preferably on a global scale.

On this view, the current system of global governance is predicated on this liberal governmentality, which subscribes to a teleological view of the evolution of international society. This "rationality" favors the application of imagined prior norms and values to streamline divergent interests, synchronize procedures, resolve exigent problems, and build consensus. The Lockean constitutional state constitutes one illustration of this logic, considering how it aligns the domestic processes of governance with the imposition of a synchronizing constitutional order (Larrinaga & Doucet 2010). Similarly, the democratic peace thesis—in essence, the notion that democracies do not fight other democracies—advances a Lockean vision of international order, to the effect that countries like the United States (especially under the Clinton administration) have used it to justify intervention for the sake of establishing more stable liberal democracies and, by implication, ensuring world peace (Lynn-Jones 1998).

In contrast to this liberal governmentality, the concept of governability does not conjure any vision of an ideal "end state" or a promise of permanent solutions to vexing global problems. This idea supports the improvisation of *minimum* conditions for the sake of maintaining order or the quality of being governable. Governability does not promote any specific notion of "good governance", but places importance on the cultivation of governing legitimacy on the part of a regime or leader, with the former considered a crucial component to the relations necessary for a government to govern.

Humanitarian or military intervention would be permissible only insofar as it is undertaken to restore—*not* impose—order-as-governability within a conflict- or disaster-afflicted country. As such, whether or not intervention contributes to governability has to be judged by local standards instead of any prior 'universal' norm. In effect, governability runs contrary to efforts aimed at attaining a specifically contrived or prescribed mode of good governance that requires going beyond minimal conditions to reconstitute local identities by externally imposing certain norms, rules and values.

Self-governance as governability

Despite China's adamant adherence to the principle of sovereignty and territorial integrity, it recognizes that governments must comply with the extant norms, rules, and values of international society for the sake of maintaining relationships. Recognizing global governance architecture does not necessarily equate to full compliance, however. China has its disagreements with the nature and substantive content of the international responsibility that each government is expected to shoulder. This disagreement centers on the question of whether a state has the responsibility to intervene when external intervention appears to be the solution to restoring good governance within a failing or fragile state. It, moreover, reflects the duty of a BoR-attuned state to refrain from altering its relationship with another state for the sake of enforcing certain rules or values.

Although China appears to be deepening its involvement in the governance of world affairs, Chinese engagement with global governance and the institutions underpinning it remains "incomplete" at best, beig riddled with tension and inconsistencies. Some have attributed this to the conflicting identities of China as a great power and a developing country (Swaine & Tellis 2000), whereas others have pointed to geostrategic factors that make China wary of a supposedly Western-centric governance architecture (Shambaugh 2011). Differences in identity and distrust together indicate a kind of sensibility, where China's inability and reluctance to fully engage in global governance derive more from its differing understanding of the relational basis for governance.

As previously mentioned, the concept of self-governance aptly highlights China's preference for minimalist intervention in global affairs. Based on the argument that ensuring socio-political stability and the welfare of the citizenry, who should seek to practice international norms on their own initiative, already amounts to a contribution to global order, self-governance entails governments to focus on the resolution of domestic problems first. Order is perceived here to emanate outwards in concentric circles from the domestic to the international realm, such that maintaining internal stability serves as the prerequisite for global stability.

Past and present Chinese leaderships, most notably under former President Hu Jintao, have consistently supported this practice through state-led discourses, such as those on building a "Harmonious World" (*hexie shijie*) and harmonious societies (*hexie shehui*), and more recent discourses on "community with shared future for mankind" (*renlei mingyun gongtong ti*) that neutralizes "Chinese dream" (*Zhongguo meng*), which prioritizes the rejuvenation (*fuxing*) of the Chinese nation (Yeophantong 2013: 357–358). Implicit in self-governance is an aversion to the forced or coerced enforcement of certain norms and values in other countries, as such interventionist actions are viewed as being unlikely to generate sustainable outcomes in target states. Also implicit in the notion is a belief in the emulation of models. That is, self-governance allows for the creation of a system of exemplarity, whereby countries should be free to "pick and choose" which aspects of another country's governance arrangements they would seek to adopt or avoid. Rather than imposing its own rules, a country can act as an exemplar for others to follow. This strategy arguably ensures a greater degree of norm diffusion and internalization because countries engage in social learning through emulation on their own terms. Raymond Dawson (2005: 79–80) stated that such action constitutes an influential way of thought as well as a long-standing practice in ancient Chinese societies, where "the acts of the famous and of the notorious [were recorded by historians in the hope that they] might provide examples for later men to follow or avoid."

Governability in the Chinese context

Chinese philosophical attachment to the cyclical perspective of governability can be traced back to Mencius (372–289 BC), who had characterized the Three Dynasties Period (c. 2070–771 BC) as being replete with illustrations of the *zhi-luan* cycle. Later historians would share similar historical accounts. In his preface to the *Brief Reader of Chinese History*, published by the Chinese Academy of Social Sciences in July 2012, former President Jiang Zemin states the necessity of "scientifically understanding and correctly using the law of history and drawing correct lessons from the experiences of order-chaos [and] rise-fall of all dynasties." Only early Republican writers had voiced some reservations regarding the application of a cyclical perspective, given that intellectuals then had sought to substitute it for a modernist view of history. They had few followers, however.

Most narratives on the historical patterns of *zhi-luan* (order-chaos) mention the reasons behind the cyclical development of history, with some entertaining an explicit focus on the question of history remaining "orderly". Indeed, classical Chinese texts offer two interesting accounts that can serve as basis for contemporary Chinese perspectives on managing domestic and external affairs. The first is derived from Confucian thought and is largely centered on the quality of leadership (or rulership). Confucius once advised that the benevolent ruler is expected to reward more and receive less to bring back order from chaos. This amounts to a domestic version of the first of the BoR principles (see Chapters 1 and 2), and its practice demonstrates how rulers should be mindful of the need to sustain harmonious relationships with their subjects under heaven. An imagined prior resemblance between rulers and their people based on such beliefs as the necessity of oneness (*yi*) to responsible governance informed such sensitivity towards harmonious relationships.

Mencius was similarly concerned with the maintenance of relationships between rulers and their subjects. He stated that the only viable way to safeguard order is to enable the population to become "self-sufficient", as a self-sufficient population is more capable of exercising their good nature as "governable" human beings. Confucius expected such a population to be sincere in subscribing to ritual, propriety, and honesty as a role-conscious society. Mencius was optimistic in his outlook and posited that "every 500 years there will be a kingly person and among these kingly persons there will be good governors of the world". He also noted how people should play a major role in identifying this kingly person, one who can enlighten the people, win their hearts, and bring them peace (understood here as a form of order). Therefore, Mencius was flexible with regard to the method of succession which could be through heredity and selection, and with the people retaining the right to revolt against an "unjust" or "incapable" ruler. Cycles of governability thus came to pass as authority was bestowed upon or revoked from the leader by the people (Pye 1985: 64).

Underlying Mencius' argument are references to how economic affluence also constitutes a condition for governability, and vice versa. The same argument continues to inspire China's Belt and Road Initiative in 21st century. The consideration of economic affluence gives rise to an alternative viewpoint based on the inevitability of economic cycles, from which governability cycles can be explained.[4] Republican thinker Liang Shu-ming (1893–1988) (2005: ch. 11) summarized the literature on such cycles and concluded with the following observation: coming after a period of order, chaos results from the corruption bred by hereditary institutions, a drop in productivity due to population increases, and the moral decline of ruling elites. Chaos breeds revolution, which the new leadership seeks to assuage and accommodate, and paves the way for another period of governability. If one were to contrast this outlook with Lockean constitutionalism, the expectation would be that it is only a matter of time before one witnesses the Lockean constitutional state retreating into a non-constitutional state of chaos.

In light of traditional Chinese thinking on the *zhi-luan* cycle, no strong distinction is found between the inner and outer realms, as would be the case if one were to adopt a perspective based on sovereign constitutionality. Sovereignty emerged as a definitive dimension of order only in the 20th century. It attributes order exclusively to relations inside sovereign borders, yet, for Confucianism, there remains one grand order where one determining factor is the perception of the population toward the incumbent leadership. Here, the population is considered politically indiscriminate, as opposed to being participatory citizens belonging to discrete domains. In the modern condition, therefore, the idea of governability has to adapt to the institution of sovereignty, in which internal and external relations are practically separate.

With the influence of sovereignty looming significant, the concepts of governability and governmentality do share one noteworthy characteristic: both stress the significance of local initiatives and individual agency in resolving the issues at hand. Their conceptual differences still result in different prognostications as to the role played by such an agency, however. To begin, the praise accorded by liberal governmentality to the free individual agency rests upon the prior taming of the population within the framework of a liberal institution. The sited sensibilities of a clan, religious sect, strongman, or guild are expected to seek alignment with the liberal state through the rationalities of governmentality. They do not work to hinder the introduction and assimilation of the liberal norms, rules, and values of global governance.

Governability thought encourages the establishment of good (i.e. selfless) leadership to improve the capacity of the local population to manage global issues that affect it. Governability advocates for domestic solutions to global problems. Thus, global norms and rules that require the transformation of local leadership and the alteration of international relationships are subject to immediate suspicion from the proponents of governability—in this case, China. Liberal governmentality focuses on the implementation and enforcement of rules to cope with exigent issues, whereas governability places emphasis on first identifying the stakeholders involved and then grouping them into a "greater self" before any viable solution is attempted. Governability focuses more on restoring self-restraint in leadership than in the external imposition of rules. A self-restraining leadership restores harmony to the society, so that a population engaged in social production need not worry about extraction either by the authorities or other powerful forces.

At this point, one might ask how such governability thinking features in the policies and foreign relations of contemporary China. The two key aspects of governability continue to stand out in China's foreign engagement today. First, if global governance aims to transform anarchy into governmentality via acts of intervention to enforce liberal values, a rising China is inclined to wait until this "global governance moment" has passed, with failures and shortcomings in the relationship being rectified in due course. Global governance is viewed as a transitory achievement or a temporary solution to the challenge of failing relationships. Some Western scholars have lamented the inadequacies and indeterminability of the current system of global governance, remaining doubtful of its capacity to keep abreast of the rapid changes across the international landscape (Finkelstein 1995: 368). Moreover, Chinese pundits have advised Beijing against becoming excessively entrenched and holding too much stake in this impermanent and imperfect system (Qin 2013: 4–18, Yu 2000: 17–24).

In accordance with China's spatial-temporal ontology, anarchy qua failing relationships becomes an attribute of the status quo that returns regardless of interventionist attempts to control it. Thus, China would benefit if we, in the time-worn words of Deng Xiaoping, were to "bide our time" and pursue self-strengthening through acts of self-governance. The Chinese believe that the issue is not a question of which norms and rules should be promoted and proliferated in international society, but rather about ensuring the capacity of countries to self-govern. But while achieving self-restraining leadership is not an easy task, from a governability perspective, global governance and its implicit support for interventionist behavior merely work to undermine local innovation and spontaneity in the long term. Proponents of global governance ask a governability thinker, "how much (human) suffering can result from waiting, and in whose interest does governability serve under an integrated leadership?" The governability way of thinking, by contrast, emphasizes the question of "how practical can externally imposed norms and rules be without a population that has faith in its leadership and which has to exercise self-responsibility for enforcing these norms and rules as a result?"

Second, unlike liberal governmentality which seeks to reconcile differences and manage "multiculturalism" through a universal discourse of governance, "difference" does not possess a particular "value" from a governability perspective. Contrary to the burgeoning scholarship that identifies the pluralism inherent in Confucian political philosophy, the idea of governability neither supports nor denounces pluralism. Local assertions of difference should be regarded as neither a valid explanation of chaos within states or, more broadly, the international system, and therefore cannot serve as justification for intervention to impose a synchronized liberal order. Nor does it serve as a convincing basis for governments to resist their duties and obligations, the fulfillment of which is necessary to maintain governable relationships irrespective of the nature of the state (i.e., regardless of whether it is feudalistic, tribal or authoritarian). National identities, as defined by ideological, religious, and cultural differences, also do not constitute a matter of concern. Difference and diversity are not to be suppressed but allowed. But although this sense of indifference toward liberal pluralism can result in a neglect of human rights issues that exist within each sovereign domain, the fact that it pushes the burden of the responsibility to reform onto the local population can have a positive impact, as they can forge their own pathways according to local, as opposed to universal, norms and conditions.

In light of the country's quest for peaceful development, the Chinese State Council issued in 2011 a White Paper on China's peaceful development. The paper contained the following remarks on the pursuit of an "independent foreign policy of peace":

> ...[C]ountries should draw on each other's strengths, seek common ground while putting aside differences, respect the diversity of the world,

and promote progress in human civilization. Dialogues and exchanges among civilizations should be encouraged to do away with ideological prejudice and distrust, and make human society more harmonious and the world more colorful...[China does not] use [its] social system or ideology as a yardstick to determine what kind of relations it should have with other countries. China respects the right of the people of other countries to independently choose their own social system and path of development, and does not interfere in other countries' internal affairs.[5]

Non-interventionism and governability

Anarchy, for the purposes of this book, is perceived as a condition of *luan* or failing relationships. The opposite of anarchy is sovereignty, which is underscored in the 21st century by Foucaultian governmentality that prepares and disciplines the population under the sovereign jurisdiction for global governance (Vrasti 2013: 49–69). Sovereignty safeguards against anarchy by dismantling it into distinct pieces of orderly space. However, the Chinese understanding of *zhi-luan* amounts to a dyadic cycle occurring over time. To the Chinese mind, the mitigation of disorder is not through the creation of synchronic rules of governance, but via the reinstatement of a governable state that is neutral to diversity and difference. This stance is not about realism, provided that the concerns for the balance of power are deliberately undertheorized vis-à-vis the discourse on order. The fear of the reappearance of *luan* and the anxiety toward its control suggest that the realist conception of anarchy is not the conceived state of nature. As with realism, no one would be interested in dictating how a country ought to be ruled if order is maintained. Beijing's foreign-policy commitments to "relations of mutual respect" and its oft-articulated "respect for the diversity of development models" mirror this attitude (Cheng 2007: 239), as does its record of consistent support to authoritarian regimes in Myanmar, Zimbabwe, and North Korea which, while invariably informed to a degree by geopolitical considerations, continues to be rationalized by the logic of governability.

Global governance and governmentality make up the international landscape in which globality and sitedness emerge as two variables whose interactions are negotiated through interventionism. Intervention in fragile states can indicate the limits of the claim of sitedness, as it is disciplinary toward the population that fails to follow the practices and prior resemblance of governmentality. Intervention, in this sense, serves as a discourse and process that allows for the pursuit of synchronizing rules that answer the call for good governance and, in so doing, defines how global and sited space should be redivided, not transcended (Cheng 2007: 239).

Furthermore, the rise of China has engendered a fundamental epistemological challenge to the amorphous concept of good governance which, as indicated earlier, is grounded in a belief in synchronicity within the global space and a universally applicable standard of the ideal state. In view of the cyclical view of history, the possibility of progress toward an ideal state, as premised upon a liberal governmentality, does not carry much normative weight. The fact that "good governance" remains hotly contested appears to further attest to these inadequacies. The most one can hope for, based on this cyclical view, seems to be the (transitory) maintenance or restoration of order within any given society. Failed American attempts to impose good governance through the establishment of "consolidated democracy" attest to this idea, as evinced by the cases of Iraq and Afghanistan where such a development path has proven elusive at best. This has led Stephen Krasner (2013) to argue that consolidated democracy is infeasible and policy-makers should instead aim for a less-than-perfect, but achievable, alternative—that is, "good enough governance" where the "physical rights of individuals" is safeguarded and the state is responsible for supplying basic public services, but where "more extensive human rights" may not necessarily be protected.

China's governability approach has also given rise to an ontological challenge, as it situates governable populations within a long cycle of history where any spatially oriented thinking would appear non-ontological. In Confucian historiography, one important aspect concerns scholars who migrate on purpose to find and serve benevolent princes, to whom they resemble in terms of values and the belief in rulership through self-restraint. Confucius was known for suffering as a result of this constant migration, as he epitomized the notion that loyalty based on residence should not exist among the learned circles. A similar sentiment was also shared by local populations. The earliest record of the people following kingly leadership can be traced to Emperor Shun (circa 21st century BC). Legend has it that, after Shun had moved to the area around Mountain Li, a village was formed in one year, a township in two years, and a city in three years.[6] The legend has since become a source of inspiration for leaders of subsequent generations to learn the "kingly way". Here, the message spotlights the critical element of virtue in governing the population as represented by thriving cities. A territorial space acquires meaning because its population chooses to stay with a leadership that restrains itself from pursuing an inherent proclivity towards power maximization, and rules with such self-restraint.

Returning to the issue of intervention, this knowledge problematizes the rationale for intervention that involves the transformation of the sited population as a permanent stage of governmentality. Governability thought flows from a view of history that is insensitive to the confrontation between synchronic governance and sited differences. It is also anti-Wendtian given China's alienation from the linear and teleological views of history, especially from Alexander Wendt's focus on the methods and processes for achieving a world state. The oft-cited (and previously mentioned) line of wisdom taken from the *Three Kingdoms*, which was not scientifically proven nor precise in its periodization, speaks to an inherent sensibility toward unity and integration and reflects a deep appreciation of "pragmatism". No solution to any issue can be deemed pragmatic unless it comes internally from an integrated leadership. Again, an integrated leadership needs to be supported by all those affected (i.e., the governed population), and only then can order be sustainably maintained. The external imposition of norms and rules risks stirring local resistance, elite cleavage, and political struggles, and thus becomes more susceptible to eventual failure.

Fragile states exemplify unsuccessful or ineffective governance, and represent the breakdown of liberal governmentality. Characterized by human rights abuses and a weak rule of law, these states have the potential to seriously undermine global governance. It is also the case that the human populations of these states would not have gone through the prior "cultural preparation" required for global governance.[7] The acceptance of interventionism, as a discourse propagated by liberal governmentality, relies on these cultural preparations that render intervention possible, indispensable, and desirable. It becomes especially powerful when these cultural preparations are enacted by governments and the constituting population. This scenario is usually seen in liberal democratic societies, where the rationale for interventionism and the globality of these issues come almost spontaneously to members of these societies. The public tends to anticipate the need for intervention even before knowing what the exact problems are in the states to be intervened. Foreign policy gains popular familiarity despite the fact that the foreign policy-making processes in most countries remain obscure and inaccessible to the general public.

In contrast, in fragile states where such cultural preparations have not taken place, "global governance" tends to be treated with suspicion, with people (perhaps aside from those with motives to strategically romanticize global governance), being more inclined to not easily accept the legitimacy of interventionism (Innes and Steele 2012, Kendall 2004). The United States' military intervention in Iraq has prompted widespread backlash. In fact, there have been reports that increasing numbers of Iraqis have been visiting Saddam Hussein's grave to pay their respects—a symbolic gesture indicative of growing nostalgia for a "strong" leader (Davis 2011). Certain observers have further argued that liberal governmentality is unsuitable for certain (non-Western) states, effectively critiquing the identification of intervention as the only solution. This relates to the adoption and implementation of principles such as the "responsibility to protect" (R2P) and "sovereignty as responsibility". Both concepts have gained currency among intellectual and policy circles; however, anxiety concerning the inability of fragile states to enact the minimal agency required for governance, casting a doubtful light on the real-world effectiveness of these principles, has similarly grown.

To China as a bystander, the physicality of most interventions problematizes their ostensible "naturalness": in other words, intervention emerges as a tangible manifestation of the "alien" forces that seek to influence the target state. This explains Beijing's constant and default aversion to engaging in interventions, even when for humanitarian purposes. The recent case of

Libya, along with past examples such as Kosovo in the 1990s and Congo in the mid-1960s, testifies to this (Huang & Shih 2014). Chinese reluctance to intervene denies resemblance between China and the prevailing governmentality by contesting the naturalness of the extant global governance system, and revealing it to be a control mechanism that favors its proponents at the expense of others.

The dilemma of whether to intervene is one that China still has to address in light of protracted conflicts, such as those in Darfur. Members of the international community have attempted to justify intervention in South Sudan based on humanitarian concerns, whereas China has stood steadfast against intervention, opting instead for dialogue and diplomatic pressure. However, amid increasing pressure to rescue its relationship with the West, China had to eventually conform by supporting the deployment of the African Union–UN Mission in Darfur. Yet, China did so only once it had gained the approval of the African Union and the consent of (reluctant) local authorities. A similar story is also seen with respect to the question of humanitarian intervention against the Qaddafi regime in Libya. China— together with four other countries, including Russia—elected to abstain from voting on UNSC Resolution 1973 and was unwilling to endorse the imposition of a "no-fly zone" over Libya. Even so, China finally lent its support to some of the UN's proposed sanctions,[8] which can be interpreted as a "gift" to sustain relationships in the broader collective interest.

China's tempered approval to intervene in these cases serve more as exceptions than the norm. Understood from a governability perspective, Beijing continues to insist that the local populations of target states should retain the power to restore their country's domestic order in their own desired way, irrespective of whether such a decision is deemed acceptable to the international community. While this mentality may seem to indicate a lack of interest on China's part to support liberal democratic ideals, it is more the case that China remains deeply skeptical of the possibility of success for any attempt to externally impose rules and policies. This is again evident from China's stance on Iraq, as epitomized by the idea of the "Three Supports" (*san ge zhichi*). Foreign Minister Wang Yi has stated that Beijing is committed to firmly supporting Iraq in safeguarding the independence, sovereignty, and territorial integrity of the country; provide assistance to the country to enhance the processes of political reconstruction and national reconciliation, whereupon the Iraqi people can "find a development path suited to their own national conditions";[9] and support the Iraqi government to oppose all forms of terrorism.[10] This diplomatic position underscores China's enduring minimalist approach to governance: that is, its commitment to maintaining governable relationships between all stakeholders involved. As such, China is less of a "revisionist" power that makes its own rules than a "status quo" power,[11] but one that is less interested in either expanding or narrowing the present scope of global governance rules.

Future of governability

Global governance, as predicated on liberal governmentality, largely serves as a driving force behind interventionism in world affairs. China is an active contributor to global governance but continues to adhere to an "independent" foreign policy of non-interventionism. Participation in global governance in various ways improvises relations between China and the West, as do those attempts that aim to mediate interventionist impulses between China, the West and fragile states. As previously explained, China's deep-seated preference for governability is to maintain order by strengthening local capacity, while leaving the pursuit of resolutions to the national governments in question. This is similar to the rationale given to China's ambitious Belt and Road Initiative, which ideally seeks to enhance the degree of governability of all recipients through sharing economic development in the form of infrastructure and new technologies, but without imposing rules that favor investors at the expense of developing host countries.

Foucaultian governmentality and global governance work in the same epistemological horizon, being both biased toward a spatially synchronized arrangement. One significant outcome is the moral responsibility that is created for states subscribing to global governance. Those who reject global governance are reduced to the periphery or labelled as a "pariah" that supposedly stands in opposition to international justice and security. Hence, the epistemological alienation felt by proponents of governability toward contemporary global governance stems not just from interventionist behavior, but from the broader liberal overtones of governmentality.

By comparison, the notion of governability, as grounded in a cyclical theory of history, does not view intervention as necessary in most cases as order and fragility are both understood as transitory attributes. Needless to say, the cyclical view that the Chinese adopt does not belong on the same epistemological plane as governmentality and global governance. This fact does not suggest that China cannot learn the rules of global governance or that it has no potential to incrementally adopt the underlying rationalities of liberal governmentality. Indeed, the governability approach and the liberal norm of governance parallel each other in some respects, such that countries may subscribe to them in different issue-areas with different targets, and at different times. However,

To conclude this chapter, it warrants note how governability or global governability thought resonates not only with the Chinese case, but may already be practiced by other countries as well. One example is taken from the area of food inspection. Food production takes place all over the world and across different sovereign territories. However, US inspectors traverse sovereign borders to engage in food inspection whose main purpose is to protect American consumers. While the spread of American food inspection practices might indicate a form of global governance (even though its standard operating procedures are unilaterally determined by the US), there is an emerging food inspection regime ostensibly based on the principle of governability—that is, whatever works should be continued but this still needs to be based on consent and consensus. Accordingly, this food inspection regime is top-down with the US bearing the costs of training and inspection. Yet, it also involves mutual cooperation and self-restraint on the part of the US and inspected countries, such that an improvised resemblance of consensus is constructed. This regime arguably has the potential to reconcile governability and global governance.

Notes

1 Xi's Key note speech can be accessed at www.herald.co.zw/president-xi-jinpings-keynote-speech-at-opening-ceremony-of-2018-focac-beijing-full-text/.
2 The UN General Assembly Resolution 2758.
3 According to Neumann and Sending (2010: 158), it is "due to the ever-increasing structural pressure exerted by liberalism...understood as a selector of why certain practices become constitutive of sovereignty...[that accounts for the gradual emergence of] the global polity of the liberal story."
4 Wang Chong (27–97 AD) of the Eastern Han Dynasty once suggested an extreme version of cycles of order and chaos. According to him, cycles are decided by time, not policy. Order within the state is a matter of fate than of capable leadership, and the political drivers of governability cycles become reduced to a superstitious quality.
5 Information Office of the State Council of the PRC, "China's Peaceful Development" (September 2011), available at: http://english.gov.cn/official/2011–09/06/content_1941354.htm (accessed 10 February 2014).
6 See "Annals of Five Emperors" in Sima, Qian, *The Record of the Grand Historian*.
7 For an example of reducing the phenomenon of failing state to backward culture, see Harrison and Huntington 2001. For further discussion, see Luke 1996.
8 See "'China has serious difficulty with part of the resolution,' envoy says," *Xinhua* (18 March 2011), available at: http://news.xinhuanet.com/english2010/world/2011–03/18/c_13784748.htm (accessed 29 June 2011); and "Libya sanctions: China's new role at the UN," *The Christian Science Monitor* (28 February 2011), available at: www.csmonitor.com/Commentary/the-monitors-view/2011/0228/Libya-sanctions-China-s-new-role-at-the-UN (accessed 5 August 2011).
9 Assistance tends to be focused on the public service and infrastructure sectors.
10 "*Wang Yi chanshi Zhongfang dui Yilake de 'San ge Zhichi'*" [Wang Yi defines China's "Three Supports" to Iraq], *CRNTT* (23 February 2014), available at http://hk.crntt.com/doc/1030/3/7/7/103037709.html?coluid=202&kindid=0&docid=103037709&mdate=0223212707 (accessed 10 June 2014).
11 This does not mention cases such as Cambodia in the late 1970s, when the Chinese military intervened in the country against Vietnamese incursion. However, Chinese interventionary action in Cambodia was undertaken as a measure to restore an imagined modicum of order within the region, which was seen as having been jeopardized by Vietnamese "aggression."

Part 3

Processes of BoR

7　Cultural memory

As a testament to the changing relationality, which China must adapt to, modern conditions have added a peculiar variety to the virtue of self-strengthening—attaining resemblance to the West in terms of modernity. Chapter 7 explores how self-strengthening qua self-governance in the modern condition transformed China into an entity that can mimic unfamiliar Western institutions, values, and even ways of life. The choice between self-strengthening, via learning from the West, and closing off alien influences, as to revert back to traditional self-strengthening, is never automatic. China has struggled between these two options throughout history, having only witnessed a call to resume "confidence of theorizing" in China since the beginning of the 21st century. In light of this nascent Chinese consciousness, whether the rising China can improvise global resemblance through learning has become a hot topic. Chapter 7 argues that cultural memory enables China to decide between learning and reverting for proper relationships.

China's rise has been a major feature of global politics since the beginning of the 21st century and has raised many questions. Going from a position of relative weakness to one of relative strength, how can a rising China and global politics improvise reciprocal relations? Will China's rise be a rational process? We follow one major subject of the relational turn—the moment of one's entry into international relations—and use historical cases for clues to answer these questions. This chapter asks whether and how China is ready to improvise adaptation to the global conditions and how a general frame of relational motivations can evolve from the discussion on China's coping with the West.

Two of the four cases took place during Emperor Xianfeng's reign (1850–1861) and the other two cases were under Emperor Guangxu (1875–1908). Emperor Xianfeng considered China as possessing a unique culture that should be separated from alien forces, whereas Emperor Guangxu accepted exchanges with the West and was willing to learn from it. Both emperors similarly faced constraints to their power in implementing their policies. We have selected two cases from each emperor to show how they acted differently from a position of strength and of weakness. This comparative study provides hints on how the 21st century rising China adapts to its expansive influence and expected duties toward global resemblance. These cases show that BoR is comparable, generalizable, and distinctive in substance.

Relational purpose: civilizational vs. cultural approach

Chapter 1 argued that relational sensibility is always rational and long-term. It simplifies the policymaking process by dodging the uncertainty involved in the calculation of national interest in the short run and concentrating on the non-apparent benefit, presumably accrued upon the stability brought by the relational security, in the long run. Relational sensibilities enable one to be patient. The concerns for relation prompt one to compromise even to a presumably weaker opponent in the short run to signal a willingness to maintain an existing relationship and confront a stronger opponent to demonstrate the determination to deny a decaying relationship.

Consider the theory of cultural memory, which moves beyond the Chinese literature and informs the division between the civilizational and cultural relationship. Cultural memory refers to the prior orientation toward a present difference in value, identity, and world order. It suits the relationality of encounter between perceived strangers, who imagine no prior resemblance, as discussed in the Introduction and Chapter 1. We accept the cultural memory division between social and individual, and between material and mental (Assmann 2006: 210–224, Erll 2008: 3–5, 2011). Cultural memory lives on the shared meanings between the members of society and the symbolic and material resources available to each in order to carry the shared meanings (Erll 2008: 7). These shared meanings and the resources used to carry them on are necessary for cultural memory to form and evolve. Nonetheless, a theoretical differentiation implicitly exists. The perception of shared meanings gives rise to the identity of a relational self. It immediately and intuitively sensitizes the difference between in- and out-groups. The cultural resources are instrumental, diffusional, and undetermined. We can divide one's take on relational sensibility into the "cultural relationship", aimed at protecting or enforcing perceived Chinese uniqueness (Gries 2004, Shih 1990), which intuitively spawns policy preference for estrangement, and the "civilizational relationship", which shows fluidity, hybridity, ambiguity, and open-endedness in that China can improvise a new resemblance to the West (Callahan 2004). Illustrating a mechanism of choice and a habit of the heart (Ivanhoe & Kim 2016), China is a comparative case of cultural memory.

The cultural relationship approach reflects the idea that the Chinese stick together because they inherited a shared system of meaning. Thus, the Chinese culture continues to prosper in the future. A Chinese person grows up, lives among other Chinese people, and internalizes the inherited shared consciousness to become Chinese. An alien is unlikely to become Chinese under the cultural approach embedded in shared memory, whereby Chinese people and culture mutually define each other. Leaders take the cultural relationship approach to maintain the perception of Chinese uniqueness by resisting foreign influences or enforcing the Chinese way during interaction with foreign nations. The uniqueness of China is taken as the intuitive suspicion toward improvisation of resemblance to those who fail to comprehend its cultural meanings. The cultural purpose to protect or enforce one's own style shall lead to tense relationships with other nations. Attempts to remain estranged reflect a long-term strategy of identity and interest.

The same threatening encounter under a cultural relationship within a learning context would incur an entirely opposite policy orientation. This would be the civilizational relationship, which may accommodate or acquire foreign practices of institutions, technology, language, cuisine, religion, and style, etc., to craft China's resemblance. China interacts by preaching or learning since cultural resources can be extensively shared. The civilizational purpose leads to more relaxed international relationships because the incurring or re-incurring shared cultural resources are conducive to mingling and openness. Unlike the cultural relationship approach, the reciprocal exchange is a historical ideal that ensures the long-term resemblance to the West despite the giving away of national resources or identities at the present time.

The same purpose can yield different short-run orientations in accordance with the perceived relative power of China. Perceived relative strength at the moment of policymaking, in combination with the cultural approach, leads to enforcement policies. This condition is called an "empire." However, perceived weakness in China's relative power under a cultural relationship produces policies of resistance and protection, which results in the "great wall." In the perception of a relatively powerful position, a China that adopts the civilizational approach improvises cultural exchanges, trivializes binary relationships and exercises patience over unresolved issues. We call this a condition of *"tianxia."* The same approach is also ready to actively acquire new practices, institutions, and kinship in the condition of "sinification" when perceiving a relatively powerless position (Nathan & Ross 1998, Shih 1990, Van Ness 1985). The cultural memory approach, together with the realist calculus of relative power, yields four generalizable possibilities, each of which sprouts a historically sensitive discourse in the Chinese context (Table 7.1).

Table 7.1 Chinese Foreign Policy Rationality

	CFP Purpose in the Long Run	Cultural	Civilizational
Relative Power in the Short Run			
High		Empire	*Tianxia*
Low		Great Wall	Sinification

Empire

A familiar intuitional memory in the Chinese worldview is the division of the world into the civilized and the alien. The Confucian saying, *yan yi xia zhi fang* (adhering to the defense of China from aliens), reminds people of the cultural self-centrism in Chinese political tradition. The great wall symbolizes the estranging state of mind. When China is considered strong, China enforces the ritual that ensures its role at the top of the hierarchy through reward or punishment. A Chinese growing up and living in a foreign land or an ethnic group living on the social and territorial margins faces two choices: to believe that one is Chinese-like to adopt voluntary cultural conversion or to deserve no attention due to the lack of cultural preparation. Visiting aliens are required to adopt Chinese practices before receiving preferential treatments. Expelling is applied to visiting aliens who violate Chinese customs or values.

History has witnessed the practice of granting much in return to a neighbor or a visitor that pays tribute. This lack of rationality improvised a shared order in which China, being at the center of the world, constitutes identities for all, and this historically intuitive order legitimizes the extraction of and unlimited access to resources in times of crisis, which are the non-apparent and incalculable benefits of hedging.

Great wall

A perceived weak China is practically in danger of intrusion by aliens. China's distinctive order in such jeopardy is that resistance/ban is needed. China's weakness does not allow confident resistance to the extent that confrontation can be merely symbolic rather than substantial. The symbolic confrontation can be a well-planned sequence of quick reactions and disengagement or the execution of internal opponents who advise compromise (Adelman & Shih 1993). Other possibilities include a claim of future revenge, a desperate but useless act of self-sacrifice to shame the arriving aliens, a strong act of self-sacrifice aimed at intimidating the arriving aliens, or over-reaction to perceived but unintended disrespect with the result of overthrowing established consensus or reconciliation.

The resistance aims to make a nationalist statement to the intruding aliens that weakness does not keep China from averting relations. The benefit these ineffective responses to the perceived and real dangers can accrue is dubious because it is neither measurable nor guaranteed. The quest for acknowledged uniqueness can still prevail over a concession policy although concession would reduce apparent loss. Adherence to such a symbolic distinction reinforces the losing side's self-awareness and preserves the drive for restoration in the long run.

Tianxia

The drive for conversion or exclusion of aliens decreases if the attitudinal orientation is toward learning, sharing, or preaching and away from intuitive estrangement or conversion. China is at the top of an open hierarchy and wants to accommodate and promote diversity and divergence in the periphery by accommodating their petty maneuvers as if the contradiction is natural and intrinsic to the human world. A selfless Chinese leadership exclusively symbolizes such harmony. The contradiction is even desired because such contradiction or alienation from Chinese values indirectly attests to China's unimposing leadership. The major motivation is to demonstrate China's all-embracing capacity to accommodate all possibilities in the spirit of the Confucian wish of *tianxia*.

Improvisation to concede apparent national interests is a way to give gifts for the sake of harmony or the transcendence of confrontation. This relational strategy ensures that China would never be in anyone else' way in that China resembles to the rest of the world in terms of their common interest. Substituting an alternative for the Chinese leadership, which preaches without any demand for synchronization, would be unnecessary.

Sinification

Nationalist resistance is not the only solution to the crisis of intrusion or containment by the West. Another option when facing unfriendly international relations under the circumstance of perceived weakness is to cut across imagined binaries. Improvising or reactivating existing resemblance between China and its opponents is a practice seen often in Chinese history. A popular method of reconnection in Chinese history is the acquisition of a mutual identity through marriage or voluntary hostage. In addition to social reconnection to transcend national boundaries for China to escape from being the target of containment, there is also civilizational learning and complying. This option is not available unless China willingly acquires and shares international means and norms. Sinification, in this sense, refers to ways to make Chinese customs easy for foreigners and foreign things easy for Chinese to understand, practice, or internalize.

The civilizational approach does not rely on externally inaccessible cultural memory to define China. China has become aware of its limitation and, so, is prepared to learn from other civilizations and comply with their practices. China can appear to be losing jurisdiction, control, or dignity when alien advisors are admired or when foreign standards are strictly observed. The civilizational purpose is to catch up with the major powers on their criteria or methods. Ironically, a hidden racial premise may undergird such openness since cultural mingling may remain merely instrumental to saving China from complete assimilation.

Methodological note on cultural memory

All groups adopt a certain degree of the cultural approach, which reinforces and reproduces prior in-group consciousness. The social identity theory demonstrated that group consciousness generates discriminative intuition that favors in-group members even where the group is artificial and temporary (Oldmeadow & Fiske 2010, Stephan & Stephan 1985). The same self-protective mechanism applies to China and elsewhere. However, despite the same 2×2 cultural mechanism, the cultural memory of different groups, each embedded in its own geo-cultural trajectory, inevitably motivates relational strategies differently. For example, a weak nation that adopts the cultural approach may resort to the improvisation of external threats or the internal segregation of certain alien components, depending on its perceived relative power, as opposed to the distinctively Chinese notions of Sinification or great wall.

The agency of its policymakers is inevitable, which is shown in the choice, change, and restoration of a purpose. A national purpose requires them to make judgments on whether they should improvise exclusion or Sinification in a specific context. Cultural memory can fail to prevail in a foreign policy event and/or in a domestic challenge. Thus, such an abortion of the previous evaluative intuition may compel policymakers to embark on a cycle of alternative memories. The civilizational approach necessarily prompts a decision on how cultural learning, sharing, or preaching should craft resemblance to whom (e.g., a neighbor, a chronic rival, a globalizer, a second powerful colonizer, and/or a stranger) it is legitimate to. The cultural memory that provides evaluative intuition is rational not because an objective calculus leads to an accurate, cost-benefit scale but because the purpose that motivates and orients policy looms accordingly. The purpose tells what relationship policymakers should strive for and targets a long-term goal. Cultural memory explains how a policy seemingly failing can appear intellectually reasonable in light of a certain purpose.

The four categories of cultural memory are universal while the substance of each category is geo-culturally distinctive. The cultural and civilizational purposes, together with the switch between them and the style of fulfilling them, make the cultural memory a proper framework to compare foreign policy motivation and show the cultural mechanisms that explain how and where a rising China can or cannot acquire global resemblance.

Case studies: short- vs. long-term

The following four cases use Emperor Xianfeng as a representative example of the cultural approach and Emperor Guangxu as one of the civilizational approach. These cases, arranged chronologically, are similar to cases in the Western historians' eyes because they reflect China's consistent resistance to the West's progressive influences. The 19th-century decision makers actually acted differently in these four cases. The issue in the first two cases was that the Chinese side intuitively refused to abide by the treaty rights of the alien to interact with the Chinese. The latter two cases reflect a shared concessional purpose and a similar strategy of intermingling to accommodate challenges or obscure differences to restore or improvise resemblances. The cases do not imply that the two emperors were consistent elsewhere, or that their court officials were in agreement with them. We attempt to explicate these four cases in terms of the quest for non-apparent national/rational interests qua relational propriety. Culture and rationality are not opposite. On one hand, cultural memory reproduces intuitively relational sensibilities that leave their marks centuries later to sustain a weakened identity. On the other hand, the sharing of cultural resources by others deliberately softens China as an object of offense.

Empire: the Arrow incident during the first war of Anglo-French alliance

A highly self-regarded China, combined with a cultural purpose, would avert crafting resemblance to aliens. The outbreak of the Arrow War in 1856 to refute unruly aliens from a lofty position led to the most serious hostile Sino-Western engagement in the 19th century. Owing to this local war in Canton, the British and French alliance went into Peking (Beijing) and razed the Summer Palace in 1860. In the history of the Qing Dynasty, this was the first time the capital city was taken over by foreigners and the first time the emperor abandoned his minister and his palace. The gravity of the events shows an absolute lack of rationality on behalf of China's foreign policymakers.

The Chinese and the Western accounts treat Liang-Kwang Viceroy Yeh Ming-chen (Ye Mingchen) (1809–1859) as a critical figure. Yeh "belonged to the last generation of Chinese imperial civil servants to grow up in a world on which Western influence had not yet begun to impinge" (Hudson 1976: XV). Contemporary and current Western scholars had difficulty rationalizing Yeh's seemingly ridiculous behavior. First, Yeh mobilized the local militia to resist the British from entering Canton as allowed by the Treaty of Nanking (Treaty of Nanjing).[1] He rejected requests by Sir John Bowring (1792–1872, Governor-General of Hong Kong 1854–1859) to meet unless he would be willing to meet in a trade house. Yeh had the intention of humiliating Bowring, who emphatically refused this offer. When Yeh's troops arrested the crew of a Chinese-owned and Chinese-manned vessel called the *Arrow* and pulled down the British Ensign (Hurd 1967: 12), the Acting Consul of Britain, Henry Parkes (1808–1881) understood this as another violation of the treaty. He ordered an attack but Yeh's militia was able to hold back the enemy and forced them into retreat. The triumphant Yeh cut the supplies to the British in Hong Kong in retaliation, which forced the British out into the sea.

However, financial support for the militia, which Yeh solicited from those who used to profit from foreign trade, ceased due to the closing of businesses. When the British came back with reinforcements, Yeh tried in vain to agitate the people of Canton, in substitution for the militia, to rise up to their own defense. He could only prepare himself for his capture at his desk with food as he declined food from Britain. His food ran out after he was transferred to Calcutta. He ended his life in a 17-day hunger-strike. In this sense, Yeh was considered an outdated traditional hardliner and did not have a sound knowledge of foreign affairs. He can be comprehended better if the cultural approach is applied to this case.

Yeh believed that the aliens and the Chinese could not interact via written arrangement. The ship remained domestic because a British Ensign could not change the fact that the *Arrow* was Chinese-owned and Chinese-manned. He similarly relied on a Chinese-manned city to deny the British from entry. Parkes had already sent a dispatch to Sir John Bowring and Commander George Elliot (1784–1863) for naval support before he received Yeh's official reply.[2] However, Yeh did not understand why Bowring used the Arrow incident to threaten him that the British must enter Canton city as these two matters were irrelevant. The only meaningful string that connected both events was that the Chinese and the aliens had to remain separated. Bowring and Parkes viewed these two issues to be the same because they were both regulated by the Treaty of Nanking.

Yeh, Bowring, and Parkes could not reach any consensus because separation and exchange are two opposite purposes. Both sides took the "empire" approach to cope with the other. Therefore, war was inevitable from both the British perspective, which could not accept any negotiations (Wong 1998), and the Chinese perspective. The war was conducive to a typical cultural purpose in Yeh's resolute position that demonstrated, consolidated, and capitalized on the presumed cultural difference.

> ...[Yeh] restrained his troops from even firing on the enemy in defense when the latter tried to capture forts on the outskirts of the city, so as to let the Cantonese see with their own eyes that the British were the aggressors. By so doing, he hoped to achieve two aims: first, that the people of Canton would be provoked and would stand to the enemy, who he thought, would realize that they had by mistake antagonized the people and would retreat; second, if the British nevertheless insisted on a military solution, the alienated people of Canton would fully back up their government in the war effort.
>
> (Wong 1976: 171)

A villain in most British foreign documents, Yeh's determination to revoke the agreed entry of the aliens made the wall of Canton into a mini Great Wall, which he mistakenly thought he could defend with the support and reinforcing of Cantonese anti-foreign sentiments (Wong 1976: 167).

Had Yeh had the level of power he thought he had, his approach would have appeared as rational as Deng Xiaoping's decision in 1982 to force Hong Kong's return from Margaret Thatcher, which was widely considered shrewd by Deng's contemporaries. Yeh's lofty style of waiting for the enemy to fire the first shot has also been the standard style of war, as reiterated in the contemporary national defense principle of "tit for tat" (*or ren bu fan wo wo bu fan ren, ren ruo fan wo wo bi fan ren*). Yeh could be faulted for miscalculating the British's military strength but he did not lack rationality. His purpose and strategy were consistent. Yeh's stylistic use of an anti-foreign sentiment was the first of its kind in Chinese modern history. Anti-foreign sentiments continued to gird the quest for national unity to a noticeable extent in the 21st century.

Great wall: the second war of Anglo-French alliance

The Arrow War and the subsequent First War of the Anglo-French Alliance should have cleansed the myth that China had military advantage. An intuitively confrontational attitude could nevertheless persist even with a foreseeable loss, as long as the emperor adopted the cultural approach. This was the case after the signing of the Treaty of Tianjin in 1858. The Treaty temporarily ended the war but not the cultural memory of the intuitively estranged West, although China could no longer sustain it.

The atmosphere of the time that surrounded Emperor Xianfeng (1831–1861) continued to be that the Chinese and the aliens had to remain separate. This compelled him to adopt an uncompromising cultural approach despite China's weakness, which he had witnessed in person during the Opium War. This would have suggested a preference for making concessions. The emperor believed that the requested stationing of alien delegations in Peking and their intention of holding all exchanges of rectifications there were unacceptable.[3] Two incidents virtually bound the emperor to a confrontational practice. One was the destruction of British warships at Taku (Dagu), and the other was the detention of Henry Parkes. During and after these incidents, the cultural rationality to assert a righteous order prevailed over the immediate battle assessment. This was the emperor's deliberate choice rather than his ignorance out of insanity.

The first defeat China suffered at the Taku garrison in 1858 showed the weakness of the gate of the Celestial Court. Emperor Xianfeng instructed the Mongolian cavalry general Sengge Linchin (1811–1865) to enhance the defense of the Taku forts and dispatched thousands of soldiers there.[4] The general's response was adamant and enthusiastic, which ultimately resulted in an irrevocable event. He first reported to the emperor that, if the representatives insisted to enter Peking, they would use their military power to deter the representatives, and "the only solution will be to encourage the soldiers and bombard their ships in order to express the Celestial Court's justice and cease their demonic aggression."[5]

The British and French delegates did not expect any engagement when they anchored at the Taku garrison in June 1859. None of them had any military preparations; thus, the British lost 89 lives and had 345 wounded from bombardments (Hurd 1967: 183). The loss and retreat inflamed the feud between China and Britain. In the fury of unexpected defeat and the insult of diplomatic failure, the Anglo-French forces came back with full preparations for war. The battle only lasted for seven days (Hurd 1967: 214–215). The gate of the Celestial Court was opened by force, and the forces thought the war was over (Hurd 1967: 216).

The bombardment in June 1859 was a political statement on the proper Chinese-alien relationship rather than an execution of a war policy. The Emperor had no such policy. The following event would appear even more absurd. Sengge Linchin retreated to Tungchow, which was 8 kilometers away from the Forbidden City, after the third battle of Taku.[6] While Prince Yi Tsai Yuen (1819–1861) and Lord Elgin (James Bruce 1811–1863) were communicating, Parkes showed up again, accompanied by Thomas Wade (1818–1895). For the Westerners, "Parkes and Wade came back thoroughly satisfied, and completely deceived" (Lane-Poole 1901: 232). The British thought they were deceived because Parkes was placed in custody by Sengge Linchin.[7] However, the emperor did not intend the incident. Sengge Linchin personally wanted to hold Parkes responsible for all the problems since 1858 (Loch 1900: 98). The actual order for Parkes' arrest was given by Prince Yi when his suggestions were declined outright by Parkes.[8] When informed of the arrest, Prince Yi stated that "…the Anglo-French forces have no strategist and the Chinese troops should be able to defeat them easily."[9] The capture of Parkes meant that this particular war could not be ended easily.

The Xianfeng Emperor was unsure if he should release Parkes because his court was full of excitement. The emperor was ultimately accountable for *yan yi xia zhi fang*. Could he act less concerned over the celestial order than the dangers of war? For millennia, Confucianism has cherished the virtue of sacrifice more than that of life when facing defeat. The virtue of sacrifice ensured that national revival would eventually succeed, and that the aliens would be defeated with the voluntary sacrifice of generations. No emperor should refuse to be a model when facing approaching aliens. Thus, his court officials caught him in a dilemma with regard to Parkes' case. The emperor appeared more determined as the opportunity to hold off the aliens from intruding the Forbidden City was decreasing. He declared that he would give up peace as long as the approaching aliens insisted to hand over the treaty to him in person.

The possibility of resuming cultural separation and punishing the aliens was so attractive that almost all court ministers suggested that the Emperor executes Parkes as they considered him a prisoner of war. These ministers proposed hundreds of useless tactics to him only to the effect of reproducing the principle of *yan yi xia zhi fang*. For instance, a prosecutor of the Shanxi Province argued that

> our soldiers should attack the foreign troops in the evening because they cannot see in the evening and they sleep like pigs. Our cavalries are superior to their cavalries because foreigners do not know how to ride horses. We should set up traps because foreigners' cannot bend their knees…[10]

The emperor actually considered escaping in this xenophobic atmosphere. For an immediate solution, he could have either allowed the Alliance to come to Peking or run away without further fighting. However, he chose neither. Instead, he resigned to fight a hopeless war unlike Yeh Ming-chen, who believed that he stood a good chance. This again suggests that the purpose was more important than the concern for security in determining the immediate choice. The emperor seemed more culpable than Yeh because he could anticipate the result better. However, the result was worse than what he had anticipated. The signing of the Treaty of Peking (Treaty of Beijing) in 1860 resulted in a cost much heavier than what would have been had they not confronted the West. The summer palace was razed, and the emperor abandoned the imperial capital and never returned to the capital. Most importantly, China had to admit that the reckless actions of their side were the cause of the war.[11]

In 1865, the Inspector-General (IG) of the Imperial Maritime Customs Service of China, Robert Hart (1835–1911), submitted his "A Bystander's Viewpoints" to the Zongli Yamen in 1865. He felt that confrontation was irrational, especially for a weak party: "These said affairs are all because the less intelligent party wanted to despise the other party and the less strong party wanted to suppress the other party.... Thus, external problems resulted from the internal side."[12]

However, following Hart is irrational from the culturalist point of view. All these calculable infringements that already happened would not be considered infringements by the aliens in the future if China had expediently accepted them to stop the allied forces. What if the emperor had understood that the war would come regardless of whether the request was met or not? The best guess is that he would not have changed his policy because he actually knew that he had no chance. This would be similar to realizing that the war was inevitable unless he complied. Such compliance would be tantamount to inviting other alien powers to follow suit. The emperor was also conscious of the shame that a treaty signed under pressure could create for him. Cultural purpose is embedded in the assumption that China and the aliens must remain estranged in order for Emperor Xianfeng to continue reproducing estrangement. However, the unavailing relational security left the surprised Yeh Ming-chen and, subsequently, his clear-headed emperor completely disempowered in a state of insanity.

These suggest to the coming generations that China succumbed to the treaty rights in 1860 not because China agreed to, but because the aliens imposed them upon China regardless of its disapproval. The deliberate choice of the emperor to suffer defeat and immensely exacerbate the cost of war to China, among other similar events, left the future Chinese generations a nationalist consciousness of wanting to restore relational propriety. Xianfeng did not anticipate the actual return of Chinese nationalism in another centennial. His deliberation could only come from his intuitive compliance with the cultural belief that his choice would eventually benefit China. Once the calculations of national interests fall on the imagined horizon of an unlimited future, any cost-beneficial analysis would appear myopic, granted that the emperor's choice in the immediate event could mean disaster. This explains the absolute separation of the aliens from the emperor. Xianfeng could never guarantee, upon his adamant insistence on separation, the emerging Chinese dream in the 21st century. His long-term rationality, albeit subconscious, was a cultural calculus that reduced his sense of shame at the time.

Tianxia: *concession of the Ryukyu islands*

The relational security embedded in a nominal hierarchy and indicated by the tribunal ritual shared by all relevant parties was essential to the graceful pose of Qing China as the center of all under heaven. However, any disturbance could destroy China's presumably graceful reign, and the rest of the world could fall into anarchical self-protection due to China's inability to control the disturbance. China must appease a disturbed regional order in the hope that its nominal superiority could constitute a prior resemblance, however thin it might be. Therefore, maintaining relational security may result in ambiguities, patience, or concessions in the short run in that a confrontational situation in which China's graceful reign is in jeopardy can be controlled. The thrust of the *tianxia* worldview is to demonstrate accommodation rather than to assert distinction. The Qing court's maneuver of cultural resources to delay Japan's annexation of Ryukyu for almost two decades illustrated a style that features ambiguity, patience, and inconsistency and a less intense approach, which is typical of the *tianxia* style.

In December 1876, the Ryukyu King sent his brother in law, Kōchi Chōjō (1843–1891), to China's Fujian Province and asked for the Qing court's help.[13] Chōjō submitted a proposal, asked the Min-Zhe (Fujian and Zhejiang) Viceroy to forward it to the Qing court, and stated that Japan did not allow Ryukyu to carry out the tribute rituals to China. Ryukyu's tribute was a sensitive issue at the time because the shaky Qing court, under the consecutive blows of foreign invasions, could still maintain a posture as the center of the world in Ryukyu's tribute relationship with the Qing Empire.

Empress Dowager Cixi (1835–1908) realized the complexity of the Ryukyu case upon hearing China's Japan Minister He Ruzhang's (1838–1891) investigation on the situation.[14] He reported that Ryukyu was ordered to stop carrying out the tribute rituals to China because Japan planned to put Ryukyu under its county system. A Japanese county should neither have diplomatic relations with China nor tribute obligations to China. Chōjō reported the detention of his king by Japan but he did not believe that China would be interested in direct confrontation with Japan to save his king, if not also for the sake of restoring a nominal relationship with Ryukyu.

Cixi did not want to further deteriorate the already tense Sino-Japanese relations, caused by China and Japan's diplomatic conflicts over Taiwan in 1874. The Ryukyu issue was highly sensitive, since the Ryukyu Islands had been China's feudatory for more than a 100 years; thus, the Qing court was supposed to protect Ryukyu from Japan's annexation. However, China would gain little if it could successfully protect Ryukyu given its relatively small size. The main challenge the court faced at the time was Japan. The Qing court needed to act like a responsible celestial state and protect its feudatory.

Minister He Ruzhang proposed three solutions: China should (1) send its Navy to Ryukyu and force it to continue the tribute rituals, (2) plan a joint attack plan against Japan with Ryukyu, and (3) ask the foreign powers' diplomatic representatives in Japan to settle the dispute.[15] These solutions would have assumed Ryukyu was not automatically Chinese and reduced China to another calculative power equal to Japan, which would have put them in an awkward position. No selfless leadership would ever be in anyone else' way but, to save the image of being on top, China needed an excuse for inaction.

Regent Prince Gong (1822–1898) asked former US President Ulysses Grant (1822–1885) to reconcile this dispute. In the eyes of Prince Gong, the former US President was more influential than the other foreign powers' diplomatic representatives in Japan because Japan was "opened" by the US Navy in the 1860s.[16] Grant was received by the Meiji Emperor, met the Minister of Public Affairs Itō, and designed a compromise. The northern islands of Ryukyu would be ceded to Japan and put under Kyushu's jurisdiction, and the southern islands of Ryukyu would be ceded to China and put under Taiwan's jurisdiction. The main island, Okinawa, would be returned to the King of Ryukyu, and Japan would release the king and his son to re-establish the Ryukyu Kingdom.[17]

This solution saved face for China, Japan, and Ryukyu, although Ryukyu suffered from Japan's partition. China was ready to take the compromise. Japan's representative Takezoe Shinichiro (1842–1917) stated that China could take the southern islands but Japan would take the northern islands and Okinawa. The Qing court declined this proposal because it did not serve the purpose of nominally continuing the Ryukyu Kingdom or the core of their tributary relationship.[18] The Qing court then discussed how to finalize this matter; both expedition and economic embargo were discussed, but none appeared proper or decent.[19]

The Qing court was unwilling to take an adamant policy toward Japan to avoid the image of losing control if Japan was not going to change its policy. This stood in contrast to Xianfeng's decision, which was to demonstrate disapproval despite having lost control. Xianfeng faced a much stronger opponent than Cixi, who saw a better chance of maintaining China's reign over the Ryukyu Kingdom, at least militarily. However, forcing a policy on Japan to restore the Ryukyu Kingdom could backfire if it was not immediately successful. This was different from her husband's situation, where surrendering would have improperly given the impression of approval. For Cixi, not showing strong disapproval could camouflage the fact that China may have already lost the Ryukyu Kingdom, which she could not have cared less about if not for the concern over relational propriety.

Cixi's most trustworthy Governor Generals and Viceroys started to discuss whether China should ally with Russia or Japan. While the choice between Russia and Japan was strategic, the debate was premised upon the wish to legitimately leave the Ryukyu issue in perpetual stagnation. Ambiguity on the Ryukyu issue could be justified if it enabled a stable relationship with Japan. The first court member who took a stance was Zhang Zhidong (1837–1909). Zhang argued as if Ryukyu was no longer the real issue:

> If Sino-Japan relations are strong enough, Japan will not lend Russia its military harbor. Thus, we should suspend the decision on the Ryukyu issue and lure Japan with better trade terms in order to persuade Japan not to ally with Russia.[20]

This argument was challenged by Chih-Li Viceroy Li Hongzhang, who also argued as if Ryukyu was no longer the real issue:

> Even if China were able to ally with Japan with pretty words and heavy bribery, China can still expect Japan to betray... Conceding to Japan would not help us resist Russia but would make us simultaneously lose to Japan and Russia. In comparison, how about we concede to Russia and deter Japan with our Russian connection?[21]

However, Nanjing Viceroy Liu Kunyi (1830–1902) had a different opinion. Liu indicated that Ryukyu should not be an issue, even though China was stronger: "The Ryukyu islands are much closer to Japan. Can we hold there forever? If we cannot, do we want to send troops again and take the islands back?"[22]

These three officials reduced the Ryukyu case to an embarrassing condition to the effect that nothing could have been properly done even if China had wanted to. Disliking this choice between Russia and Japan, where picking one side would place China against the other, Cixi decided to move beyond alliance building, as she had no confidence in diplomatic alliance. Seeing a large strategic picture, which illuminated the impossibility of the Ryukyu issue, she set the issue aside and focused on strengthening China's naval power. A civilizational approach of accommodation under which China stood in the way of no one else's apparent interests was Cixi's preferred choice. Displeasure toward Japan and readiness to incorporate Japan's unfriendly encroachment could coexist. This became and remained to be the policy thrust until the 21st century.

Neither Zhang nor Li favored a strong policy on the Ryukyu issue because no such policy could guarantee the restoration of the disturbed order without the risk of failing the test of China's doubtful reign over all under heaven. They both looked for a long-term policy that could lure or discipline Japan back to China's world order, which should transcend mutually excluded sovereign domains. China's lack of determination on the Ryukyu issue was out of a deliberate calculus that reflected a civilizational wish for China to be big enough to accommodate all the petty maneuvers in the periphery and actually achieve its high status, which sufficiently demonstrated its inclusiveness via an enhanced trade relationship. Inaction covered the possible incoming loss of a workable relationship and awaited restoration in the long run. This imagination that Japan could still find a place in the Chinese world order postponed China's eventual falling prey to all major powers almost 20 years later after the Sino-Japanese war in 1894.

A similar encroachment took place in France's military action in An Nan (Vietnam) and Taiwan. The Qing reacted strongly to engage France on the battlefield, which indicates that the *tianxia* approach was not consistently applied under Emperor Guangxu. This was perhaps the first major war that China did not lose. China yielded the suzerainty of An Nan to France to preserve this unusual parity with a European power on the battlefield. As long as China's disapproval at France's encroachment was successfully shown, the emperor moved quickly to avoid escalation by making a territorial concession to reproduce the pretension that territorial possession in An Nan and Ryukyu was only a minor issue in all under heaven. To whom, how much, and in what style China should yield were discrete under the *tianxia* approach. Culturally, yielding was neither imperative nor necessarily culpable.

Sinification: appointment of Hart

Reconnection, aimed at establishing a reciprocal relationship via the incurring of shared cultural resources that can obscure China as a distinctive object of exploitation, can be sewn through transnational characters. Foreign advisors have played critical roles in modern China for over a century. Sir Robert Hart, the Inspectorate General of Customs during the Qing Dynasty, personified the transnational nature of the institution of customs administration. He started his career in China in 1854 as an assistant interpreter of Britain's Ningbo Consulate. After nine years, he was appointed Inspector General (IG) by Prince Gong and held the post until he passed away in 1911. He single-handedly established the modern customs system for China. Hart sinicized the institution of international commerce for China and demonstrated that such an efficient and incorrupt institution could adapt to Chinese conditions for the Chinese to use. He was the "most powerful Westerner in China for decades" (Spence 1969: 128).

However, his aborted appointment as Chief of Navy Command was met with a surprise among Western observers and skepticism from Chinese intellectuals for a century. Why would an alien be allowed such power over vital national interests, especially when Hart endeavored to comment on China's internal issues in his "Bystander's View"? Zhejiang Governor-General Ma Xinyi (1821–1870) was among the most skeptical as he argued that Hart "actually planned to distribute foreign troops in China... If we sanction his proposal, foreigners could control the court and sabotage China."[23]

Hart was Irish but was appropriate for the post because of his involvement in the acquisition of China's first steamer fleet, the Flotilla project, in 1861 (Gerson 1972: 151–176), although he had not yet been appointed as an IG then. The project failed, but the Ryukyu issue reminded the Qing government of the importance of naval power for China. After 18 years of peace, China became interested in powerful battleships rather than flotillas. However, when Hart showed the provincial leaders "big-gun gunboats" while being considered as the chief inspector of coastal guards, Jiangsu Governor-General Shen Baozhen (1820–1879) said that the big-gun gunboats "cannot steam against a headwind on sea and cannot go fast with wind and tide in favour – further, that they cannot work their guns except in smooth water, and that they are not fit for deep water fighting."[24]

Shen's concerns reflected little knowledge of western technologies although he was famous for his open-minded attitude toward learning from the West. Shen acted lukewarmly because of Robert Hart. Xue Fucheng (1838–1894) explained their shared concerns: "Robert Hart is insidious and manipulative. Although he enjoys a high-ranking post and a high salary, Hart still protects Westerners' interests." Xue criticized, "Hart already controls the customs service and collects tariff tax. If he is put in charge of coastal defenses, China's navy and revenues will be completely controlled by Hart."[25] Hart's attempt to control the Chinese Navy was stopped by Shen and Xue. Shen and Xue had reasonable grounds for their opposition to Hart's appointment, as his predecessor, IG Horatio Nelson Lay (1832–1898), sought direct authority over the Qing's military affairs for the sake of administrative centralization. Shen's and Xue's doubt, albeit reasonable, resulted in the destruction of the Southern fleet by the French Navy in 1884 and the Northern fleet by the Japanese Navy in 1895. China's coastal defenses were not fully re-built until the 21st century.

The subsequent Boxer Rebellion threw Cixi and Emperor Guangxu (1871–1908) into refuge and forced them to head for Xian on 15 August 1900, a few hours before the Eight-Nation's Army stormed the Forbidden City. The city was occupied by the alliance for over a month, and a hefty indemnity was served to the imperial palace. Two consecutive defeats testified to the failure of the previous four decades and the wisdom of Hart's critics. However, a belated rationale of Hart's appointment re-emerged at the Empress and the Emperor's "Hunt to the West" (*Xishou*), which took almost four months. They realized that an intimidating negotiation was awaiting them.

Li Hongzhang was aware of his own limitations and suggested that "Hart is the best candidate of consultant for negotiations with the powers but he is also a victim of the Boxer rebellion. The Throne has to bestow significant honor upon him in order to convince him to go."[26] Hart's reaction enacted his role in reconnecting China into a large relationship: "The IG has been given so much honor by the Court so he does not have the heart to watch the situation deteriorating with folded arms."[27] Cixi immediately consented and decreed that "...Her Majesty gladly appointed Prince Qing and the IG plenipotentiaries for negotiations with the foreign powers."[28]

Hart's task was to convince the foreign powers not to destroy the Manchu empire because they needed to reach a consensus on how to punish China seriously enough to deter it from planning another xenophobic mass movement. Hart began by publishing essays in *The Times*. He first analyzed for his readers why the Boxer Rebellion remained possible despite four decades of self-strengthening. He then disputed the idea to partition China or install a new dynasty (Hart 1901: 84). His conclusion appealed to the importance of reconnecting China to the rest of the world:

> The only practical solution, in the interest of law and order and a speedy restoration of the tranquility that makes life and commercial relations safe and profitable, is first of all to leave the present dynasty where it is and as it is, and let the people of China deal with it themselves when they feel its mandate has expired.
>
> (Hart 1901: 99)

Hart, Prince Qing, and Li Hongzhang manufactured the signing of the Boxer Protocol, which reaffirmed Fairbank's account of the post-1860 recruiting of Hart's service as a "Manchu-Chinese-Western 'synarchy'" (Fairbank, Bruner & Matheson 1975: 465). Hart was the only Westerner conferred of the title of *Taizi Shaobao* (Guardian of the Heir-Apparent) in the aftermath.[29] Hart was flattered by the gesture, which he viewed as equal to the leading reformers of the time, Zhang Zhidong and Yuan Shikai (1859–1916); thus, he commented, "the Chinese say [of] a big honor."[30] Hart made the imperial customs service suitable for Chinese norms and enjoyed himself being sinified. Synarchy was the quintessential illustration of civilizational approach for a perceived weak China that was in need of Western knowledge.

Robert Hart retired seven years after the signing of the Boxer Protocol, but the Qing court insisted that he remained the IG, which meant he could return to China and direct the Customs Service whenever he liked. *The Times* commented on his retirement that "if in the conduct of diplomatic negotiations he sometimes chose to consider that primarily he owed a duty to his Chinese associates, we are not now disposed to criticise him on that account."[31] Hart had witnessed the confusions and struggles in China and endeavored to direct it back to the Western world.

China unaware of its responsibilities

Robert Hart's analysis in 1865 concluded:

> ...Although Westerners were happy that the resulting treaties could settle everything, local authorities usually violated the articles' contents.

Westerners then suspected that this was because their higher ranking officials were not aware of these treaties, but the higher ranking officials did not understand what the Westerners thought. Thus, military engagements occurred again, and this caused that all sorts of treaties would be sent to Peking.[32]

Treaties and various kinds of global legal responsibilities continue to rock China's position against intervention in certain target states in the 21st century. This reminds us that China's "higher ranking officials were not aware of these" responsibilities.

The Chinese cultural memory that prefers stable long-term relationships has led to a non-apparent mode of rational thinking. This cultural memory enables an interest calculus to center on the improvisation of relationships to oblige reciprocity. China is ready to compromise on such apparent national interests as territory, power, energy, or economic gain in order to substantiate and stabilize an imagined relation. For the sake of credibility, China is prepared to resort to violence when necessary to demonstrate its determination to restore what it perceives to be a proper relationship. These behaviors enacted China's resemblance to the other party in terms of shared interest calculus that symbolized a greater self.

Thus, China's choice between civilizational and cultural approaches echoes the same challenges faced by the Qing court. It is one between the open-ended exchange of cultural resources, to become embracive and sociable, and the intuition of adhering to the shared meaning among the Chinese population to remain distinctive and lofty. Such a necessity of choice challenges all nations and is not Chinese in essence. Thus, merely the substance of cultural memory is distinctively geo-cultural. The mechanism of cultural memory through which a choice emerges is general.

The relative power in one's possession constrains the choice in the short run. China's rise today forms a significant contrast to the decline of the Qing dynasty, which makes *tianxia* and the empire a more credible choice than either the sinification or the great wall. Table 7.2 juxtaposes the non-apparent yet long-term and rational interests of the four cases against the national interest calculus that ignores temporality. This non-apparent rationality emerges into four practices under the four conditions that the crossing of the two different purposes and the two different levels of relative power produces. The last row of Table 7.2 displays the Chinese performance in response to the arrival of global governance.

The equivocal decision between the cultural and the civilizational relationships that plagued China's performance at the moment of its entry to IR has characterized China's attitude toward rules of IR ever since. The critical attitude regarding global governance today is still determined by the choice of relationship. The civilizational relationship does not abhor global governance. Under civilizational sensibilities, global governance proceeds upon willing learning and practice at each site with China readily conceding

Table 7.2 Rational and Non-apparent National Interests across the Four Cases

	First War of Anglo-French Alliance	Second War of Anglo-French Alliance	Japan's Subjugation of the Ryukyu Kingdom	Negotiation with the Eight-nation Alliance
Rational interest	National security	Peace and independence	Power balance and order	Regime security
Rational policy	Abiding by the treaty rights of foreigners to enter Canton	Conceding to the rights of entry to Peking	Confronting Japan through diplomatic and military means	Trusting only the Chinese nationals
CFP condition*	Empire	Great Wall	*Tianxia*	Sinification
CFP purpose	Conversion or Exclusion	Resistance or disengagement	Concession or patience	Compliance or relationship
CFP practice	War	Escape	Inaction	Synarchy
Non-apparent Rationality	Promote anti-foreignism	Disapprove exchange	Disguise disharmony	Obscure boundary
Non-apparent Interest	Control	Restoration	Status quo	Survival
Contemporary disposition	Distinction consciousness	Independence consciousness	Harmony consciousness	Openness consciousness
Global governance	China model	Autarky	Non-intervention	Self-governance

Source: Authors

* CFP: Chinese foreign policy

on the delay, revision, and rejection of international rules by the local regimes. However, the cultural relationship engrains the morale for the promotion of the China model and the Chinese Dream when China is relatively strong, yet resorts to separatist autarky when China is relatively weak. The Chinese dream may become generous and tolerant as the cultural relationship shifts toward the civilizational relationship.

The above comparative study of the two periods and four cases has demonstrated that, through cultural memory, diplomatic history proceeds upon the undecidability of the long-term purpose and the calculable short-term power in possession. Whichever purpose China chooses, enhancing Chinese officials' awareness of international responsibilities is not helpful. Even under the civilization relationship, China prefers to allow room for local regimes to enact the rule of global governance in accordance with their own interpretation and needs. However, China will challenge global governance with an alternative option of the China model if it possesses power with a cultural sensibility toward intuitive difference. The same can be said about any other nation's global policy. What and how the China model asserts its effects are the subjects of yet-to-come agenda.

Notes

1 Article II, Treaty of Nanking, 1842. Statistical Department of the Inspectorate General of Customs, 1917: 352.
2 FO 228.213, Parkes to Bowring and Elliot Despatch No. 150, October 8, 1856.
3 Emperor Xianfeng to Grand Councillors, March 25, 1859, XF YWSM, Vol. IV: 1329.
4 Emperor Xianfeng to Grand Councillors, March 9, 1859, XF YWSM, Vol. IV: 1304.
5 Sengge Linchin to Emperor Xianfeng, April 2, 1859, XF YWSM, Vol. IV: 1337.
6 Sengge Linchin to Emperor Xianfeng, August 24, 1860, XF YWSM, Vol. VI: 2138.
7 Sengge Linchin to Emperor Xianfeng, September 18, 1860, XF YWSM, Vol. VII: 2322.
8 Prince Yi to Emperor Xianfeng, September 17, 1860, XF YWSM, Vol. VII: 2319.
9 Emperor Xianfeng to Grand Councilors, September 17, 1860, XF YWSM, Vol. VII: 2321.
10 Zhu Chao to Emperor Xianfeng, September 21, 1860, XF YWSM, Vol. VII: 2348.
11 Article I, Treaty of Peking, 1860. See Author n.a.: 433.
12 Hart, 1880/2007: 1668, (henceforth, the citation manner is TZ YWSM).
13 Ding, June 24, 1877/1934: 16.
14 *Qingshilu*, June 24, 1877: 716-1~716-2.
15 Prince Gong, April 10, 1879, *Qingji Waijiao Shiliao*, Vol. XV: 11.
16 Prince Gong, July 7, 1879, *Qingji Waijiao Shiliao*, Vol. XVI: 19.
17 Prince Gong, September 29, 1879, *Qingji Waijiao Shiliao*, Vol. XVI: 21.
18 Prince Gong, July 26, 1880, *Qingji Waijiao Shiliao*, Vol. 21: 25.
19 Chen (2012: 97–100) discusses Li Hongzhang's anxiety toward any engagement with the presumably subordinate Japan over trivial values.
20 Zhang, November 3, 1880, *Qingji Waijiao Shiliao*, Vol. 24: 1–3.
21 Li, November 11, 1880, *Qingji Waijiao Shiliao*, Vol. 24: 3–6.

22 Liu Kunyi, November 30, 1880, *Qingji Waijiao Shiliao*, Vol. XXIV: 15–16.
23 Ma Xinyi, November 27, 1866, in *Jindai zhongguo dui xifang ji lieqian renshi ziliao huibian*, Vol. 2.2: 687–692.
24 Hart to Campbell, 261, Z/8, October 11, 1879, IG in Peking Vol. I: 306.
25 Xue, August 10, 1879, *Yongan wenbian*, Vol. II: 53–55.
26 Li Hongzhang to Cixi, August 6, 1900, *Xixun Dashiji*, Vol. I: 31–33; quoted from Wang & Wang (1934: 4021–4022).
27 Natong to Cixi, August 26, 1900, *Xixun Dashiji*, Vol. I, 10; *Qingji Waijiao Shiliao*, Vol. IV: 4010.
28 Cixi to Hart, August 27, 1900, *Xixun Dashiji*, Vol. I, 16; *Qingji Waijiao Shiliao*, Vol. IV: 4013.
29 Cixi Edict, December 11, 1901, *Xixun Dashiji*, Vol. XI, 27; *Qingji Waijiao Shiliao*, Vol. IV: 4283.
30 Hart to Campbell, Z/914, December 15, 1901, Chen Xiafei and Han, 1990: 603.
31 *The Times*, April 23, 1908.
32 Hart, TZ YWSM: 1668, 1672–1673.

8 Psychological efficacy

The influence of cultural memory occasionally prompts a nation to ignore the disadvantaged power asymmetry and intuitively reverts to separation or autonomy from the influence of another nation. The long-term rationale of the weak party is to reimagine a resemblance of interest calculus between the two that is independent from asymmetry. The intuitive tendency toward confrontation in those serious conditions does not ensure that the actual act of confrontation follows where asymmetry is too obvious to ignore. Chapter 8 studies the psychological mechanism that enables the weak party to overcome the disadvantaged asymmetry and resist the continuing relationship for the sake of reimagining resemblance.

IRT lacks a specific processual analysis of the social relationship where a justifiable resistance of the weak leads to action. Constructive IR stresses the importance of a collective identity that bounds all the consenting states to a certain degree (Wendt 1999). The manner in which smaller states utilize collective identity to force a concession from the greater power is intrinsic to the reproduction of a collective identity. This is how studies on East Asian international relations suggest to achieve order through influence, not coercion (Goh 2011, Kang 2007). Influence is a two-way process to the extent that smaller states can refuse to bear resemblance to the stronger side to reconstitute the latter's self-identity by reduced resemblance. The mechanism that explains the actual decision of the weak party to exert unyielding pressure is worth studying. In this chapter, we gather from a social survey in Taiwan three mechanisms that can lead to the adoption of confrontation, namely, peace efficacy, determination, and legitimacy. In brief, smaller states can believe in their power to sway the policy of larger states.

Resistance under asymmetry as a puzzle

Resistance can be either drastic or subtle. Any act to defy the wish of the strong party is regarded as tacit resistance. We argue that the weak party can resort to confrontation and expect concessions from the other side. The stronger the peace efficacy the weak party owns, the more resolute it can confront the strong party. Peace efficacy is a matter of social relations. The greater self-consciousness may have double effects. It contributes to one party's confidence in the social relationship and enhances the feeling of control over peace resolution despite the confrontational approach it adopts in face of the strong party. However, a thick consciousness of the greater self may reversely restrain the level of resistance of the weak party. Cultural intuition orients its consciousness toward resistance, and an ambiguous message is sufficient to convey resistance, because no such ambiguity exists in the normal exchange of the two parties. However, such resistance can be denied or repaired relatively easily.

Take Pyongyang as an example. IR theory, which focuses on the balance of power (BoP), holds that Kim Jong-un's options in dealing with the US are either bandwagoning, which he defied, or balancing against the US with China's support, which he risked losing. If Kim has considered China as a potential threat, his China policy has neither been bandwagoning nor balancing until a reconciliation he suddenly initiated in Summer 2018, four years into his term. The confrontation policy of Taiwan toward China is a strong example of an asymmetric relationship (Christian 2002, Ross 2006), although literature has consistently considered the US as the major (real) actor behind Taiwan in a triangular frame (Gilley 2010, Ross 2002). However, the confrontational position taken by Lee Teng-hui and his successor Chen Shui-bian is theoretically unexplained (Corcuff 2012). This confrontational stance is intriguing because the US was unsupportive of the confrontational policy. The relationship between Vietnam and China is another example of an asymmetric relationship (Womack 2006). However, the incorporated perspective of the weak party under study is more interpretive than empirical.

The academic interest in Chinese tributary and hierarchical systems has increased recently in the literature and has focused mostly on the systemic structure or great powers, rather than the asymmetric ones (Callahan 2008, Kang 2003–4, Yan 2011). Nevertheless, a study attempted to explain China's relationship with Myanmar according to BoR theory, which argues that Myanmar does not adhere to BoP, nor does it embrace bandwagoning as an alternative approach to China (Huang 2015). Hedging is not always relevant because countries such as Vietnam or Myanmar can adopt a confrontational approach in coping with China (Butterfield 1996, Fan 2010, Vuving 2006, Zhu 2011). Taiwan, whose internal cleavage discredits the assumption of a unitary actor that a calculative policy for hedging requires, (Chu 2011, Wu 2011) has likewise resorted to confrontation occasionally. The weak party possesses a sense of efficacy whenever self-restraint is the conscious duty of the strong party in the relational context.

BoR relies on the relational stability with China that entails no specific power threat to maintain a peaceful relationship that transcends ideological contrast, border dispute, bloc confrontation, and ethnic complexity. The history of Sino–Myanmar relations is the best example of this definition. BoR seems effective in ensuring that the strong party practiced self-restraint. Self-restraint keeps the strong party from resorting to force to secure a manageable bilateral relationship embedded in mutually congruent practice and stability. Thus, for a long period of time, the blunt impudence of Pyongyang in dealing with Chinese affairs engenders compromises from China that equally or increasingly cherishes relational security.

This chapter aims to determine how a weak party can practically possess the sense of efficacy to confront a strong counterpart in an asymmetric relationship. In line with BoP, asymmetry in this book refers to the lack of BoP between two interacting states or the inability to achieve balance. The confrontational policy is the expressed taking of a position by a party via rhetoric or action that is understood by both parties as a means to oppose the position of the other. This definition renders the social relationship perception significant to understanding confrontation as a challenge through enhanced efficacy. The process is tantamount to a policy in which a weak party engages in independent hard balancing with no chance of long-term success. Theory of hedging assumes that hard balancing occurs through the indirect form of military build-up for deterring (Hiep 2013: 351–356) instead of confronting. Therefore, theory of hedging fails to explain the adoption of confrontation by a weak party.

A case study offers suggestions on how Taiwan can rely on asserting a proper relationship with China to cope with China's inclination to use force in resolving the unification issue. Taiwan is selected because a society-based psychological analysis of the bilateral relationship is possible, as evidenced by a social survey that reveals the psychological mechanisms that the Taiwanese constituency adopts to attain BoR with China. The survey in Taiwan investigated whether the respondents are confident that peace with China can be maintained under various conditions instead of requiring them to answer questions derived from hypothetical cases of confrontation. The questions focused on whether respondents think they can attain or effectively maintain peace by adopting a confrontational policy or electing a party inclined to a confrontational policy. Their answers served as proxies for confrontational behavior.

The survey discussion provides a generalizable clue to an occasional confrontational policy that weak parties adhere to by identifying psychological mechanisms rather than power mechanisms that allow or prevent confrontation. The survey yielded three efficacy variables in formulating the BoR attitudes of the Taiwanese constituency toward China, all of which could have universal implications. These variables are *peace efficacy, determination*, and *legitimacy*. *Peace efficacy* is related to the relevance of an expected outcome of change, in time or the ruling party, to control peace with China. *Determination* is concerned with the relevance of one's psychological readiness for confrontation to control a proper relationship. *Legitimacy* is associated with the relevance of consolidating popular opinion to control a proper relationship.

BoR approach to asymmetric confrontation

The following discussion on the psychological mechanisms of weak powers to challenge strong powers also contributes to the literature on small state foreign policy by: (1) offering processual instead of structural explanations; (2) focusing on confrontational behavior rather than smart ways of managing security issues; (Chong 2010, Maass 2014) and (3) rationalizing bilateral as opposed to multilateral policies of asymmetric parties. The literature on foreign policy of small states attempts to answer the question related to small state power or influence by empirically correlating the concept with structural factors (Charles et al. 1997, Ingebritsen, Neumann & Gstöhl 2006, Maass 2017, 2009, Panke 2010, Vital 1967, Zahariadis 1994). The widely recognized structural factor is systemic configuration, which is usually described in terms of the number of contending greater powers that engenders room for maneuvering by small states in between and the sizes of the small and medium states in the system that favor collective actions (Baldacchino 2012, Fox 1959, Midlarsky & Park 1991). The domestic conditions of small states in question are equally important, which are often related to their historical backgrounds, policy-making frameworks, participation of populations, (Hey 2003) and levels of economic development (Amstrong et al. 1998). However, cases seem contingent upon idiosyncratic factors. In short, actual practices perceived through the lens of structural analyses do not allow generalizations.

By contrast, the literature of relational IR encourages the identification of processual mechanisms that connect structures to behavior and acknowledges the uncertainty of decisional contexts. In other words, the resulting policy may still be compliant even with the presence of structural factors that favor an assertive policy, or vice versa. Thus, processual mechanisms through which contesting policy behavior can emerge should be identified. This task calls for an agenda to discover the psychological mechanisms through which confrontation makes the most sense. Psychological mechanisms do not explain how policy makers adopt them, but they present the process of how things happen, thereby revealing dynamic and agency relations.

Relational security is a type of "felt security" (Sroufe & Waters 1977) that deviates from the impression that security depends on power. It refers to a state of mind that requires the readiness to adopt confrontation at times, regardless of the available power. Relationally secure actors perceive an environment that is comfortable and supportive of their pursuit of interests and recognize minimal threat from the pursuit of interests by other actors (Devine 1995, Sleebos, Ellemers & de Gilder 2006). A relationally secure national actor possesses an acknowledged and accepted role in the international order. The image of being a trustworthy actor observing the norms of its expected role is essential in maintaining relational security (Levinger 1983). This image provides the actor with the duty to protect its role and the associated relationships through forgiveness or punishment (Younger, Piferi, Jobe & Lasler 2004) even though the actor possesses limited power to fulfill its duty.

BoR is relevant in explaining cases where internal conditions across weak countries lead to a quest for a new relationship by renouncing the self-restraint that supports the continuation of the existing relationship. The internal conditions of the strong or weak party become irrelevant under BoP. However, even the internal conditions of the weak party under BoR can be consequential. The sense of efficacy of the weak party can be enhanced under BoR because revenge, punishment, and rebellion generate dominance and control in the weak party rather than military security (Baumeister 1997, Yoshimura 2007). The internal determination suggests that the weak party provides the strong party an incentive to appease the former and improve their long-term relationship. Therefore, whether the weak party believes that the strong party protects the peaceful relationship between them explains the former's adoption of the confrontational policy.

In Taiwan, the BoR adaptation emerged in accordance with the shift of the internal politics of identity toward Taiwan's independence from the administration of Lee Teng-hui (Hughes 2011, Jacobs 2012). Confrontational BoR purports to revise a relationship perceived as outdated. Pointing to the disadvantage of BoP in Taiwan and its national interest of optimizing progressive economic opportunity, rational choices highlight a less confrontational policy than those adopted by Lee (1988–2000) and his successor Chen Shui-bian (2000–2008) (Chow 2012) or Tsai Ing-wen (2016–present). Chen employed the extreme measure to compel the US to publicly denounce its provocative pro-independence policy. China is deemed sensitive to the preservation of the image of a greater-China identity, such that it provided numerous economic concessions to Taiwan during the eight-year term of Ma Ying-jeou (2008–2016), who decided to cease the pursuit of independence. The pampering proceeded despite the reiteration of Ma that reunification is not a cornerstone of his policy.

The threats that typically compel the weak party to take a confrontational approach as a powerful warning to the strong party are infringements on territorial integrity, ruling ideology, or political institution. The weak party has the option, for the sake of maintaining or creating a proper relationship, to use a drastic threat to compel the strong party to devote serious attention to the need of the weak counterpart and repair the relationship accordingly. This is a kind of negative gift-giving. Defining the gravity of the threat requires judgment and skill. Thus, the strong party is as much in a position to decide as the weak party. The inevitability of human decision in managing proper relationships suggests that a proper relationship is one that comprises mutually congruent role expectations, which do not always vary with changing power balances or national interests. The process through which the weak party can manipulate BoR to demand a change makes the study of BoR attractive.

BoR efficacy in Taiwanese attitudes toward China

BoR contrasts sharply with BoP to the extent that conflict is not a contingency of power politics. The threat to resort to conflict is a method of conflict resolution available to all nations regardless of their power. Thus, BoR seeks subjective rather than objective explanations to situations in which a strong state tolerates and adapts to the challenges posed by its counterpart in an asymmetric relationship. The China policy of Taiwan is a typical case of an asymmetric relationship faced with the challenge of losing balance. Historically, the BoR between China and Taiwan emerged at the end of the Chinese Civil War, which ensued as the defeated Kuomintang established an exile regime in Taipei. The legitimacy of both regimes originated from their shared, alleged commitment to reunite China. This commitment to one China defined the imagined resemblance between China and Taiwan, which enabled them to rule their respective domains. Both would lose legitimacy without their shared goal of reunification. Their mutual expectations of each other were renegades of their own China.

The extreme asymmetry of power that privileged China was balanced by the US support for the Kuomintang. The US enforced the containment policy from the 1950s to the 1960s. However, the predominance of the US superpower did not deter either side from engaging in military clashes in defiance of the containment policy. Clashes, which reflected the ongoing Civil War, were necessary for both sides to maintain the image of one China. The coupling of the BoP between China and the US, as well as the BoR between China and Taiwan, diminished when the Sino–US rapprochement in the early 1970s shook the BoP that kept Taiwan in a military balance. Taiwan maintained self-restraint via its pretentious claim over mainland China to keep the other pillar of the relationship balance intact. This BoR deteriorated as Taiwan moved toward the option of independence in the 1990s, as symbolized by the election of the pro-independence President Lee Teng-hui.

The adaption of Taiwan to its internal conditions and the challenge of the asymmetric relationship can be a harbinger for the general asymmetric relationship because of the following: (1) the asymmetry of power between the two sides is evident, (2) under the nascent circumstance of identity change, Taiwan holds an absolutely contrary policy position regarding its desire for independence from the People's Republic of China (PRC), (3) a consistent record of arms purchase from the US ensures the capability of Taiwan to deter actions from China, (4) the shared Chinese culture and Han ethnicity between the two sides allow China to appeal to Chinese nationalism, and (5) the prevalence of the peace issue as a top campaign agendum in Taiwan after Martial Law was lifted in 1987 (Bush 2013, Cheng 1993, Wei 2012). In lieu of armed unification, both sides have alternated between compromise and confrontation for more than three decades since the adoption of the national peace goal by the post-Cultural Revolution leadership (Sheng 2002).

Taiwan has been gradually resorting to a pro-independence platform since the early 1990s. The cyclical climax of the confrontation was reached the second time during the term of Chen (2000–2008), who defied US advice and escalated the pro-independence agenda. Consequently, China was compelled to accept the change in the internal value of Taiwan (i.e., averting unification) to maintain a harmonious relationship with Taiwan that is presumably conducive to a long-term unification agenda. China's approach was to work through the US (See Chapter 3). Chen failed to win the support of the US, and his successor had to adjust, which resulted in their withdrawal from the pro-independence pursuit. Chen and his supporters project a sense of efficacy regardless of the lack of power of Taiwan or the discouragement of the US to execute a political campaign that a BoP veteran believed had slight chances of success (Mearsheimer 2014). Nevertheless, China arranged a series of economic concessions for Taiwan after Chen stepped down. China displayed a strong will to keep a low profile and settle for a peaceful policy. Chen anticipated China's unwillingness to confront him. The interaction between the two sides can allude to the weak-party strategy in an asymmetric relationship.

The 21st Century Foundation in Taiwan randomly selected 1,000 households based on the official population book to serve as respondents in a face-to-face interview during the fall of 2013.[1] Ten questions focused on the Taiwan–China asymmetric relationship and the BoR efficacy on Taiwan's side. The BoR efficacy refers to the sense of control over the long term, presumably a peaceful prospect of the Taiwan–China relationship. The survey questions explored five potential psychological mechanisms: willingness to fight (D1/D4), commitment to building a national defense (D2/D8), confidence in the pro-independence party (D3/D5), confidence in public opinion (D7/D9), and attitudes toward time (D6/D10). The questions were intended to generate a sense of efficacy among the Taiwanese constituency regarding crafting a new relationship with reunification-seeking China. The imagined resemblance between Taiwan and China from the former's perspective, as assumed by the survey questions, is a vaguely defined peaceful autonomy from the governing influence of the PRC.

Determining how the sense of control over peace is related to the confrontational pro-independence policy in Taiwan can assist in discovering the psychological mechanism of the weak party that chooses to confront the strong party. These five psychological processes suggest the readiness of the Taiwanese respondents in terms of confrontation with China. They attend to the interaction between independence and peace as two values and study which is more important, whether the values can be made compatible, and how these can be made compatible. The results suggest the following. First, independence is more imperative than peace when juxtaposed against each other, indicating a confrontational tendency. Second, a small portion of the population believes that peace and independence can be compatible. Third, all three potential strategic instruments do not receive a high opinion, which questions the belief that independence and peace can be compatible. The three strategic instruments include electing a party inclined toward confrontation, articulating the popular will at the poll, and awaiting a bright future.

"Willingness to fight" requests the respondents to evaluate how far they are willing to go to assert a new relationship with China. Statistics show that a high proportion of the population is psychologically prepared to wage war for the cause of independence. "Commitment to national defense" measures how far people are willing to go physically to prepare for a confrontation with China. It compares the constraints of two interest calculi, namely, tax payment and a good relationship with China, and shows that tax payment is a higher constraint than a good relationship with China. "Confidence in the pro-independence party" asks the respondents to assess whether a ruling party inclined for confrontation can exert better control over China's Taiwan policy. "Confidence in public opinion" asks the respondents to judge whether the popular will in Taiwan can deter China from resorting to military means. Finally, "attitudes toward time" indirectly measures the level of confidence and comfort of the respondents toward waiting as a method of achieving peaceful independence.

Factor analysis of the ten questions yielded three factors: *peace efficacy*, *determination*, and *legitimacy*. *Peace efficacy* shows a good fit among five variables, suggesting that time (i.e., the future), party (the pro-independence Democratic Progress Party), and willingness to resist invasion are positively related. The variable of democratic independence is also positively associated but to a lesser degree. Therefore, peace efficacy is a salient issue that can divide the population into optimistic or pessimistic attitudes. From the psychological perspective, trust in the capability of the pro-independence party to control the exchanges and negotiation with China, the expectation of the eventual independence of Taiwan, and the willingness to resist invasion belong to one idea. People reveal their level of peace efficacy through the expressed level with which they can enhance or lose control over the pursuit of independence. Table 8.1 reveals that more people believe in low efficacy to the extent that the pro-independence party has a slight impact on China, time is not on the side of Taiwan, and the people are unwilling to fight against invasion. People lack BoR efficacy in a low peaceful prospect for independence. Nevertheless, owning peace efficacy is a plausible psychological mechanism to enable a confrontational policy (Table 8.2).

Determination indicates a strong relationship between the willingness to fight to assert the pro-independence position and the inclination to purchase arms with or without tax increase. This factor includes a positive association between the willingness to initiate a pro-independence war and the support for military preparation, which highlights the determination to make the relationship proper through the unilateral effort of Taiwan. The approval of an enhanced defense budget reveals the willingness to support a pro-independence war. The lack of support for the defense budget reflects

Table 8.1 Relationship Efficacy of Taiwan's China Policy[a]

No.	Questions	Cases	Pros	++	+	Cons	−	−−
D1	If the government conscripts people to have war with China to achieve independence, people have the right to deny conscription.	900	50.6	7.3	43.4	49.4	42.4	7.0
D4	If China resorts to armed unification and the government gives up fighting, the people should continue to fight by all means.	890	54.8	10.1	44.7	45.2	40.3	4.9
D7	If a majority of Taiwanese expressively support independence, China will renounce the use of force as a means of unification.	884	19.9	1.0	18.9	80.1	68.2	11.9
D9	If a majority of Taiwanese expressively support unification, China will renounce the use of force as a means of unification.	855	44.9	3.9	41.0	55.1	49.9	5.3
D2	Even if arms purchase causes tension with China, Taiwan should still proceed with the purchase.	911	68.1	8.9	59.2	31.9	30.1	1.7
D8	If arms purchase requires a higher tax, people should still give support.	924	33.5	1.9	31.6	66.5	55.6	10.9
D3	If the ruling party is the DPP, China will not force unification.	843	27.8	1.6	26.2	72.2	66.0	6.1
D5	If the DPP carries out openness to and exchange with China, people should feel safer.	856	37.3	3.3	34.0	62.7	56.2	6.5
D6	The longer the current situation lasts, the more bargaining chips Taiwan will have against China.	818	33.9	2.2	31.7	66.1	59.4	6.7
D10	Taiwan will eventually become independent despite China's opposition.	853	46.3	4.8	41.4	53.7	47.7	6.1

Source: All three tables in this paper were generated from the survey, which is composed of interviews with 1,000 households randomly selected from the official population statistics sponsored by the 21st Century Foundation in Taiwan in Fall 2013. The data set can be requested at the following email address: Yu-cheng Kao <kaoyucheng@gmail.com>
a   ++: strongly agree, +: agree, −: disagree, −−: strongly disagree.

the unwillingness to wage a pro-independence war. *Peace efficacy* requires the assessment of the intentions of China, whereas *determination* is mainly an internally shaped psychological propensity, which may not be affected by

Table 8.2 Factor Analysis of the Peace Efficacy Survey

	Factors		
	Peace efficacy	*Determination*	*Legitimacy*
D5 If the DPP carries out openness to and exchange with China, people should feel safer.	0.709	−0.017	0.044
D10 Taiwan will eventually become independent despite China's opposition.	0.660	0.060	0.015
D3 If the ruling party is the DPP, China will not force unification.	0.655	−0.213	0.060
D4 If China resorts to armed unification and the government gives up fighting, the people should continue to fight by all means.	0.554	0.363	−0.219
D6 The longer the current situation lasts, the more bargaining chips Taiwan will have against China.	0.544	0.132	0.050
D8 If arms purchase requires a higher tax, people should still give support.	0.064	0.704	0.113
D1 If the government conscripts people to have war with China to achieve independence, people have the right to deny conscription.	0.140	−0.639	−0.089
D2 Even if arms purchase causes tension with China, Taiwan should still proceed with the purchase.	0.257	0.611	−0.308
D9 If a majority of Taiwanese expressively support unification, China will renounce the use of force as a means of unification.	−0.102	0.053	0.789
D7 If a majority of Taiwanese expressively support independence, China will renounce the use of force as a means of unification.	0.432	0.008	0.659

Source: See Table 8.1.
Extraction method: Principal Component Analysis.
Rotation method: Varimax with Kaiser normalization.
a   Rotation converged in five iterations.

the power of China. BoR prevails over BoP in the mind of the people, to the extent that the strength of *determination* is internally shaped regardless of the superior power of China. With the owning of determination as a psychological mechanism, the population's perception of the relational purpose (i.e., becoming independent) is a strong incentive to provide guidance to the policy.

Legitimacy is the ironic combination of pro-independence and pro-unification public opinions that serve as a vehicle of the BoR efficacy to initiate a confrontation with China. The support via polling for either independence or reunification is positively associated in terms of the effect on the attitude of China toward the proper relationship with Taiwan. The support for a particular relationship with China via public polling is a strong statement regarding the democratic legitimacy of such relationship. However, factor analysis shows that the articulation of a specific position (pro-independence vs. anti-independence) does not enable people to gain or lose their sense of control. Sheer standing together with fellow citizens in unity (on whichever position) is the source of power. Therefore, the people will possess the sense of efficacy to affect the proper relationship with China as long as they have confidence in democratic legitimacy. If they lack such confidence, their BoR efficacy will lessen, and the support for an increase in national defense will increase.

BoR efficacy and IR theory

The ability of a weak nation to control its international relations attests to its level of efficacy to pursue national interests. The level of efficacy of a weak nation under BoP almost entirely depends on its ability to forge alliances. However, the sense of efficacy of the weak nation is inevitably constrained by the necessity of demonstrating its value to potential allies, which are strong nations. The BoR system provides opportunities for the weak nation to improve its level of efficacy by maneuvering its relationship with the strong nation, especially in their bilateral relationship. This strategy relies on the use of cultural memory, as discussed earlier in the last chapter. However, the level of efficacy is not automatically enhanced. Mechanisms must be put in place to enable the weak nation to assert its wish to protect or change the relationship. The sense of efficacy to achieve a particular mode of relationship is also the sense of efficacy to maintain peace, because any military confrontation in the short run is unfavorable to the weak party. Institutional or intellectual devices must be available for the weak party to signal its use or renouncement of self-restraint. In Taiwan, these devices can include identity strategy, national defense, party politics, polling, and patience with time. Specifically, the BoR efficacy of Taiwan in relation to China refers to the sense of control over peace via certain institutional and intellectual mechanisms while asserting a confrontational policy for independence. The three psychological mechanisms at work in the factor analysis are efficacy, determination, and legitimacy.

The typical strategy offered by BoP theory for the weak party adheres to the following alternatives: balancing by building an alliance with a third party, bandwagoning with the strong party, and hedging (from a revised BoP point of view) (Hiep 2013: 335–338). Balancing and bandwagoning rely on the calculation of power and, therefore, cannot explain the unilateral confrontational approach taken by the weak party in the asymmetric relationship. Hedging is an alternative to BoP because it allows a mix of balancing and bandwagoning on the basis of a long-term assessment. However, the rationale for hedging is incompatible with the confrontational approach acceptable to the BoR strategy. For the BoR strategy, confrontation initiated by the weak party assures a long-term relationship that provides stability and reciprocity. Therefore, the strong party must be convinced that the new long-term relationship is proper and beneficial to both sides. However, hedging does not consider the sense of legitimacy of the strong party. Thus, the unilateral and independent confrontation launched by the weak party, such as Vietnam, which may appear unintelligent because of the lack of power or a powerful ally, as prescribed by the hedging strategy, can be a necessary sacrifice to ensure future cooperation in line with the BoR strategy (Ninh 1998).

The three factors of *efficacy, determination,* and *legitimacy* allude to the psychological mechanisms of how a weak party challenges the wishes of a strong party. However, in the actual case of Taiwan, individual questions show a limited disposition for confrontation, except for a significant portion of the population that believes in resorting to violence for independence and investment in military build-up. The factor analysis reveals the psychological mechanisms that could have generated a sense of BoR efficacy. The survey generated a total of three factors, namely, *determination* (D1, D2, and D8), *peace efficacy* (D3, D4, D5, D6, and D7), and *legitimacy* (D9 and D10). *Determination* suggests an internally generated drive for independence that can be powerful enough to transform confrontation into a desirable option. This drive is neither a function of power politics nor an interest calculation. It may fail badly in reality, though. The psychology of *peace efficacy* is based on confidence, the level of which is mediated by the pro-independence party and the expectation for the future. Owning positive peace efficacy necessarily leads to the tendency to adopt a confrontational approach.

BoR efficacy, as indicated by *peace efficacy* and *determination,* distinguishes relational security from hedging that is exclusive to the national security of the party seeking to avoid confrontation. Relational security is an interest of both strong and weak parties. No strong party desires a partner that will be difficult to cope with in the long run and will accommodate resistance to a certain extent (Path 2012). The proper level of resistance depends on the judgment over the long-term effect on the relational security of the strong party. The quest of the strong party for relational security explains the rational power of the weak party in taking a confrontational approach.

Peace efficacy may relate to the concerns of power politics because it involves a calculus of future BoP between Taiwan and China (D6). This future power calculus is independent of the existing level of power but contingent upon *determination* (Dreyer 2000, 1999, Tkacik 2008). The factor analysis already shows that *peace efficacy* and *determination* describe two separate psychological processes. Thus, the inclination to resort to drastic means is statistically unrelated to the assessment of the future. Someone who possesses a pessimistic outlook shows the determination to take non-peaceful means or another who possesses weak determination to feel optimistic about achieving a proper relationship via pro-independence party leadership.

Unrelatedness of *legitimacy* to *peace efficacy* and *determination* has been shown statistically. *Legitimacy* offers an additional dimension, which examines the rationale of the confrontational approach. *Legitimacy* suggests that the weak party can expect tolerance from the strong party if the legitimacy efficacy is present among the constituency (Hugh 2013, Rigger 2011, 1999). Nonetheless, *legitimacy* is a mode of resistance if the sole purpose of holding democratic elections or polls is to acquire the legitimacy required in articulating a position, the popular support of which is not well conveyed on other dimensions, such as strong determination and optimistic peaceful prospect. The level of confidence in legitimacy and in one's determination or peaceful prospect belongs to different psychological processes. The legitimacy factor gives a clue to the availability of another separate mechanism to adjust the confrontational policy intended for the strong party.

Finally, a cluster analysis is available. Table 8.3 shows that dividing Taiwanese respondents into five categories according to their reactions to questions that encapsulate the influence of the three factors is statistically proper. Each category shows a peculiar manner of determining whether the three factors are convincing. No factor is universally convincing to the five groups, which indicates the psychological limits of the Taiwanese constituency to unite on any single strategic orientation that asserts the difference of Taiwan from China via confrontation. Nonetheless, *legitimacy* has registered significance in at least three groups, which gives it the potential of becoming a leading factor in facing the imagined China threat. The last group holds an absolutely optimistic attitude with regard to the confrontation with China. If the fifth group enlists the three factors to support resistance, each of the other four groups is alienated for its own reason. Alienation caused by any of the three factors leads to their withdrawal. Thus, the aggressive fifth group is left on its own. However, increased political support may arise in backing the pro-independence stance if the last group learns from the experience and focuses on legitimacy.

Table 8.3 Cluster Analysis of the Factors of Prospect, Determination, and Legitimacy

	Clusters				
	1	*2*	*3*	*4*	*5*
Peace efficacy	−1.18971	−1.00673	−1.99811	3.15974	2.65793
Determination	3.26743	−3.04177	−1.31731	−1.93070	2.80144
Legitimacy	−3.80399	−2.86320	2.10100	.99904	2.15015
%	21	27	19	16	17

Source: See Table 8.1.

Conclusion

Each relationship has its own historical trajectory and normative conventions. However, the way the weak party manages the relationship with the strong party is comparable. This chapter generates three factors that allude to the psychological mechanisms through which the weak party may acquire a sufficient sense of efficacy to confront China. The actual substance of the *determination, peace efficacy*, and *legitimacy* of one state is different from those of the other state. *Peace efficacy* advises the researcher to seek the institutional and intellectual mechanisms through which the local constituency establishes or loses confidence in their capability to convince China away from the use of force when they assert a change in the proper relationship or restore the existing one violated by China. *Determination* looks for ways to enhance or reduce the readiness to fight China. The purchase of arms is only one option. Troop movement or provoking China's enmity with the US or Japan can be another. *Legitimacy* points to the use or loss of features that China cannot resist recognizing, such as polling, family history, shared ideology, and Third World status, as in the case of Taipei, Pyongyang, Hanoi, and New Delhi, respectively.

Efficacy does not lead to reality. Policy propensity based on enhanced efficacy does not produce the capacity to create the desired result. Efficacy explains why the weak party in an asymmetric relationship can challenge the strong party despite the lack of capacity for balancing or bandwagoning. Efficacy makes BoR a plausible theory, as the challenges of the weak party primarily tackle relational security that is meant to benefit both parties in the long run. *Peace efficacy, determination*, and *legitimacy* explain the psychological mechanisms of efficacy generation. Other factors may be discovered through other case studies. The stabilized asymmetric relationship is in itself a value for both parties. The weak party can always attempt a confrontational policy. At what point this happens is contingent on its judgment and sense of efficacy.

Note

1 The survey data used in this chapter were provided by the 21st Century Foundation. The request to access the data set were addressed to Mr. Yuchen Kao at Kaoyuchen@gmail.com. Some conditions may be applicable.

9 Institutional style

The bilateral sensibility that prevails in the BoR, which provides the weaker party some leverage in influencing the stronger party through the dyadic self-constituted by the bilateral relationship, may not be the first choice of the weaker party in managing the relationship with the stronger party. The risk of facing retaliation instead of concession from the stronger side is not insignificant, even though a confrontational approach may compel the stronger party to yield for the sake of long-term stability. Psychologically, the weaker side may still prefer a multilateral setting to dissolve the disadvantage of the asymmetry to some extent. Nevertheless, the advantage of sheer number owned by small parties is likewise hardly effective in pressuring the stronger party into compliance with a multilateral decision against its will. If the weaker party prefers a multilateral solution regardless of its sometimes-greater influence in an actual bilateral exchange, the stronger party may prefer a bilateral to a multilateral solution to avoid multilateral interference, which ironically yields more to a weaker party of strong efficacy.

For a stronger party, coping with controversies in a relationship, symmetric and asymmetric, reduces the complexity by restricting the process to a bilateral frame. The concession made in a bilateral as opposed to a multilateral relationship does not automatically apply to arrangements with other smaller parties. Moreover, the stronger party may think that it can monopolize the dyadic relationship. The real process rarely meets the expectations of the stronger party and may result in a better than expected solution for the weaker party. The stronger party could resort to unilateralism upon the frustration that the reciprocal relationship seems beyond reach in facing the resistance of the weaker party. One nation that unilaterally enforces the bilateral role expectations for the other nation to follow is an ironic performance that is largely unnoticed in the current literature. Chapter 9 calls this "uni-bilateralism," which gives a twist to common BoR practice.

From "harmonious world" to "communities of shared future"

Given the structural uncertainties generated by China's rise, understanding Chinese international relations requires comprehending the institutional style, (Elias 1982, Goh 2011) in addition to cultural memory and psychological efficacy, to determine how interactive processes have evolved across policy changes. We describe a typology that bridges Chinese and relational IR, including a comparison scheme that is compatible with processual relationality for understanding Chinese institutional style and developing detailed theoretical propositions in the future. From the relational perspective, we define Chinese "institutional style" as the Chinese self-restraint tactic of institutionalizing imagined resemblance of identity and interest between nations. We discover the Chinese form of self-restraint as consisting of unilateral methods for achieving a bilateral relationality that imposes China's self-centric concessions on other parties without their prior consent, which contradicts the bilateral ideal of relational equality. However, we do not wish to deny the ability of liberal societies to do likewise.

Researchers who use structural and relational perspectives disagree in their analyses of China's rise. Multilaterally, Western-dominated rules and institutions facilitate China's international integration (Ikenberry 2008). Bilaterally, American engagement with China encourages China to act as a responsible power (Zoellick 2005). However, even among optimists who welcome China's multilateral efforts, some believe that China only uses multilateral and bilateral means to support its own national interests and bides its time for opportunities to resist and revise the established order (Medeiros & Fravel 2003). Thus, they view with suspicion examples such as China's endeavor to establish the multilateral Asian Infrastructure Investment Bank (AIIB) (Heilmann, Rudolf, Mikko & Buckow 2014, Raby 2015, *The Economist*, 11 November 2014).

In October 2013, Chinese President Xi Jinping used the term "striving for achievement" (*fenfa youwei*) when he described a new policy for dealing with China's neighbors, which reduces China's "harmonious world" foreign policy to a secondary platform (Yan 2014). The new policy moves away from multilateralism and seemingly toward unilateralism (Johnston 2013) but retains the spirit of a harmonious world through its inclusion of a mission statement regarding the creation of "communities of common destiny" (later "communities of shared future"), which include China and its individual neighbors. The new policy sanctions an unusual combination of bilateralism and unilateralism, with multilateralism primarily serving the bilateral rather than the multilateral purposes one may expect from a responsible major power (Yan 2014). This practice could even apply to the AIIB, which is a multilateral institution based on bilateral agreements for individual investment projects (Wang 2015). This does not preclude China from multilateral efforts elsewhere. The idea of "shared future" denotes China's willingness to contribute to the welfare of other parties, thus rendering American efforts to contain China redundant and irrelevant.

IR scholars have analyzed multilateralism in terms of collective security and cooperation among three or more actor-states, bilateralism as reciprocal bonds between two states, and American unilateralism as preemptive intervention. Chinese foreign policy has been consistently distinguished from multilateralism (van der Putten 2013) despite the country's active participation in UN peacekeeping efforts and President Xi's proclaimed commitment to multilateralism (Chen 2014). China experts deem this preference for a mixed bilateral/unilateral approach as having its roots in China's experiences with Western powers at the end of the Qing dynasty and in a culturally sensitive Sino-centrism that is "less receptive to Western advocacy of multilateralism and security through co-operation on arms control and disarmament" (Kuik, Li & Ling 2017, Yuan 1999: 86). Samuel Kim, a veteran China watcher, reached the same conclusion two decades ago: "In most domains, [China] seems to be propelled by unilateralism in bilateral clothing, with a little Asian multilateral regionalism" (Kim 1995: 469, 477).

The abstract but multilateral harmonious world theme that emerged in 2005 under Hu Jintao is no longer convincing in the contexts of multiple maritime disputes with China's neighbors and a lukewarm attitude toward global governance. "Striving for achievement" emerged when Chinese foreign policy was increasingly perceived as assertive, expansive, and self-revealing. Chinese foreign policy critics do not view Xi's bilateral goals and unilateral calls for achievement as credible. However, the critics fail to acknowledge the uncertainties that a rising China must deal with in an environment marked by asymmetrical capacities. Pressure for an increasingly powerful China to demonstrate self-restraint should be viewed as internally and internationally challenging.

The three approaches differ in their ideal state conceptualizations and methods for achieving them but are similar regarding the extent to which they address conflict resolution in an anarchical world that views China's rise as a structural problem "out there." However, Chinese unilateral-bilateral shifts suggest an alternative solution that transcends, acknowledges, or appeals to distinctions between China, its neighbors, and the world at large. Chinese advocacy for a sense of community with its neighbors as an institutional ideal testifies to its view of other countries as part of its world and not as problems "out there." Compromising on multilateral norms rather than complying with them involves a different kind of self-restraint, one that emphasizes the method of coexistence over conversion.

Many worldviews of China subscribe to a bilateral order that emphasizes an idea, such as tributary dyad, class struggle, or strategic partnership. However, the relational analyses of such bilateral preferences require recognition that China can apply unilateral methods to achieve a bilateral ideal state. Those unilateral methods imply anarchy, but adherence to a bilateral order restricts anarchy. This requires distinctions between ideal states and the methods used to achieve them. "Ideal state" refers to desired relationality. Thus, unilateralism may be linked with a Middle Kingdom consciousness, bilateralism with a "community of common destiny" that consists of China's immediate neighbors, or multilateralism in the form of UN peacekeeping. However, "method" refers to processual relationality, which is contingent upon the degree of self-restraint while practicing a relationship to achieve the ideal state. Methodic unilateralism emphasizes China's self-initiated or self-centered effort to achieve an ideal state, methodic bilateralism emphasizes the mutual consultations required to achieve the three ideal states, and methodic multilateralism emphasizes the formation of a collective resolution. We argue that China represents a uni-bilateral model, in which the unilateral method is used to achieve the bilateral ideal state.

Assuming the adoption of the unilateral method, which defies intersubjectivity, a predominantly US-initiated multilateral ideal state prefers universal rules to connect those independent national actors reluctant to follow the US leadership, whereas a China-initiated bilateral ideal state aims at stable and reciprocal relationships, even with those unwilling to meet China's expectations. Achieving ideal states via unilateral methods requires considerable confidence and trust in the unilateral actor. The reputation of the American practice of uni-multilateralism is dependent on consistently prescribed standards, effective monitoring, and interventions in response to perceived wrongs. Regarding the Chinese practice of uni-bilateralism, credibility is based on self-restraint and a willingness to disregard differences with the other side, as well as an inclination toward compromise to craft resemblance of identity and interest, regardless of the relative power of the other party, or toward confrontations aimed at restoring it.

Institutional mechanisms

We define *institutional mechanism* as the incurrence or renunciation of self-restraint that affects one state's self-perceptions and interactions with other states in accordance with an agreed set of rules and goals (Hodgson 2006, McAdam, Tarrow & Tilly 2001). Bilateralism and multilateralism underscore the view that state preferences for certain goals or methods are not exclusively about power or interest calculations but also about how states improvise resemblance between them. Each of the three methodic mechanisms can be used to achieve all three ideal states. This appears to be especially true for unilateral ideal states. John Mearsheimer (2001) analyzes how a major power is dependent on its own efforts to achieve peace by achieving dominance and describes how unilateral processes can be used to achieve a unilateral ideal state of hegemonic stability. By contrast, Stephen Rock (1989) explains how bilateral processes were used to preserve unilateral peace during the hegemonic power transition from the UK to the US after World War II. Robert Keohane (1984) asserts that Western countries that benefited from the existing hegemonic order willingly participated within a multilateral framework to sustain a unilateral order led by the US. This is an example of how method, not relative power, determines how a nation is constituted by an existing unilateral, bilateral, or multilateral order. China's or US' image of being assertive is more informative to observing national actors than one's rivaling ideology in assessing one's

Table 9.1 Ideal States and Methods associated with the Institutional Mechanisms of Unilateralism, Bilateralism, and Multilateralism

Method \ State	Unilateral Peace	Bilateral Peace	Multilateral Peace
Unilateralism	Medium unilateralism, i.e., Mearsheimer's (2001) "tragedy of power"	Hard uni-bilateralism, i.e., Tow's (1999) "San Francisco system"	Hard uni-multilateralism, i.e., Van Ness's (2004) "Bush Doctrine"
Bilateralism	Soft bi-unilateralism, i.e., Rock's (1989) "hegemony transfer"	Medium bilateralism, i.e., Womack's (2006) "asymmetric model"	Hard bi-multilateralism, i.e., Gaddis's (1986) "long peace"
Multilateralism	Soft multi-unilateralism, i.e., Keohane's (1984) "after hegemony"	Soft multi-bilateralism, i.e., Wang Jixi's (2005) "six-party talks"	Medium multilateralism, i.e., O'Brien et al.'s (2000) "global governance"

Source: Authors.

relations with the international society and these actors. While the ideal state may be subject to prior inter-subjectivity, the method to achieve them may not be (Table 9.1).

The three institutional methods can all contribute to the ideal state of reciprocal bilateralism as an ideal state. William Tow (1999) describes the San Francisco system in which the US single-handedly initiated and established a series of bilateral defense treaties via its unilateral interactions with individual partners. Brantley Womack (2006), for example, traces the changes and continuity in the asymmetrical model used to describe the ongoing and evolving bilateral relationship between China and Vietnam for nearly 2,000 years, and Wang Jisi (2005) describes how multilateral Six Party Talks were used to support bilateral conflict resolution between the US and North Korea.

The multilateral ideal state in which national actors abide by shared rules has likewise been analyzed in terms of all three approaches. Peter Van Ness (2004) asserts that the unilateral enforcement of anti-terrorism laws under the Bush Doctrine attests to America's unilateral approach to multilateralism. The analysis of John Gaddis (1986) on Cold War alliances rooted in a bipolar system gives a detailed example of the bilateral method of achieving multilateral conflict resolution. The use of multilateral methods to establish multilateral cooperation has been the focus of a number of global governance studies in the area of economics (O'Brien, Goetz, Scholte & Williams 2000).

Most US–China confrontations have focused on ostensible contradictions between multilateral and bilateral ideal states, such as the contradictions between free passage and the China–Philippines territorial dispute. The US adherence to free passage on the East and the South China Sea is inadequate for understanding the instances of unilateral style of enforcement, such as China's establishment of the East China Sea Air Defense Identification Zone, which is targeted at Japanese claims of sovereignty in the region. Chinese unilateralism can be compared with American unilateralism, to the extent that the bilateral and multilateral orders they each pursue do not necessarily contradict each other. Arguably, the escalation and perceived threat result from methodic unilateralism instead of the contrast between free passage and the air defense zone. However, their use of unilateral method can appear mutually threatening despite the insufficient evidence that either the US disapproves China's territorial claims or China interferes with the free passage.

The US-China relationships contrast the Sino-Vietnamese relationships, which ostensibly focus on China's bulling style. However, Vietnam adopts a shaming technique that reproduces China's superior position (Hiep 2013, 2014). Having no intention to transform China's methodic unilateralism, Vietnam's contention pertains primarily to the contents of the ideal state— who owns what.

Moreover, Chinese methodic unilateralism challenges the intersubjective spirit of bilateralism that China desires, whereas American methodic unilateralism harms the spirit of democratic processes that the US favors. The air defense zone can be viewed as a unilateral method for China to cope with bilateral territorial disputes with Japan while coincidentally undermining US-supported multilateral relationality. China's use of a unilateral method disregards its inability to gain Japanese cooperation[1]; China has never openly expressed an intention to recover the Senkaku (Diaoyu) islands, only a desire for acknowledgement from Japan that a dispute exists (Wang 2013). China demonstrates that a dispute exists but does not resolve the dispute (See Chapter 4). This serves as evidence that processual relationality supersedes a calculus of power. The same can be said of US unilateralism in the form of sending ships into areas claimed by China to honor a multilateral order regarding public seas despite knowing that China's protest would complicate the norm of free passage (US/CHINA CNO Discussion Readout 2015). In the abovementioned sense, the method apt for the ideal state parallels the personality apt for the ideology.

Multilateralism

Multilateralism literature does not differentiate between the multilateral ideal states of peace or conflict resolution and the multilateral methods used to achieve them. Ruggie (1992) observed that discussions of multilateralism typically address the value and institution of peace and the methods used to resolve conflicts. Specifically, multilateralism is a collective process that involves three or more states that are in agreement with "generalized principles of conduct ... without regard to the particularistic interests of parties or the strategic exigencies that may exist in any specific occurrence" (Ruggie 1993: 11). Multilateral discourses have addressed the end of the fundamental ideological competition (Fukuyama 1992), interdependency, and great cooperation among nation-states. The need for collective action theoretically requires multilateral agreement. The US always takes unilateral initiatives to push for multilateral action, though. Relational turn literature has stated that underlying multilateral discourses are considered a liberal democratic means through which self-restrained nation-states yield political power. However, the US imposes unilateralism instead of democratic participation, which ensures that all multilateral rules or "common interests" fit with its own values and actions, which underscore the difficulty of applying multilateral methods to crafting a same identity for all. Therefore, in practice, leadership and self-restraint are the two most important parameters that define multilateral processes.

International organizations, such as the League of Nations, the United Nations, and NATO, have failed to transcend the governments' fear of "subordinating themselves to a common authority" (Bull 1997, 45). While national leaders may express appreciation for relational security, in practice, the ideal state of multilateral peace requires strong leadership in order for different relationalities to emerge. Kindleberger (1981) and Olson (1965) are political economists who address the need for a single leader to provide collective goods and punish free riders to protect common interests (Lepgold 1998). The failure of participants to practice self-restraint damages efforts made in the name of multilateralism.

The most serious problem that post-WWII international organizations are facing has been enforcement, because all countries have incentives to engage in opportunistic behavior by reneging on their commitments to liberalization (Yarbrough & Yarbrough 1986). Enforcement is dependent on the American ability to bring all other actors on board (Haass 1999); thus, collective action analysts continue to debate whether cooperation is possible during and after the decline of a dominant hegemonic power. Keohane (1984) describes Western countries' multilateral tolerance of hegemonism in the interest of conflict resolution during the decline of a dominant power that is willing to participate in police actions. He supports the idea of hegemonic indispensability by stressing that cooperation is possible after hegemony "because shared interests can lead to the creation of regimes" (50). Keohane believes that hegemonic leadership and a multilateral framework are equally important. The multilateral consensus among Western countries has supported unilateral US hegemonism, which, in turn, has supported a broad multilateral liberal order in the rest of the world. This two-step mechanism—from multi-unilateralism to uni-multilateralism— means that American unilateralism is an ideal state for Western countries concerned about a liberal order and is a valid method for promoting liberal ideals outside the West.

Bilateralism

IR scholars have overlooked the distinctions between bilateral ideal states and the bilateral methods used to achieve them. A bilateral ideal state of conflict resolution can exist between two national actors regardless of the power balance involved. Bilateral methods are most commonly reflected in the self-restraining behaviors of two parties to improvise their resemblance of identity and interest. Second-track diplomacy is a well-known technique to breed the bilateral consciousness between any two historical rivals that begin to appreciate self-restraint in each other due to the recognition that the other side is increasingly willing to sustain the second-track process in itself over a long period of time. Self-restraint makes sense when two sides are ready to conceive of their togetherness as a "greater self" instead of focusing on their respective short-term interests. In addition to bilateral, the method used to achieve a bilateral state may be unilateral or multilateral. For example, China's or any country's tactical use of self-restraint to oblige the other side toward a bilateral relationality enlists a unilateral method in disguise. Mikhail Gorbachev engaged in unilateral self-restraint to mitigate security problems between the Soviet Union and the US. Last, but not least, using multilateral processes, such as the Six-party Talks, to build confidence and create bridges between two parties, i.e. Washington and Pyongyang, attests to the application of multilateral methods to achieve a bilateral ideal state.

Many bilateral conflict resolution researchers have analyzed the mutually assured destruction (MAD) strategy and confidence building as a method for achieving peace. Once considered a Cold War defense doctrine (George & Smoke 1974, Kahn 1960), the primary rationale behind MAD was deterrence, with both the US and the Soviet Union understanding that a nuclear conflict would completely destroy both countries (Schelling 1966). However, a "security dilemma" scenario in the form of a never-ending arms race could occur if the two sides view nuclear competition in the same manner (Jervis 1978). China entered this environment by unilaterally renouncing first use or use against a non-nuclear enemy (Pan 2015). This kind of self-restraint is an example of unilateralism rather than of building bilateral confidence. Regarding confidence-building, a bilateral approach requires mutual agreements and information exchanges concerning military forces and armaments to reach an ideal state of mutual predictability. Such a state can be applied to an arms race, trade barriers, or agricultural subsidies. The main defects of confidence-building as a method are resource asymmetry and misunderstandings due to structural factors, which are another facet of the security dilemma (Friedman 2013, Nathan & Scobel 2012).

Another example of a bilateral ideal state is the relationship between the United States and Japan (Pempel 2004). Japan has "safeguarded key constitutional prohibitions and independent military capabilities that have allowed it to retain a measure of autonomous security vis-à-vis the United States" (Hughes & Akiko 2004: 59). The US unilaterally created Japan's constitutional self-restraint to establish a sense of trustworthiness. The situation is more complex in Europe, where both bilateral and multilateral approaches have been used, for example, Germany's use of multilateral methods to stabilize its relationship with the US (Gould & Krasner 2003, Kupchan 1998). According to Gould and Krasner, Germany's leaders have chosen to enmesh their country in multilateral institutions to make it appear less threatening to the US. European multilateralism is based on a foundation of general trust, whereas the bilateral security framework in Asia has evolved through partnerships initiated unilaterally by the US to enlist the support of strategically important countries. A "general trust" with a multilateral disposition may produce stronger commitments (Rathbun 2012), whereas "strategic trust" that involves individual Asian countries entails American self-interest calculations that disregard self-restraint at times. Most of today's bilateral agreements in Asia have been established according to America's Cold War containment strategy (Nau 2002). Relationships between certain Asian countries (for example, Japan and South Korea) remain difficult due to unresolved historical grievances, which block the development of a "general trust" or even "generalized principles of conduct" that are often prior to multilateral frameworks (Katzenstein 2008, Ruggie 1993).

America's China policy shows a preference for engagement over containment. Its bilateral approach to China entails confidence-building mechanisms, such as a "mutual intelligence collection" and security dialogues aimed at creating an ideal state of mutual understanding that avoids miscalculations (Ross 1999). The ideal state is multilaterally defined according to frameworks such as the 1968 Nuclear Non-Proliferation Treaty (NPT), the 1996 Comprehensive Test-Ban Treaty, and the Zangger Committee (the implementation arm of NPT export control provisions). These efforts require considerable compromises on the part of the US. However, China's rise and related challenges to American dominance have caused the US to occasionally return to a unilateral approach that affects compromises made elsewhere. Despite the occasional examples of self-restraint, the US is primarily a unilateral actor attempting to convince China that supporting a US-defined ideal multilateral state is in China's best interests.

Unilateralism

For unilateralism, the ideal state is stability maintained by a "world police," which is a role that the US has essentially played since WWII. It likewise practices unilateralism in the name of anti-terrorism. Its emerging self-role in East Asia is rebalancing in the 21st century. Washington uses a mix of multilateral, bilateral, and unilateral tactics to ensure a form of unilateralism that supports its interests in global issues and regularly vetoes efforts promoted by other states. During the Cold War, its bilateral method consists of enlisting support from Asia's national actors, South Korea and Japan, with which it has bilateral defense agreements. In the current age of global governance, these bilateral relationships are the methodic bases for interventions aimed at synchronizing the world with American values. Using unilateral methods to achieve a unilateral ideal state is only possible for a superpower.

Distinguishing between soft and hard unilateralism is possible. Where the number of actors involved in achieving an ideal state is greater than the number subscribing to it, there is a soft process. Soft Unilateralism is time consuming because other actors external to the ideal state are equally involved in achieving it. The American use of multilateral UN to promote a unilateral policy of sanctions on Syria, for example, illustrates "soft" unilateralism, and its use of unilateral mobilization to impose a multilateral war on terror illustrates a "hard" example. Soft unilateralism based on a multilateral method is methodologically open-ended and has a high likelihood of failure in terms of synchronizing the actions and wishes of other nations to fit in with US goals. The same can be said about Chinese versions of hard and soft unilateralism.

The historical and philosophical bases of Chinese uni-bilateralism, as opposed to the American uni-multilateralism, can be analyzed on three levels of cultural memory. The first involves traditional values as a reference for a Chinese bilateral ideal state and the unilateral method used to achieve it. Self-restraint and gift-giving have been used as the method, and the middle kingdom and *tianxia* concepts have been used as foundations for different versions of the ideal state (Jacques 2009, Ren 2010, Zhao 2005). The second level incorporates modern Chinese strategic thinking into the materially and emotionally vulnerable consequences of invasion by imperialist forces (Callahan 2012). The memory of past invasions encourages China to rely on tactics such as unilateral self-restraint to achieve stable reciprocal relationships without expressing concern for any rules of governance. Deng Xiaoping's advice on "concealing one's ability and biding one's time" is a modern example. The third level describes contemporary Chinese behavioral patterns as reflective of the country's current rise, which illustrates capacity-status discrepancies and entails nostalgia for the middle kingdom as a restored ideal state (Jacques 2009).

Understanding distinctions between bilateral ideal states and unilateral methods helps China watchers appreciate the country's shifts between hard and soft Chinese unilateralism. One example of soft unilateralism, or bi-unilateralism, is when China and the UK negotiated the return of Hong Kong for the sake of China's reunification as the unnegotiable ideal state. After reunification, China's unilateral enforcement of one-country-two-system with Hong Kong to make a peculiar bilateral relationship between them is reversely an example of hard unilateralism or uni-bilateralism. China's hard uni-bilateralism is likewise familiar to Indian and Vietnamese, who experienced China's method of unilateral withdrawal of troops from land captured during armed conflicts to enforce bilateral ceasefire. The same hard unilateralism characterizes China's competition in the territorial dispute on the South China Sea in the 21st century.

China's quest for bilateral ideal state additionally relies on the bilateral method. China and its neighbors do not always clash over national interests. For example, China and Myanmar maintain a peaceful relationship that transcends serious differences in alliances, ideology, regime type, immediate interests, and complex ethnic issues along a shared border. Another example is China's refusal to fully use its influence with Pyongyang on the issue of nuclear proliferation. Its relationships with Myanmar and North Korea do not fit well with any existing model of alliance, exchange, or strategy. China has made territorial concessions to both countries by defying power balances.

This bi-bilateralism disappears in China's unilaterally crafted confrontations with stronger power and concessions given to weaker powers (Huang & Shih 2014). In practice, China's uni-bilateralism often means confrontations over relatively minor issues. For instance, it interprets the visits of Japanese politicians to the Yasukuni Shrine as a disregard for reciprocity and as evidence of malicious intent. In another example involving Japan, China unilaterally announced the creation of an Air Defense Identification Zone over disputed areas between the two countries. Other examples involve maritime disputes with Japan, Vietnam, and the Philippines. The symbolic importance of these territorial claims informs China's anxiety toward the unavailing of bilateralism. China also has unilaterally broken off relations with nations that have hosted the Dalai Lama, supported Taiwanese pro-independence leaders, or sold weapons to Taiwan, which was at the center of two missile crises in 1995 and 1996. However, these kinds of heated confrontations can cool down quickly once China judges that they sufficiently deter the other side from further encroaching the proper bilateral relationship.

Uni-bilateralism easily suffers from communication failure, which was the reason for the 1969 border clash between China and the Soviet Union (Wich 1980). This communication failure suggests that unilateralism is not a credible, albeit less time consuming in the short run, method to achieve bilateral ideal. The following sequence can be used to explain how China's conflict resolution approach fails within the cycle of hard and soft bilateralism (Shih & Yin 2013):

1   Beijing unilaterally compromises on a certain point that involves (occasionally core) national interests to demonstrate its willingness to reproduce an imagined string of resemblance to each other.
2   The other party neither refuses nor accepts.
3   Beijing unilaterally perceives that the two sides have achieved a harmonious greater self.

4   The other party's external and internal politics compel it to publicly express its non-compliance with China's unilateral role expectations.
5   Beijing reacts strongly and presents its self-perceived restraint as justification for imposing sanctions.
6   The other party views Beijing's symbolic sanctions as confirmation of its malicious intentions.

Transforming bilateral relationships with historic adversaries, such as Vietnam and the US, to create a "community of shared future" is a task that the Chinese President Xi Jinping is at least talking about. He requests for a new cycle of soft bilateralism that allows other parties to decide when and how to join the middle kingdom in creating a greater self. Such a cycle alone does not explain how soft bilateralism may turn into hard or uni-bilateralism, that is, the stage at which China imposes its middle kingdom as an ideal state in the form of unilateral concessions and sanctions. It must consider the judgments of Chinese leaders regarding the responses of other parties, especially in terms of whether ongoing events indicate that China's soft bilateralism runs into a bottleneck, if not a deadlock.

Uni-bilateral practices in Chinese foreign policy

China, which uses uni-bilateral institutional practices to bind itself with its partners, has a long history of alternating concessions with pressure to encourage other actors to agree to its terms. China's unilateral self-restraint enforces a resemblance of interest and identity to the other party, hence a greater-self, which obliges it to reciprocate where China may need. China's unilateral renouncement of self-restraint reduces the other party to a target of anger and put pressure on it to respond to China congruently. Since China cannot sustain perpetual anger, and therefore restoration that comes with concessionary reward is always possible, other actors often ultimately go along with Chinese agendas despite the annoyance they feel about being pressured. China now has a calculating "little self" (i.e. the reflexive self) that decides when sufficient punishment has been meted out so that it can resume relationships based on its own version of how the other should resemble to China. In the Chinese style of altercasting, concessions are offered to overcome indifference, to camouflage suspicions, and to distract criticism from other negotiating parties. Whether those concessions are real or nominal, China often succeeds in making strong impressions in terms of relational agendas that emphasize the greater self (i.e. the constituted self), and that encourage the other side to acknowledge its expected duty toward China. From China's perspective, maintaining proper relationships requires other actors to accept a permanent position of self-restraint that acknowledges the resemblance of identity and interest to China. If other actors are capable, they can exert uni-bilateral pressure on China in return.

In most cases, these improvised resemblances are less about material interests than about the principles that China uses to evaluate how other actors perceive it as a trustworthy partner. However, China rarely follows a fixed standard. On the territorial dispute, often the ideal state for China is to have both sides stay ambiguous enough to allow different interpretation and maintain the greater-self pretension. The same applies to one China principle aiming not at a state of complete severance of relations with Taiwan or Tibet by the target state, but at removal of any title that carries sovereign implications for them. Such requests are usually followed by some kind of gift-giving action. The only bilateral ideal states that have little to do with territory or one-China principle are with both Koreas, where China and the two neighbors negotiate over how much China should shape their respective relations with the US.

In the rest of this section we will consider seven examples, most of which are about Chinese uni-bilateralism, the first being Sino-U.S. relations. The "one-China" principle is part of an ideal-state relationship that American arms sales to Taiwan violate. Officially, the U.S. refuses to discuss these sales with China on the pretext that they are guided by its Taiwan Relations Act. After each sale, China responds by severing military exchanges and accusing the U.S. of a serious betrayal, but after an undetermined period of time it resumes the exchanges. In 2011 they were resumed during planning sessions for Chinese President Hu Jintao's visit to the States, indicating a symbolic visit enjoying priority over a core interest (Wei 2011, also see Chapter 3). Arms sales and the one-China principle have become so institutionalized in this bilateral relationship that it is easy to perceive them as part of an enduring cycle of pressure and concession, with both capable of unilaterally triggering a turn.

The second example is Sino-Mongolian relations, in which the two sides appear to be involved in intensive economic interactions. However, Mongolia's ongoing efforts to build closer ties with the U.S., Japan, India and Korea are viewed as evidence of a quest for reduced dependence on both China and Russia. For China, an important and unacceptable aspect of this particular relationship is Mongolia's links with the Dalai Lama—a large number of Mongolian Buddhist nuns are trained in Dharamsala. The Dalai Lama's visit to Ulaanbaatar in 2016 incurred immediate economic sanctions, but China resumed its investments and aid packages within a few weeks upon securing a nominal self-critical statement from the Mongolian side.[2] A realist analysis might assume that India or Japan would have provided aid to Mongolia if major investment projects were threatened. Regardless of how Beijing calculated power balances while deciding if or when to resume aid, this example of Chinese uni-bilateralism touches on issues involving Tibetan Buddhism, anticipated concessions, the unpredictable timing of concessions, and the perceived need for a bilateral resolution.

Sino-Vietnamese relations are a third example, with maritime disputes now accepted as chronic. Over time, confrontations between the two sides have taken on an appearance of ritual (albeit one holding enormous emotional frustration for the Vietnamese side), with each escalation followed by one or more joint activities meant to neutralize differences. Activities include visits by Vietnamese leaders to China, joint military drills, the opening of a Confucius Institute, and Chinese investment in Vietnamese infrastructure projects. In 2014, China installed and operated a drilling platform in disputed waters, and thousands of Vietnamese fishermen protested the action. China suddenly withdrew the platform, claiming that its "scientific task" had been completed.[3] Vietnam's only possible response was to "name and shame China" into making concessions (Hiep 2014). Apparently, the goal for China was to demonstrate Vietnam's incapability of enforcing its own claims or resisting Chinese claims to the disputed area, as well as to reinforce a sense of territorial integrity that China perceives as foundational. Vietnam's habitual resistance and anticipation of Chinese concessions are key factors in this instance of bilateral relationship, in which China makes Vietnamese territorial selfhood an intrinsic component of its agenda.

Sino-Filipino relations serve as the fourth example. China's economic exchanges with and promises of investment in the Philippines coincide with territorial ocean disputes that are played up in the Chinese media. In 2012, China took control of the Scarborough Reef after the Philippines withdrew its vessels as a typhoon approached. China enacted a boycott of bananas shipped from the Philippines after Manila presented its case to an international court of arbitration.[4] The Philippines received a favorable verdict, which was followed by a large-scale Chinese military exercise. This case is an example of simultaneous uni-bilateral maneuvering on the part of both sides. For China, its motivation was similar to that enacted for Vietnam— there is no open challenge to China's claim, but this does not require official acknowledgement by the Philippines. A new administration in Manila decided to not pursue the verdict, a decision followed by economic and anti-terrorist aid from China, which are so immediate and large as if they are to make up the loss of relationship in the past four years.[5] Filipino fishermen were also given permission to work near the Scarborough Reef.

In Sino-Japanese relations, Japan is engaging in uni-bilateralism by injecting the Senkaku Islands (Diaoyu Dao) issue into its bilateral agenda,[6] thus expressing how its relations with China should constitute Japan's identity. China used to the ideal state, practiced by both sides, of shelving full resolution of the dispute. As this looks unlikely, China resorts to continuing to patrol the seas between the two countries and unilaterally declaring an Air Defense Identification Zone.[7] However, China's purpose can be no more than returning to the acquiesced state of no resolution. Remaining silent on the claim is the same duty that China imposes on the other side in the South China Sea, except that China does not enjoy the same favorable power balance in the skies over the Sea of Japan. For China, the ideal state on the Diaoyu Dao issue is to remove it from the bilateral agenda while on the South China Sea, take the claim only off Vietnam's or the Philippines' agenda.

The sixth example is Sino-India relations—another case of clashing uni-bilateral approaches. It serves as an example of soft uni-bilateralism, since the two sides rely on multilateral frames in response to bilateral territorial disputes. Apparently neither side is capable of convincing the other to enact a shared reciprocal pattern, despite the presence of similarly patterned compromise and pressure trajectories. The multilateral dimension looms large because China and India, as the world's two largest developing nations, carry certain expectations in terms of offering themselves as alternatives to the world's existing superpower. BRICS (Brazil, Russia, India, China, South Africa) association politics came into play with the territorial standoff over Doklam in 2017, which emerged when India accused China of invading an area belonging to Bhutan to build a road (Jha 2017). The standoff de-escalated in part due to the forthcoming BRICS summit to be held in Xiamen, China—an incentive for speedy resolution. Apparently, each side anticipated that the other would retreat in the interest of a successful summit. China terminated its road construction project (at least temporarily) after holding military exercises in the area,[8] and India reciprocated with a troop withdrawal. It is very likely that the dispute will reemerge in due course. From the Chinese viewpoint, the Doklam incident was initially an Indian rather than Chinese coup. It involved a cycle of an anticipated concession on India's part, the imposition of an Indian agenda on China, and self-identification of both sides based on a patterned, bilateral and long-term relationship.

The next example is Sino-South Korean relations, an example of aborted bilateralism on the part of China. The deployment of THAAD missiles in South Korea are perceived as threatening bilateral relations because China is well within their range. This is much more of a Sino-U.S. issue.[9] The imposition of sanctions on Korea by China to express its dismay with U.S.-Korean relations would defeat the purpose of bilateral (or trilateral) maneuvering. We have argued earlier that China's multilateral policy tends to be either passive (involving ritual, abstention and absence) or normative (as in the case of exemplification of the China model). The only other options are distinctly negative and potentially destructive, involving anti-hegemonic pronouncements, vetoes of intervention policies, and boycotts of global governance organizations (Grant 2009, Williams 2001). If China makes Sino-South Korean relations triangular, it drastically diminishes the potential for fruitful bilateral relations by making it difficult to execute institutional acts in anticipation of new patterns or in support of existing patterns. When Chinese anger eventually cooled down, sanctions were cancelled in the interest of restoring bilateralism.[10]

Note that Sino-North Korean relations share some similarities with Sino-India relations, with the weaker party imposing its uni-bilateralism on the stronger party. The two sets of bilateral relations are also comparable in terms of the extent to which China is using soft versions of uni-bilateralism. In the case of North Korea, China at one time facilitated bilateral relations between North Korea and the U.S. within the context of Six Party Talks. Today, multilateralism presumably relieves China from having to take a measure of responsibility for North Korea's nuclear weapons development plans, while allowing Beijing to maintain reasonable relations with Pyongyang. However, Kim Jong-Un is clearly practiced in enforcing his own uni-bilateral maneuvers, launching missiles and testing nuclear devices just as China is preparing to host important international events,[11] but retreating immediately with a series of submissive visits to China. China could not resist the temptation for becoming a superior in this improvised/renewed brotherhood. North Korea is successfully improvising resemblance of identity and interest to China, despite the large power imbalance between the two nations.

Conclusions

Numerous IR researchers have made the dual observations that (a) China shows willingness to follow a multilateral line in its handling of disputes and foreign relations (Courmont 2012, Kuik 2005, Wang 1999, Wu & Lansdowne 2008, Wuthnow, Li & Qi 2012, Yuan 2000), and (b) China's increasing involvement in multilateralism is mostly limited to economics and not security issues (Wang 1999) based on its traditional preference for bilateralism (Goldstein 1997/98). For example, China signed a Declaration on the Conduct of Parties in the South China Sea in 2002 but only after it rejected a highly restrictive draft proposed by the Association of Southeast Asian Nations (ASEAN). Beijing rejected a South China Sea Code because the code would require multilateral negotiations, and China wanted to reserve the right to engage in bilateral negotiations concerning South China Sea disputes (Xiong 2012). Two examples of Chinese multilateralism are the Shanghai Cooperation Organization and the AIIB. However, such multilateral attempts to mitigate American influence have not caused it to shun bilateralism.

   Different scholars have reached different conclusions about the nature of China's increasing involvement in multilateral institutions (Wuthnow, Li & Qi 2012). Pessimists view it as a tactic in defense of national interests, whereas optimists describe it as a "New Diplomacy" that involves "a less confrontational, more sophisticated, more confident, and, at times, more constructive approach toward regional and global affairs" (Medeiros & Fravel 2003, 22). However, China's choice of a bilateral framework covers its aversion to multilateral processes aimed at synchronizing rational thinking among multiple parties. China's preference for uni-bilateral approaches to conflict resolution makes it difficult to win the trust of weak parties, such that it must make unilateral concessions (at least those that China deems proper) to demonstrate its intentions and trustworthiness. For example, the complexity of Chinese attitudes has allowed Vietnam to exert "the power of the weak" (Hensengerth 2010, Thayer 2010). According to the Chinese perspective, its good deeds are rarely acknowledged and are sometimes used as targets for criticism. China has criticized Vietnam for forgetting past acts of generosity and relational bonds. However, from the Vietnamese perspective (which is much in line with Chinese bilateralism), a weaker party must rely on moral shaming to force a settlement with China (Hiep 2014).

China frequently congratulates itself for unilateral concessions ostensibly made in the name of reciprocity. Cited examples include territorial settlements in which China received 50 percent or less of the contested territory, and the approval of a code of conduct in 2002, which was negotiated by the ASEAN and China, the draft language of which was primarily written by the ASEAN (Ye & Li 2009: 172). From a Southeast Asian perspective, such shifts from bilateral to multilateral approaches are not specifically about multilateralism, because most countries perceive China–ASEAN discussions as bilateral while relieving pressure for truly multilateral negotiations that involve the US and other Western powers. However, China rejected a multilateral approach because, as Yang Jiechi argues, "it will only make matters worse and the resolution more difficult." The best way to resolve such disputes is "for countries concerned to have direct bilateral negotiations on the basis of equality and mutual respect" (Yang 2010).

In the IR discipline, the relational turn concept supports studies of international institutions by attending to actual practices that nations use in their interactions. These practices produce different forms of processual relationality based on the unilateral, bilateral or multilateral foreign policy styles of the nations involved. Institutionally connected nations tend to interact with consensual self-restraint, which transcends certain short-term interests and power concerns. That is, they negotiate within the constraints of mutually constituted relationality. However, they can still disagree on how to enforce and reproduce mutual relationality given the enforcement issues representative of highly sophisticated differences between institutions as ideal states and methods. These refined differences clarify what remains to be explained in the current emphasis on relationality: the adoption of a method, the evolution of an institutional ideal, or the processes of conflict and conflict resolution.

We disagree with claims that China's increasing involvement in multilateral IR serves as a substitute for its bilateral practices. However, more soft bilateralism may be expected, which will possibly result in China's incapacity to reach consensual bilateralism. The Chinese preference for bilateralism and the American preference for multilateralism diverge over international rule formation because of China's inclination to bypass rules to breed reciprocity and accommodate differences in values, institutions, and interests. However, both states show willingness to use unilateral methods to support their institutional ideals, whether they are bilateral or multilateral. This relational analysis regarding China's rise clarifies what is being disputed. For example, conflicts between the US and China over the details of institutional ideal states are less relevant to their unilateral style of enforcing their expected order. In another example, the conflict between China and Vietnam centers on the substance of bilateral relationality, that is, different views on what should constitute the proper state between the two stylistically self-restraining nations.

Notes

1 Two US bombers were immediately sent to penetrate the Air Defense Identification Zone following the announcement of its creation. China made no attempt to intercept them.
2 *Voice of America*, "China Claims That Mongolia Admits Mistake; Economic Stick Works Again?" 21 December 2016, www.voachinese.com/a/mongolia-dalai-lama-china-20161221/3644691.html, accessed 29 September 2017. This break was much shorter than the six-year period of sanctions placed on relations with Norway between 2010 and 2016 in response to the Nobel committee's decision to award its Peace Prize to the imprisoned democracy activist Liu Xiaobo. See, *New York Times*, "Norway and China Restore Ties, six Years After Nobel Prize Dispute", 19 December 2016, www.nytimes.com/2016/12/19/world/europe/china-norway-nobel-liu-xiaobo.html, accessed 29 September 2017.
3 *BBC News*, "China's Drilling Platform Number 981 Operations End in the Paracel Islands and is Moved to Hainan Island," 16 July 2014, www.bbc.com/zhongwen/trad/china/2014/07/140716_china_haiyangshiyou981_hainan, accessed 29 September 2017.
4 *BBC News*, "Review China: Sino-Philippines' Confrontations on the Scarborough Reef," 17 May 2012, www.bbc.com/zhongwen/trad/focus_on_china/2012/05/120514_cr_southchinasea, accessed 29 September 2017.
5 *Liberty Times*, "Full Affinity Toward China: Duterte Says Shelving the South China Sea Verdict," 18 December 2016, http://news.ltn.com.tw/news/world/paper/1063069, accessed 29 September 2017.
6 *Epoch Times*, "Japanese Cabinet Meeting Confirms Nationalization of Senkaku Island," 10 September 2012, www.epochtimes.com/b5/12/9/10/n3679216.htm, accessed 29 September 2017.
7 *BBC News*, "China Announces Making East China Sea Air Defense Zone", 23 November 2013, www.bbc.com/zhongwen/simp/china/2013/11/131123_east_china_sea_air_defence, accessed 29 September 2017.
8 Bannedbook Website, "China and India Withdraw Military at the Same Time? So It Is: The Inside Story of Secret Negotiation for Military Withdrawal," 29 August 2017, www.bannedbook.org/bnews/zh-tw/topimagenews/20170829/814398.html, accessed 29 September 2017.
9 *ETNEWS*, "Why Does China Oppose THAAD? US Media Says: Radar Will Weaken China's Deterrence Capability," 13 March 2017, www.ettoday.net/news/20170313/883551.htm, accessed 29 September 2017.
10 *ETNEWS*, "China Refuses to Withdraw Its THAAD Sanction; South Korea Entrepreneur Are Disappointed," 11 July 2017, www.ettoday.net/news/20170711/964055.htm?t=%E4%B8%AD%E5%9C%8B%E6%8B%92%E6%92%A4%E8%96%A9%E5%BE%B7%E5%88%B6%E8%A3%81%E3%80%80%E5%8D%97%E9%9F%93%E4%BC%81%E6%A5%AD%E5%A4%B1%E6%9C%9B, accessed 29 September 2017.
11 For example, just three hours before China's hosting of the BRICS event in Xiamen on 3 September 2017, North Korea launched its sixth nuclear test. See http://news.ltn.com.tw/news/world/breakingnews/2183539, accessed 29 September 2017.

Part 4
Identities of the theory

10 A plausible post-Western theory

The discovery of the BoR system is made possible by revisiting Chinese cultural resources. However, this cultural route does not preclude other cultural systems from gaining their own access to BoR. The parallel of the BoR and the BoP and the concomitant judgmental process that moves decision makers back and forth acknowledge their distinctive and shared qualities. The possibility of reverting to an alternative epistemology gives BoR an ambiguous Western and non-Western identity. Chapter 10 reflects upon the unstable identities of BoR as a theory. BoR is post-Western because it qualifies its ubiquity in accordance with the cultural resources of the nation in question. It is Western because all Western civilizations can exercise BoR. No clear forward-moving history exists between the West and the non-West despite a trend at a particular decision site toward a fixed goal, which may be the pursuit of improved security, high modernity, or a clear identity.

The quest for a postcolonial identity that neither belongs to Western international relations nor to an indigenous past cannot fully capture the thematic spirit of BoR because of such an identity's historiographical necessity of being forward-moving and the spatial necessity of ultimately being binary, not relational. The spatial sensibility of IRT and its critics epistemologically limits the potential of IRT from fully appreciating the power of agency that lies in exerting patience, natural cycles, altercasting, and destruction. The noticeable concept of hybridity presumes the existence of a spatially discernible site or body to engage in recombination to attain postcolonial selfhood. The implied Hegelian synthesis in the evolution of hybridity disregards the nationhood constituted by relationality that cannot house a self-contained hybrid to engage in synthesizing.

How does a hybrid site that is hybrid in space and time recognizes shifts and cycles leads to post-hybrid relations? We argue in this chapter that BoR is not just a post-Western IR theory to the extent that multiple relations constitute the self. If the deconstruction of the hegemonic discourse contributes to the integrity of hybrid subjectivity, the further deconstruction of hybrid subjectivity reveals the lingering binary, othering, and hegemony, which BoR relates positively as well as negatively. BoR complicates and qualifies the agenda of hybridity. Given that relationality transcends territoriality,

BoR fits well into the category of post-hybridity, where no forward-moving historiography or romanticized subjectivity is claimed.

Spatiality of IR reconsidered

Hybridity, a highly popular concept in international, ethnic, migrant, cultural, and civilizational studies of the 21st century and a key component of post-Western and non-Western identities, is losing its critical potential because no one is not hybrid anymore (Hutnyk 2000: 36) and because awareness of hybridity may encourage violence. A plausible explanation lies in the concept's preoccupation with spatiality (Kraidy 2004). We believe the irony of "hybrid violence," cosmopolitan as well as indigenous, must be acknowledged to move beyond the self-other binary. The cosmopolitan hegemonic power claims to represent the highest form of hybridity, namely, qua globalization, and vows to protect globalization by targeting failing states and terrorist forces. In this conceptual strike back, neo-conservatism in the cosmopolitan center claims hybridity, while an indigenous, hybrid product of the Cold War acquires nationalist and religious fundamentalism. Hybrid actors at both levels can refuse further improvisation of relationship and abandon the flexibility expected of a hybrid cosmopolitan and postcolonial relation. The former sense often took the modes of urbanization or "global city," whereas modes of sited identification were taken in the latter. The latest snap of globalization shows further overlapping between those two. The faddish and political use of hybridity conflates discursive postcoloniality and its material condition. Recovering the ontological insecurities addressed by postcolonial hybridity requires a specific notion that can show the potential danger of all things being hybrid, but anti-relational.

Hybridity used to denote the unfortunate incapacity of a postcolonial actor before hybridity became an indicator of cosmopolitanism to escape the scrutiny of the established canon (Delanty 2006, Neilson 1999, Ong 1998, Sajed 2010). A hybrid actor recognizes but evades his or her own inferiority (Cabán 1998, Fanon 1986, Paolini, Elliott & Moran 1999). However, hybridity has turned into a subversive celebration of the unavailing indoctrination of any orthodoxy or canon. It is the evidence of sited subjectivity or agency, whose unique genealogy cannot be entirely subsumed by simulating the sanctioned orthodox. Hybridity's own suppressive potential emerges in its political call for such sited subjectivity that generates new binary. Ironically, since 911, the Bush Doctrine has insinuated hybridity as a feature of globalization that fully exposes the unanticipated practice of "hybrid fundamentalism" in both terrorism and neoconservatism.

Therefore, the question is not just about how one has been synthetic of one's own sited geo-cultures and the encountered/assimilated hybrid civilizations, rather, it is about what happens afterward (Arxer 2008). The undecidable conditions allude to the suppressive potential of agents of hybridity, which aborts BoR's bilateral sensibilities in hybridity's applauded potential for emancipation. We intend to further develop theory of hybridity to recover its original critical power, as registered in the teachings of Fanon (1986), Said (1993), and Bhabha (1994). We propose the concept of post-hybridity to understand the cycles of hybrid dominance and hybrid tolerance and examine the dangerous and emancipative potential of hybridity.

As a reminder of the post-Western pursuit of the other dark side of its emancipative intent, theory of BoR belongs to the category of post-hybridity. This chapter aims to bring forth a temporal perspective to supplement the overly spatial sensibility registered in the quest for a synthetic kind of sitedness in post-Western IR theory, reflect upon the danger of hybridity to become binary, and release hybridity's burden of emancipation in a cyclical mode of historiography. Such historiography transcends obsession with the geo-culture of space that emerges in the post-Western pursuit of sitedness while cautioning against the use of genealogy or linearity to implicate sitedness. The Newtonian ontology that undergirds the culture of space and linear time has been the root image of the Western worldview (McMullin 2001) to the effect that the post-Western quest for sitedness risks reproducing prior hegemony by relying similarly on geographical binary to mark and illustrate hybridity.[1] This is the source of confusion that renders globalization hybridity and postcolonial hybridity anti-relational. While each postcolonial site, being "differently different" (Bilgin 2012), resists synchronizing pressure under the circumstance of global governance, sitedness may inadvertently reproduce the prior self-other dichotomy to imagine a Newtonian process of forces colliding in a demarcated space to make a new combination.

Post-hybridity is emerging to show how hybridity may generate pressure on the collective actor to present itself as a synthetic identity and win acknowledgment in a largely capitalist, multi-cultural world (Jameson 1991). Hybridity rejects the possibility of "purity," which neither starts from a rigid "self" nor sees the external as an "other." Post-hybridity is not optimistic in its awareness of multilayer cultural memory, resemblance, and non-synthetic and yet cyclical historiography, which are aforementioned dimensions of BoR. Katz (2013) calls this trans-hybridity, with a focus on cultural transformation in spatial and temporal aspects. Theory of BoR adopts the epistemology of post-hybridity in the temporal and cyclical sense to remind us of the prior resemblance of absolute space or time that may return in post-Western IRT. The discussion continues with a case of post-hybridity, that is, the intellectual history of Hong Kong.

Synthetic hybridity in IR

Emergence of sited hybridity

Mainstream IRT has talked about a horizontal community of "the self" as the international order or a vertical process of "othering" as the imperial order (and its reaction) (Keene 2002), but hardly anything "in-between" has existed until recently. The postcolonial approach has brought IRT to witness the "post-Western" standpoint. Unlike "non-Western" IR (e.g., Acharya & Buzan 2009) or the claims for national reconceptualization of own worldviews, the post-Western self is aware of being "in-between." The sense of "unhomeliness" (Bhabha 1994), together with the idea of "provincialization" (Chakrabarty 2000/2007), became the major strategy for their engagement (e.g., Shani 2007, 2008, Vasilaki 2012). What all experts may share is a critical reassessment of IRT and its re-formulation from the point of in-betweenness. Continuous criticism is in tandem with the notion of "identity as iteration" (Bhabha 1994: 12).

One challenge for post-Western IR comes from its foundation, that is, of where the international are. The idea of hybridity may entail "in-betweenness" in the spatial and temporal sense. However, an error may occur when (mis)interpreting in-betweenness exclusively as the first in the process. The same pitfall of "ending up reproducing the very hegemony they set out to critique" may remain if one regards hybridity as a philosophical and empirical project against the process of a pure, fixed, and totalizing identity and theorization and if one takes hybridity only in the spatial sense (Shani 2008: 723), which shows the irony that a hegemony has to be hybrid or, at times, *vice versa*. It may convert attempts of non- or post-Western IR into a pursuit toward intellectual dominance based on sited hybridity.

Another hurdle is determining how to relocate the postcolonial actors' own critical practice with less, if not without, Western-centeredness. The problem with it is not that criticism comes from the West, but that its mode of practice is considerably influenced by their prior resemblance in terms of commitment to modernity (Gay 1979). Criticism has been regarded as the "struggle against the absolute state" (Eagleton 1984/2005: 9) and "the continuation of politics by other means" (Eagleton 2003/2004: 29). As a counterpart of absoluteness, the idea of plurality is another normative pillar. The criticism has been linked with "the political" in an organic manner, which constitutes an antagonistic field (Mouffe 1993/2005) and aims at bringing "the political" back (Edkins 1999). This thought is expressed in the postcolonial discourse when Fanon iterates his criticism toward white universalism (Fanon 1986) or when Said argues "there are two sides" and identifies three themes of resistance (Said 1993, 1994). The post-Western IRT has likewise been pursued as the "democratization" of the discipline (Chen 2011: 3), and the idea of hybridity has been a major strategy.

Contrary to BoR's stress on improvised resemblance, the wisdom here is to improvise lack of resemblance. A materialized site and a synthetic hybridity to conveniently represent it are the strategic prerequisites to participate in the democratization of IR. It may also go along with a similar line of postcolonial thought, given that Spivak called for temporary essentialism as a strategy. Nevertheless, a site is still needed, which is a matter of criticism and identity. Once we accept the first point of challenge and see hybridity as the strategic representation of a spatial site, any activity of post-Western IR may cause a fundamental deadlock that post-Western is already the acutest version of prior binary.

In such a situation, perceiving the emergence of hybrid fundamentalism is ironic. The rejection of purity qua fundamentalism may be commonly shared among hybridity, post-hybridity, and non-/post-Western IR. Onto-logically, post-hybridity may mean no synthetic subjectivity to own a site or no site to synthesize subjectivity in the long run. Epistemologically, it attends to the changing times of the world as well as improvisation of rela-tions. Finally, methodologically, it may suggest dialectic conversion, even rupture, instead of the genealogy that is oriented toward Newtonian ab-solute time, as a different mode of critical engagement that may transcend sited "critics."

Dangers of post-hybridity

Globalization generates political pressure in all actors to eagerly claim hy-bridity. Thus, the BoR makes a foreign policy a necessity of any national actor to constantly improvise resemblance to each other according to their differently different self-identity. The opposition of hybridity to purity requires either the imagination of an object of purity or the disregard for the object's post-hybrid conditions. For example, former Taiwanese Pres-ident Lee Teng-hui once justified his pro-Taiwan independence campaign by alleging that Taiwan was no longer a part of feudal (i.e., pure) China and imposing a curb on his countrymen from investing in China (Cheung 1998: 118–120). Pure feudalism is no longer existent, but making hybridity a foundation of non-Chinese subjectivity seems his only choice (Corcuff 2012: 56–58). China's adoption of the one-country-two-system formula to reunite with Hong Kong was a deliberate exercise of hybridity made of socialism and capitalism on the one hand and Chinese and British on the other. The last case suggests that reunification does not damage the degree of hybrid-ity. This innocence of being always hybrid breeds the first danger of post-hybridity as the green light to exercise a conquest of any kind.

The conquest of a presumably hybrid target is not for its purification be-cause the conquering subject is already hybrid. All postcolonial nations owe their postcoloniality to the historical forces of colonialism, which brought modernity to the indigenous society. Immigrants who chase after the mod-ern lifestyle to rise from a subaltern identity transform hosting societies into hybrid societies, albeit portrayed in the highly prestigious term "cosmopol-itan." Cosmopolitanism is not described as transcendental but is close to a network among global subalterns. The colonial scope is usually more hy-brid than any particular postcolonial identity and even takes hybridity as an ideal (Andrews 2012). American intervention that has arrived in the name of global governance transcends and synthesizes hybrid conditions with the most magnificent scope.

Cosmopolitanism originally assumed and aimed at overcoming members' purity to tie them together. Such culture has become a site against parochial nationality by proposing denationalized citizenship (e.g., Sassen 2006: Chapter 6). Cosmopolitanism is a counterpart of a particular type of sited identity, namely, nationality. It values a kind of space that cities may best represent. Thus, no cosmopolitan culture is without a city culture. Three implications follow. First, hybridity becomes a vital factor for cosmopolitanism while the latter becomes the site for the former. Second, everything may become hybrid because it requires a cosmopolitan culture or the culture of global cities, and we are fixated with a culture of space. Finally, such hybridization may take networking as a non-material mode of urbanization, which is important because cosmopolitanism is primarily a spatial site necessary to move beyond mere material urbanization. However, given sovereign entitlement to intellectual property rights, it is finally reduced to networking owned by sites.

Another danger is the internal conquest. Resemblance to another national actor can discredit a claim to hybridity, because hybridity cannot be conveniently defined by a real or imagined opposition to purity. Confucian Vietnam and Confucian Korea breed scholarship that painstakingly improvised all trivial variations from Chinese Confucianism to present an indigenously synthetic cultural legacy.[2] The second danger that post-hybridity rests in the tendency to protect the image of hybridity among local leaders who point fingers at others for being traitors of indigenous identity. Traitors are those who declare resemblance to presumably alien cultures and civilizations to undermine synthetic identity and risk the loss of sited distinction.

Internal conquest takes place globally even though the spread of hybridity should have deprived any attempt at conquest or the morale to do so. No conquest can be complete or effective in setting up the future direction of the conquered population. Internal conquest gains momentum wherever a site, allegedly one of a kind, acquires a synthetic identity. This makes, for example, Inner Mongolians in China not Mongolian in the eyes of contemporary Mongolian citizens, and Han Chinese in China a different race than Han Chinese in Taiwan in the eyes of pro-Taiwan independence activists (Brown 2004, Bulag 2004: 109). Mongolian and Taiwanese civilizations are celebrated to be nobly hybrid but synthetic in their own way.

Conquests do not always result in dominance or exploitation. Cosmopolitanism is a tolerant and ongoing mechanism that constantly embraces another different component via soft conquest, soft intervention, or soft governance (Brandsen, Boogers & Tops 2006, Koremenos 2001, Schelkle 2007), as discussed in the notion of governability in Chapter 6. Cosmopolitanism and military campaigns often arise from the same colonial leadership at different times or on different issues, whereas isolation and openness compose the two postcolonial modes of self-synthesizing over different times or issues as described in Chapter 7. Pre-WWII Japan's approach to Taiwan attests to the former cycles of cosmopolitan assimilation and military annihilation

(Ching 2001), and contemporary Singapore's approach to China testifies to the latter cycles of closure and access (Klingler-Vidra 2012).

Figure 10.1 portrays two modes of evolution. All components under hybridity combined into a unique synthetic subject, which evolves from Time 1 to Time 2 in the genealogy of the same synthetic subject despite the addition of new components and the adaptation of old components. The subject defines the way to combine civilizational identities under hybridity. However, under post-hybridity, the process is dialectical with only one particular identity that takes the lead each time. The identity discourse defines the non-synthetic subject under post-hybridity.

Hybridity, composed of at least two pure civilizational components simultaneously, loses behavioral relevance to a certain extent because actors are no longer the hybrid of two inconsistent sets of standards represented exclusively by place. One cannot simply sit between the United States and China because the values and self-understanding of the two places are not internally consistent or even expressible without serious distortion. For example, Korea may represent Confucianism, Buddhism, and Christianity. Confucianism, Buddhism, and Christianity can all use Korea (or China, Japan, and Taiwan) as models in that Korea (or others) becomes temporally divided. Hybridity that is not territorially embedded is unfamiliar to the literature. Saying Korea is a hybrid of these religions is more familiar than saying that these religions are hybrids of Korea, China, Japan, and Taiwan to change sitedness into a style that makes their relations, in addition to difference, pertinent to practices.

A multilayered set of identities of this temporal nature moves the control away from the sited (sovereign and non-sovereign) subjectivity, which the literature on hybridity has attempted to philosophically praise and empirically demonstrate. Under the conditions of post-hybridity, the territorially irrelevant call or urge of a particular mode of self-identification answered by indigenous leadership decides what reigns for the time being and which actors to relate. This pushes essentializing identity into inessential role-playing. For example, the same Korean intellectuals could take pride in the recognition of their English-written scholarship by their American colleagues at one moment but denounce liberalistic suspicion toward nationalism at the next moment to promote Korean unification as the utmost life goal of all Koreans. Relation constitutes each role-play, which is incurred by the practices of the other party according to the time and the issue. Multilayered

Hybridity
A+B+C...(Time 1) → A+B+C...(Time 2) →...

Post-hybridity
A, b, c...(Time 1) → B, a, c...(Time 2) →...

Figure 10.1 Synthetic vs. Non-synthetic Hybridity
(Source: Authors)

values and identities do not oblige a synthetic solution to all acquired and internalized values and identities. They may surface and submerge dialectically without a scientifically decidable pattern because the emergence of the other side is, to an extent, random.

Non-synthesis and resemblance

BoR requires a national actor to adapt to a variety of bilateral relationships without necessarily abiding by specific rules. Thus, non-synthetic hybridity can well characterize the transcendence of BoR processes over their own sitedness. The theme of non-synthesis defines the extent that post-hybridity may be different from hybridity. Post-hybrid identities must be practically re-incurred, while the power of hybrid identity comes mainly from discourse. The three factors that make post-hybridity epistemologically different are its multilayeredness, memory, and resemblance. They are all counterparts of the major tenets of hybridity, which are subjectivity, uncertainty, and difference. More fundamental differences exist between the spatial and temporal epistemology. They share one imagination that ontology changes. However, hybridity may focus on spatial change through a sited subjectivity, whereas post-hybridity is interested in its temporal cycle that requires neither synthetic subjectivity nor forward time.

Multilayeredness may describe coexisting strings in our identity. Its starting point is the recognition that no identity is a *tabula rasa* in the geographical and cultural sense. Postcolonialism does not simply support the plurality of identity as postmodern writers often argue (Bhabha 1994: Chapter 12). Our identity can be a discontinuous construct. Thus, identity cannot be fully understood through discourse analysis and discursive re-interpretation is not really powerful in subverting hegemony. Multilayeredness suggests that our identity and existence belong to more than one temporal dimension, in this sense, it is dissimilar to plurality. What further differentiates multilayeredness from plurality is the rejection of the synthesis premised upon a sited subjectivity. In the international context, subjectivity is sometimes connected to nationalism, which constitutes the affiliation of the self to a particular political community. The theme of plurality requests all to subscribe to a high level of identity. For example, in Taiwan, this means shelving the consciousness of where one's ancestor comes from (e.g., aboriginal, dynastic migrant, Japanese colonial, or civil war refugee) to improvise equal resemblance as a "new Taiwanese" (Fan 2011: Conclusion).

The problem with plurality is that it always assumes a particular line of liberalism (Gray 2002) and is oriented toward civic nationalism, which is reproduced to the effect of synthetic subjectivity that cannot reflect the multilayeredness and open-endedness of non-synthetic dialectics. It can extend such nationalism under a new banner of "cosmopolitan culture." Thus, a similar difficulty can be identified in the current mode of cosmopolitan citizenship because of its reduction to citizenship, not because of its cosmopolitan character. Multilayeredness, which is composed of a contemporary thesis and many anti-theses, is proposed to avoid the pressure of sited synthesis. Non-synthetic multilayeredness enables one to appreciate the return of a lost anti-thesis, which includes notorious Fascism, despite its disappearance for a long period of time. Any anti-thesis can be retrieved to obscure the identity of a particular site or personality. In Taiwan, the aboriginal may re-identify with the Polynesians, the dynastic Han heirs with the aboriginal, the postcolonial subjects with the colonial Japanese, and the civil war refugees with the Chinese.

Cultural memory instead of uncertainty is a ground to remain cognizant of multilayeredness so that all anti-theses can potentially be re-enacted. Its principle is that all are capable of (re)incurring an imagined past. In the world of hybridity, the social formation of the subject may take place via the infliction or totalization by one character over the other. The future is always uncertain, one cannot return to the past, which results to "unhomelyness" (Bhabha 1994). Such synthesizing pictures often stress the fact that two symbiotic stories can be told (Hollis & Smith 1991) from the same identity discourse at the same time. However, cultural memory may suggest that the practical, as opposed to the discursive, switches between the thesis and that a non-symbiotic anti-thesis can be conscious and abrupt.[3] For example, Lee Tenghui turned himself from a Communist to a Christian or from a follower of Chinese unification to a leader of Taiwanese independence. His re-identification with Japanese colonialism resulted from more than just uncertainty. He was recalling a distinct and solid past from memory. Similarly, the modern history of Okinawa reflects the island's cultural memory, which explains the fact that oppositions toward the USA, Japan, and China have always existed in tandem with a sense of affiliation toward any of them.

What may be the link between multilayeredness and memory is the third tenet of resemblance. Resemblance describes how the incurring of an earlier layer may occur to reconnect with those others who were conceived of as belonging to a different other. The concept is contrasted with "difference." The cyclical practices of multilayered theses reflect the duty of the subjects to fulfill their social roles as time changes. Therefore, the duty is not about how different the subject is from the other but about how the subject copes with time and its context as constituents of his or her relational self. Moreover, the act to reconnect is always improvisational because the subject is expected to hold multilayered identities. To provide another East Asian example, note that growth, nuclear weapons, comradeship, national unification, regime stability, and family history, to name just a few, all inspire cycles of resemblance in Pyongyang in reference to China, the Chinese Communist Party, South Korea, and kinship (Kim 2011: 26–27). Each cycle emerges out of a discernable rationale at a certain time, whether it is socialism, nationalism, or comradeship.

The post-hybrid capacity for resemblance informs the non-synthetic dialectics of a site, person, or history to switch identities as the constituting relations shift. However, an allegedly synthesized hybrid site relies on re-interpretation to resist domination. Genealogy is the basic method of cultural sociology to track how one hybrid condition evolves with a traceable string (Mukerji 2007), which leads to uncertain and yet sited subjectivity. Hybridity proceeds with participants and observers who provide symbiotic yet contradictive meanings to the same practice. However, incurred resemblance is what characterizes the post-hybrid subject exercising cycles of plausible canons one after another because the reigning one fails to achieve success or because altercasting out of the arriving encounter demands performance. Democratic Taishao turned to imperialist Showa in the aftermath of the Washington Conference because it was perceived to have subjected Japan to US dominance (Nish 2002: 26). Genealogy between different canons is unnecessary in this particular change because democracy and imperialism were parallels in history rather than hybrid at the same site. Changes were not merely discursive but were practical under the post-hybrid condition.

Therefore, the idea of post-hybridity projects an epistemology to think in a temporal manner. Hybridity does not discard social ontology in a temporal sense (Bhabha 1994: 6). Fanon and Bhabha mentioned that the problem of "the location of culture" is one of the "ambivalent temporality of modernity" (Ibid.: 239). However, the IRT has showed that social ontology has been interpreted in the sense of belonging, which tends to see identity in terms of "where" rather than "when."[4] Thus, post-hybridity can be close to the Derridean idea of différance, which states that the present and the presence are always a mixture of temporally different existences. Social ontology must deal with Bhabha's question on modern ambivalent time, which is "often ignored" in the tradition of stressing spatiality (Id.). Differences in terms of identity can only emerge as such from prior relations of the self. Thus, genealogy is the proper method to explain the evolution of sited hybridity. However, multilayeredness and resemblance via the strategic incurring of memory make post-hybridity a temporal process of dialectics and rupture. This process can be called, as in Chapter 6, "cyclical view of history," which is discussed further in the case study of Hong Kong, a site ironically characterized by both cosmopolitanism and postcolonialism.

Post-hybridity identity case of Hong Kong

The dangers of hybridity reside primarily in the desire for new binary and conquest. It can arise internally from an imagined sitedness to gather, as a cosmopolitan center does, another exotic model to enhance the universality of the center. The US intervention in the Middle East is the archetype of a cosmopolitan center that seeks dominance over sites of different civilizations via an allegedly multicultural institutional frame (Cheng 2012: 7). Internally imagined sitedness can sever, as an independent subaltern does, trans-border resemblance(s) to protect a distinctive hybrid identity.

Singapore's pursuit of a non-Chinese identity via a national English curriculum represents a quintessential case of self-reconstruction (Stroud & Wee 2011).

The externally triggered action transcends the sited distinction and presses actors constantly in response to altercasting that is externally prepared (e.g., human rights, economic growth, nationalism, and peace). Nations are merely agents of cycles, for example, China's coping with Myanmar, North Korea, Vietnam, and the Philippines dissolves the nation into different modes of relationships, each embedded in a prior series of bilateral trajectories. Subjectivity is no longer premised upon the ability to re-appropriate civilizational mingling for the use of national self-actualization. From a historical perspective, almost all national actors demonstrate the intellectual capacity for dialectical change in accordance with the demand of the time.

Postcolonial Hong Kong is distinctive in its ostensible combination of Chinese, British, American, and other Asian civilizational resources. Chinese immigrants have arrived in different generational cohorts in over 300 years, and nascent immigrants joined from Southeast Asia after the Cold War. Hong Kong is a typical site of non-synthetic hybridity. Canonic thoughts and beliefs that sustain differing identity strategies of Hong Kong's intellectual and elite strata remain tenaciously within their own genealogy with their own imagined tradition and self-identity. Thus, Hong Kong exemplifies a geo-cultural path that the literature on hybridity has not seriously considered. Hong Kong's geo-cultural path is different from hybridity because Hong Kong's identity encompasses non-synthetic, lingering Confucian, Christian, liberal, patriotic, and other identities that exist parallel to one another rather than merging into a certain hybrid identity. Thus, the allegedly hybrid identity of Hong Kong can disintegrate at any time because of re-imagined or re-enacted traditions. The non-symbiotic parallel identities support a cyclical view of history rather than the celebrated postcoloniality that moves Hong Kong irrevocably away from any fixed past.

However, Hong Kong would *not* be considered essentially distinct in the postcolonial literature, given that Hong Kong embraces both postcolonialism and cosmopolitanism. The two agendas do not move in the same direction. Postcolonial historiography stresses variety, whereas historiography on globalization stresses synchronized practices and representations. They similarly conceive a local history that moves forward on its own track and denies any possibility of reproducing prior canonic thoughts or hegemonic values. The postcolonial agenda treats this forward move either as one into or away from a global agenda or a little of both. The contemporary history of Hong Kong illustrates this as a move away from any specific meaning of being Chinese.

At this seemingly nontypical hybrid site Hong Kong, two popular modes of historiography are readily available to approach its geo-cultural history. One is the "end-of-history" kind of historiography that expects a linear and progressive evolution toward an individualist, civilian culture that can engender resemblance to European modernity and transcend sitedness. The other is the challenging deconstructive historiography that emerges in different schools of deconstruction, including those that advocate "postcolonial modernity," "multiple modernities," and "post-Western international relations." Both modes, however, fail. Neither of the two options can cope with the paralleling, coexisting, and non-confrontational cultural, religious, and political identities in Hong Kong after its return to China in 1997. The rise of the confrontation between pro-democratic and pro-Chinese forces brings forth an unfamiliar challenge because one can detect incongruence in imagined resemblance to China that enter different temporal layers. The two forces hardly synthesize despite a hybrid outlook of the agent. Each appears in cycles contingent upon the context and judgment of the agent. Thus, the case of Hong Kong has wide philosophical implications, to the extent that indigenous and colonial thoughts considered mixed during cultural encounters *do not* substitute each other. Instead, they parallel or layer each other.

The capacity for intellectual return or appeal to a perceived past string cannot be a phenomenon specific only to Hong Kong. Therefore, postcolonial hybridity fails to appreciate powerful prior intellectual foundations to which later generations can resort. Incurring an alternative origin to situate a different contemporary identity is always possible because of the longevity of human intellectual history. Hong Kong demonstrates this constant re-appealing that takes place on the basis of solid traditions in Confucianism, Christianity, and patriotism, in addition to the familiar liberalism and anti-Communism. Chineseness has become difficult to define, and attempts at doing so generate bitter feelings because none of the above intellectual identities have mixed well. Thus, hybridity is a misleading notion because of the lack of reference to the intellectual mechanism that brings back the past. The past in the present is always reimagined, and such a past is portrayed in postcolonial literature as being for a contemporary purpose. The epistemology of hybridity treats the cultural past in Hong Kong that encompasses all these prior identities as sheer strategic resources that can be enlisted by contemporary people for their own purposes. It omits the nature of culture as an internalized memory that inspires a spontaneous action.

Consider, for example, a past intellectual resource such as Confucianism. Confucianism has implanted a cultural memory that enables contemporary people to naturally and instantaneously respond to Communist symbols with a ready aversion that imposes barriers on certain strategic options. Given that the above process constitutes an intuitive response, the response would not be considered a strategic choice. However, if Confucianism would ally with Christianity to be anti-Communist, this connection would constitute an improvisation. Postcolonial hybridity only focuses on the latter while omitting the former.

Cycles make a legitimate concept only if arriving civilizations each remain in their own momentum. In the modern history of Hong Kong, cycles should at least include Chinese immigrants that arrived in Hong Kong in separate waves, colonial immigrants, and missionaries. The result has been coexisting non-synthetic intellectual resources embedded in Confucianism, anti-Communism, Christianity, nationalism, and liberalism. These resources parallel, not merge, in a community undergirded by the geological demarcation of the colony and the Cold War camp. These values could each replace one another contingent upon the event, the political condition, the individualized experience, and the choice of the agent. Thus, Hong Kong's intellectual history illustrates an entirely unfamiliar yet potentially ubiquitous postcolonial condition that the notion of hybridity is not nuanced enough to catch.

Chinese immigrants in Hong Kong have avoided sited identity. This does not mean that they did not gain sitedness, instead, it illustrates that they preferred a distinctive non-Hong Kong identity until the 21st century. The first cohort of Chinese immigrants consisted of Chinese who lost the political battle during the Manchurian (Qing) conquest of China. The overthrowing of the Qing Dynasty brought another generation of Confucian scholars that remained loyal to the dynasty. They despised the colonial Hong Kong population and naturally became the faithful ally of the cultural conservatives in China, who were opposed to those characterized as Westernizers, modernizers, or cultural revolutionaries. Lu Xun, an important leader of the May Fourth Movement, was critical of these Hongkongnese Confucians whom the colonial administration found an ironic ally in its attempt to deprive the labor movement of its legitimacy. The Communist revolution in 1949 brought in another cohort of Confucian immigrants, who were anti-Communist. The most recent intellectual Chinese immigrants arrived after the suppression of the Pro-democracy Movement in 1989, likewise anti-communist but hardly Confucian.

The different generations of Confucian immigrants multiplied the cultural layers in Hong Kong as each carried with them a peculiar mission of restoration. Their ideological enemies have varied widely over the years, from Manchurians and Westernizers, to Communists and, finally, to the Communist party-state. Hong Kong has never been a real home for these immigrants despite most of them having spent the rest of their lives there. Nostalgia for certain Chinese cultural identities combined with an aversion to the current regime made the immigrants unfit for both the colonial lives in Hong Kong and the possible new lives in China. The wished temporality of their stay in Hong Kong kept them from attending issues that practically affected them. Nevertheless, they always stood firm against colonialism in the beginning.

Synthesis or mutual conversion has not occurred despite the brief alliance between the British colonial government and Confucian scholars during the Republican period, during which the Chinese Department was established at the Hong Kong University. The colonial government did not intend to reproduce a particular kind of Chinese relationality for Hong Kong. Thus, pedagogy under colonialism had no patriotic goal but prepared the population for capitalist competition. Nevertheless, prior imagined resemblance to China remained strong through the practice of Chinese cultural life as well as the exodus of Chinese refugees and the ubiquitous appropriation of Chinese cultural symbols. However, indigenous Chinese and colonial British components and different cohorts of Chinese immigrants did not synthesize. Both are more than just cultural resources for use in accordance with the context and judgment. They make a hybrid repertoire of cultural memory that can be triggered into action for achievement often of opposite ends, such as Chinese patriotism and colonial modernity. The concept of cultural memory refers to the evaluative intuition that generates agency for action. A non-synthetic kind of cultural memory in Hong Kong is destined to cause cycles in identity strategy in the population and in each individual.

The above situation made it possible for people like Szeto Wah (1931–2011) to be a leader of the pro-democracy movement after 1989 and a determined patriot. Szeto's simultaneous critical perspective on the Chinese Communist Party rule and his unreserved leadership in campaigning for the recovery of the Diaoyu Islands' sovereignty from Japan embarrassed his followers, who could often only agree with one of his two positions. University professors specialized in China studies have to rely on the different layers of imagined resemblance to Chineseness to research their Chinese subjects empathically, practice activism in Hong Kong, engage Western colleagues professionally in academic conferences, and re-appropriate their network in Singapore, Taipei, or among Chinese diaspora elsewhere. Their intellectual capacity of adaptation and shifting reveals the non-synthetic hybrid condition they are in. Thus, all the cultural resources can prevail on their own and make the dialectics of cultural memories an ongoing process.

Non-synthetic hybridity can be illustrated by the mutually estranging relationship between the different generations of Chinese immigrants to Hong Kong. In favor of liberal democracy, the latest anti-Communist generation of the 1990s does not possess the same anti-Communism embedded in Confucianism of the early days. This generation was also different from the one brought forth separately by the Church tradition, which included Sinology but not Confucianism. The cohort that arrived after the Communist takeover largely experienced the war with Japan during childhood. Their strong patriotism alienated them from the cultural nationalism that arrived a generation earlier or the China watchers who came to Hong Kong to solidify American containment. Chinese scholars who have come to Hong Kong during the last two decades with a professional resemblance to the Western academics are lukewarm to anti-Communism, which makes them block communication with the earlier nationalist cohort. Moreover, intellectuals who were raised in Hong Kong can represent yet another indigenous layer with resemblance of liberal and nationalist discourses. The values, identities, and cultural memories in the culturally hybrid Hong Kong can emerge and submerge separately. Thus, improvisation has become an inevitable process of life that depends on the pragmatic concerns and evaluative intuition of the actor.

Hong Kong's case makes Singapore or differing Chinese diasporic communities cases of comparison. Singapore has Chinese immigrants who arrived in different cohorts. The first generation arrived amidst the transformation of a dynastic China into a republic, whereas the second generation grew up during the anti-Japanese war. Even though the second generation has preserved major intellectual resources that sustained certain prior Chinese humanities and identities, it watched the third generation drift away from Chineseness. The leadership under Lee Kuan Yew initially suppressed Chineseness to improvise an indigenous resemblance to a non-Chinese neighborhood, a cosmopolitan resemblance to the multi-racial and religious components in the nation, and a Cold War resemblance to potential communist sympathizers among Chinese patriots. Granted that the third generation was bred according to English pedagogy, Lee can revitalize resemblance of Chineseness to China first under the disguise of Asian values and then upon the fast-rising Chinese economy. New Chinese immigrants began to arrive from the Chinese mainland before the start of the new century to make a non-synthetic parallel to those who had come from Hong Kong a decade earlier. The evolving non-synthetic hybridity causes integrative problems.

Conclusion

To negotiate a proper relationship in a bilateral network, each relationship according to its own characteristics requires conscious improvisation. Such a BoR strategy hardly appreciates sited subjectivity, which asserts identity-based role conceptions and acts upon an imagined environment that reproduces self-identity. BoR can also arise from a memory that is deeper than merely pragmatism. No easy defensive mechanism can guarantee guarding against violence, suppression, or self-centrism other than relational self-restraint under such a BoR system. Self-restraint prepared by BoR is mainly contingent upon external role expectations. Therefore, it is not sited but differently incurred upon the altercasting of the other party under different bilateral circumstances.

A post-hybrid community of black and white is not as gray as it appears from a distance. Approaching closely, we see more and more clearly (or unclearly) a combination of members turning black or white at different points of time on different agendas in different degrees. (Figure 10.2) A politically correct mobilization may gather those in the correct color at a time and silence others in the wrong color. An alternative trigger may reverse the color. Social science agendas ought to study what makes a trigger and prepares performance of politically correct self-restraint. This is not linear historiography, nor pluralist historiography, nor indigenous historiography. This is instead a relationally cyclical or dialectical historiography. Given its improvisational characteristics, abrupt change and sticky constant coexist;

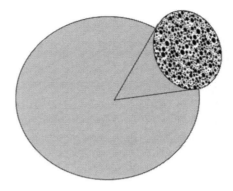

Figure 10.2 Individualized Post-hybrid Historiography
Source: Authors; designed by Alice Yen-ting Liu

distinctive black and distinctive white makes no binary; and agency for self-reconstitution attracts no attention.

Another observation from the case of Hong Kong may be added in its relation to (post-)Western IR. IR theory has been the theories of and among sited identities. Hong Kong shows that such framework in the study of global relations or globalization is narrow in its scope and analysis. Even Hong Kong's case may make a post-Western mode of IR inquiry insufficient, as the post-Western literature sees the uncertainty of a particular identity in a spatial aspect. Presumably uncertainty testifies to local agency. In post-Western IR, the agenda has still been a matter of reinterpreting sited identity. The newest addition to the inquiry is the possibility of temporal resemblance out of strategic improvisation and cultural memory. Although some works have attempted to achieve such reinterpretation (Ling 2013, Sassen 2006), bringing time/history back to IR theory but in a different sense is necessary. Thus, a cyclical view of history may become a gentle reminder to reflect upon how one may re-situate the self, the other, and the world within the theories embedded in relational sensibilities.

Notes

1 The possible sites that can reproduce existent borders and generate new ones include India, the Caribbean, Eurasia, the Andes, China, Japan, and Southeast Asia (Tickner & Blaney 2013).
2 For a comparison between these especially separate Confucianism, see Richey (2013).
3 A case for such practical use of memory through "the balance of relationship" or "the balance of role" was presented through the example of the urban Chinese. See Shih (2013: 88).
4 Post-colonial literature enlists words that indicate our existence in any spatial sense, such as "site," "displace," "home (and the world)," "unhome," and "space."

11 Plausible Chinese theory[1]

American relations instead of international relations

Despite the continuing prevalence of realism in Chinese IR circles, relation has emerged as a plausible alternative to the extent that morality is becoming a prominent element in Chinese realism. However, scholars elsewhere have difficulty believing this development. Not only does the Anglophone IR suspect the practically inconsequential notion of *tianxia* as an ontological device to control, but the Sinophone IR also regards it as the CCP's legitimating discourse. In this light, Chapter 11 reviews Taiwanese scholarship on Chinese new IR thinking that is similarly suspicious.

The Taiwanese research can be understood as a quest for relational security that is strategically girded by American hegemony but culturally lured by Chinese alternatives, with an additional emotional/historical string attached to Japan. The previous chapter contends that BoR embraces post-hybridity, which in Taiwanese scholarship on Chinese IR rings the bell of danger, embedded in nationalist fundamentalism, rather than emancipation provided by the hybrid institution of one country and two systems. For Taiwanese IR scholars, Chinese historical and philosophical resources at best reconfirm the existence of a Chinese threat from realist perspectives. Such perspectives reject the relevance of good will or relation in IR and support Taiwan's quest for independence from Chinese influence. In practice, relational purposes pertaining to Taiwan's relationship with China constitute Taiwanese IR scholarship.

This chapter begins with a theoretical discussion on Taiwan's improvised abortion of prior resemblance to China in terms of Taiwan's peculiarity vis-à-vis China, pertaining to a civilizational identity (e.g., modernity, democracy/human rights, etc.), a national identity (e.g., strategic alliance-ship, anti-China regulations, and civic nationalist discourse), and an ethnic identity (e.g., aboriginal kinship, 400-year historiography, etc.), which explains why none of them works well. It advances four claims. First, new concepts, such as harmony, *tianxia*, or non-traditional/new security, do not change Taiwanese academic evaluations of Chinese new IR or shake the realist mode of analysis concerning the BoP. Second, the potential of China's new

IR to deconstruct Taiwanese resemblance to the US in terms of American values and security community represents an intellectual threat. Third, the improvised/aborted Taiwanese relation with China is divided more between exclusion and mingling than between balancing and bandwagoning in Anglophone IR. Fourth, intellectual and political exits are existent, emerging, and possible for subaltern Taiwan.

Whom to patronize?

Between national and civilizational Taiwan

A rich repertoire of discourses and cultural perspectives can support a non-synthetic variety of reviews on Chinese IR perspectives in Taiwan. This scenario leads to the anxiety of any author who regards himself/herself as Taiwanese, because his/her choice of perspectives confronts different selections of others. This could expose an enacted role identity to a necessarily dissenting audience. Each of these differing perspectives originates outside Taiwan, and enlisting authoritative information from its foreign source enables improvisation of resemblance to a potential ally in order to avoid or disguise confrontational identity politics for the sake of political correctness inside.

Therefore, an IR publication in Taiwan stimulates the imagination of a double audience from Taiwan and the presumed source countries of IR perspectives. The effects of such audiences became increasingly complicated after the intensified interactions between China and Taiwan in the 1990s. A real audience exists in Taiwan and China, whereas an imagined audience exerts influence from the US and Japan. Different sets of audience demand different imaginations of mutual resemblance, which leads to multiple bilateral concerns. The real audience judges the appropriateness of an IR piece in terms of whether it incorporates a separatist or non-separatist stance. The imagined audience may serve two functions. One is to camouflage, obscure, and change the identity of those who are not ready to claim a stance. The other is to assert, reproduce, and refocus individuals who are determined holders of separatist or non-separatist positions.

American IR literature is dominant among all intellectual sources. Almost all IR scholars in Taiwan reiterate the troika of realism, liberalism, and constructivism (Chiu & Chang 2012). American IR literature is a perfect platform for Taiwanese and Chinese IR scholars to establish a dialogue. However, new Chinese IR perspectives evolved as the exact result of critical reviews on American IR. Taiwanese IR scholars who first emerged in the 1970s and who were cultured in American IR twice as long as their Chinese counterparts have been consistently alienated from any critical reflections. The rare dissenting views in Taiwan originate from the faddish cultural studies. They are borrowed from the mini post-structural turn in American IR research, which pre-dates that of China by two decades and loses its advantage because the nascent Chinese IR attracts enormous attention globally.

Taiwan has depended on the US to deal with Communist China since the end of the Chinese Civil War. Such all-round political and strategic dependence is widespread in Taiwan, resulting in the defensive consciousness against China. Embedded in American IR, the intellectual justification to such dependence legitimizes and comforts the Kuomintang's (KMT) reign in Taiwan upon its alleged mission to recover the Chinese Mainland from communism. IR provides Taiwan with an epistemological resemblance to the US in terms of universalism that intellectually empowers a small Taiwan that is losing its physical battle with China to acquire an external and eternal as well as equal perspective. Intellect and politics are incompatible owing to the contradiction between the idea that knowledge on China presupposes an external (i.e. neutral, objective, and unrelated) position of observation and the civil war legacy that democratic Taiwan remains an internal competitor in China. Thus, this improvised intellectual universalism in Taiwan achieved monopoly after the Civil War was discontinued.

The pro-independence Democratic Progressive Party (DPP) came to power in 2000. It sought a substitute that could naturally coincide with the concept of a universal Taiwan that neither belongs to nor is belittled by China. Liberalism marks such an improvised ideological difference between China and Taiwan, whereas realism aborts political resemblance to China so that defending liberalism, as opposed to imposing it, externalizes China as other. Taiwan's universalist identity has two components: Taiwan's imagined Americanness and China's un-Americanness. The latter is reinforced by efforts to build indigenous IR schools in China. Facing nascent epistemological determination to confront US universalism in China, Taiwan has not responded to the call for global IR, non-Western IR, or post-Western IR with any noticeable enthusiasm lest this creates China's competitive edge in IR. The similar inattention among Chinese scholars to these calls for IR fails to enhance Taiwan's courage to look away from American mainstream IR. All the Taiwanese can think with comfort is that the Chinese IR composes an attempt to replace the US leadership.

This situation explains why the Ministry of Foreign Affairs in Taipei has spent a significant budget on two intellectual endeavors for over an entire decade since the beginning of the century. One endeavor is the launch of the Taiwan Democracy Foundation, which aims to develop the country as a nominal symbol for, and in contrast to China's resistance to, global democratization. The other endeavor is the holding of endless conferences and workshops on all types of triangular relations (e.g., the Taiwan–US–China relationship), where a game theory matrix can transform Taiwan into an equal national player, an opportunity that is not available in practice. Both efforts establish resemblance to American scholarship.

Universalism in scholarship connotes a civilizational identity that transcends local or regional historiography and has a track that is older than the Chinese Civil War. If Americanness in Taiwanese IR confirms that Taiwan is external to China from strategic and ideological points of view, then Taiwan's former superior obsession with a civilizational sensibility can date back to pre-War colonialism under Japan. The quest for a modern identity has led to vicissitudes in Japanese modern history but left a permanent mark in Taiwan. Postcolonial intellectuals in Taiwan remain alert to their achieved modernity ahead of China. However, the irony of history was that Japan eventually opted for a reincarnation of East Asia by expelling the white race out of the continent (Goto-Jones 2005) as well as that the defeat in war pushed Japan back to accept American protection. Many pro-independence scholars in Taiwan were pleased that Taiwan's enlisted contribution, albeit once to the losing side of Japan, was ultimately registered in a level of (American) civilization higher than that of China.

As the colonial model for Taiwan, Japan relies on the US in dealing with China. IR writers in Taiwan primarily cite American literature, not always immediately including the Japanese. Nevertheless, they resemble each other in terms of the irony of relying on the US to demonstrate independence from China. This irony ensures that the Japanese and the Taiwanese intellectual strings stay closely informed about each other and almost strategically tie both of them to an inexpressible but clear hierarchy of intellectual alliance, with the US on top and Taiwan at the bottom. This background sets up the epistemological parameters for scholars in Taiwan to read new IR thinking from China.

However, Taiwanese scholars are beginning to disperse along the trend of globalization, albeit in small numbers. They can write from Europe, America, or elsewhere in Asia. Moreover, writing for international publishers makes an imagined audience into a real one. A joint project that can simultaneously include Americans, Europeans, Australians, Japanese, Chinese, or all of them compels the Taiwanese to move beyond domestic politics and consider whether they want to exercise academic resemblance to critical IR that will undermine American dominance. These are exceptions to the trend presented in the remainder of this chapter.

Perceptions of Chinese new IR thinking in Taiwan

Compared with their Japanese and Western counterparts, the nascent IR thinking of China resonates differently among Taiwanese academics. Given its persistent perception that China is not the right model to emulate as far as the birth of modern Westphalian IR is concerned (Kayaoglu 2010: 193–217), Japan's IR circle has not paid attention to the latest development of the "Chinese School" (Chen 2011: 463–492). Such disinterest, along with Western IR communities' surging interest in the opposite, can be considered two sides of the same coin, as the latter is very much preoccupied with confirming the impossibility/undesirability of indigenous theory-building in China (Snyder 2008: 28–31). IR scholarship in Taiwan tends to be attracted to the possibility of Chinese new IR thinking as an alternative to mainstream Eurocentric IR theories while using American/Western IR as the benchmark to affirm that such a possibility is far from being materialized.

A case in point is Chao and Hsu's (Chao & Hsu 2009: 1–44) study on the theoretical and policy implications of China's "harmonious world" under its fourth generation (i.e., Hu-Wen) leadership. Chao and Hsu indicate that "harmonious world" as a new vision of international order and diplomatic thinking serves Beijing's purpose of constructing a favorable international environment necessary for China's economic development. They illustrate how "harmonious world" theory is designed to assure the international community that China is a status quo power and emphasize the importance of respecting cultural differences to shield the communist regime from external pressures. Beijing's calls for the democratization of international relations and multilateral mechanisms for reciprocal cooperation likewise seek to constrain the US hegemony and highlight China's growing importance. Chao and Hsu applaud that "harmonious world" is conducive to the improvement of China's international image and is theoretically grounded by realism and constructivism. Hu (2012: 3–16) argues that "harmonious world" is a result of learning and innovation in Chinese foreign policy, which is compatible with neo-liberal institutionalism's focus on international cooperation and multilateral organizations. None of the aforementioned authors maintains that China has succeeded in developing an original IRT with "Chinese characteristics." This insufficiency is attributed to "harmonious world" remaining a soft-power instrument of the communist leadership to sustain regime legitimacy at home and shape a favorable environment abroad; that is, "harmonious world" is more of a form of Chinese ideology than a theory (Chao & Hsu 2009: 29–30, Hu 2012: 16).

Two observations can be made here. First, if "harmonious world" is also "for someone and for some purposes (Cox 1996: 27)," then it is unclear why being "problem-solving" automatically disqualifies it as an original thinking, not least because "problem-solving" theories are abundant in the West.[2] Moreover, Taiwanese political scientists commonly look at new thinking and practices in Chinese foreign policy through the American microscope, which is typically a realist prespective (Chang 2006, 323–340, Chao & Hsu 2009, Chiu & Chang 2012, Chu & Tung 2010: 135–158, Hu 2012). For example, Chao and Hsu are skeptical of China's (as a rising hegemon) willingness to observe the cooperative principles of a "harmonious world" when dealing with the declining US at the expense of its national interest, which would be obtainable through coercive means (Chao & Hsu 2009: 31). They consider China an offensive realist whose strategic choice is strongly shaped by its power position of adopting an offensive posture when strong and a defensive one when weak. Rather than seeing the introduction of the notion of "new security" as Beijing's learning of the post-Cold War trend in "deepening" and "broadening" the meanings of security (Booth 2005), Hu reduces the "new security" notion to a soft-power instrument for shaping an external security environment in China's favor. Embedded in the prior resemblance of autonomous state, China's security interests are, according to the literature, fixed, pre-given, and immune to its social interactions with other states.

Yu and Chang (2011: 46–83) indicate that research on neo-liberalism in China has not reached the status of theoretical innovation because Chinese IR scholars rely on notions from "Western proto-type theory" (e.g., transaction cost) rather than their traditional culture and values to explain the origins of international cooperation and institutions. Nevertheless, the (structural) realist paradigm in the study of China's foreign policy has reached its limits in the age of economic interdependence and regional integration, which explains neo-liberalism's popularity among Chinese IR scholars. They mention that the development of neo-liberalism in China has exceeded the stage of copying, thus leading to reflections in the field of Chinese IR and efforts to draw on Chinese history, culture, and philosophy by including other academic subjects. Yu and Chang note that Western "democratic peace theory" conceives democracy as a new standard of civilization. They point out that whether the so-called harmonious peace inspired by traditional Chinese political thought could go beyond the "democratic peace" or only has limited applicability within what used to be the Sino-centric world in contemporary East Asia depends on the extent to which Chinese academics can materially and ideationally substantiate the "harmonious peace" alternative. Without examining how and why these imported notions have been translated, modified, and appropriated in China, the West remains the sole and superior reference point for Taiwanese political scientists to judge the (im)maturity of Chinese new IR thinking.[3]

Chang and Chen's (2012: 89–123) other recent research on the alleged emergence of the "Tianxia system" reveals caution against China-centric ontology. Some Chinese academics have started drawing upon ancient Chinese philosophical thought and diplomatic experience to rethink questions contemporary IR theory and international order are facing. Thus, they indicate that the rise of China is relevant for the development of new schools, ontologies, and methodologies for IR theory (Chang & Chen 2012: 91). The "universality" of the "Tianxia system" that does not seek to unite the world under a market economy and liberal democracy echoes Beijing's "harmonious world," which calls for the peaceful coexistence of plural civilizations and different political systems.[4] Rather than dismissing growing literature on the "Tianxia system" as a part of "China's discursive networks of power" (Callahan 2008: 757–758, Chang 2011)"[5] Chang and Chen (2012: 98) remind us that Zhao Tingyang first proposed his Tianxia philosophy in 2003, two years before President Hu Jintao's "harmonious world" speech in the United Nations General Assembly. Contrary to the common perception held in Taiwan's IR community (and elsewhere), they maintain that PRC officials did not engineer the rise of the present Tianxia discourse as an exercise of Chinese soft power.

Based on some basic features of the tribute system and its foreign-policy relevance for China's neighbors, people ask why Tianxia literature has not generated great interest among Taiwanese IR scholars in studying relations across the Taiwan Strait. Chang and Chen (01: 96–97) indicate that, as long as the weak counterparts followed the principle of "*shida*" (serving the great and powerful) and maintained their resemblance to the Chinese court in terms of ritual, China typically did not intervene in their domestic affairs and adopted a generous economic policy of "*houwang bolai*" (giving more and getting less) toward them (Chang & Chen 2012: 96–97). This brings us back to the conclusion of Taiwan's increasing incorporation into Sino-centric cosmology. Critics argue that hierarchical relations were confirmed when Taiwan ("vassal state") submitted to the paternal Chinese state ("suzerain") by upholding the so-called one-China principle (i.e., a ritual of presenting "tribute"); the Taiwanese were then granted trade privileges as gifts from Beijing ("son-of-heaven"). Secondary political entities historically enjoyed immense latitude within the tributary order regarding their economic, cultural, and even military affairs. This perspective helps to understand why Chinese leaders formulated the "one country, two systems" proposal in dealing with Taiwan the way they did (which precludes Beijing from exerting domestic control over the island) and why they have been willing to entertain issues pertaining to Taiwan's "international space" if Taipei adheres to the one China principle. (Chen 2012: 480) The sales of US arms to Taiwan has been an irritant in PRC–US relations not necessarily because the weapons systems and platforms would pose an insurmountable challenge to the People's Liberation Army's (PLA) ability to coerce or conquer Taiwan;[6] rather, the existence of such arms sales exposes Taiwan's role as a security protégé of the US, thus violating the *shida* principle and disrupting the island's hierarchical relations with China.

Chang and Chen (2012) conclude that the current traces of the revival of the tribute system and the Tianxia worldview insufficiently support the claim that Beijing consciously pursues a strategy to construct a new Tianxia system that may provide the emerging "Chinese School" with a real-world foundation for theory-building. However, they do so by developing some empirical indicators to measure the extent to which China and four of its former vassal states can interact within such a system. Their project attempts to "connect history, extract concepts from historical experiences while relating them to modern IR studies, and finally operationalize these concepts so as to confirm the requirements of positivist research" (Chang & Chen 2012: 92–93). Despite their China-centric ontological orientation, they remain under the influence of a Euro-centric epistemology that aspires to contribute to the betterment of social science by revising the laws on a universal behavioral pattern (Shih & Chang 2011: 280–297).

New "China threat" to Taiwanese relational security

The previous section illustrates the mixed reception of Chinese new IR thinking in Taiwan. Taiwanese academics have closely followed various emerging Chinese alternatives, from "new security" to the more recent "Tianxia system." However, they remain unimpressed by the indigenous theory-building on the other side of the strait, and their realist or Euro-centric mode of analysis remains unshaken. Taiwanese scholarship is a prac-tice of BoR in response to the Taiwanese political incumbent's endeavor to abort resemblance to China as much as possible. It denies new scholarship to reproduce its own resemblance to American IR.

However, IR scholarship in Taiwan did not always maintain this ambiv-alent attitude toward the study of Chinese foreign policy. The Civil War discourse used to prevail in guiding policy thinking and scholarship to re-produce an absolute rival relationship. Until the 1980s, the field was domi-nated by a completely different generation of scholars, whose ontology and epistemology may be considerably more "non-Western" than contempo-rary critical IR scholarship, which is largely informed by poststructuralism or post-colonial studies originated in the West. Experts in "bandit stud-ies" (the name reserved for China studies after the KMT's defeat on the mainland) focused on CCP ideology and propaganda when studying PRC's foreign policy, which points to its consistent principles and flexible tactics. KMT-associated scholars drew upon CCP history and official documents, the thinking and remarks of its leaders, and their civil war experiences against the CCP, enabling them to empathize with their archenemy,[7] with a level of sophistication hardly matched by today's social and scientific IR theory-armed China pundits (Kuo & Myers 1986).

This generation of scholars did not emerge out of a geocultural vacuum.[8] As self-therapy to compensate for its incompetence in representing China politically in the aftermath of the Chinese Civil War, the KMT-ruled Re-public of China (ROC) in Taiwan assigned the island a role as represent-ative of "authentic" Chinese culture. This strategy was familiar to some second-tier tributary states, such as Vietnam, Korea and Japan, which have also insisted that they were the "real" China. This tendency is not surpris-ing given that they were socialized by a Tianxia worldview that allowed for peripheries to become the center as long as they could demonstrate their cultural and moral superiority in promoting social harmony. Chiang Kai-shek responded to Mao Zedong's series of campaigns that began with the Great Leap Forward in 1958 followed by the Great Proletarian Cultural Revolution in 1966. He launched the much less noticed Chinese Cultural Renaissance Movement from Taiwan to "bring order out of chaos" (*bo luan fan zheng*); the CCP's ultimate downfall was deemed inevitable because it destroyed Chinese culture. Given that scholars of the KMT-backed "ban-dit studies" were epistemologically illiterate in engaging English-language works on Chinese foreign policy and determined to represent China cultur-ally, they may have been "the most conscious China-centrists ever" (Shih and Chang 2011: 290).

This "(Communist) China threat" had a new twist after the pro-independence turn in Taiwan during the administrations of Lee Teng-hui

(1988–2000) and Chen Shui-bian (2000–2008). The PRC was not simply seen as a civil war (i.e., internal) enemy; it gradually emerged as a Chinese "other" against which a democratizing Taiwan struggled for its independent statehood.[9] Unlike the "bandit studies" generation, whose mission was to sustain Taiwan as the *best* part of China to support the ROC's pretense of representing the whole China, contemporary Taiwanese political scientists are increasingly evaluating China in light of its (alleged) differences with Taiwan by employing Euro-centric theories and methodologies. This tendency is to the extent that Taiwanese scholars improvise resemblance to their Western counterparts so as not to be reduced (in the eyes of the Western academic) to being a pre-modern, non-universal, and non-rational actor. Speaking the same language is similar to becoming an equal colleague in the English-speaking academic community (Shih 2007: 218).

The virtual absence of non-Western IR theory in Taiwan indicates as much of Western IR theory's hegemonic status as the local scholarship's choice to appropriate its assumed universalism for achieving different purposes (Chen 2011: 12). The total acceptance of American/Western IR theory reflects a self-empowering improvisation through which the Taiwanese resemblance to the US/West, allowing some of the Taiwanese scholars (and the emerging Taiwanese state) to look at China from a separate, universalist, and superior position. Offspring of the "bandit studies" generation are under the pressure brought by the pro-independence turn in Taiwanese politics. Their complete adoption/mastering of American/Western theories and methods, such as strictly anonymous review procedures, can shield them and their research on China's foreign policy from the charge of being politically incorrect (Shih & Chang 2011: 292–293). The obsession with Western theories and the embedded Euro-centric epistemology exhibited by Taiwanese IR scholarship ironically reveals that defining China is the common (and ultimate) purpose of theorization.

Given that Taiwanese relational security has depended heavily on American theories, values, and "extended deterrence," the recent development of Chinese new IR thinking becomes an unexpected source of the "China threat" because it possesses the potential to deconstruct Taiwan's relations with the US. If a "Chinese School" emerged as a feasible alternative to mainstream American IR theories, which would require recognition that human ideas and experiences are ontologically equal regardless of their national or civilizational background, then the strategy of Taiwanese scholars to appropriate the latter's alleged scientific universalism would be questioned as an identity practice to improvise Taiwan's abortion of resemblance to political China. If Chinese nascent IR thinking remains a "derivative discourse" of Western modernist social science that leaves the logic of colonial modernity intact (Chatterjee 1986), it will challenge a popular imagery held by Taiwanese IR scholarship regarding China's un-Americanness, thus blurring the assumed difference between IR studies in Taiwan and China. As shown in the previous section, when Taiwanese academics reach the conclusion that Beijing's promotion of "harmonious world" was a sophisticated realist-cum-constructivist exercise of soft power and the development of neo-liberalism in Chinese IR community has been beyond the stage of mere theory-copying (Chao & Hsu 2009), the aforementioned appropriation strategy backfires because these academics admit that their mainland counterpart have also mastered American theory and diplomacy.

How to cope with China? Beyond balancing and bandwagoning

In their study on the state of the field in Taiwan, Chiu and Chang (2012) lament that IR theory-informed research on Chinese foreign policy remains in its infancy; that is, compared with "the rising quality and quantity of IR studies in Mainland China, Taiwanese scholars will face a serious challenge if they cannot take advantage of their existing Western academic training combined with their grasp of Chinese history". Chiu and Chang mention that feasible IR theorizing requires researchers to consider Chinese characteristics and empathize with China. However, Chiu (2011: 11) caution that it would be too "limited and narrow" to use Chinese terminology for studying Chinese foreign policy without "making comparative reference to Western IR theory". This remark captures the general tendency of Taiwan's IR scholarship toward Chinese IR categorized by a mixture of exclusion and mingling. This section illustrates that such ambivalence is discernible in Taiwan's broad strategic behavior toward the PRC, behavior that has no proper expressions in Western IR jargon, such as balancing or bandwagoning.

In the face of China's military build-up, Taiwan's US arms procurement does not fit well into the classical category of balancing. However, the tendency for Taiwanese officials and strategists to be more interested in the symbolism of such procurement than in the actual fighting capability those weapons and equipment purchases could add to Taiwan's military is not new even to American security analysts. A 1999 RAND report mentioned that President Lee regard US weapons "more as symbols of reassurance and resolve than as key components of a larger force structure designed to attain genuine warfighting objectives" (Swaine 1999). Specifically, purchasing US weapons has been essential in establishing and maintaining Taiwan's imagined resemblance to the strong in terms of identity and interest, providing Taiwan with a certain confidence to be independent vis-à-vis China.[10] The imagined resemblance does not require a substantial military alliance with Washington, an enhanced inter-operability with the US armed forces, or even weapons and platforms on active service in the US's own arsenal. Taipei's decision to procure 150 outdated F-16 A/B fighters offered by the Bush administration in 1992 is a case in point. The aircraft were not the advanced C/D version used by the US Air Force and were not even equipped with some of the originally designed systems for firing and control upon delivery, yet politicians and the general public in Taiwan were highly satisfied with the deal. The KMT government's first (semi-)official talks with Beijing since the end of the Chinese Civil War in 1993 became acceptable to Taiwan in part because of the morale-boosting F-16 sale.

The US arms sales acquired more salience in the formation of Taiwanese identity after 2000. To acquire a massive arms package approved by Washington in 2001, the pro-independence DPP government adopted a special budgetary program (under the rubric of "Three Major Military Procurement Projects") in June 2004. Despite the failure to push the special budget bill in the Legislative Yuan, the DPP government's campaign rhetoric for the budget was effective in the (re)production of a peace-loving, pro-US Taiwanese identity that is threatened by the warlike Chinese given that the further deterioration of the cross-strait military balance would make PRC aggression highly likely. (Chen 2009) Since 2004, the Chen administration has been advocating the importance of coping with the mounting "China threat" by passing the special defense bill. However, Taipei allowed its annual defense budget as a percentage of GDP to shrink every year, from 3.8 percent in 1994 to 2.1 percent in 2006 until 2007. The relational security is entirely discursive.

The greatest significance of the US arms sales to Taiwan is not the utility of the particular weapons systems in terms of addressing the unfavorable military balance across the Taiwan Strait; it is the way in which the arms sales themselves confirm that Taiwan belongs to a community of which China is not a part. Taipei's irrational behavior of non- or under-balancing becomes intelligible when we recognize that staying as a security partner of the US has satisfied Taiwan's relational security need. Whether and how far Washington is a credible guarantor against the "China threat" is a separate and secondary issue.

Taipei's lack of a hard balancing behavior under the incumbent Ma administration is rather self-evident. The KMT traces its roots back to the mainland, and President Ma himself was born in Hong Kong. However, the simple "pro-China" explanation prompts more questions than it clarifies: Why is there no noticeable about-face in Taipei's security policy with respect to the PRC (e.g., bandwagoning) when the KMT is in the position to do so (i.e., controlling both the executive and legislative branches)? Why bother to reiterate calls for the US to sell Taiwan F-16 C/D jet fighters whenever Ma and his officials meet American guests and stress that Taipei's policies do not lean toward Beijing when receiving Japanese politicians and journalists?

An improving tie with Beijing means that Taipei has a great need to stabilize its long-term relationships with Washington and Tokyo. This stabilization is typically done through improvising abortion of resemblance of interest and identity between Taiwan and China in front of American and Japanese audience, real or imagined. Under two pro-independence administrations, Taiwan's emergence as a "subject in history" (i.e., no longer some other polity's peripheral territory or appendage) was promoted by resorting to the island's non-Chineseness (Lynch 2006: 150–180). The DPP government treated the processes of charting a developmental course autonomously and of de-Sinification as a synonym. In addition, Taiwan's colonial Japanese experiences and aboriginal inhabitants served as important reference points to confirm such non-Chineseness, even though Imperial Japan also imposed peripherality on the islanders, and Malayo-Polynesian aborigines are ethnic minorities in a Taiwan society dominated by Han Chinese. After regaining political power in 2008, the KMT government slowed down the DPP's de-Sinification programs and sought to revitalize the island's own Chineseness that bears no resemblance to Chineseness of the PRC.

In his 2011 New Year's Day message, "Building Up Taiwan, Invigorating Chinese Heritage," President Ma indicated that Taiwan's past development and the ROC's centennial history have been so intertwined that building foundations for another "century of prosperity" requires the consolidation of "our collective homeland."[11] Some of Ma and KMT supporters believe that the ROC on Taiwan represents a Chinese state that is more legitimate than the PRC. The sources of such legitimacy are traced back to the prior relations of the ROC as the "true" inheritor of the Xinhai Revolution of 1911, which overthrew the Qing Dynasty, and the ROC's sacrifice and victory in the War of Resistance against Japan (1937–1945). "Taiwan has never experienced anything like mainland China's Cultural Revolution" and preserves "the roots of the Chinese culture intact over the past six decades." Thus, Ma brands the ROC as "the standard-bearer at the leading edge of Chinese culture" that successfully combines the openness and innovation of a maritime culture and the Confucian values. This self-perceived "authentic" Chineseness helps explain why Ma was waging an undeclared little war that pitched its Taiwan Academy against Beijing's Confucius Institute around the world.[12] Since 2009, Ma held public ceremonies to worship the Yellow Emperor, a legendary figure seen as the initiator of Chinese civilization and the ancestor of all Han Chinese (Sina News China 2012), and Genghis Khan days before he handed the regime to the pro-independence incomer Tsai Ing-wen in 2016. Both are traditional rituals performed by self-proclaimed rightful rulers of China.

Another important source of legitimacy often invoked is the level of freedom and democracy enjoyed by ROC citizens. Ma describes Taiwan as "a paragon of democracy for the Chinese-speaking world" whose experience can "serve as a reference for the future development of mainland China."[13] In his 2011 National Day speech, titled "A Century of Struggle, a Democratic Taiwan," Ma maintained that "'The Republic of China' is more than the name of a nation; it also stands for a free and democratic way of life, and serves as a model for those living in other ethnic Chinese societies who yearn for freedom and democracy."[14] In this regard, Taiwan's "authentic" Chineseness mingles with its Americanness as a vanguard of the US-led anti-Communist camp during the Cold War and a "model" of US democracy promotion in the post-Cold War era (Cocke 2005: 2008). Taipei's Ministry of Foreign Affairs repeatedly stresses that the near worldwide visa exemptions or landing visa status granted to the

Taiwanese is a testament to the international respect Taiwan receives. The inclusion of Taiwan in the US Visa Waiver Program was boasted by the Ma administration as evidence that its foreign policy is "in the right direction" and that the Taiwan–US bilateral relationship is "at their best in 60 years" (Shan & Shih 2012).

This "at-their-best" assertion has acquired a mantra-like status in Taipei's foreign policy circle. Taipei's latest decision to sign a fishery agreement with Tokyo prohibiting Taiwanese fishing boats from entering the Japanese-controlled 12-nautical-mile belt of water surrounding the contested islands (in acquiescence to Japan's sovereignty over them despite statements to the opposite) can be interpreted as an act to balance its relationships with China and Japan and a show of resolving territorial disputes peacefully (in contrast to Beijing's more high-profile patrolling in the East China Sea) in front of the international audience (Shih 2013).

The difference of Taiwan with the PRC has been demonstrated through the discursive construction of a "better China," which, contrary to the prevailing "China threat theory" associated with the mainland, is capable of conducting cordial working relationships with the United States/West and Japan and is welcomed by the international community. Taiwan's foreign and security policy as an identity construction practice during Ma's term is not qualitatively different from that of the Chen administration, because the Taiwanese self remain defined against the PRC through the creation of a series of binaries (e.g., authentic Chinese culture/disrespect for tradition, model of democracy/authoritarian resilience, pro-US/anti-US, pro-Japan/anti-Japan, international acceptance, and respect/international suspicion and distrust). Can Taiwan ever rise above its "relational security dilemma" and start appreciating Chinese new IR thinking and practices in their own right?

Conclusion: the im/possibility of transcendence in subaltern Taiwan

On October 11, 2011, the day after the anniversary of the ROC and during the national celebration, President Ma Ying-jeou conferred the Order of Brilliant Star with Grand Cordon on former US Defense Secretary Donald H. Rumsfeld for his leadership in global anti-terrorism and the US support for arms sales to Taiwan during his term. Ma's peace-loving statements strongly contradicted the reputation of his awardee. Rather than for peacemaking, Rumsfeld is well known for his military acts, such as his deliberate misinformation for the purpose of launching a war in the Middle East, ruthless ignorance of the sacrifice of civilian lives, and subsequent instruction to use torture on prisoners of war. Nevertheless, Ma's recognition of Rumsfeld's achievements incurred neither criticism nor anxiety from the infamously critical opposition group. The irony of Taiwan's appeal to the value of peace, as exposed by the inappropriate conferring of an award to

Rumsfeld, is a harbinger of Taiwanese scholars' insensitivity toward new IR perspectives in the PRC.

This chapter examined the ways in which Chinese IR's emerging indigenous theories and concepts have been received by Taiwan's IR scholarship. Under the influence of various legacies combined, namely, Japanese colonial rule, Chinese Civil War, and the US-led Cold War, IR scholars are attentive but not sensitive to the development of new IR thinking on the other side of the Strait. Taiwanese academics tend to evaluate nascent Chinese IR thinking through American (and typically realist) lens rather than make use of their resemblance of Chinese language, history, and culture and join their mainland colleagues in building feasible alternatives to mainstream, Euro-centric theories for genuinely "global" IR studies. Despite their subsequent conclusion that speaking of indigenous IR theory-building in China or a plausible "Chinese School" remains premature, these Chinese alternatives unexpectedly pose an epistemological threat to Taiwanese IR scholarship. These alternatives can reveal that the universality associated with American/Western IR (through which Taiwan obtains a sense of superiority over China) is at best limited, or that Chinese scholars also have acquired a good command of American theories and methods (obscuring the assumed differences between Taiwan and China). Academics and practitioners of IR in Taiwan appear to be good disciples of American realism, concerning themselves with the BoP when facing China's rise. Akin to their ambivalent attitude toward Chinese new IR thinking, this chapter illustrated that Taipei's actual foreign policy behavior toward the PRC is not so much about balancing (or, for that matter, bandwagoning) in a classical sense but more about how to balance Taiwan's relationships with China and the US/Japan. The quest for relational security has rendered Taiwan's overall approach to China a mixture of mingling and exclusion, both politically and intellectually.

This situation leads us to an epistemological and political question as to whether Taiwanese IR scholarship should or could understand new ideas and practices in China's external relations given that they are unfiltered and unconstrained by any national (Chinese or Japanese) and civilizational (Confucian or Western) conditions. From the perspective of Western IR, contemplating such a possibility is fruitless because the nation-state remains the dominant unit of analysis in international politics. Postcolonial IR is not interested in the possibility of transcendence because it celebrates hybrid identities capable of switching between different situations. However, scholars in Chinese study communities, especially those located in China's immediate neighborhood, have confronted the same question well before the current "China fever" in IR discipline, and some creative suggestions have been offered.

Chapter 4 discussed the relevant case of Takeuchi Yoshimi, who proposed Asia as a method of constantly *becoming* a different entity (Takeuchi 2005), and Mizoguchi Yuzo, who maintained that studying China serves as a way for Japan to learn how to understand a different nation based on the latter's own historical subjectivity without taking any specific standpoint. The chapter also offered an analysis on Tsai Pei-huo, an intellectual and political activist in colonial Taiwan who resorted to "East Asia" for transcending colonial Japaneseness. Becoming an East Asian in Taiwan was an exercise of constant self-denial, being neither Chinese nor Japanese. Tsai focused on the relationship between Japan and China without opposing Europe/the West. Thus, his East Asia was non-threatening to the West. Becoming an East Asian only required one to retreat far beyond all national conditions.

This viewpoint does not imply that pursuing Tsai's East Asia as a method of constant self-denial would be easy. The fact that Tsai's writings have been largely ignored in contemporary Taiwan indicates that the academic and political climate is more concerned with improvising abortion of semblance between Taiwan and China than with the transcendence of their relationship. An East Asian has difficulty consciously exercising conceptual retreat in their daily life permeated by national politics. The temptation of power eventually led Tsai to serve in the KMT government as a minister-without-portfolio in the early 1950s, thus forfeiting his nascent East Asian identity. Nevertheless, Tsai's thinking and activities demonstrate that intellectual and political exits to Taiwan's "relational security dilemma" (i.e., choosing between China and the US/Japan) are intellectually possible. Rather than treating new IR thinking in China as an external process, Taiwanese IR scholarship may not permanently overlook the possibility of transcendence when engaging Chinese IR.

Notes

1 Surnames precede given names for all East Asian individuals in this chapter's main text.

2 Chen (2011: 1–23) demonstrates the necessity for any feasible "non-Western" IR theory to be also critical theory, but this line of argument is not pursued in the aforementioned writings.

3 The same problem can be found among leading figures of the would-be "Chinese School." Qin writes, "The American IRT [IR theory] tells Chinese scholars that theorizing about important thoughts is a sign of disciplinary maturity. If persistent efforts are made, it will be inevitable for Chinese IRT, with local experience and universal validity, to emerge and grow" (Qin 2011: 253). One must ask what modes of theorizing are preferred or considered valid, who decides which thoughts are important, and how much theorizing is enough to claim maturity.

4 Ibid. Chang makes a distinction between Tianxia as an ancient Chinese ideal and worldview embodied in the tribute system and as a contemporary concept that seeks to construct a new world system, but some do not hold such a distinction (for example, see Zheng 2013: 127–152). On the Tianxia system, see *inter alia* by Zhao (2011).

5 Chang's (2011: 28–42) article makes a more pertinent observation that the popularity of the Tianxia discourse has more to do with the desire of Chinese scholars to build *Chinoiserie* theories against Western ones than with any concerted instructions from the Chinese government.

6 The military balance across the Taiwan Strait has tilted in Beijing's favor since the mid-2000s, and this trend is unlikely to be reversed even with the continuation of US arms sales to Taiwan at their current level of quality and quantity. (Chen 2009: 69–119).

7 For example, see Yin (1973, 1984), and Kuo (1975).

8 Their story deserves detailed treatments in writings on IR knowledge production, such as in Tickner and Wæver's article (2009).

9 Shih (2007: 699–716) argues that before the island's democratization and the rise of independence movement, Taiwan had already discursively emerged as a separate entity outside of China when the KMT sought to co-opt the American post-Vietnam War Newly Industrialized Countries' discourse that assigned Taiwan a new identity as a development model for China.

10 For example, many Taiwanese involved in the February 28th, 1947 uprising against the KMT's misrule were wearing old Japanese military uniforms and believed that Chinese soldiers would not dare fire at them (Lai, Myers & Wou 1991).

11 The text of Ma's speech "Building Up Taiwan, Invigorating Chinese Heritage" is available at www.president.gov.tw.

12 Introduction about the Taiwan Academy can be found at http://taiwanacademy.tw.

13 Ma, "Building Up Taiwan, Invigorating Chinese Heritage." For critical IR scholarship, describing Taiwan as having an image (not an identity) of being a democracy is highly accurate. See Shih (2007).

14 The text of Ma's speech "A Century of Struggle, a Democratic Taiwan" is available at www.president.gov.tw.

12 A plausible Western theory

This chapter deals with two contradicting messages regarding the obstacles of the BoR to transcend civilizational and national divides. One major obstacle to overcome before BoR can contribute to the evolution of IRT points to the Orientalist tendency in contemporary social sciences to consider non-Western theories as scientifically irrelevant, given that non-Western intellectual traditions are weak in offering a universally applicable methodology. However, Orientalist mentality does not need to exclude non-Western theories. Equally discriminatory attitudes are found toward Western scholarship in the non-Western world, but such mentality does not affect non-Western scholars' learning of Western social sciences and theories, nor does learning from the West always dissolve the discriminatory attitude in the non-Western world even for those who appreciate learning from the West.

Another obstacle is the mere unfamiliarity of Western social scientists with non-Western theories, making them incapable of explaining their own world comprehensively and deeply. Such lack of paradigmatic access to comparative knowledge elsewhere hinders a balanced explanation of the phenomena that Western social sciences set out to explain. Analyzing and explaining are the two major tasks of Western social science. Thus, anyone who criticizes Western Orientalism and the resulting distortion of non-Western phenomena must present non-Western theories in ways that are functional to the overall enhancement of analytical and explanatory capacity. Criticism would be redundant for non-Western theorists who are determined to maintain a binary scope of knowledge equipped with its own distinctive (or absent) ontology and epistemology. Nevertheless, the Western world for centennials received and appropriated non-Western theories just as the non-Western world did with the Western theories, albeit more frequently in the most recent century.

Our book attempts to cope with the second obstacle, which assumes that BoR is an international theory that contributes to the analysis and explanation of IR and foreign policy-making anywhere. Thus, we present BoR as a non-Western theory that comes from a distinctive cultural, philosophical, and historical trajectory and a Western theory in accordance with the social science discourse. This endeavor is a translation of Confucian intellectual legacy into contemporary social science. We understand that no translation is perfect or politically innocent. Our purpose of translation constrains our work. That said, our main purpose is to improve IR's explanatory capacity in those aspects where social scientists can benefit from the studies of relationality, bilateralism, and historiography informed by cycles. Chapter 12 draws lessons from previous attempts at appropriating non-Western theories. Such sorting alludes to how BoR may be received in the Anglophone world and inspires the pursuit of global IR.

The quest for global IR is not complete until it simultaneously tracks the so-called Worlding of the "provincialized" West. We consider the appropriation of non-Western theories by the West an important subject to gather the ways in which Chinese theories are translated, interpreted, and applied in the Anglophone world. We identify four plausible ways in which theory travels from the non-West to the West: (1) unrelated or outdated conventions, (2) an exotic but useful resource in a specific context, (3) a culturally specific access to universal knowledge, and (4) an independent source of universal knowledge. We use Sun Tzu's *The Art of War* and the notion of Tianxia as our examples. We suspect that most readers in the West tend to cross these different routes to varying degrees. This critical examination of the reception of Chinese theories enables us to see that Western social sciences attain, or fail to attain, from Chinese theories an inspiration to reproduce self/other identities, although not always successfully. Orientalism may be registered in the exchanges. Nevertheless, paradigmatic ignorance characterized by usual parochialism, rather than Orientalism, is the obstacle to the appreciation of relationality. Paradigmatic ignorance is epistemologically remediable.

IR as a post/Western site

Global IR seeks to obscure and yet connect the distinctive imaginations of the West and the non-West. Thus, our discussion contributes to global IR by equalizing the West and the non-West epistemologically. The typical post-Western method is to World the subaltern non-Western sites and indirectly provincialize the West. We hope to reversely show the Worlding practices of the West in its encounter and appropriation of non-Western resources. By treating the West as another non-Western site, one deconstructs Euro-centrism and Orientalism not by denying their discursive imperialism or conducive intervention in historical expansion of the West but by demonstrating how different the Orientalist can be in each different Western geo-cultural way. Orientalism without a fixed form suggests that cultural ignorance does not immediately determine the intellectual capacity to learn or exclude. This is the Western counterpart of what Chapter 7 revealed to be the Chinese attitudes toward the arriving imperialism, namely, civilizational versus cultural approaches. The following discussion addresses the significance of re-Worlding the West to enrich the appeal of global IR.

Tickner (2013: 628) noted that the reasons for "IR's resilience as a (neo) imperial field have yet to be examined systematically and empirically." This book joins a critical line of IR scholarship aiming to decolonize the discipline. Jones (2006: 7–9) suggested that IR can be decolonized by exploring the political, ontological, and historical foundations of the discipline, critically examining how it came to be configured as it is and what sorts of power relations are at play in the evolution of the discipline.

We critically examine the ways in which the IR thinking in China traveled to the West. We can gain a deeper understanding of how the West acquires an intellectual perspective or resource and where the lacunas are. We can judge whether appropriations and lacunas are products of Orientalism or of sheer paradigmatic ignorance. Paradigmatic ignorance implies a responsibility in the non-Western world, whose academics fail to provide enough materials to juxtapose, provincialize, or nullify the generalization based upon Western empirical findings. If Western IR cannot be given the chance to fathom the cultural significance of the notion of Tianxia, for example, how can it proceed with self-criticism without misreading relational ontology by the Tianxia worldview into an ostensible universalization of BoP?

One particular mode of debate on gender bias in the history of Chinese literature is illuminative and noteworthy. Kang-I Sun (1997) disputed the widespread impression that gender bias plagued the Western acknowledgment of female poets in the Ming and Qing dynasties. She showed how male and female poets during the two dynasties were mutually supportive. Sun did not deny that the society was generally patriarchal, though a boom of female poets was discovered during those few hundred years. She even found that poets used to write in the voice of the opposite gender, implying a style that by no means intimated gender. However, such female poets and their works are not known to the West. Thus, Chinese students of Chinese literature in Western academia resort to postcolonialism and feminism in their critical review of their Western colleagues for the latter's impression of gender suppression during the two dynasties. Sun believed that Chinese students are responsible for making the ready sources in Chinese available to their Western colleagues. She extended her argument to a parallel debate regarding Western scholarship on the Chinese literature that arguably commits Orientalism, which neglects the relevance of Chinese characters to the structure of beauty. Sun believed that this lack of sensitivity to characters is not due to Orientalism but rather to sheer paradigmatic ignorance. Therefore, Chinese scholars interested in explaining beauty should incorporate the literary features of characters into the structure of analysis rather than advocating irreconcilability.

Thus, Sun believed that reproaching Orientalism or postcolonialism is not needed despite the widespread Orientalist attitudes in the profession. Once enough materials exist in English, even Orientalists understand their limitation and search for a new methodology to accommodate what the current methodology fails to cope with. Thus, we tend to think that identifying the routes of non-Western civilizational resources that enter Western sites is important to examine and reconstruct the Worlding strategy of the West. Tracking the Worlding of the West prompts a process of re-Worlding to allow the West to become more tolerant culturally and more comprehensive scientifically by designating four routes in accordance with "how useful" they appear to different agendas and "how universal" they are. Four routes inducted from the reading of the literature embody four Worlding strategies:

1   Denial (neither universal in fulfilling functions nor useful to out-groups, for example, the West) that *The Art of War* or Tianxia should not make an agenda.
2   Exotic (useful to out-groups under specific conditions but not universal in fulfilling all functions) that *The Art of War* or Tianxia could be peculiarly heuristic or alarming.
3   Collusion (not useful to out-groups but universal in fulfilling functions) that *The Art of War* or Tianxia could reach similar knowledge from an unintelligible perspective.
4   Absorption (universal in fulfilling functions and useful to out-groups) that *The Art of War* or Tianxia independently contributes to eternal knowledge (Table 12.1).

These four plausible routes, by which *non-Western theory* may have traveled in the Anglo-American world, runs the risk of being accused of Orientalism to different degrees. Nevertheless, the four routes that are well-informed by Chinese traditions can contribute to Western scientific thinking to determine where and how a Chinese tradition is functional to the explanation of behavior. Among others, universalism is perhaps the least Eurocentric, and yet, we do not argue that universalism is ethically better than a culturalist approach as presented in other routs. The aspects of Chinese relationality could be peculiar and unique. The potential of a useful exchange with and a contribution to Western theorization is clear wherever solid non-Western scholarship participates in translating non-Western traditions to establish applicable and accessible structures of explanation to all. Orientalism and wild appropriations are inevitable wherever readers are preoccupied with their own agendas and their own paradigmatic ignorance. In what follows,

Table 12.1 Routes for the West to Appropriate the Non-West

Function/knowledge	Out-groups (the West) Useful	Not Useful
Universal	Absorption	Collusion
Not Universal	Exotic Culture	Denial

this chapter will explore two examples respectively: (1) the reception of *The Art of War,* and (2) the appropriation of Tianxia in the Anglosphere.

Translation of *The Art of War* in the West

The Art of War is perhaps one of the very few non-Western strategic texts that has been widely translated and well known to the Western world.[1] The book was brought to the Western world in the 1700s, when it was translated into French. Rumor has it that Napoleon Bonaparte was the first leader to study and implement Sun Tzu's teachings in Europe. Together with Carl von Clausewitz' *On War* and Antoine-Henri de Jomini's *Art of War,* the book is said to be among the most important classics in the field of Strategic Studies. The book is also widely referred to by lawyers, businessmen, and sports coaches to get the upper hand in cases, negotiations, and games.[2]

It is however noted that the serious study and research on non-western strategic thinking are hugely underdeveloped compared with the schools of thought embedded in European traditions. For instance, in his book *Strategic Thinking,* prominent British strategic scholar Philip Windsor (2002) traces the origins of strategic thinking in medieval and modern Europe. He makes no reference to any non-Western strategic thought. Two possible explanations for the absence of non-Western strategic thought can be identified. The first explanation is closely related to the familiar self–other dichotomy and is concerned about the self-identity of the West. Chris Goto-Jones, in his study on non-European philosophy, asks why non-Western philosophy is considered futile. He views the history of philosophy as part of Euro-Americans' search for their cultural identity (Goto-Jones 2005b: 38). The second reason is the methodical caution against anachronism. Texts can be used anachronistically in two ways. The first one is prochronism, which refers to cases where one analyzes historical text such as *The Art of War* with relatively new concepts such as "strategy" and "tactics" that did not exist at that time. The second one of anachronism is called parachronism, which refers to a situation wherein one utilizes classical concepts and theories to analyze the current warfare. It is wrong because there is an error in dating, and the text is outdated and obsolete (Drop 2012). Those works that disregard any of non-Western strategic thought belong to the first route, the denial.

Today, *The Art of War* has many different translations in the Anglosphere (Drop 2012). In 1910, the British Sinologist Lionel Giles produced the first English translation of *The Art of War.* Thirty-four years later, the second translation was published by Arthur Sadler (1944), a Japanologist from Australia. In 1963, Samuel B. Griffith, who served in the US Marine Corps during the Pacific War and retired from service in 1956, published the third main translation in the Anglo-American world, which was reprinted over the past decades. In the 1980s, another important translation by Thomas Cleary (1988) appeared. Since the 1990s, another two important translations were produced by Sinologists, Roger Ames (1993) and John M. Minford (2002). The majority of these translations see *The Art of War* as a useful source.

For instance, the first translation by Giles is dedicated to his brother, Captain Valentine Giles, a professional soldier. Giles states that "a work 2400 years old may yet contain lessons worth consideration by the soldier of today ..." (Giles transl. 1910/1999: ii). Evidently, Giles sees *The Art of War* as useful resource, which may represent a universally valuable knowledge of war, revealing the forth route mentioned above – the absorption. From this perspective, Chinese strategic thinking does not only represent a typically Chinese view of war and peace; instead, its lessons and relevance are universal. We could be losing an opportunity to enhance our understanding of the warfare if we disregard non-Western strategic ideas. The more we learn about the ideas hidden in those multiple locations, the closer we might come to understanding of the nature of the warfare. To a certain degree, Sun Tzu's strategic thought is even more relevant ever today when compared to Clausewitz or Jomini, largely as a result of the advancements in the nature of warfare in the last half century. The Giles version of the text for instance is about 60 pages, whereas the English translation of Clausewitz's *On War* is roughly ten times longer. Meanwhile, Sun Tzu's thinking is much broader in its interpretation of the concept of war, preferring diplomacy or other non-military means to achieve the will of the state, and relying on force only as a last resort. The brevity and breadth of Sun Tzu's text has enabled it to retain its influence over military strategy, regardless of advancements in technology and the nature of international relations.

In a similar manner, Sadler's translation is also inspired by the Pacific War when Australia was fighting against the Japanese (Drop 2012), whose strategic thinking, according to Sadler, was hugely influenced by Classical Chinese military culture. As expressed by Sadler, "The writings of these strategists [Chinese military classics] have not only been regarded as authoritative by their own countrymen, but have also been carefully studied and followed by the Japanese experts ever since medieval times, and are much quoted in their writing" (Sadler 1944/2009). This was demonstrated during the Russo-Japanese War, in which the admiral of the Japanese fleet, Togo Heihachiro, defeated the Russian Navy, supposedly largely through the teachings of Sun Tzu's strategic thinking. *The Art of War* is useful because it can facilitate the Western military strategists to understand what and how their enemies think in order to confront them. Sadler evidently sees *The Art of War* as a useful source, but, unlike Giles, he deems it culturally-bounded, not universal. That is to say, he approaches it via the second route elaborated in the previous section – a useful if exotic and culturally-bound source.

Most translations by Sinologists belong to the second route that proposes various schools of "Eastern wisdom." Cleary interprets the text of Sun Tzu as defensive Taoist in character (Johnston 1999, 4). He suggests that *The Art of War* is "permeated with the philosophical and political thought of the *Tao-te Ching*" (Cleary 2000: 20), the most important classical work of Daoism (Taoism). Moreover, for Cleary the Classical Chinese language has some special peculiarities, and he states that he would have been therefore "able to generate at least three possible translations" of this "Oriental classic" (Clearly 2000: 35; also in Drop 2012). This suggests that Cleary believes that one can only understand *The Art of War* by being familiar with the Daoist classics and the multiple layers of Classical Chinese.

Similarly, Ames suggests that we need to understand Sun Tzu on his own (cultural) terms. Ames sees *The Art of War* as a philosophical text.[3] Ames notices that "military philosophy was a common topic in many of the works on political philosophy in ancient China and thus should be seen as part of the process of developing a distinctive Chinese philosophy, not as a separate field of military thought" (Johnston 1999: 5). Ames' argument is succinctly summarized by Johnston,

> [M]ilitary action provides a metaphor for all other types of human behavior, and that in Chinese tradition military action was 'applied philosophy'. His basic argument is that in both civil and military action the consummate actor is one whose character tries to achieve order through harmonizing himself with changing circumstances. In contrast to Western assumptions that there are two worlds – a perfect, predestined, independent world that will be created through purposeful action, a teleology – ancient Chinese philosophy assumed that order already existed in things, and was not imposed on things. The Dao was not a teleology, but a recognition of the completeness of existing reality. Harmony arose from 'personal cultivation and refinement' whether in the civil or military arenas. (Johnston 1999: 5-6)

In such way, there are "the differences between Chinese and Western philosophical traditions" (Johnston 1999: 5). Ames is accordingly interested in the cultural presuppositions of the text.

Nevertheless, it is noted that the juxtaposition of the Eastern and Western tradition does not necessarily suggest that Sun Tzu's thoughts only represent a typical Chinese form of warfare and life. Rather, its lessons can be universal. Minford believes that *The Art of War* has universal value, or in Minford's own words: "it lends itself to infinite applications" (Minford 2002: xi). Minford says in an interview

> [The] whole manner of Sun Tzu's book *The Art of War* is that of a handbook or manual for life ... Among other subjects treated, The Art of War deals in a very intuitive and general (almost abstract) way with the workings of natural, human and interpersonal dynamics ... In this respect it has great interest and value for *all people and all ages*. (Mindfod interview)

Minford echoes Griffith's view on Sun Tzu, whose translation was intended to bring the lessons that Sun Tzu teaches to the attention of Western audiences. Griffith's work (1963) can be divided into three major parts: firstly, an introduction, which contains discussions regarding the origin of the text and its author, elaboration on the warring states period and *The Art of War*'s relation to this period, Sun Tzu's view on warfare and his subsequent influence on Mao Zedong; then, there is the actual translation of the thirteen chapters, containing all of Sun Tzu's maxims on warfare; lastly, Griffith adds four appendices that contain remarks, respectively, on Wu Ch'i (about 440 B.C—n.a.) (an ancient Chinese commander who is often associated with Sun Tzu), Sun Tzu's influence on Japanese military thought, *The Art of War*'s reception in the West, and short biographies of the ancient Chinese commentators who were cited in the thirteen chapters. Griffith too points out the timeless relevance of Sun Tzu's work. In a sense, Griffith's aim becomes apparent from three things: firstly, the foreword written by the famous British strategist, Sir Captain Basil Liddell Hart (1895–1970), who criticizes Western negligence towards the valuable lessons of Sun Tzu; secondly, Griffith's various comparisons between successful applications of Sun Tzu's theories by modern armies in Asia and Allied command in WWII, which failed to take note of this; and thirdly, Griffith's description of various failed attempts to properly translate and introduce *The Art of War* in the West.

On the one hand, Griffith apparently sees *The Art of War* as representative of a typical East Asian form of strategy. He addresses the age of the work, which has had a profound influence on the strategic thought of Mao Zedong as well as the military doctrine of the Chinese army, and subsequently inspired the revolutionary guerrilla war movements in North Vietnam and elsewhere in the Third World.[4] Griffith considers many of Mao's writings and tactics to be inspired by *The Art of War*, since many of the People Liberation Army's (PLA) tactics in their fight against the KMT and the Japanese follow Sun Tzu's maxims, and multiple remarks in Mao's writing appear to paraphrase Sun Tzu. Griffith's translation also briefly focuses on the Korean War, where the PLA managed to gain initial success by applying Sun Tzu's theories; this reference, in combination with his account of the battle between the Chinese communists and nationalists reflect his belief in the applicability of Sun Tzu to modern warfare. Moreover, his remarks on the work's influence on military thought in East Asia also contain a description of how Sun Tzu's theories guided military figures throughout Japanese history (Griffith 1963: 169-177). The second appendix elaborates on the Sun Tzu's impact in Japan, which dates back well before 760 AD. Griffith claims that *The Art of War* directly influenced the strategic thought of various famous Japanese generals, including Minamoto Yoshitune (1159–1189) and Tokugawa Ieyasu (1543–1616) (ibid.: 170, 173). Griffith uses the Japanese campaigns in Malaya and Northern China during the Second World War as examples of Japanese tactics inspired by Sun Tzu's maxims. He also uses these examples to criticize Western military commanders for not having taken note of this strategic doctrine sooner. He explains that it was only after Allied command started to apply unconventional tactics that they were able to effectively fight off the Japanese army (ibid.: 177-178).

On the other hand, Griffith also maintains that this Chinese type of strategic thinking can be applied universally. The second appendix of his translation, on the Western reception of Sun Tzu's work, continues to criticize Western negligence towards the military value of *The Art of War*. Griffith lists a number of largely unsuccessful attempts made at translating and introducing Sun Tzu by various Western scholars, once again criticizing the disregard of Western audiences towards the book. According to Johnston, Griffith "saw his text as a tool for influencing senior US military and political leaders about how to deal with revolutionary warfare in the Third World" (Johnston 1999: 3). In order to achieve his main objective – proving the timeless and universal value of Sun Tzu's maxims – Griffith shows the myriad of occasions throughout time where Sun Tzu's ideas on strategy formed an essential part of creating winning conditions (Wu Ch'i, Sun Pin, Mao, the Japanese army, etc.) both on and off the battlefield. Consequently, Griffith's account of *The Art of War* allows Sun Tzu's holistic understanding of strategy, applicable to any conflict scenario, to come to its full right. Griffith aptly displays how Sun Tzu's theories on the importance of terrain, morale, maneuvering, and knowledge of the circumstances were decisive in both ancient and modern conflicts, in some cases even allowing those at the brick of defeat to turn the tide (as was the case for Mao). The main strength of this particular work on Sun Tzu lies in its ability to effectively use historical examples to prove the timelessness of methodical strategic thought as presented by Sun Tzu. It proved that proper strategic method, even if conceived 2500 years ago, still holds merit today and most likely in the future too.

Griffith's goal is also reflected in Basil Liddell Hart's foreword. Hart is the one who really put *The Art of War* firmly on the intellectual map of Anglo-American strategic and military studies (Drop 2012). Obviously, Hart regards *The Art of War* as a timeless and universal resource. From his perspective, *The Art of War* bolsters his own critique of a certain type of Western strategic thinking. As Johnston observes,

> Hart used Sun [Tzu] to justify his critique of Clausewitz for his over-emphasis on the so-called 'direct' approach, defined as the massive application of military power at the enemy's 'center of gravity'. Liddell Hart blamed Clausewitizian thinking for the disastrous violence of the First World War. (Johnston 1999: 3)

John Boyd (1927-1997) is another strategic theorist in the Anglosphere whose thinking is shaped by Sun Tzu. Boyd, the inventor of the so-called "OODA" loop model, which sees conflict as time-competitive observation-orientated decision-action cycles (Lind 1985: 5–6, cited in Robert B. Polk 2010: 257), is regarded as one of the most important strategists of the twentieth century. One of his most important contributions is his emphasis on the dimension of time in conflict interaction, which was already highlighted by Sun Tzu 2000 years ago. Hence, as Osinga argues, Sun Tzu "must be considered the true conceptual, albeit ancient, father of Boyd's work" (Osinga 2007: 35). In sum, similar to Hart, Boyd also regards *The Art of War* as an access point to aspects of universal truth that are new to the West. In contrast to Hart, who uses Sun Tzu's strategic thinking to critique Clausewitz, Boyd adopts Sun Tzu's strategic thinking to develop his own theory. As such, both Hart and Boyd's appropriations of *The Art of War* span the second and forth routes to varying degrees. This suggests that, Orientalism aside, universal learning takes place regardless. This amalgamation, in a way, is analogous to Alastair Iain Johnston's way of thinking.

In his 1995 book *Cultural Realism*, Johnston attempts an extensive study of the grand strategy and strategic preferences of China. By studying the Ming dynasty and its strategic customs – a period where China witnessed virtually permanent conflict, Johnston's study firstly charts a group of didactic military handbooks – "Seven Military Classic", which includes *The Art of War*, a quintessential benchmark in Chinese thought on strategy and security canonized in the 11th century AD – in this scrupulous manner to determine whether a specific strategic preference can be found in the texts (Johnston 1995: 40). Johnston then turns his study to the actual practiced strategy of the Ming Dynasty, its military policy makers, and the empirical evidence of conflicts on the northern border with the Mongols. Johnston's work is associated with the "strategic culture" approach within Strategic Studies.

The term "strategic culture" was invented in the nineteen seventies during the cold war when the former Soviet Union was said to demonstrate a different nuclear strategy that had a tendency towards a more offensive use of force, a tendency deeply rooted in Russia's expansionist history and autocratic culture (Johnston 1995a: 32). Scholars of strategic culture oppose the assumption of IR theory that strategies of security by state actors can be explained through a framework in which the core behavior of state actors is ahistorical and non-cultural, with rational decisions guided by the overriding imperative of survival. They instead emphasize "the weight of historical experiences and historically-rooted strategic preferences" that "tends to constrain responses to changes in the 'objective' strategic environment, thus affecting strategic choices in unique ways" (ibid.: 34).

Johnston (1995) discerns three phenomena of Chinese strategic culture. First, a Chinese grand strategic culture exists, most probably in the form of a parabellum paradigm, paralleling the realpolitik we generally associate with classical European foreign policy. Second, this strategic culture is built upon a strong belief in ultimate flexibility (*quan bian*), resorting to defensive strategies when conditions are unfavorable while using offensive strategies if circumstances permit. Third, there is another Chinese strategic culture, the more renowned Confucian-Mencian paradigm, which serves as a symbolic strategic culture, reinforcing the authority and credibility of the military elite. Nevertheless, this does not mean that Chinese leaders automatically make different strategic choices than their Western counterparts. This is because certain elements of different strategic cultures can overlap; in our example this overlap is the *parabellum* paradigm. Johnston explains that the mix of paradigms in Chinese strategic thought will often lead to strategic outcomes similar to those a structural realist would predict. In other words, it is the same reality and the same realist approach lauded in the culturally specific narrative. Johnston therefore concludes that realism is a very persuasive and powerful theory, as it developed independently in both Europe and China (Johnston 1995: 242).

In a nutshell, Johnston's cultural realism proves the difference between the East and West while at the same time reconfirming the generality of Western thinking, including its assumption of the universality of the logic of strategy. The implication is clear: by rendering it unnecessary for the West to become familiar with the ways generalized strategic patterns have been accessed in the East. Johnston's study of ancient Chinese strategic thought can therefore be regarded as the basis for more cross-cultural analysis to determine whether other strategic cultures produce similar results. His approach therefore represents the third route since Chinese strategic teaching is not useful to the West, but it nonetheless attests to the existence of a general pattern of strategic behavior.

The appropriation of Tianxia

Thus, the reception in the English literature of the nascent popularity of Tianxia can be evaluated in the Chinese IR literature. We will show that how the Anglophone literature adopts the first, i.e. the obsolete, and the second, i.e. the culturalist/collusive route in accepting Tianxia. Tianxia became a focus of debate since the publication of Zhao Tingyang's book. Zhao (2006, 2009) promoted the idea of Tianxia as a philosophy of a world system that transcends the perspective of a nation state so that all must look at all, without excluding anyone. This mindset is pertinent to the practice of the BoR. Tianxia, which is literally all under-heaven, is a historically and culturally embedded expression of the belief that all are bound to relate. It has supported narratives of novels, movies, and soap operas throughout contemporary history in the 21st century. Chinese scholars have inconsistently acquired and appropriated the notion in answering the call for the Chinese School of IR.

Some studies have been willing to see Tianxia provide a plausible vehicle to a general pattern exercised everywhere with other paralleling intellectual discourses that enable their subscribers to adopt the same behavior pattern. (Wang 2017, Zhang 2015) However, these studies are written by predominantly Chinese authors in English. No such literature in English has considered Tianxia a universal frame to explain contemporary IR. The majority of the literature on Tianxia has focused on its potential as a resource for various sakes. An implied reference to habitus connects various interpretations of Tianxia—conceiving of it as a kind of revisionist ontology. These include its use by a rising China to shelf liberalism and a China that increasingly strives to co-opt its neighbors in compliance with the historical practice of Middle Kingdom. These positive and critical discussions portray Tianxia as a legitimating theme to undergird a hierarchical world order. Welcome or not, the use of the concept is a Chinese way of expanding/exporting to the rest of the world.

The most ardent critics of Tianxia, William Callahan, and a favoring reflectivist, Martin Jacques, have similarities and differences between them. The difference is basically evaluative. Callahan (2008, 2009) is anxious toward the destiny of Tianxia discursively being just another hegemonic construction that silences neighboring nations in Southeast Asia. Jacques (2009) is curious about the changes Tianxia could bring to rescue the country from the collapse of global governance. Accordingly, Tianxia represents a different kind of discursive empire or hegemony to justify China ruling at the top. For Callahan, though, Zhao would appear to be a grand strategist and matrix designer to dissolve the identities of different nations to preserve their relationality in Tianxia. This would give China great room to maneuver for the submission of others in the name of benefiting them. Thus, China would reign from above with discretion but without responsibility. In short, Tianxia either represents an exotic access to understanding a distinctively Chinese practice of hegemony or it colludes to reproduce exclusively for China the same hegemony elsewhere.

The similarity between Callahan and Jacques lies in the shared treatment of Tianxia, according to the exotic route, as a lens to be appropriated strategically to cope with China's order/interest. China appears as an owner of an initiative, an agency, and a different identity. Neither attends to the lack of substantive reference in the discourse on Tianxia to the principles that should re-order the current IR. The only clue found in Tianxia is the preference for some clear hierarchy in the social sense that either silences the representation of national difference or preserves peace between differing nations. Silence and peace are often two sides of one coin. Silence and peace indicate the epistemological collusion between Callahan and Jacques to exclude the aspect of cultural memory and the associated relational sensibilities.

Such lack of substantive principles of governance, which our theory of BoR explains, produces the image of a rising China to be primarily territorial expansion, as opposed to consolidation of value. Both authors recognized the Chinese's stress on temporality but treated temporality as a dispensable discursive resource than a cultural necessity. Without a sharable norm, China on the rise could only be conceived of as a territorial empire. The empire rules with its dominant capacity by either force or benevolence. Tianxia might lean toward benevolence. However, benevolence is unhelpful for the member nations to anticipate consequences. China would be perceived as a territorial empire that abides by improvised expediency. Under BoR, though, peace and harmony guaranteed by China are at best relational values that are tantamount to the deconstruction of neoliberal governmentality. Whoever abhors neo-liberalism may find relational values are gospels; and whoever accepts it, would dread Tianxia instead.

In Zhao's own version, Tianxia is in sharp contrast to the ontology composed of nation states, which would seemingly have no use of Tianxia. That is, Tianxia is not something the nation states use to attain goods and power. It is not a scheme to evaluate the world conditions so that the nation can develop a grand strategy to cope with it and even transform it, a standard to determine whether or not specific states are on the correct tracks to be rewarded or rectified, or a synchronizing procedure to reconcile differing identities and practices that cause conflict. Thus, nothing ontological would be relevant since all stay what they are internally. Neither is Tianxia a helpful epistemology that can assist in goal setting, rulemaking, or policy making. It is not useful for national leaders who oversee exclusively national interests. Tianxia merely provides the thin prior resemblance between all, in terms of all bound to relate, that necessitates all to improvise practical relationships. It parallels but not replaces neo-liberalism.

Zhao intends that Tianxia serves the world, which includes the West and all those actors that the ontology of nation state has temporarily trapped. Zhao believes that, in the ontology of Tianxia, the entirety of IR makes the unit of analysis, and no sub-system unit, such as the nation state, distracts the analysis from the systemic level. Thus, nation states each focus on their own roles in Tianxia rather than watching one another's internal conditions. The relationship between the part and the whole prevails over those between the parts. Nation states, including China, do not acquire their role identities independently from Tianxia. It is a system of all bound to relate and its constituting nations come into being simultaneously. Anarchy only emerges wherever imagined resemblance is aborted. Tianxia as resemblenace of Dao or Way is inside the roles of all nations.

Tianxia embraces a philosophy of relation, in which no nation affects other nations without reformulating the relations of the system. Therefore, no rules can survive any enforcement because the rule-followers are in themselves no longer the same. Any move taken by China to affect others has an immediate consequence on Tianxia. Given the extent that Tianxia is ontology, it owns China in the same degree it owns its neighbors. The ultimate rationale for any constituting nation of Tianxia is to preserve all the components to preserve the whole, and vice versa. With or without the knowledge of Tianxia, the West's paradigmatic ignorance of its own partiality cannot exclude the repercussion of its all-round interventionary governance from feeding back to the very existence of its own identities.

The Anglosphere may conceive of Tianxia differently and think of it as a strategic resource to change and silence the neighbors. This approach points to the rise of a Sino-empire equipped with a legitimizing intellectual resource. Zhao realizes that Tianxia is not for the subscribers of the nation state to comprehend. It still makes a good sense if Zhao intends that Tianxia serves more to restrain China, or any actor that rules, than the West. The implicit law is that order is genuine only where states are free from control. This echo's Adam Smith's "an invisible hand." Such a metaphor indicates that the Western nations may have already exercised Tianxia unknowingly. Nonetheless, the West can retrieve this knowledge by watching how China exercises its self-restraint to engage in altercasting toward the West. Eventually, the West will philosophically connect and appreciate the availability of a paralleling ontology of relation.

In the mainstream IR, Tianxia contrarily appears exotic and functional only to the public relations of a rising China to soothe and silence its weaker neighbors, if not useless at all in advancing IR theorization. Tianxia is credibly universal only when China, alongside its neighbors, acts systematically with self-restraint in accordance with the philosophy of Tianxia and exemplifies the inevitable and ubiquitous relational couplings for the rest of the world to appreciate their own relational necessities. After all, relation as a given ontology is not contingent on the realization of the nation state. China's long-term interests rest upon its responsibility to perform Tianxia so everyone else can see their relational roles with China and everyone else under Tianxia to ensure their long-term interests. At that stage, the West will be able to adopt the universalist route to explain more of its own IR than it can today.

BoR ready for Western re-appropriation

Studying the West as an ontologically provincial site requires the study of its Worlding strategy. Recording the Worlding strategy of a Western site is an indirect and strong method to provincialize it. An epistemologically Worlded site evolves through a wanted or unwanted encounter and the concomitant strategic choice. The re-Worlding of a site via the encounter of the external and a choice of approach is the same with all Western and non-Western sites. The West and the non-West contribute to the Worlding of each other by providing unfamiliar resources to the other (e.g., Tianxia or Westphalia). They enhance the Worlding of each other by re-appropriating the other to help achieve spreading, which explains the different versions of Orientalism in reading Sun Tzu or Tianxia.

The explanation on how the subaltern sites penetrate or fail to penetrate the West is no longer missing. Otherwise, the hiatus leaves the West in a discursively essentialized, centralized, and privileged site. Without the West being simultaneously re-Worlded, the post-Western quest is not more than an affirmative action program that reproduces the imagined West as a shared reference. To move beyond, the post-Western quest must tackle how the West, as an incoherent sum of sites, has appropriated different non-Western resources differently.

Epistemological equality can be achieved between Western and non-Western sites or between hegemonic and subaltern sites. The West must restore its multiplicity for the post-Western agenda to disclose its provinciality. Provincializing and Worlding become two sides of one coin once the Worlding of a Western site becomes a point of scholarly interest. No site is in itself global, yet all sites give and take via an encounter and a choice. To World an intellectual site such as China, which that first generated a genealogy of Tianxia, is to provincialize Tianxia at a different site so that Tianxia gains different meanings everywhere. Provincializing an intellectual site such as China is also Worlding a Western site, such as a provincial site, via an entirely different reinterpretation of Tianxia.

BoR is another example. Toward the end of this discussion, we provide the metaphor of chopsticks to illustrate how commonplace and widespread the appropriation of non-Western resources is. Consider the use of chopsticks as an art of eating (or a mechanism to relate, improvise, or resist). One could decide to make the use of chopsticks a universal art that can be taught to all for eating any food and yet it brings forth different sequences, sociability, and enjoyment. Chopsticks could be reversely conceived of as an outdated utensil to be extensively substituted and jettisoned. Between the two extremes, the third could be the exotic practice of learning chopsticks as exclusively for eating Asian food. Last, ethnic epistemology could also define chopsticks and other Western utensils as good for all foods but only proper for a specific ethnic population to use.

This book suggests that the study of IR requires cross-cultural communication. IR scholars in the Anglo-American world, while promoting their field of study in a way that does not seriously engage with alternative conceptions, risk widening misunderstanding and setting the stage for hostility, resulting in the deterioration of legitimacy of the field. Chinese scholars determined to look for alternatives entirely outside of social science epistemology risk nullifying their criticism of Western IR agenda as if two independent agendas were not supposed to be interactive after all. We hope this book connects Chinese, primarily Confucian, resources and Western IR for those who continue their dedication in explaining social science through the incorporation of bilateralism, historiography embedded in cyclical view, relational role, order as the state of nature, cultural memory, and post-hybridity. We also hope to help them understand non-Western, specifically Chinese, IR and those puzzles in Western IR that are currently either left unexplained or incorrectly explained.

BoR is a highly relevant approach to the study of Chinese IR where bilateral relation readily comes to mind. However, BoP must remain on duty to cope with actors with whom reciprocity appears to have broken down. Western IR will inevitably adapt once BoR begins to make sense to Western

IR through deep empathy with a Confucian order or its social science translation. It will appropriate BoR for its own practical use, analyze Chinese foreign policy in BoR terms, and understand Western IR differently in some cases and more comprehensively in others. Moreover, previously unnoticed and sporadic sensitivities toward the bilateral relations, the feelings for the other side, or even the occasional adoption of alternative epistemology and ontology can be detected in Western IR. This situation would release Western IR from the methodological rigidity in regarding elements outside the BoP frame as irrelevant, idiosyncratic, or wrong and save the ontology of Western IR in its entirety.

Notes

1 The book is an ancient Chinese text from the late 4th century BC. It is separated into thirteen chapters, each of which focusing on different aspects of waging war.
2 Sun Tzu and his advice on battle, is well known also in other disciplines, such as management sciences, where scholars have similarly cited the man and his work intensively, believing his military stratagem can be extensively applied anywhere else that engages in some kind of contest.
3 Ames' version used a version of *The Art of War* found in the *Yin Que Shan* manuscript and Mawangdui's script (Drop 2012).
4 Vietnamese leaders Ho Chi Minh and Vo Nguyen Giap studied the Art of War closely during the war of independence against the French.

In lieu of a conclusion—four caveats

Major IR theories tend to contrive binaries of self and other. They do so predominantly through adopting a statist ontology, which stresses the inevitability of actors to independently enhance interests each exclusively for their own benefit. Statism of this kind naturally leads to mutual estrangement and, hence, engenders the psychological state of mistrust, fear and aggression. Accordingly, it justifies social regression.

We, contrarily, recognize the general need of all to relate, which they do through various imagined resemblances between them. Therefore, we propose a relational therapy for the pathetic binaries of 'inside' and 'outside,' and 'self' and 'other'. We argue that such a relational therapy must be historical as well as cultural. This brings us to propose the method of comparative relational studies. This method incurs two different modes of relationality; (1) (the mode of) prior relationality and (2) (the mode of) improvised relationality. Prior relationality alludes, for example, to the characteristics of a normal 'state'. The existence of this concept of relational 'state' makes the evolution of multilateral regimes possible. The literature of the relational turn is keen on tracing this type of processes. Improvised relationality, then, seeks to stabilize mutual expectations between incongruent identities. It is most effective in coping with bilateral relationships that require nuanced and practiced care. Confucianism, for instance, preaches propriety and rituals to achieve ubiquitous bilateral stability. Both modes of relationality, however, similarly require self-restraint on all sides to attain relational security.

All actors necessarily engage in both types of relations, each in their own style. Tianxia and natural rights are examples of prior relations, and respectively inform the cultural memories of East Asia and Europe. Tianxia is a thin relation, which shuns institutions or norms beyond symbols and rituals to enable harmony between all. It requires improvisations of relationship in specific contexts, usually bilateral, to substantiate the sense of resemblance between actors. Such imagined resemblance obliges reciprocity that is essential to self-actualization. In contrast, the belief in natural rights qua liberalism is much thicker since it has already developed many long trajectories of norms and institutions. Thus, strangers can relate under these prior cultural circumstances.

For those not sharing prior resemblance or those in quest of specific relationships under a thin prior relation, improvisation is necessary. The most convenient improvised relation can be established through gift giving because gift giving, in the Confucian context, is a show of sacrifice to reproduce a 'greater-self' consciousness. Particularly sacrifices that answer a correctly perceived need of the other party symbolize resemblances of interests and identity between them.

To reiterate, the above logic, already intensively discussed in the book, is a way to concisely respond to the two most familiar challenges we have encountered in the process of BoR theory building. Namely, BoR is either challenged for being guilty of epistemological China-centrism, defeating the purpose of developing a general theory, or biased against China's multilateral sensibilities, which loom increasingly apparent in the process of China rising. The former challenge further incurs the question of the identity of the BoR theory and calls for engagement with post-Western IR, non-Western IR and global IR. The latter is related to an additional question of relationship being just another item of national interest or a kind of soft power calculus.

To begin, we see the irony that China-centrism--understanding the world through Chinese lenses—used to be a solution to Euro-centrism. This has been noticeable in the field of modern history, sociology and indigenous psychology. From the image of a rising China emerged the perception of a China threat and the delusion of permeating Chinese sharp power. Consequently, China-centrism became a bad thing. Through our development of the BoR theory, however, we echo the earlier call for a China-centric method to understand those who presumably behave on behalf of China. Still, BoR is not just about China. It is through the Chinese case that we discovered the significance of improvised resemblance as a general mechanism of both establishing and stabilizing relationships. Improvisation of resemblance in accordance with the conditions of the other side suggests that Chineseness is constituted by dynamic processes rather than by any stable contents. Methodological China-centrism therefore leads to a kind of Chineseness that is epistemologically undefinable and useless. This could be dreadful, though, to those who religiously believe in integrity, identity, and consistency. BoR suggests that all identities are post-identities that evolve and bifurcate through practices. Alternatively, BoR calls for a future agenda of post-Chineseness to indicate how all actors improvise their relationships with China as well as how China improvises its relationships with others. Consequently, rather than essentializing 'China' and 'Chineseness,' China-centrism as used by us by all means complicates the concepts.

Second, we have not argued that China owns no multilateral sensibilities at all. We have just argued that Tianxia is too thin as a prior relation to coach policy. This is because, as we have shown, the concept of Tianxia, if understood correctly, amounts to no more than a cosmological metaphor illustrating that all are bound to relate. Tianxia deliberately remains discursively thin so that nations do not have to intervene in one another's internal arrangements, institutionally or practically –i.e. they do not have to change/convert others. This ensures that actors remain resembling to one another in terms of their commitment to harmonizing relationships everywhere. In its own way, China observes rules of most multilateral regimes. However, China partakes in little prior resemblance (i.e. neoliberalism) through which Western nations jointly develop these regimes. Therefore, China's participation often appears half-hearted, practically always incomplete, and untrustworthy. In fact, though, observing rules for the time being can be a practice of improvised resemblance to the EU. We urge to use the degree of imagined prior resemblance between nations to explain the strength of passion for multilateralism. Lower degrees push nations to additionally resort to bilateral gift giving to make up for the embarrassing lack of feelings for the multilateral regimes.

The notion of relation that is embedded in the division of prior and improvised resemblance endorses the post-Western pursuit to highlight the constitution of BoR by non-apparent national interests as well as long-term calculus at the expense of the immediate gain. BoR studies show how multilateral rules can be appropriated in a bilateral setting, but this is not enough. In addition to its post-Western characteristics, BoR studies demonstrate how epistemologically parties of asymmetric relationships are equal due to the mutual constitution of their identities. Regardless of the level of power one possesses, nations are relational so that appropriations of relations are intersubjective. Therefore, BoR transcends binaries of East and West, multilateral and bilateral, and great and small nations. It is not only post-Western, but also post-post-Western since subaltern and hegemonic powers are mutually constituted to transcend nonnegotiable categories embedded in geo-cultural sitedness.

Finally, relational IR is far from soft power or interest calculation to the extent that relations constitute and govern all that belong to it. As a result, no actor is completely on its own. Any calculus necessarily and always incorporates other relational selves, positively as well as negatively, and knowingly as well as unknowingly. Under a relational circumstance, exertion of soft power reproduces a prior relational culture that usually triggers dialectical repercussions and often even backfires. Thus, soft power that assumes that China's core national interests are distinctive is incompatible with BoR (especially in Chapter 3) according to which the ultimate purpose of appearing to have core national interests is either to give them up at the right time as gift to the other party or insist on them to punish the other party for betraying relationships. The ultimate test of Chinese soft power is not about influencing the preference of the other party to the benefit of China, but about practically transcending binary and rendering China's soft power an obsolete subject.

References

Acharya, Amitav. 2007. State Sovereignty After 9/11: Disorganized Hypocrisy. *Political Studies* 55(2): 274–296.

Acharya, Amitav and Barry Buzan. 2009. *Non-Western International Relations Theory: Perspectives On and Beyond Asia*. London, UK: Routledge.

Adelman, Jonathan and Chih-yu Shih. 1993. *Symbolic War: The Chinese Use of Force, 1840–1980*. Taipei: Institution of International Relations.

Adler, Emanuel. 2008. The Spread of Security Communities: Communities of Practice, Self-Restraint, and NATO's Post-Cold War Transformation. *European Journal of International Relations* 14(2): 195–230.

Adler-Nissen, Rebecca. 2014. *Opting out of European Union: Diplomacy, Sovereignty and European Integration*. Cambridge, MA: Cambridge University Press.

Ames, Roger T. Transl. 1993. *Sun-Tzu: The Art of Warfare*. New York: Ballantine Books.

Ames, Roger T. 1985. The Common Ground of Self-cultivation in Classical Taoism and Confucianism. *Tsing-hua Journal of Chinese Studies* 17(1–2): 65–97.

Ames, Roger T. Transl. 1993. *Sun-Tzu: The Art of Warfare*. New York: Ballantine Books.

Amstrong et al., Harvey.1998. A Comparison of the Economic Performance of Different Micro-states, and between Micro-states and Larger Countries. *World Development* 26(4): 639–656.

Andrews, Nathan. 2012. Globalization, Global Governance, and Cosmopolitanism: A Critical Exploration of European Practice. *CEU Political Science Journal* 7(4): 411–433.

Angle, Stephen C. 2009. *Sagehood: The Contemporary Significance of Neo-Confucian Philosophy*. Oxford: OUP.

Archer, Margaret. S. 1996. *Culture and Agency: the Place of Culture in Social Theory*. Cambridge, MA: Cambridge University Press.

Arxer, S. L. 2008. Addressing Postmodern Concerns on the Border: Globalization, the Nation-state, Hybridity, and the Social Change. *Tamara Journal* 7: 179–199.

Assmann, Aleida. 2006. Memory, Indivdual and Collective. In E. Goodin and C. Tilly. Eds. *The Oxford Handbook of Contextual Political Analysis*. Oxford: OUP, 210–224.

Author n.a. 1969. Lin Biao on the Sino-Soviet Boundary Question: An Excerpt from Lin Biao's Political Report to the Ninth Congress of the Chinese Communist Party. *Studies in Comparative Communism* 2(3–4): 187–189.

Author n.a. 2011. 'China has serious difficulty with part of the resolution,' envoy says. *Xinhua*, 18 March. http: //news.xinhuanet.com/english2010/world/2011-03/18/c_13784748.htm accessed 29 June 2011.

Author n.a. 2011. Libya sanctions: China's new role at the UN. *The Christian Science Monitor*, 28 February. www.csmonitor.com/Commentary/the-monitors-view/2011/0228/Libya-sanctions-China-s-new-role-at-the-UN accessed 5 August 2011.

Author n.a. 2011. Waijiaobu fayanren Ma Chaoxu jiu Meiguo zhengfu xunbu dui tai jun shou jihua chanming zhongfang yanzheng lichang [MOFA Spokesman Ma Chaoxu Expounds the Serious Positions of China towards the U.S. Government's Announcement of Planned Arms Sales to Taiwan] September 22. http: //news.xinhuanet.com/world/2011-09/22/c_122069644.htm accessed 16 July 2013.

Author n.a. 2012. Three Years Later, Ma Ying-jeou Hosts the Ceremony of the Yellow Emperor Mausoleum Again. *Sina News* (China), April 3.

Author n.a. 2014. Wang Yi chanshi Zhongfang dui Yilake de 'San ge Zhichi'" [Wang Yi defines China's 'Three Supports' to Iraq], CRNTT, 23 February. http: //hk.crntt.com/doc/1030/3/7/7/103037709.html?coluid=202&kindid=0&docid=103037709&mdate=0223212707 accessed 10 June 2014.

Author n.a. year n.a. Xueer. In *Confucian Analects* [*Lun yu*].

Axelrod, Robert. 1984. *The Evolution of Cooperation*. New York: Basic Books.

Ayoob, Mohamm. 2002. Humanitarian Intervention and State Sovereignty. *The International Journal of Human Rights* 6(1): 81–102.

Bajoria, J. 2010. *The China-North Korea Relationship*. Council on Foreign Relations, October 7. www.cfr.org/china/china-north-korea-relationship/p11097 accessed 21 July 2013.

Baldacchino, Godfrey. 2012. Governmentality is All the Rage: The Strategy Games of Small Jurisdictions. *The Round Table* 101(3): 235–252.

Baldwin, David. 2004. Power and International Relations. In W. Carlsnaes, T. Risse, and B. A. Simmons. Eds. *Handbook of International Relations*. Thousand Oaks, CA: Sage, 273–297.

Barbalet, Jack M. 2014. Greater Self, Lesser Self: Dimensions of Self-Interest in Chinese Filial Piety. *Journal for the Theory of Social Behaviour* 44(2): 186–205.

Barbalet, Jack. 2001. *Emotion, Social Theory, and Social Structure: A Macrosociological Approach*. Cambridge, MA: Cambridge University Press.

Barr, Michael. 1999. Lee Kuan Yew: Race, Culture and Genes. *Journal of Contemporary Asia* 29(2): 145–166.

Bastiaan, Apeldoorn van and Naná de Graaff. 2012. Corporate Elite Networks and US Post-Cold War Grand Strategies from Clinton to Obama. *European Journal of International Relations* 18(2): 1–27.

Baumeister, Roy. 1997. *Evil: Inside Human Cruelty and Violence*. New York: W. H. Freeman & Co.

Bays, Daniel H. 1978. *China Enters the Twentieth Century: Chang Chih-tung and the Issues of a New Age, 1895–1909*. Ann Arbor, MI: University of Michigan Press.

Behr, Hartmut. 2014. *Politics of Difference: Epistemologies of Peace*. Oxon: Routledge.

Berling, Trine Villmsen. 2012. Bourdieu, International Relations, and European Security. *Theory and Society* 41: 451–478.

Bhabha, Homi. 1994. *The Location of Culture*. London, UK: Routledge.

Bilgin Pinar. 2012. Security in the Arab World and Turkey: Differently Different. In Arlene Tickner and David Blaney. Eds. *In Thinking International Relations Differently*. London, UK: Routledge, 27–47.

Billoud, Sébastien. 2011. *Think Through Confucian Modernity: A Study of Mou Zongsan's Moral Metahysics*. Leiden: Koninklijke Brill NV.

Böhmelt, Tobias. 2009. International Mediation and Social Networks: The Importance of Indirect Ties. *International Interactions* 35(3): 298–319.

Borchrt, Thomas. 2008. Worry for the Dai Nation: Sipsongpannā, Chinese Modernity, and the Problems of Buddhist Modernism. *The Journal of Asian Studies* 67(1): 107–142.

Bourdieu, Pierre. 1977. *Outline of a Theory of Practice*. Cambridge, MA: Cambridge University Press.

Bourdieu, Pierre and Loïc Wacquant. 1992. *An Invitation to Reflexive Sociology*. Cambridge: Polity Press.

Bourdieu, Pierre. 1977. *Outline of a Theory of Practice*. Cambridge: Cambridge University Press.

Brandsen, T., M. Boogers and P. Tops. 2006. Soft Governance, Hard Consequences: The Ambiguous Status of Unofficial Guidelines. *Public Administration Review* 66(4): 546–553.

Breiger, Ronald L., Eric Schoon, David Melamed, Victor Asai, and R. Karl Rethemeyer. 2014. Comparative Configurational Analysis as a Two-mode Network Problem: A Study of Terrorist Group Engagement in the Drug Trade. *Social Networks* 36: 23–39.

Brook, Timothy. 1994. Rethinking Syncretism: The Unity of the Thee Teachings and Their Joint Worship in Late-imperial China. *Journal of Chinese Religion* 21(1): 13–44.

Brooks, Stephen G., G. John Ikenberry, and William C. Wohlforth. 2012/13. Don't Come Home, America: The Case against Retrenchment. *International Security* 37(3): 7–51.

Brown, Melissa. 2004. *Is Taiwan Chinese? The Impact of Culture, Power and Migration on Changing Identities*. Berkeley, CA: University of California Press.

Buchanan, Allen. 1999. Internal Legitimacy of Humanitarian Intervention. *Journal of Political Philosophy* 7(1): 71–87.

Bulag, Uradyn. 2004. Inner Mongolia: The Dialectics of Colonization and Ethnicity Building. In M. Rossabi, Ed. *Governing China's Multi-ethnic Frontier*. Seattle, WA: University of Washington Press, 84–116.

Bull, Hedley. 2012/1977. *The Anarchical Society: A Study of Order in World Politics*. London, UK: Macmillan.

Burgess, J. Peter. 2002. Ethics of Humanitarian Intervention: The Circle Closes. *Security Dialogue* 33(3): 261–264.

Burke, Peter. 1991. Identity Processes and Social Stress. *American Sociological Review* 56(6): 836–849.

Burkitt, Ian. 2016. Relational Agency: Relational Sociology, Agency and Interaction. *European Journal of Social Theory* 19(3): 322–339.

Bush, Richard. 2013. *Uncharted Straits: The Future of China-Taiwan Relations*. New York: Brooking Institution Press.

Butterfield, Andrew. 1996. *Vietnamese Strategic Culture and the Coming Struggle for the South China Sea*, M.A. Thesis, Naval Postgraduate School.

Buzan, Barry. 2004. *From International to World Society? English School Theory and the Social Structure of Globalisation*. Cambridge, MA: Cambridge University Press.

Buzan, Barry. 2010. China in International Society: Is "Peaceful Rise" Possible? *The Chinese Journal of International Politics* 3: 5–36.

Cabán, Pedro. 1998. The New Synthesis of Latin American and Latino Studies. In Frank Bonilla, Edwin Meléndez, Rebecca Morales and María de los Angeles Torres. Eds. *Borderless Borders: U.S. Latinos, Latin Americans, and the Paradox of Interdependence.* Philadelphia, PA: Temple University Press, 195–215.

Caldwell, Dan. 2009. The Legitimation of the Nixon-Kissinger Grand Design and Grand Strategy. *Diplomatic History* 33(4): 633–652.

Callahan, William. 2004. *Contingent States: Greater China and Transnational Relations.* Minneapolis, MN: University of Minnesota Press.

Callahan, William. 2008. Chinese Visions of World Order: Post-hegemonic or a New Hegemony?" *International Studies Review* 10(4): 749–761.

Callahan, William. 2009. Tianxia, Empire and the World: Soft Power and China's Foreign Policy Discourse in the 21st Century. In W. Callahan and E. Barabantseva Eds. *China Orders the World? Soft Power, Norms and Foreign Policy.* Washington, DC: Woodrow Wilson Center Press.

Callahan, William. 2012. *China: Pessoptimist Nation.* Oxford: Oxford University Press.

Calmes, Jackie and Steven Lee Myers. 2013. Obama and Xi Tackle Cybersecurity as Talks Begin in California. *The New York Times.* June 7: A5.

Campbell, David. 1992. *Writing Security: United States Foreign Policy and the Politics of Identity.* Minneapolis, MN: University of Minnesota Press.

Cao, Ruichen. 2011. Xifang da guo jueqi shijiao xia zhongguo hai quan yu haiyang da zhanlue tanxi [Analysis of China's Sea Power and the Oceanic Grand Strategy in the Western Perspectives of the Rise of Major Power] *Journal of Dalian Maritime Affairs [Dalian haishi daxue xuebao]* 5: 92–95.

Cao, Xun. 2009. Networks of Intergovernmental Organizations and Convergence in Democratic Economic Policies. *International Studies Quarterly* 53(4): 1095–1130.

Carlson, Allen. 2005. *Unifying China: Integrating with the World.* Stanford, CA: Stanford University Press.

Carr, Edward Hallett. 2008. *What is History?* Camberwell: Penguin.

Central Party School Research Centre for Socialist Theory with Chinese Characteristics. 2014. Deeply Grasp the Rich Contents and Characteristics of the China Dream. [Shenke bawo zhongguo meng de fengfu neihan he tezheng] June 26. http://gd.people.com.cn/n/2014/0606/c123932-21364842.html accessed 15 September 2014.

Cha, Victor. 2009. What Do They Really Want?: Obama's North Korea Conundrum. *The Washington Quarterly* 32(4): 119–138.

Cha, Victor. 2012. Powerplay: Origins of the U.S. Alliance System in Asia. *International Security* 34(3): 158–196.

Chakrabarty, Dipesh. 2000/2007. *Provincializing Europe: Postcolonial Thought and Historical Difference.* Princeton, NJ: Princeton University Press.

Chan, Serina. 2011. *The Thought of Mou Zongsan.* Leiden: Koninklijke Brill NV.

Chan, Steve. 1978. Chinese Conflict Calculus and Behaviour: Assessment from a Perspective of Conflict Management. *World Politics* 30(3): 391–410.

Chan, Wing-Cheuk. 2008. On Mou Zongsan's Idealist Confucianism. In Qingsong Shen and Kwong-loi Shun Eds. *Confucian Ethnics in Retrospect and Prospect.* Washington, DC: The Council for Research in Value and Philosophy, 171–184.

Chan, Wing-Tsit. 1957. Neo-Confucianism and Chinese Scientific Thought. *Philosophy East and West* 6(4): 309–332.

Chang, Ching-tai, 2006. Shi lun zhonggong xin anquan guan de lilun yu shijian [A Study of the Theory and Practice of Communist China's New Security Concept]. *Saint John's Bulletin* [*Shen yuehan xuebao*] 23: 323–340.

Chang, Chishen, 2011. Tianxia System on a Snail's Horns. *Inter-Asia Cultural Studies* 12(1): 28–42.

Chang, Teng-chi and Chen Ying-shi, 2012. Chaogong tixi zai xian yu tianxia tixi de xinqi? Zhongguo waijiao de anli yanjiu yu lilun fansi [Revitalization of the Tribute System and the Rise of the 'Under-Heaven System'? Case Studies and Reflections on China's Diplomacy]. *Mainland China Studies* [*Zhong guo dalu yanjiu*] 55(4): 89–123.

Chang, Yen-hsien, and Shih-hung Chen. Eds. 2012. *Taiwan zhuquan yu waijiao gongshi [Taiwan's Sovereignty and Diplomatic Offensive]*. Taipei: Wu San-lin Foundation for Taiwan Historical Materials.

Chao, Chien-min and Chih-chia Hsu. 2009. Zhong gong disidai lingdao jiti de hexie shijie guan: lilun yu yihan [China's Harmonious World: Theory and Significance]. *Prospect Foundation Quarterly* [*Yuanjing jikan*] 10(1): 1–44.

Charles, Dame Eugenla. 1997. *A Future for Small States: Covercoming Vulnerability*. London, UK: Commonwealth Secretariat.

Charon, Joel. 2004. *Symbolic Interactionism: An Introduction, An Interpretation, An Integration*. Boston: Pearson.

Charvet, John. 1997. The Idea of State Sovereignty and the Right of Humanitarian Intervention. *International Political Science Review* 18(1): 39–48.

Chatterjee, Partha. 1986. *Nationalist Thought and the Colonial World: A Derivative Discourse*. Oxford: Oxford University Press.

Chaziza, Mordechai and Ogen S. Goldman. 2014. Revisiting China's Non-Interference Policy towards Intrastate Wars. *Chinese Journal of International Politics* 7(1): 89–115.

Chaziza, Mordechai and Ogen S. Goldman. 2004. Revisiting China's Non-Interference Policy towards Intrastate Wars. *Chinese Journal of International Politics* 7(1): 1–27.

Chen, Ching-chang. 2009. When Is China's Military Modernization Dangerous? Constructing the Cross-Strait Offense-Defense Balance and U.S. Arms Sales to Taiwan. *Issues & Studies* 45(3): 69–119.

Chen, Ching-chang. 2012. The Im/possibility of Building Indigenous Theories in a Hegemonic Discipline: The Case of Japanese International Relations. *Asian Perspective* 36(3) 463–492.

Chen, Ching-chang. 2011. The Absence of Non-Western IR Theory in Asia Reconsidered. *International Relations of the Asia-Pacific* 11(1): 1–23.

Chen, Ching-Chang. 2012. The 'Loss' of Ryukyu Revisited: China's No Use of Compellence in the Sino-Japanese border Dispute, 1877–1880. *Afrasia Symposium Series Studies on Multicultural Societies* 1: 87–105.

Chen, Jie. 2002. *Foreign Policy of the New Taiwan: Pragmatic Diplomacy in Southeast Asia*. Cheltenham: Edward Elgar Publishing LimitEd.

Chen, Xiafei and Han Rongfang. Eds. 1990. *Archives of China's Imperial Maritime Customs: Confidential Correspondence between Robert Hart and James Duncan Campbell, 1874–1907*. Beijing: Foreign Languages Press Beijing.

Chen, Zhi. 2014. 'Xi Jinping meets with UN secretary-general Ban Kimoon'. *Xinhua News*. www.gov.cn/guowuyuan/2014-02/07/content_2584753.htm accessed 10 March 2014.

Cheng, Grace. 2012. The Relationship between Nationalism and Human Rights: An Introduction to the Dimensions of Debate. In G. Cheng Ed. *Nationalism and Human Rights: In Theory and Practice in the Middle East, Central Europe, and the Asia Pacific.* New York: Palgrave Macmillan, 1–20.

Cheng, Joseph. 2007. How China Deals with the 'China Threat' Perception. In Joseph Cheng. Ed. *Challenges and Policy Programmes of China's New Leadership.* Hong Kong: City University of Hong Kong Press.

Cheng, Tun-jen. 1993. Democracy and Taiwan-mainland China Ties: A Critique of Three Dominant Views. *East Asia* 12(1): 72–89.

Cheung, Gordon. 1998. *Market Liberalism: American Policy toward China.* New Brunswick, NJ: Transactions.

Ching, T. S. Leo. 2001. *Becoming Taiwanese: Colonial Taiwan and the Politics of Identity Formation.* Berkeley, CA: University of California Press.

Chiu, Chin-yih. 2013. Zhuiyi gu wang huitan de ruogan mi xi [Recollection of a Few Untold Strings of the Gu-Wang Meeting], speech, Memorial Seminar on the Twentieth Anniversary of the Gu Wang Meeting, April 28.

Chiu, Kun-hsuan. 2011. China's Multilateral Diplomacy in Its Surrounding Areas: Theory and Practice. *Prospect Journal* 6: 1–24.

Chiu, Kun-shuan and Teng-chi Chang. 2012. A Review of the Studies on China's Foreign Policy in Taiwan: Opportunities and Challenges. Presented at the Conference on Taiwanese Political Science: Review and Prospect, Institute of Political Science, Academia Sinica, Taipei, August 7.

Chodorow, Nancy. 1991. Toward a Relational Individualism: The Mediation of Self through Psychoanalysis. In N. Chodorow. Ed. *Feminism and Psychoanalytic Theory.* New Haven: Yale University Press, 109–130.

Chong, Alan. 2010. Small State Soft Power Strategies: Virtual Enlargement in the Cases of the Vatican City State and Singapore. *Cambridge Review of International Affairs* 23(3): 383–405.

Chow, Peter. Ed. 2012. *National Identity and Economic Interest: Taiwan's Competing Options and Their Implications for Regional Stability.* New York: Palgrave MacMillan.

Christian, Thomas. 2002. The Contemporary Security Dilemma: Deterring a Taiwan Conflict. *The Washington Quarterly* 25(4): 5–21.

Chu, Teh-feng and Hui-ming Tung. 2010. Zhonggong jueqi de lilun yu shiji: guoji guanxi lilun de jianshi yu fenxi [A Study on the Theory and Practice of China Rising: Reviewing and Analyzing from International Relations Theory]. *Fuxinggang Bulletin* [*Fuxinggang xuebao*] 100: 135–158.

Chu, Zhaofeng. 2011. The Beginning and Subsequent Development of the South China Sea Issue' [Nanhai wenti de lailong qumai], *Junshi Shilin* [Martial Historical Facts].

Chua, Daniel Wei Boon. 2015. *Konfrontasi: Why It Still Matters to Singapore.* RSIS Commentary 054 (March 16).

Chung, Jae Ho and Myung-hae Choi. 2013. Uncertain Allies or Uncomfortable Neighbours: Making Sense of China-North Korean Relations, 1949–2010. *Pacific Review* 26(3): 243–264.

Clearly, Thomas. 1998/2000. *The Art of War: Complete Texts and Commentaries.* Boston: Shambhala Press.

Cocke, Chris. 2005. Taiwan Democracy a Model for Middle East: Wolfowitz. *China Post* (Taipei), February 5.

Cocke, Chris. 2008. Taiwan a Model for Asia: European Parliament Taiwan Caucus Chairman. *Central News Agency* (Taiwan), January 17.

Collins, Gabriel et al. 2008. *China's Energy Security: The Impact on Beijing's Maritime Policies*. Annapolis, MD: Naval Institute Press.

Confucius' *Spring and Autumn Annals [Chun qiu]*.

Copeland, D. 1996. Economic Interdependence and War. *International Security* 20: 5–41.

Corcuff, Staphane. 2012. The Liminality of Taiwan: A Case Studies in Geopolitics. *Taiwan in Comparative Perspectives* 4: 34–64.

Coser, Lewis. 1995. Role-set theory and Individual Autonomy. In Judith R. Blau, Rose Laub Coser, Norman Goodman. Eds. *Social Roles and Social Institutions: Essays in Honor of Rose Laub Coser*. New Brunswick: Transactions.

Cottam, Martha. 1986. *Foreign Policy Decision Making: The Influence of Cognition*. Boulder, CO: Westview.

Cottam, Martha. 1994. *Image and Intervention: US Policies in Latin America*. Pittsburgh: University of Pittsburgh Press.

Courmont, Barthelemy. 2012. Promoting Multilateralism or Searching for a New Hegemony: A Chinese Vision of Multipolarity. *Pacific Focus* 27(2): 184–204.

Cox, Robert. 1996. A Perspective on Globalization. In J. H. Mittelman. Ed. *Globalization: Critical Reflections*. Boulder, CO: Lynne Rienner, 21–113.

Cranmer, Skyler J., Tobias Heinrich and Bruce A. Desmarais. 2014. Reciprocity and the Structure Determinants of the International Sanctions Network. *Social Networks* 36(Special Issue): 5–22.

Crossley, Nick. 2010. *Towards Relational Sociology*. London, UK: Routledge.

Danchev, Alex. 1998. *Alchemist of War: The Life of Basil Liddell Hart*. London, UK: Phoenix Giant.

Davis, Aaron C. 2011. At Shrine to Hussein, Nostalgia for a Strong Leader. *The Washington Post*, 20 May, www.washingtonpost.com/world/war-zones/at-shrine-to-saddam-hussein-in-iraq-nostalgia-for-a-fallen-leader/2011/05/18/AFvW7u7G_story.html accessed 15 March 2014.

Davis, Bret, Brian Schroeder and Jason M. Wirth. Ed. 2011. *Japanese Continental Philosophy: Conversations with the Kyoto School*. Bloomington: Indian University Press.

Dawson, Raymond. 2005. *The Chinese Experience*. London, UK: Phoenix Press.

Delanty, Gerard. 2006. The Cosmopolitan Imagination: Critical Cosmopolitanism and Social Theory. *The British Journal of Sociology* 57: 25–47.

Dellios, Rosita. 2011. International Relations Theory and Chinese Philosophy. In Brett McCormick and Jonathan H. Ping. Eds. *Chinese Engagements: Regional Issues with Global Implications*. Robina: Bond University Press, 63–93.

Deryer, June. 1999. The Defense of Taiwan: A View From Afar. In James R. Lilley and Larry Wortzel. Eds. *China in the Twenty-First Century*. Carlisle, PA: Strategic Studies Institute, 289–320.

DeVido, Elise A. 2009. The Influence of Chinese Master Taixu on Buddhism in Vietnam. *Journal of Global Buddhism* 10: 413–458.

Devine, Patricia G. 1995. Prejudice and Out-group Perception. In A. Tesser. Ed. *Advanced Social Psychology*. New York: McGraw-Hill, 466–524.

Dimen, Muriel. 2012. Perversion Is Us? Eight Notes. In Lewis Aro and Adrienne Harris. Eds. *Relational Psychoanalysis, Volume 2: Innovation and Expansion*. New York: Routledge, 257–292.

Ding, Richang. 1934. Mindu hejing deng zou liuqiu qianshi rugong riben gengzu gingzhi Banlizhe fu shangyu" (Fujian-Zhejiang Viceroy He Jing and his staff reported that Ryukyu sent the representatives for tribute rituals to China but Japan stopped them), 24 June 1877. In Wang Yanwei and Wang Liang. Eds. *Diplomatic Materials of the Late Qing* [Qingji waijiao shiliao].

Do, Thien. 1999. The Quest for Enlightenment and Cultural Identity: Buddhism in Contemporary Vietnam. In Ian Harris. Ed. *Buddhism and Politics in Twentieth-Century Asia*. London, UK: Pinter, 254–283.

Donati, Pierpaolo. 2010. *Relational Sociology: A New Paradigm for the Social Sciences*. London, UK: Routledge.

Dorff, Cassy and Michael D. Ward. 2013. Networks, Dyads, and the Social Relations Model. Presented at the Annual Meeting of the Political Networks Conference (June 13–16).

Dpelteau, Franscois. 2008. Relational Thinking: A Critique of Co-Deterministic Theories of Structure and Agency. *Sociological Theory* 26(1): 51–73.

Dpelteau, Franscois. 2013. What Is the Direction of the Relational Turn? In Christopher Powell and Franois Dpelteau. Eds. *Conceptualizing relational sociology: Ontological and Theoretical Issues*. Basingstoke: Palgrave, 163–186.

Dreyer, June. 2000. China's Attitude Toward the Taiwan Relations Act. In Jaw-Lin Joanne Chang and William W. Boyer. Eds. *United States-Taiwan Relations: Twenty Years after the Taiwan Relations Act*. College Park, MD: University of Maryland Series in Contemporary Studies 156(1), 203–230.

Dreyer, June. 2004. Encroaching on the Middle Kingdom? In Christopher Marsh and June Teufel Dreyer. Eds. *U.S.-China Relations in the Twenty-First Century: Policies, Prospects, and Possibilities*. Lanham, MD: Lexington Books, 85–104.

Drop, Hein. 2012. How Sun Tzu Conquered Great Britain and the United States of America. Unpublished manuscript.

Eagleton, Terry. 1984/2005. *The Function of Criticism*. London, UK: Verso.

Eagleton, Terry. 2003/2004. *After Theory*. London, UK: Penguin Books.

Edkins, Jenny. 1999. *Poststructuralism and International Relations: Bringing the Political Back In*. Boulder, CO: Lynne Rienner.

Elias, Norbert. (1982). *Über den Prozeß der Zivilisation. Soziogenetische und psychogenetische Untersuchungen [Power and Civility: The Civilizing Process]*. Trans Edmund Jephcott, Vol. 2. New York: Pantheon Books.

Eliasoph, Nina and Paul Lichterman. 2003. Culture in Interaction. *American Journal of Sociology* 108(4): 735–794.

Emirbayer, Mustafa. 1997. Manifesto for a Relational Sociology. *American Journal of Sociology* 103(2): 281–317.

Epstein, Mark. 1989. Forms of Emptiness: Psychodynamic, Meditative and Clinical Perspectives. *The Journal of Transpersonal Psychology* 2: 61–71.

Er, Connie. 2007. Taiwan's Ports Can Also Take Open, Pragmatic Route. *The Straits Times* June 15.

Eriksen, Stein S. 2011. State Failure' in Theory and Practice: The Idea of the State and the Contradictions of State Formation. *Review of International Studies* 37: 229–247.

Erll, Astrid. 2008. Cultural Memory Studies: An Introduction. In Astrid Erll and Ansgar Nunning. Eds. *Cultural Memory Studies: An International and Interdisciplinary Handbook*. Berlin: de Gruyter, 1–17.

Erll, Astrid. 2011. *Memory in Culture*. London, UK: Palgrave Macmillan.

Ervin, Laurie H., and Sheldon Stryker. 2001. Theorizing the Relationship Between Self- Esteem and Identity. In Timothy J. Owens, Sheldon Stryker, and Norman Goodman. Eds. *Extending Self-Esteem Theory and Research*. Cambridge, MA: Cambridge University Press, 29–55.

EU Official. 2003. Commission Policy Paper for Transmission to the Council and the European Parliament: A Maturing Partnership – Shared Interests and Challenges in EU-China Relations, 2003. http: //europa.eu/legislation_summaries/ external_relations/relations_with_third_countries/asia/rl4(207_en.htm accessed 10 July 2013.

Evans, Paul. 2010. Historians and Chinese World Order: Fairbank, Wang and the Matter of 'Indeterminate Relevance'. In Yongnian Zheng. Ed. *China and International Relations: The Chinese View and the Contribution of Wang Gungwu*. London, UK: Routledge, 42–57.

EWS. 2012. China hopes Russia-India ties conducive to Asian stability. 2012.12.26, http: //news.xinhuanet.com/english/china/(2012-12/26/c_13(2065055)htm accessed 8 January 2013.

Fairbank, John King. Ed. 1968. *The Chinese World Order: Traditional China's Foreign Relations*. Cambridge, MA: Harvard University Press.

Fairbank, John King, Katherine Frost Bruner and Elizabeth Macleod Matheson. Eds. 1975. *The I.G. in Peking: Letters of Robert Hart, Chinese Maritime Customs, 1868–1907*. Cambridge, MA: The Belknap Press of Harvard University Press.

Fan, Hongwei. 2010. Zhong Mian Bianjie Wenti De Jiejue: Guocheng Yu Yingxiang [The Settlement of China–Burma Border Disputes: Course and Impact]. *Southeast Asian Affairs [Nanyang wenti yanjiu]* 143: 36–45.

Fan, Joshua. 2011. *China's Homeless Generation: Voices from Veterans of the Chinese Civil Wars, 1940s–1990s*. New York: Routledge.

Fang, Tien-sze. 2014. *Asymmetrical Threat: Perceptions in India-China Relations*. Oxford: Oxford University Press.

Fang, Tony. 2012. Ying Yang: A New Perspective on Culture. *Management and Organization Review* 8(1): 25–50.

Fanon, Frantz. 1986. *Black Skin, White Mask*. London, UK: Plito.

Fewsmith, Joseph. 2011. Debating 'the China Model'. *China Leadership Monitor* 35, www.hoover.org/publications/china-leadership-monitor/article/93636, accessed 22 May 2014.

Finkelstein, Lawrence S. 1995. What Is Global Governance? *Global Governance* 1(3): 367–372.

Finnemore, Martha and Kathryn Sikkink. 1998. International Norm Dynamics and Political Change. *International Organization* 52(4): 887–917.

Foucault, de Michel. 2004. *Naissance de la Biopolitique: Cours au Collège de France (1978–1979)*. Paris: Hautes études.

Fox, Annette B. 1959. *The Power of Small States: Diplomacy in World War II*. Chicago, IL: University of Chicago Press.

Freeman, Lawrence. 2013. *Strategy: A History*. Oxford: Oxford University Press.

Freeman, Linton. 1979. Centrality in Social Networks Conceptual Clarification. *Social Networks* 1(3): 215–239.

Freiberg, Aaron. 2012. *A Contest for Supremacy: China, America and the Struggle for Mastery in Asia*. New York: W. W. Norton & Company.

Friedman, Edward. 2013. 'Building New Vital Mutual Interests for a Better Future: A Commentary on Wang Jisi and Kenneth Lieberthal's Addressing US-China Strategic Distrust'. *Journal of Contemporary China* 22(80): 367–378.

Fu, Charles Wei-hsun. 1973. Morality or Beyond: The Neo-Confucian Confrontation with Mahāyāna Buddhism. *Philosophy East and West* 23(3), 375–396.

Fukuyama, Francis. 1992. *The End of History and the Last Man*. New York: Free Press.

Gaddis, John. 1986. The Long Peace: Elements of Stability in the Postwar International System. *International Security* 10(4): 99–142.

Garver, John W. 2006. China's Decision for War with India in (1962). In Alastair Iain Johnston and Robert S. Ross. Eds. *New Directions in the Study of China's Foreign Policy*. Stanford, CA: Stanford University Press, 106.

Gay, Peter. 1979. *The Enlightenment: An Interpretation (Book One)*. New York: W.W. Norton.

George, Alexander L. and Richard Smoke. 1974. *Deterrence in American Foreign Policy: Theory and Practice*. New York: Columbia University Press.

Gerson, Jack. 1972. *Horatio Nelson Lay and Sino-British Relations, 1854–1864*. Cambridge, MA: Harvard University Press.

Giddens, Anthony. 1984. *The Constitution of Society: Outline of the Theory of Structuration*. Cambridge, MA: Polity Press.

Giles, Lionel. Transl. 1910/1999. *Sun Tzu on the Art of War*. Torrance, CA: Heian Int.

Gilley, Bruce. 2010. Not So Dire Straits: How the Finlandization of Taiwan Benefit US Security. *Foreign Affairs* 89(1): 44–60.

Gilligan, Carol. 1993. *In a Different Voice: Psychological Theory and Women's Development*. Cambridge, MA: Harvard University Press.

Goh, Evelyn. 2011. Institutions and the Great Power Bargain in East Asia: ASEAN's Limited Brokerage Role. *International Relations of the Asia-Pacific* 11(3), 373–401.

Gold, Thomas, Douglas Guthrie and David Wank. 2002. *Social Connections in China: Institutions, Culture and the Changing Nature of Guangxi*. Cambridge, MA: Cambridge University Press.

Goldstein, Avery. 1997/98. Great Expectations: Interpreting China's Arrival. *International Security* 22(3): 36–73.

Goldstein, Avery. 2005. *Rising to the Challenge: China's Grand Strategy and International Security*. Stanford, CA: Stanford University Press.

Gong, Prince. 1879. Zongshu zou meiguo qian zongtong hancheng zai riben shangban qiushi zhe" [Zongli Yamen reports that former US President is discussing the Ryukyu issue in Japan now], *Diplomatic Materials of the Late Qing [Qingji waijiao shiliao]* 26 (29 September).

Gong, Prince. 1879. Zongshu zou meiguo qian zongtong zai riben tiaochu liuqiushi yiu banfa zhe" [Zongli Yamen reports that former US President knows how to solve the Ryukyu issue in Japan]. *Diplomatic Materials of the Late Qing [Qingji waijiao shiliao]* 26 (7 July).

Gong, Prince. 1879. Zongshu zou yifu he ruchang hanshu riben zugeng liuqiu rugong yian xiangji zhuaoban zhe" [Zongli Yamen instructed He Ruzhang how to deal with Japan and Ryukyu]. *Diplomatic Materials of the Late Qing* [Qingji waijiao shiliao] 15 (10 April).

Gong, Prince. 1880. Zongshu zou riben feimie liuqin yian quanguo qianzong nijia tiaoting shiyi zhongbian qingjian dayuan shangban zhe" [Zongli Yamen reports that the situation that Japan annexed Ryukyu has changed so China should send high-ranking official to interfere into this issue], *Diplomatic Materials of the Late Qing* [Qingji waijiao shiliao] 21 (26 July).

Goto-Jones, Chrisopher. 2005a. *Political Philosophy in Japan: Nishida, the Kyoto School, and Co-Prosperity.* London, UK: Routledge.

Goto-Jones, Christopher. 2005b. If the Past is a Different Country, Are Different Countries in the Past?" *Philosophy* 80 (311): 29–51.

Goto-Jones, Chrisopher. Ed. 2007. *Re-Politicising the Kyoto School as Philosophy.* London, UK: Routledge.

Gould, Erica and Stephan Krasner. 2003. Germany and Japan: Binding Versus Autonomy. In Kozo Yamamura and Wolfgang Streeck. Eds. *The End of Diversity? Prospects for German and Japanese Capitalism.* Ithaca, NY: Cornell University Press, 51–88.

Goulding, Jay. 2002. 'Three Teachings Are One': The Ethical Intertwinings of Buddhism, Confucianism and Daoism. In Xinyan Jiang. Ed. *The Examined Life—Chinese Perspectives.* Bingham: Global Academic Publishing, 249–278.

Grant, Charles. 2009. Liberalism Retreats in China. Briefing Note for the Centre for European Reform, www.cer.org.uk/sites/default/files/publications/attachments/pdf/2011/bn_china_july09-1114.pdf accessed 2 November 2015.

Gray, John. 2002. *Two Faces of Liberalism.* New York: The New Press.

Gries, Peter. 2004. *China's New Nationalism: Pride, Politics and Diplomacy.* Berkeley, CA: University of California Press.

Griffith, Samuel B. 1963/1971. *Sun Tzu: The Art of War.* Oxford: Oxford University Press.

Guillaume, Xavier. 2002. Foreign Policy and the Politics of Alterity: A Dialogical Understanding of International Relations. *Millennium* 31(3): 1–26.

Gupta, Krishna Praksha. 1971. China's Theory and Practice of Intervention. *China Report* 7(12): 12–27.

Haass, Richard. 1999. What to Do with American Primacy. *Foreign Affairs* 78(5): 37–49.

Hafner-Burton, Emilie M., Miles Kahler and Alexander H. Montgomery. 2009. Network Analysis for International Relations. *International Organization* 63(3): 559–592.

Hammerstorm, Erik. 2012. Science and Buddhist Modernism in Early 20th Century China: The Life and Works of Wang Xiaoxu. *Journal of Chinese Religion* 39: 1–32.

Hao, Yufan. 2010. Yong dazhanlve dapo Zhongguo waijiao beidong [Breaking China's Passive Diplomacy by Building Grand Strategy]. *Global Times* [*Huanqiu shibao*], September 17. http: //world.people.com.cn/BIG5/12757519.html.

Harnisch, Sebastian. 2012. Conceptualizing in the Minefield: Role Theory and Foreign Policy Learning. *Foreign Policy Analysis* 8(1): 47–71.

Harrison, Lawrence E. and Samuel Huntington. Eds. 2001. *Culture Matters: How Values Shape Huamn Progress.* New York: Basic Books.

Hart, Robert. 1880/2007. 'Juwai Pangguan Lun' (Bystander's Viewpoint), Tongzhichao Choban Yiwu Shimo [The Complete Account of the Management of Barbaric Affairs during the Tongzhi Reign]. Peking, 1880, Reprinted Beijing: The Chinese Bookstore.

Hart, Robert. 1901. *These from the Land of Sinim: Essays on the Chinese Questions.* London, UK: Chapman & Hall.

Hattori, Tomohisa. 2003. Giving as a Mechanism of Consent: International Aid Organizations and the Ethical Hegemony of Capitalism. *International Relations* 17(2): 153–73.

Hehir, J. Bryan. 1979. The Ethnics of Non-intervention: Two Traditions. In Peter G. Brown and Douglas Maclean. Eds. *Human Rights and US Foreign Policy: Principles and Applications*. Lexington, KY: Lexington Books, 121–139.

Heilmann, Sebastian, Moritz Rudolf, Huotari Mikko and Johannes Buckow. (2014). China's Shadow Foreign Policy: Parallel Structures Challenge the Established International Order', *China Monitor*, 18, www.merics.org/fileadmin/templates/download/-china-monitor/China_Monitor_No_18_en.pdf accessed 20 May 2015.

Heine, Steven. 2001. After the Storm: Matsumoto Shirō's Transition from 'Critical Buddhism' to 'Critical Theology'. *Japanese Journal of Religious Studies* 28(1–2): 133–146.

Hensengerth, Oliver. 2010. *Regionalism in China-Vietnam relations: Institution-building in the Greater Mekong Subregion*. London, UK: Routledge.

Hesig, James and John Maraldo. 1995. Eds. *Rude Awakenings: Zen, the Kyoto School and the Question of Nationalism*. Honolulu: University of Hawai'i Press.

Hey, Jeanne A. K. 2003. Introducing Small State Foreign Policy. In J. A. K. Hey. Ed. *Small States in World Politics: Explaining Foreign Policy Behavior*. Boulder, CO: Lynne Rienner, 1–11.

Hiep, Le Hong. 2014. Chinese Assertiveness in the South China Sea: What Should Vietnam Do? *The National Interest* (15 May). http://nationalinterest.org/blog/the-buzz/chinese-assertiveness-the--south-china-sea-what-should-10468 accessed 22 May 2018.

Hiep, Le Hong. 2013. Vietnam's Hedging Strategy against China since Normalization. *Contemporary Southeast Asia* 35(3): 333–368.

Hiep, Le Hong. 2014. Chinese Assertiveness in the South China Sea: What Should Vietnam Do. *The National Interest* (15 May). http: //nationalinterest.org/blog/the-buzz/chinese-assertiveness-the-south-china-sea-what-should-10468, accessed 22 May 2014.

Higgins, Tory. 1987. Self-Discrepancy: A Theory Relating Self and Affect. *Psychological Review* 94(3): 319–40.

Hindess, Barry. 2004. Liberalism, What's in a Name?" In Wendy Larner and William Walters. Eds. *Global Governmentality: Governing International Spaces*. London, UK: Routledge, 23–39.

Ho, David Y. F. 1998. Interpersonal Relationships and Relational Dominance: An Analysis Based on Methodological Relationalism. *Asian Journal of Social Psychology* 1(1): 1–16.

Ho, David Y. F. and C. Y. Chiu. 1998. Collective Representations as a Metaconstruct: An Analysis Based on Methodological Relationalism. *Culture and Psychology* 4(3): 349–369.

Hodel, Mike. 2008. The Scramble for Energy: China's Oil Investment in Africa. *The Journal of International Policy Solutions* 9: 50–54.

Hodgson, Geoffrey M. 2006. 'What are Institutions?' *Journal of Economic Issues* 40(1): 1–25.

Hollis, M, and S. Smith. 1991. *Explaining and Understanding International Relations*. Oxford: Clarendon Press.

Heisig, James W., and John C. Maraldo. Eds. 1995. *Rude Awakenings: Zen, the Kyoto School, and The Question of Nationalism*. Honolulu: University of Hawaii Press.

Hsu, Francis. L. K. 1971. Psychosocial Homeostasis and Jen: Conceptual Tools for Advancing Psychological Anthropology. *American Anthropologist* 73(1): 23–44.

Hsu, Jing. 1983. Asian Family Interaction Patterns and Their Therapeutic Implications. *International Journal of Family Psychiatry* 4(4): 307–320.

Hsu, Jing. 1985. The Chinese Family: Relations, Problems and Therapy. In Wen-Shing Tseng and David Y. H. Wu. Eds. *Chinese Culture and Mental Health*. Orlando, FL: Academic Press, 95–112.

Hu, Jintao. 2012. Report to the 18th CPC National Congress. November 16. www. china.org.cn/china/18th_cpc_congress/2012-11/16/content_27137540_11.htm accessed 21 July 2013.

Hu, Jingtao. 2005. Build Towards a Harmonious World of Lasting Peace and Common Prosperity. President of the People's Republic of China presented at the United Nations Summit, New York (September 15).

Hu, Ming-yuan, 2012. Zhong gong jiangou hexie shijie de zhanlue yihan: xun ziyou-zhuyi de guandian [The Strategic Implications of China's Building a Harmonious World: From Neo-Liberalism Perspectives]. *Defense Journal* [*Guofang zazhi*] 27(4): 3–16.

Huang, Chiung-chiu. 2015. Balance of Relationship: The Essence of Myanmar's China Policy. *The Pacific Review* 28(2): 189–210.

Huang, Chiung-chiu and Chih-yu Shih. 2014. *Harmonious Intervention: China's Quest for Relational Security*. Surrey: Ashgate.

Hubbard, Jamie and Paul Loren Swanson. 1997. Eds. *Pruning the Bodhi Tree: The Storm Over Critical Buddhism*. Honolulu: Hawaii University Press.

Hudson, G. F. 1976. Foreword. In John Y. Wong. Ed. *Yeh Ming-chen: Viceroy of Liang Kuang (1852–1858)*. Cambridge, MA: Cambridge University Press, xv–xviii.

Hugh, Christopher. 2013. *Taiwan and Chinese Nationalism: National Identity and Status in International Society*. London, UK: Routledge.

Hughes, Christopher and Fukushima Akiko. 2004. U.S.-Japan Security Relations: toward Bilateralism Plus?' In Krauss Ellis and Thomas J. Pempel. Eds. *Beyond Bilateralism: U.S.-Japan Relations in the New Asia-Pacific*. Stanford, CA: Stanford University Press, 55–86.

Hughes, Christopher. 2011. Negotiating National Identity in Taiwan: Between Nativization and De-Sinicization. In R. Ash, J. W. Garver and P. B. Prime. Eds. *Taiwan's Democracy: Economic and Political Challenges*. London, UK: Routledge, 51–74.

Hui, Victoria. 2005. *War and State Formation in Ancient China and Early Modern Europe*. New York: Cambridge University Press.

Hui, Victoria. 2008. How China Was Ruled? *American Interest* 3(4): 44–52.

Hui, Victoria. 2012. Confucianism and Peacemaking in Chinese History. In Susan A. Nan, Zachariah C. Mampilly and Andrea Bartoli. Eds. *Peacemaking: From Practice to Theory*. Santa Barbara: Praeger, 211–227.

Huntington, Samuel. 1997. Democracy for the Long Haul. In Larry Diamond, Marc F. Plattner, Yun-han Chu, and Hung-Mao Tien. Eds. *Consolidating the Third Wave Democracies: Themes and Perspectives*. Baltimore, MD: Johns Hopkins University Press, 3–13.

Hurd, Douglas. 1967. *The Arrow War: An Anglo-Chinese Confusion, 1856–1860*. London, UK: Collins.

Hutnyk, John. 2000. *Critique of Exotica: Music Politics and the Culture Industry*. London, UK: Pluto Press.

Hwang, Alvin, Ann Marie Francesco and Eric Kesslear. 2003. The Relationship between Individualism–collectivism, Face, and Feedback and Learning Processes in Hong Kong, Singapore, and the United States. *Journal of Cross-Cultural Psychology* 34(1): 72–91.

Hwang, Kwang-kuo. 1987. Face and Favor: The Chinese Power Game. *American Journal of Sociology* 92(4): 944–974.

Hwang, Kwang-kuo. 2012/2011. *Foundations of Chinese Psychology: Confucian Social Relations*. New York: Springer.

Hwang, Kwang-Kuo and Jeffrey Chang. 2009. Self-Cultivation: Culturally Sensitive Psychotherapies in Confucian Societies. *The Counseling Psychologist* 37(7): 1010–1032.

Hwang, Kwang-kuo. 2013. Linking Science to Culture: Challenge to Psychologists. *Social Epistemology: A Journal of Knowledge, Culture and Policy* 27(1): 105–112.

Ikenberry, John. 2000. America's Liberal Grand Strategy: Democracy and National Security in the Post-war Era. In Michael Cox, G. John Ikenberry and Takashi Inoguchi. Eds. *American Democracy Promotion: Impulses, Strategies, and Impacts*. Oxford: Oxford University Press, 103–126.

Ikenberry, John. 2008. The Rise of China and the Future of the West. *Foreign Affairs* 87(1): 23–37.

Information Office of the State Council of the PRC. 2011. China's Peaceful Development. September, http: //english.gov.cn/official/2011-09/06/content_1941354.htm accessed 10 February 2014.

Ingebritsen, Christine Iver Neumann and Sieglinde Gstöhl. 2006. *Small States in International Relations*. Seattle: University of Washington Press.

Innes, Alexandria Jayne and Brent J. Steele. 2012. Governmentality in Global Governance. In David Levi-Faur. Ed. *The Oxford Handbook of Governance*. Oxford: Oxford University Press, 716–729.

Ivanhoe, Philip J. and Sungmoon Kim. Eds. 2016. *Confucianism, a Habit of the Heart: Bellah, Civil Religion, and East Asia*. New York: CUNY Press.

Ivanhoe, Philip. 2004. Filial Piety as a Virtue. In Alan K. L. Chan. Ed. *Filial Piety in Chinese Thought and History*. London, UK: Routledge Curzon Press, 189–202.

Jackson, Patrick Thaddeus and Daniel Nexon. 1999. Relations before States: Substance, Process and the Study of World Politics. *European Journal of International Relations* 5(3): 291–332.

Jacobs, Bruce. 2012. *Democratizing Taiwan*. Leiden: Brill.

Jacques, Martin. 2012/2009. *When China Rules the World: The End of the Western World and the Birth of a New Global Order*. New York: Penguin.

Jaggar, Alison. 1995. Caring as a Feminist Practice of Moral Reason. In Virginia Held. Ed. *Justice and Care: Essential Readings in Feminist Ethnic*. Boulder, CO: Westview, 179–202.

Jahn, Beate. 2007. The Tragedy of Liberal Diplomacy: Democratization, Intervention, Statebuilding. *Journal of Intervention and Statebuilding* 1(1): 87–106.

Jameson, Fredric. 1991. *Postmodernism, or the Cultural Logic of Late Capitalism*. Durham, NC: Duke University Press.

Jervis, Robert. 1978. Cooperation under the Security Dilemma. *World Politics* 30: 167–214.

Jha, Saurav. 2017. China's Creeping Invasion of India. *The Diplomat* (6 July) http://thediplomat.com/2017/07/chinas-creeping-invasion-of-india/ accessed 29 September 2017.

Johnson, Ina. 2002. The Application of Buddhism Principles to Lifelong Learning. *International Journal of Lifelong Education* 21(2): 99–114.

Johnston, Alastair Iain. 1995a. Thinking about Strategic Culture. *International Security* 19 (4): 32–64.

Johnston, Alastair Iain. 1998/1995. *Cultural Realism: Strategic Culture and Grand Strategy in Chinese History*. Princeton, NJ: Princeton University Press.

Johnston, Alastair Iain. 1999. Sun Zi Studies in the United States. www.tinyurl.com/kato55z accessed 10 June 2017.

Johnston, Alastair Iain. 2008. *Social States: China in International Institutions, (1980–2000)*. Princeton, NJ: Princeton University Press.

Johnston, Alastair Iain. 2013. 'How New and Assertive is China's New Assertiveness? *International Security* 37(4): 7–48.

Jones, Branwen G. Ed. 2006. *Decolonizing International Relations*. UK: Rowman & Littlefield Publishers.

Joseph, Jonathan. 2010. The Limits of Governmentality: Social Theory and the International. *European Journal of International Relations* 16(2): 223–246.

Josey, Alex. 1974. *Lee Kuan Yew: The Struggle for Singapore*. Singapore: Angus and Robertson.

Kahn, Herman. 1960. *On Thermonuclear War*. Princeton, NJ: Princeton University Press.

Kang, David. 2003/04. Hierarchy, Balancing, and Empirical Puzzles in Asian International Relations. *International Security* 28(3): 165–180.

Kang, David. 2007. *China Rising: Peace, Power, and Order in East Asia*. New York: Columbia University Press.

Karlsson, Krister. 2011. China & Peacekeeping: Contributions to UN Peace Operations from 2000–2010 and the Theory of Offensive Realism. Minor Field Study Report. Uppsala: Department of Peace and Conflict Research, Uppsala University.

Katz, Paul. 2013. Repaying a Nuo Vow in Western Hunan: A Rite of Trans-Hybridity? *Taiwan Journal of Anthropology* 11(2): 1–88.

Katzenstein, Peter. 2008. *Rethinking Japanese Security: Internal and External Dimensions*. London, UK: Routledge.

Katzenstein, Peter. Ed. 2012. *Sinicization and the Rise of China: Civilizational Processes beyond East and West*. London, UK: Routledge.

Kalvaski, Emilian. 2013. The Struggle for Recognition of Normative Powers: Normative Power Europe and Normative Power China in Context. *Cooperation and Conflict* 48: 247–267.

Kalvaski, Emilian. 2018. Guanxi or What Is the Chinese for Relational Theory of World Politics. *International Relations of the Asia-Pacific* 18(3): 397–420.

Kayaoglu, Turan. 2010. Westphalian Eurocentrism in International Relations Theory. *International Studies Review* 12(2): 193–217.

Keene, Edward. 2002. *Beyond the Anarchical Society: Grotius, Colonialism and Order in World Politics*. Cambridge, MA: Cambridge University Press.

Kendall, Gavin. 2004. Global Networks, International Networks, Actor Networks. In Larner Wendy and William Walters. Eds. *Global Governmentality: Governing International Spaces*. London, UK: Routledge, 59–75.

Kennedy, Paul. 1987. *The Rise and Fall of Great Powers*. New York: Vintage Books.

Keohane, Robert. 1984. *After Hegemony*. Princeton, NJ: Princeton University Press.

Keohane, Robert and Joseph Nye. 1987. Power and Interdependence Revisited. *International Organization* 41(4): 725–753.

Khong, Yuen Foong. 2013. The American Tributary System. *Chinese Journal of International Politics* 6(1): 27–28.

Kieschnick, John. 2003. *The Impact of Buddhism on Chinese Material Culture*. Princeton, NJ: Princeton University Press.

Kim, Samuel. 1995. China's Pacific Policy: Reconciling the Irreconcilable. *International Journal* 50(3): 469–477.

Kim, Yong Ho. 2011. *North Korean Foreign Policy: Security Dilemma and Succession*. Lexingtong: Lanham.

Kindleberger, Charles P. 1981. Dominance and Leadership in the International Economy. *International Studies Quarterly* 25(3): 242–254.

King, Alexander and Bertrand Schneider. 1991. *The First Global Revolution: A Report of the Council of Rome*. New York: Pantheon Books.

King, Ambrose. 1985. The Individual and Group in Confucianism: A Relational perspective. In D. J. Munro. Ed. *Individualism and Holism: Studies in Confucian and Taoist Values*. Ann Arbor, MI: Center for Chinese Studies, The University of Michigan, 57–70.

Kissinger, Henry. 2011. *On China*. New York: The Penguin Press.

Kleinman, Arthur. 1986. *Social Origins of Distress and Disease: Neurasthenia, Depression and Pain in Modern China*. Berkeley, CA: University of California Press.

Klingler-Vidra, R. 2012. *The Pragmatic "Little Red Dot': Singapore's US Hedge against China* IDEAS Reports. In K. Nicholas Ed. SR015. LSE IDEAS. London, UK: London School of Economics and Political Science.

Klotz, Audie. 1995. *Norms in International Relations: The Struggle against Apartheid*. Ithaca, NY: Cornell University Press.

Kohli, Atul. 1991. *Democracy and Discontent: India's Growing Crisis of Governability*. Cambridge, MA: Cambridge University Press.

Koremenos, Babara. 2001. Loosening the Ties that Bind: A Learning Model of Agreement, Flexibility. *International Organization* 55(2): 289–325.

Kraidy, Marwan. 2004. From Culture to Hybridity in International Communication. In M. Semati. Ed. *New Frontiers in International Communication Theory*. Lanham, MD: Rowman & Littlefield, 247–262.

Krasner, Stephen. 1999. *Sovereignty: Organized Hypocrisy*. Princeton, NJ: Princeton University Press.

Krasner, Stephen D. 2013. Seeking "Good-Enough-Governance" – Not Democracy. *Reuters*. 23 September, http://blogs.reuters.com/great-debate/2013/09/22/seeking-good-enough-governance-not-democracy/ accessed 27 January 2019.

Kuah-Pearce, Khun Eng. 2014. Understanding Suffering and Giving Compassion: *The Reach of Socially Engaged Buddhism into China*. Anthropology & Medicine 21(1): 27–42.

Kuik, Cheng-chwee. 2005. Multilateralism in China's ASEAN Policy: Its Evolution, Characteristics, and Aspiration. *Contemporary Southeast Asia* 27(1): 102–122.

Kuik, Cheng-Chwee, Ran Li and Sien Ngan Ling. 2017. The Institutional Foundations and Features of China-ASEAN Connectivity. In Lowell Dittmer and Chow Bing Ngeow. Eds. *Southeast Asia and China: A Contest in Mutual Socialization*. Singapore: World Scientific, 247–278.

Kuo, Hua-lun, 1975. *Zhong gong shi lun* [*History of the Chinese Communist Party*]. Taipei: Institute of International Relations, 4 volumes.

Kuo, Tai-chun and Remon Myers. 1986. *Understanding Communist China: Communist China Studies in the United States and the Republic of China, 1949–1978*. Stanford, CA: The Hoover Institute Press.

Kupchan, Charles. 1998. After Pax Americana: Benign Power, Regional Integration, and the Sources of a Stable Multipolarity. *International Security* 23(2): 40–79.

Lagerkvist, Johan. 2012. China's New Flexibility on Foreign Intervention: Seeking Global Clout, China's Position on Sanctity of Sovereignty Evolves. *YaleGlobal* (May 29), http: //yaleglobal.yale.edu/content/chinas-new-flexibility-foreign-inter vention accessed 25 May 2014.

Lai, Tse-han, H. Ramon Myers and Wei Wou. 1991. *A Tragic Beginning: The Taiwan Uprising of February 28, 1947.* Stanford, CA: Stanford University Press.

Lake, David. 2009. *Hierarchy in International Relations.* Ithaca, NY: Cornell University Press.

Lake, David. 2009. Relational Authority and Legitimacy in International Relations. *American Behavioral Scientist* 53(3): 331–353.

Lampton, David. 1997. A Growing China in a Shrinking World: Bejing and Global Order. In Ezra Vogel. Ed. *Living with China.* New York: W. W. Norton, 120–140.

Lampton, David. 2008. *The Three Faces of Chinese Power: Might, Money, and Mind.* Berkeley, CA: University of California Press.

Lane-Poole, Stanley. 1901. *Sir Harry Parkes in China.* London, UK: Methuen & Co.

Larrinaga, Miguel de and Marc G. Doucet. 2010. Governmentality, Sovereign Power, and Intervention: Security Council Resolutions and the Invasion of Iraq. In Miguel de Larrinaga and Marc G. Doucet. Eds. *Security and Global Governmentality Globalization, Governance and the State.* Oxon: Routledge, 96–110.

Larson, Deborah Welch and Alexei Shevchenko. 2011. Status Seekers: Chinese and Russian Responses to U.S. Primacy. *International Security* 34(4): 70–76.

Laruelle, Marlène. 2008. *Russian Eurasianism: An Ideology of Empire.* Baltimore: The Johns Hopkins University Press.

Lee, Kuan Yew. 1988. *The Singapore Story: Memoirs of Lee Kuan Yew.* Singapore: Times Editions Pte Ltd. and the Straits Times Press.

Lee, Kuan Yew. 2000. *From Third World to First: The Singapore Story: 1965–2000.* New York: HarperCollins Publishers.

Lemke, Thomas. 2007. An Indigestible Meal? Foucault, Governmentality and State Theory [Unpublished Manuscript].

Lepgold, Joseph. 1998. NATO's Post-Cold War Collective Action Problem. *International Security* 23(1): 78–106.

Leung, Kwok. 2008. Chinese Culture, Modernization and International Business. *International Business Review* 17(2): 184–187.

Levinger, George. 1983. Development and Change. In Harold H. Kelley, et al. Eds. *Close Relationships.* New York: W.H. Freeman and Company, 315–359.

Li, Hongzhang. 1880. Zhidu li hongzhang zou riben yijie liuqiuan qianshe gaiyue zheyi huanyun zhe" [Zhili Viceroy Li Hongzhang reports that Japan attempts to change the trade agreement with China in order to wants to finalize the Ryukyu issue but China has to reconsider Japan's terms]. *Diplomatic Materials of the Late Qing* [*Qingji waijiao shiliao*] 24 (November 11).

Li, Peter Ping. 2012. Toward an Integrative Framework of Indigenous Research: The Geocentric Implications of Yin-Yang Balance. *Asian Pacific Journal of Management* 29: 849–872.

Liang, Shu-ming. 2005. *The Essence of Chinese Culture [Zhongguo wenhua yaoyi].* Shanghai: Shanghai People's Press.

Liberthal, Kenneth. 2007. How Domestic Forces Shape the PRC's Grand Strategy and International Impact. In Ashley Tellis and Michael Wills. Eds. *Domestic*

Political Change and Grand Strategy, Strategic Asia, 2007–2008. Washington, DC: The National Bureau of Asian Research, 29–68.

Lin, Hongyu. 2012. The Difficult Conditions of Chinese Maritime Strategy: Cause and Policy. [Zhongguo haiyang zhanlve kunjing: chengyin yu duice] *Contemporary International Relations [Xiandai guoji guanxi]* 8: 14–16.

Lin, Jin-shu. 2009. The Status quo of Sino-North Korean Trade and the Countermeasures. *Journal of Yanbian University (Social Science)* 1: 37–43.

Lin, Limin. 2012. Pojie bian hai kunju shi zhongguo da zhanlue qi dai jiejue de shiji mingti [Breaking up the Predicament at the Maritime Borderline is the Urgent Issue of the Century to Be Resolved]. *Contemporary International Relations [Xiandai guoji guanxi]* 8: 41–42.

Lin, Tsung-Yi, Wen-Shing Tseng and Eng-Kung Yeh. Eds. 1995. *Chinese Societies and Mental Health.* New York: Oxford University Press.

Lind, William. 1985. *Maneuver Warfare Handbook.* Boulder and London, UK: Westview Press.

Ling, Lily H. M. 2002. *Postcolonial International Relations: Conquest and Desire Between Asia and the West.* New York: Palgrave Macmillan.

Ling, Lily H. M. 2014. *The Dao of World Politics: Towards a Post-Westphalian, Worldist International Relations.* New York: Routledge.

Lionel, Giles. Transl. 1910/1999. *Sun Tzu on the Art of War.* Torrance, CA: Heian Int.

Lipson, Michael. 2007. Peacekeeping: Organized Hypocrisy. *European Journal of International Relations* 13(1): 5–34.

Liu, Kunyi. 1880. Jiangdu liu kunyi zou liuqiuan yisujie riyue yishenzhong tuwei zhe" [Nanjing Viceroy Liu Kunyi reports that the Ryukyu should be ended immediately and China should be very careful when it signs agreement with Japan]. *Diplomatic Materials of the Late Qing [Qingji waijiao shiliao]* 24 (November 30): 15–16.

Loch, Henry. 1900. *Personal narrative of Occurrences during Lord Elgin's Second Embassy to China in 1860.* London, UK: John Murray.

Lonsdale, David. 2007. *Alexander the Great: Lessons in Strategy.* London, UK: Routledge.

Lopez, Donald Jr. 2008. *Buddhism and Science: A Guide for the Perplexed.* Chicago, IL: University of Chicago Press.

Lucinescu, Alexandru. 2010. Humanitarian Intervention, Sovereignty and the UN Charter in the International Liberal Order 3.0. *Journal of East European & Asian Studies* 1(3): 401–418.

Luke, Timothy. 1996. Governmentality and Contragovernmentality: Rethinking Sovereignty and Territoriality after the Cold War. *Political Geography* 15(6–7): 491–507.

Luo, Guanzhong. 2001. *Moss Roberts. Transl. Romance of the Three Kingdoms.* Beijing: Beijing Foreign Languages Press.

Luttwak, Edward and Stuart L. Koehl. 1991. *The Dictionary of Modern War.* New York: Gramercy.

Lynch, C. Daniel. 2006. *Rising China and Asian Democratization: Socialization to "Global Culture" in the Political Transformations of Thailand, China, and Taiwan.* Stanford, CA: Stanford University Press, 150–180.

Lynn-Jones, Sean. 1998. Why the United States Should Spread Democracy. *Discussion Essay 98–07.* Center for Science and International Affairs, Harvard University, http://belfercenter.ksg.harvard.edu/publication/2830/why_the_united_states_should_spread_democracy.html accessed 10 February 2014.

Ma, Ying-Joey. year n.a. Building Up Taiwan, Invigorating Chinese Heritage. At www.president.gov.tw.

Ma, Lian. 2013. Thinking of China's Grand Strategy: Chinese Perspectives. *International Relations of the Asia-Pacific* 13(1): 155–168.

Ma, Lin. 2012. Zhong Yue Shouci Kuajie Haishang Soujiu Yanxi [The First Sino-Vietnam Interstate Rescue Drill Has Been Held]. *Wenweipo* [*Wenhuibao*]. August 30. http: //paper.wenweipo.com/(2012/08/30/CH1(208300012)htm accessed 23 July 2013.

Ma, Xinyi. 1866. Fengchen yangren chengdi juwai pangguan lu xinyi lunlue zhi yongyi bingchen ziqiang zhice" (Hart's Purpose of the Bystander's View and How to Self-Strengthen). *Jindai zhongguo dui xifang ji lieqian renshi ziliao huibian* 2(2): 687–692.

Ma, Ying-jeou, year n.a. A Century of Struggle, a Democratic Taiwan. www.president. gov.tw.

McAdam, Doug, Sidney G. Tarrow and Charles Tilly. 2001. *Dynamics of Contention.* New York: Cambridge University Press.

Maass, Matthias. 2009. The Elusive Definition of the Small State. *International Politics* 46(1): 65–83.

Maass, Matthias. 2014. Fight for Survival: Systemic Causes of Small State Survival and Proliferation. *International Politics* 51(6): 709–728.

Maass, Matthias. 2017. *Small States in World Politics: The Story of Small State Survival, 1648–2016.* Oxford: Oxford University Press.

Mair, Victor. 2008. Soldierly Methods: Vade Mecum for an Iconoclastic Translation of *Sun Zi bingfa. Sino-Platonic Papers* 178.

Maoz, Zeev, Lesley G. Terris, Ranan D. Kuperman, and Ilan Talmud. 2006. International Relations: A Network Approach. In Alex Mintz and Bruce M. Russett. Eds. *New Directions for International Relations: Confronting the Method-of-Analysis Problem.* Lanham, MD: Lexington Books, 35–64.

Marcussen, Kriste. 2006. Identities, Self-Esteem, and Psychological Distress: An Application of Identity-Discrepancy. *Sociological Perspectives* 49(1): 1–24.

McHale, Shawn. 2004. *Print and Power: Confucianism, Communism, and Buddhism in the Making of Modern Vietnam.* Honolulu: University of Hawaii Press.

McMullin, Ernan. 2001. The Impact of Newton's Principia on the Philosophy of Science. *Philosophy of Science* 68: 279–310.

Mead, George Herbert. 1934. *Mind, Self and Society: From the Standpoint of a Social Behaviorist.* Chicago, IL: Chicago University Press.

Mearsheimer, John. 2001. *The Tragedy of Great Power Politics.* New York: Norton.

Mearsheimer, John. 2006. China's Unpeaceful Rise. *Current History* 105(690): 160–162.

Mearsheimer, John. 2014. Say Goodbye to Taiwan. The National Interest (March-April), http: //nationalinterest.org/article/say-goodbye-taiwan-9931.

Medeiros, Evan and Taylor Fravel. 2003. China's New Diplomacy. *Foreign Affairs* 82(6): 22–35.

Midlarsky, Manus I. and Kun Y. Park. 1991. *Major-Minor Power Wars, 1495–1815.* Champaign-Urbana, IL: Data Development in International Research.

Minford, John M. Transl. 2002. *Sun Tzu: The Art of War.* London: Viking.

Minford, John M. Interview, Sonshi: https://www.sonshi.com/john-minford-interview.html accessed 27 February 2017.

Ministry of Finance, Republic of China. 1973. Minutes of Discussion between Ministers of Finance of Singapore and Republic of China, September 10.

Mizoguchi, Yuzo. 1999. *zhongguo zuowei fangfa* (*China as Method*). Trans. LIN You-chong. Taipei: National Institute for Compilation and Translation.

MOFA (Ministry of Foreign Affairs of the PRC). 2003. China's EU Policy Paper, www.fmprc.gov.cn/eng/topics/ceupp/t27708)htm, 12 July.

Moran, Peter. 2005. Structural vs. Relational Embeddedness: Social Capital and Managerial Importance. *Strategic Management* 26(12): 1129–1151.

Mott, William H. and Jae Chang Kim. 2006. *The Philosophy of Chinese Military Culture: Shih vs. Li*. New York: Palgrave.

Mouffe, Chantal. 1993/2005. *The Return of the Political*. London, UK: Verso.

Mukerji, Chandra. 2007. Cultural Genealogy: Method for a Historical Sociology of Culture or Cultural Sociology of History. *Cultural Sociology* 1: 49–71.

Nair, Deepak. 2019. Saving Face in Diplomacy: A Political Sociology of Face-to-face Interactions in the Association of Southeast Asian Nations. *European Journal of International Relations*. https://doi.org/10.1177/1354066118822117

Nathan, Andrew and Andrew Scobell. 2012. *China's Search for Security*. New York: Columbia University Press.

Nathan, Andrew and Robert Ross. 1998. *The Great Wall and the Empty Fortress: China's Search for Security*. New York: W. W. Norton.

Nau, Henry. 2002. From Bilateralism to Multilateralism. In Henry Nau. Ed. *At Home Abroad: Identity and Power in American Foreign Policy*. Ithaca, NY: Cornell University Press, 152–189.

Needham, Joseph. 1991. *Science and Civilisation in China*. Cambridge, MA: Cambridge University Press.

Neilson, Brett. 1999. On the New Cosmopolitanism. *Communal/Plural: Journal of Transnational and Cross-Cultural Studies* 7: 111–124.

Neumann, Iver B. and Ole Jacob Sending. 2010. *Governing the Global Polity*. New York: University of Michigan Press.

Neumann, Iver. 2011. Entry into International Society Reconceptualized: The Case of Russia. *Review of International Studies* 37(2): 463–84.

Nexon, Daniel and Thomas Wright. 2007. What's at Stake in the American Empire Debate. *American Political Science Review* 101(2): 253–271.

Nexon, Daniel. 2008. The Relational Turn in the Study of World Politics. Paper Presented at the American Political Science Annual Meeting, Boston, Massachusetts, August 28–31.

Ng, Yu-kwan. 2011. Juedui wu yu zhexue guannian de dianfan [Absolute Nothingness and the Paradigms of Philosophical Concepts]. *Satyabhisamaya: A Buddhist Studies Quarterly* [*Zhengguan*] 56: 5–28.

Ni, Eryan. 2008. U.S Arms Sales to Taiwan Poison Sino-U.S. Military Exchanges. [Mei dui tai junshou duhua zhong mei junshi jiaoliu] *Wenweipo* [*Wenhuibao*], October 9. http: //paper.wenweipo.com/2008/10/09/WW0810090003.htm.

Ninh Kim. 1998. Vietnam: Struggle and Cooperation. In Muthiah Alagappa. Ed. *Asian Security Practice: Material and Ideational Influences*. Stanford, CA: Stanford University Press, 445–476.

Nish, Ian. 2006. *Japanese Foreign Policy in the Interwar Period*. Westport: Praeger.

Nishitani, Keiji. 1983. *Religion and Nothingness*. Berkeley: University of California Press.

Noesselt, Nele. 2012. Is There a 'Chinese School' of IR? *GIGA Working Paper* No. 188.

Nye, Joseph. 1995. East Asian Security: The Case for Deep Engagement. *Foreign Affairs* 74(4): 90–102.

Nye, Joseph. 2013. Work with China, Don't Contain it. *The New York Times*. January 26: A19. www.nytimes.com/(2013/01/26/opinion/work-with-china-dont-contain-it.html?_r=0 accessed 28 January 2013.

O'Brien, Robert, Anne Marie Goetz, Jan Aart Scholte and Marc Williams. 2000. *Contesting Global Governance: Multilateral Economic Institutions and Global Social Movements.* Cambridge, MA: Cambridge University Press.

Oldmeadow, Julian A. and Susan T. Fiske. 2010. Social Status and the Pursuit of Positive Social Identity: Systematic Domains of Intergroup Differentiation and Discrimination for High- and Low- Status Groups. *Group Processes and Intergroup Relations* 13(4): 425–444.

Olson, Mancur. 1965. *The Logic of Collective Action.* Cambridge, MA: Harvard University Press.

Ong, Aihwa. 1998. Flexible Citizenship among Chinese Cosmopolitans. In P. Cheah and B. Robbins. Eds. *Cosmopolitics: Thinking and Feeling Beyond the Nation.* Minneapolis: Minneapolis University of Minnesota Press, 134–162.

Osinga, Frans. 2007. *Science, Strategy and War: The Strategic Theory of John Body.* Abingdon: Routledge.

Osondu, Adaora. 2013. Off and On: China's Principle of Non-Interference in Africa. *Mediterranean Journal of Social Science* 4(3): 225–234.

Paal, Doulas. 2010. China: Reaction to Taiwan Arms Sales. January 31. http: //carnegieendowment.org/2010/01/31/china-reaction-to-taiwan-arms-sales/3zc7 accessed 16 July 2013.

Pan, Chengxin. 2018. Toward a New Relational Ontology in Global Politics: China's Rise as Holographic Transition. *International Relations of the Asia-Pacific* 18(3): 339–367.

Pan, Zhenqiang. 2015. A study on China's no-first-use nuclear policy. *Air & Space Power Journal* 9(1): 12–24.

Pang, Zhongying. 2009. China's Non-Intervention Question. *Global Responsibility to Protect* 1: 237–252.

Panke, Diana. 2010. Small States in the European Union: Structural Disadvantages in EU Policy-making and Counter-strategies. *Journal of European Public Policy* 17(6): 799–817.

Paolini, Albert. J., Anthony Elliott and Anthony Moran. 1999. *Navigating Modernity: Postcolonialism, Identity, and International Relations.* Boulder, CO: Lynne Rienner.

Path, Kosal. 2012. China's Economic Sanctions against Vietnam, 1975–1978', *China Quarterly* 212: 1040–1058.

Pempel, Thomas J. 2004. Challenges to Bilateralism: Changing Foes, Capital Flows, and Complex Forums. In S. Krauss and Thomas J. Pempel. Eds. *Beyond Bilateralism: U.S.- Japan Relations in the New Asia-Pacific.* Stanford, CA: Stanford University Press, 1–36.

Perliger, Arie and Ami Pedahzur. 2011. Social Network Analysis in the Study of Terrorism and Political Violence. *PS* 44(1): 45–50.

Piao, Shenghe. 2011. Dezui Libiya Fankangjun Zhanho Chongjian Zhong E Meifen? (Displeasing the Libyan Rebel China and Russia Out of the Postwar Reconstruction). *cn. Chosun.com*, August 25th. http: //bbs.aboluowang.com/viewthread.php?tid=47807 accessed September 3, 2011.

Pittman, Don Alvin. 2001. *Toward a Modern Chinese Buddhism: Taixu's Reforms.* Honolulu: University of Hawaii press.

Polk, Robert B. 2000. A Critique of the Boyd Theory: Is it Relevant to the Army? *Defense Analysis* 16(3): 257–276.

Porter, Patrick. 2007. "Good Anthropology, Bad History: The Cultural Turn in Studying War. *Parameters*, Summer 2007.

Preston, Peter. 2007. *Singapore in the Global System: Relationship, Structure and Change*. Oxon: Routledge.

Pye, Lucian W. 1985. *Asian Power and Politics: The Cultural Dimensions of Authority*. Cambridge, MA: Belknap Press of Harvard University Press.

Pye, Lucian. 1990. China: Erratic State, Frustrated Society. *Foreign Affairs* 69: 56–75.

Qi, Xiaoying. 2011. Face: A Chinese Concept in a Global Sociology. *Journal of Sociology* 47(3): 279–96.

Qin, Yaqing. 2018. *A Relational Theory of World Politics*. Cambridge, MA: Cambridge University Press.

Qin, Yaqing. 2013. Quanqiu zhili shiling yu zhixu linian de chongjian [Global Governance Failures and Reconstructing the Idea of Order] W*orld Economy and Politics* [*Shijie jingji yu zhengzhi*] 4: 4–18.

Qin, Yaqing. 2009a/2009. Guanxi benwei yu guocheng jiangou: jiang zhongguo linian zhiru guoji guuanxi lilun [Relationality and Processual Construction: Bring Chinese Ideas into IRT]. *Social Sciences in China* [*Zhongguo shehui kexue*] 3: 69–86.

Qin, Yaqing. 2009b. Development of International Relations Theory in China. *International Studies* 46(1–2): 185–201.

Qin, Yaqing. 2010. International Society as a Process: Institutions, Identities, and China's Peaceful Rise. *The Chinese Journal of International Politics* 3(2): 129–53.

Qin, Yaqing. 2011. Development of International Relations Theory in China: Progress Through Debates. *International Relations of the Asia-Pacific* 11(2): 235–257.

Qin, Yaqing. 2011. Rule, Rules, and Relations: Towards a Synthetic Approach to Governance. *Chinese Journal of International Politics* 4(2): 117–145.

Qin, Yaqing. 2012. Culture and Global Thought: Chinese International Theory in the Making. *Revista CIDOB d'Afers Internacionals* 100: 67–89.

Qingshilu [The Qing Emperors' Daily Records].

Raby, Geoff. 2015. China's AIIB Bank: Part of a Much Bigger Master Plan. *The National Interest*, 28 April.

Randall, Adrian and Andrew Charlesworth. Eds. 2000. *Moral Economy and Popular Protest: Crowds, Conflict and Authority*. Basingstoke: Macmillan.

Rathbun, Brian. 2012. *Trust in International Cooperation: International Security Institutions, Domestic Politics, and American Multilateralism*. Cambridge, MA: Cambridge University Press.

Redshaw, Sarah. 2013. Feminist Preludes to Relational Sociology. In Christopher Powell and François Dépelteau. Eds. *Conceptualizing Relational Sociology: Ontological and Theoretical Issues*. New York: Palgrave Macmillan, 13–26.

Ren, Xiao. 2010. Traditional Chinese Theory and Practice of Foreign Relations: A Reassessment. In Yongnian Zhang. Ed. *China and International Relations: The Chinese View and the Contribution of Wang Gungwu*. Abingdon: Routledge, 102–116.

Ren, Xiao. 2015. China's Former Diplomat: China Has China's Reasons. Interview, the BBC News Chinese version, www.bbc.com/zhongwen/trad/china/2015/03/150312_china_marine_disputes accessed 27 October 2015.

Renolds, Robert. 2007. How Does Therapy Cure? The Relational Turn in Psychotherapy. *Counselling, Psychotherapy, and Health* 3(2): 127–150.

Renshon, Jonathan. 2015. Losing Face and Sinking Costs: Experimental Evidence on the Judgment of Political and Military Leaders. *International Organization* 69(3): 659–695.

Richey, Jeffrey. 2013. *Confucius in East Asia: Confucianism's History in China, Korea, Japan, and Viet Nam*. Ann Arbor, MI: Association for Asian Studies.

Rigger, Shelley. 1999. *Politics in Taiwan: Voting for Democracy.* London, UK: Routledge.

Rigger, Shelley. 2011. *Why Taiwan Matters: Small Island, Global Powerhouse.* Lanham, MD: Rowman and Littlefield.

Rinpocije, Kalij. 1986. *The Dharma.* Albany: S.U.N.Y. Press.

Ritzinger, Justin. 2014. The Awakening of Faith in Anarchism: A Forgotten Chapter in the Chinese Buddhist Encounter with Modernity. *Politics, Religion & Ideology* 15(2): 224–243.

Robinson, Fiona. 1997. Care: Ethics, Feminist Theory, and International Relations. *Alternatives* 22(1): 113–133.

Rock, Stephen. 1989. *Why Peace Breaks Out: Great Power Rapprochement in Historical Perspective.* Chapel Hill: University of North Carolina Press.

Romila, Thapar. 1996. *Time as a Metaphor of History: Early India.* New Delhi: Oxford University Press.

Roseman, Ira. 1984. Cognitive determinants of Emotion: A Structural Theory. *Review of Personality and Social Psychology* 5(1): 11–36.

Ross, Robert. 1999. Engagement in US China Policy. In Alastair I. Johnston and Robert Ross. Eds. *Engaging China: The Management of an Emerging Power.* London, UK: Routledge, 176–206.

Ross, Robert. 2002. Navigating the Taiwan Strait: Deterrence, Escalation Dominance and US-China Relations. *International Security* 27(2): 48–85.

Ross, Robert. 2006. Explaining Taiwan's Revisionist Diplomacy. *Journal of Contemporary China* 15(48): 443–458.

Roy, Dennis. 2005. Southeast Asia and China: Balancing or Bandwagoning? *Contemporary Southeast Asia* 2(2): 305–322.

Ruan, Ming. 2000. Xin zhengfu de liangan zhengce: guancha yu zhanwang [The New Government's cross-Strait Policy—Observation and Prospect]. *Prospect Quarterly* [Yuanjing jikan] 1(3): 179–200.

Ruggie, John. 1992. Multilateralism: The Anatomy of an Institution. *International Organization* 46(3), 561–598.

Ruggie, John. 1993. *Multilateralism Matters: The Theory and Praxis of an Institutional Form.* New York: Columbia University Press.

Ruggie, John Gerard. 1993. *Multilateralism Matters: The Theory and Praxis of an Institutional Form.* New York: Columbia University Press.

Sadler, Arthur L. Transl. 1944/2009. *The Chinese Martial Code.* Tokyo: Tuttle Publishing.

Said, Edward. 1993. *Culture and Imperialism.* New York: Vintage Books.

Said. Edward. 1994. *Representations of the Intellectual.* London, UK: Vintage UK.

Sajed, Alina. 2010. Postcolonial Strangers in a Cosmopolitan World: Hybridity and Citizenship in the Franco-Maghrebian Borderland. *Citizenship Study* 14(4), 363–380.

Sassen, Saskia. 2006. *Territoriality, Authority, Rights: From Medieval to Global Assemblages.* Princeton, NJ: Princeton University Press.

Sawyer, Ralph D. Transl. 1993. *The Seven Military Classics of Ancient China.* Boulder, CO: Westview Press.

Sawyer, Ralph. Transl. 1994. *Sun Tzu: The Art of War.* Boulder, CO: Westview Press.

Schelkle, Waltraud. 2007. EU Fiscal Governance. Hard Law in the Shadow of Soft Law. *Columbia Journal of European Law* 13: 705–731.

Schelling, Thomas. 1996. *Arms and Influence.* New Haven: Yale University Press.

Scott, James. 1976. *The Moral Economy of the Peasant: Rebellion and Subsistence in Southeast Asia.* Princeton, NJ: Princeton University Press.

Selg, Peeter. 2016. Two Faces of the 'Relational Turn'. *PS: Political Science & Politics* 49(1): 27–31.

Sending, Ole Jacob and Iver Neumann. 2006. Governance to Governmentality: Analyzing NGOs, States, and Power. *International Studies Quarterly* 50(3): 651–672.

Senn, Martin and Christoph Elhardt. 2013. Bourdieu and the Bomb: Power, Language and the Doxic Battle over the Value of Nuclear Weapons. *European Journal of International Relations* 45: 530–547.

Shambaugh, David. 2011. Coping with a Conflicted China. *The Washington Quarterly* 34(1): 7–27.

Shan, Shelley and Hsiu-chuan Shih. 2012. "KMT Denies Ex-US-Officials Claims. *Taipei Times*, April 2.

Shan, Shelley and Hsiu-chuan Shih. 2012. US Grants Taiwan Visa-Waiver Status. *Taipei Times*, October 3.

Shani, Giorgio. 2007. Provincializing" Critical Theory: Islam, Sikhism, and International Relations Theory. *Cambridge Review of International Studies* 20(3): 417–433.

Shani, Giorgio. 2008. Towards a Post-Western IR: The Umma, Khalsa Panth, and Critical International Relations Theory. *International Studies Review* 10(4), 722–734.

Sharf, Robert. 1993. The Zen of Japanese Nationalism. *History of Religions* 33(1): 1–43.

Sheng, Lijun. 2002. *China and Taiwan: Cross-strait Relations under Chen Shui-bian.* Singapore: Institute of Southeast Asian Studies.

Shih, Chih-yu and Teng-chi Chang. 2011. The China Studies That Defend Chineseness: The Im/possibility of China Centrism in the Divided Sino-phone World. In Herbert S. Yee. Ed. *China's Rise – Threat or Opportunity?* London, UK: Routledge, 280–297.

Shih, Chih-yu and Chiung-chiu Huang. 2013. *Balance of Relationships: A Confucian Routes to Systemic IR.* Paper Presented at International Studies Association Annual Meeting, San Francisco, California, April 3–6.

Shih, Chih-yu and Chiung-chiu Huang. 2013. Preaching Self-Responsibility: The Chinese Style of Global Governance. *Journal of Contemporary China* 22(80): 351–365.

Shih, Chih-yu and Jiwu Yin. 2013. Between Core National Interest and a Harmonious World: Reconciling Self-Role Conceptions in Chinese Foreign Policy. *Chinese Journal of International Politics* 6(1): 59–84.

Shih, Chih-yu. 1990. *The Spirit of Chinese Foreign Policy: A Psychocultural View.* New York: St. Martin's Press.

Shih, Chih-yu. 2007. *Democracy (Made in Taiwan): The "Success" State as a Political Theory.* Plymouth: Lexington Books.

Shih, Chih-yu. 2010. The West That Is Not in the West: Identifying Self in Oriental Modernity. *Cambridge Review of International Affairs* 23: 537–560.

Shih, Chih-yu. 2011. Taiwan as East Asia in Formation: The Subaltern Appropriation of the Colonial Narrative. In Gunter Schubert and Jens Damm, Eds. *Taiwanese Identity in the 21st Century. Domestic, Regional and Global Perspective.* London: Routlege 2011, 237–257.

Shih, Chih-yu. 2012. *Civilization, Nation and Modernity in East Asia.* London: Routledge.

Shih, Chih-yu. 2013. *Sinicizing International Relations: Self, Civilization and Intellectual Politics in Subaltern East Asia.* London, UK: Palgrave.

Shih, Chih-yu. 2014. Relations and Balances: Self-restraint and Democratic Governability under Confucianism. *Pacific Focus* 29(3): 51–73.

Shih, Hsiu-chuan. 2013. Taiwan, Japan Ink Fisheries Agreement. *Taipei Times,* April 11.

Shimizu, Kosuke. 2009. *Nishida Kitaro and Japan's Interwar Foreign Policy: War Involvement and Culturalist Political Discourse. Working Paper Series* 44. Kyoto: Arasian Centre for Peace and Development Studies.

Shimizu, Kosuke. 2014. Materializing the 'Non-Western': Two Stories of Japanese Philosophers on Culture and Politics in the Inter-war Period. *Cambridge Review of International Affairs* 28(1): 3–20.

Sima, Qian. *Shi Ji* [*The Record of the Grand Historian*].

Simon, Robin. 1992. Parental Role Strains, Salience of Parental Identity, and Gender Differences in Psychological Distress. *Journal of Health and Social Behavior* 33(1): 25–35.

Singh, Swaran. 2013. The Chinese Grand Strategy: Insisting Multiple Choices and Not Putting All Eggs in One Basket. [Zhongguo waijiao dazhanglue: jianchi duobian xuanze bu ba jidan quan fangjin yige lanzi]. Interviewed by Tang Lu, December 28. http: //mil.eastday.com/eastday/mil/node3510/userobject1ai757527. html.

Slaughter, Anne-Marie. 2009. America's Edge: Power in the Networked Century. *Foreign Affairs* 88(1): 94–113.

Sleebos, Ed, Naomi Ellemers and Dick de Gilder. 2006. The Carrot and the Stick: Affective Commitment and Acceptance Anxiety as Motives for Discretionary Group Efforts by Respected and Disrespected Group Members. *Personality and Social Psychology Bulletin* 32: 244–255.

Snyder, Jack. 2008. Some Good and Bad Reasons for a Distinctively Chinese Approach to International Relations Theory. Presented at the Annual Meeting of the American Political Science Association, Boston, August 28–31.

Spence, Jonathan. 1969. *To Chang China: Western Advisers in China.* New York: Little, Brown and Company.

Spengler, Oswald. 1991. *The Decline of the West.* Oxford: Oxford University Press.

Spivak, Gayatri Chakravorty. 1985. Three Women's Texts and A Critique of Imperialism. *Critique Inquiry* 12(1): 235–161.

Sroufe, Alan and Everett Waters. 1977. Attachment as an Organizational Construct. *Child Development* 48: 1184–1199.

Statistical Department of the Inspectorate General of Customs. 1917. *Treaties, Conventions, Etc., between China and Foreign States* 1, 2nd edition. Shanghai: Statistical Department of the Inspectorate General of Customs.

Stephan, Walter and Cookie White Stephan. 1985. Intergroup Anxiety. *Journal of Social Issues* 41(3): 157–175.

Stern, Maria and Marysia Zalewski. 2009. Feminist Fatigue(s): Reflections on Feminism and Familiar Fables of Militarisation. *Review of International Studies* 35(3): 611–630.

Stone, Jacqueline. 1999a. Some Reflections on Critical Buddhism Jacqueline. *Japanese Journal of Religious Studies* 26(1–2): 159–188.

Stroud, Christopher and Lionel Wee. 2011. *Style, Identity and Literacy: English in Singapore*. Bristol: Multilingual Matters.

Sun, Ge. 2003. *Zhuti misan de kongjian* [*The Space with Pervasive Subjectivities*]. Nanchang: Jiangxi Education Press [Jiangsu jiaoyu chubanshe].

Sun, Kang-I. 1997. Ming-Qing Women Poets and the Notions of "Talent" and "Morality." In Theodore Huters, R. Bin Wong, and Pauline Yu. Eds. *Culture & State in Chinese History: Conventions, Accommodations, and Critiques*. Stanford, CA: Stanford University Press, 236–258.

Swaine, Michael and Taylor Fravel. 2011. China's Assertive Behaviour—Part Two: The Maritime Periphery. *China Leadership Monitor* 35: 1–29.

Swaine, Michael D. and Ashley Tellis. 2000. *Interpreting Chinese Grand Strategy*. Santa Monica: Rand.

Swaine, Michael. 1999. *Taiwan's National Security, Defense Policy, and Weapons Procurement Process*. Santa Monica: RAND.

Takeuchi, Yoshimi. 1967. Yoakeno Kuni (Country of the Dawn). In *Takeuchi Yoshimi Zenshū* (Takeuchi Yoshimi Complete Works) 4. Tokyo: Chikuma Shobō, 424–441.

Takeuchi, Yoshimi. 2005. *What Is Modernity? Writings of Takeuchi Yoshimi*. Transl. Richard Calichman. New York: Columbia University Press.

Tan, Sor Hoon. 2008. Modernizing Confucianism and 'New Confucianism'. In Kam Louie. Ed. *The Cambridge Companion to Modern Chinese Culture*. Cambridge, MA: Cambridge University Press, 135–154.

Tanaka, Stephen. 1993. *Japan's Orient: Rendering the Past into the Future*. Berkeley: University of California Press.

Tang, Shiping and Yunling Zhang. 2005. China's Regional Strategy. In David Shambaugh. Ed. *Power Shift: China and Asia's New Dynamics*. Berkeley, CA: University of California Press, 54–74.

Tao, Jiang. 2002. A Buddhist Scheme for Engaging Modern Science: The Case of Taixu. *Journal of Chinese Philosophy* 29(4): 533–552.

Taylor, Ian. 2006. China's Oil Diplomacy in Africa. *International Affairs* 82(5): 937–959.

Thayer, Carlyle. 2010. Vietnam and Rising China: The Structural Dynamics of Mature Asymmetry. *Southeast Asian Affairs* 1: 392–409.

The Economist. 2014. Why China is creating a new "World Bank" for Asia, 11 November www.economist.com/blogs/economist-explains/2014/11/economist-explains-6 accessed 20 May 2015.

Thies, Cameron. 2010. Role Theory and Foreign Policy. In Robert A. Denemark. Ed. *The International Studies Encyclopedia* 10. West Sussex: Wiley-Blackwell, 6335–6356.

Thies, Cameron. 2013. *The United States, Israel, and the Search for International Order: Socializing States*. New York: Routledge.

Thies, Cameron. 2014/2013. *The United States, Israel, and the Search for International Order*. New York: Routledge.

Thucydides. 1996. *The Landmark Thucydides: A Comprehensive Guide to the Peloponnesian War*. Transl. Richard Crawley. In Robert B. Strassler. Ed. New York: Free Press.

Tickner, Arlene. 2013. Core, Periphery and (Neo)imperialist International Relations. *European Journal of International Relations* 19(3): 627–646.

Tickner, Arlene and David Blaney. Eds. 2013. *Claiming the International*. London, UK: Routledge.

Tickner, Arlene and Ole Wæver. Eds. 2009. *International Relations Scholarship Around the World*. London, UK: Routledge.

Tickner, Irene and David Blaney. 2012. *Thinking International Relations Differently*. London, UK: Routledge.

Tkacik, John, Jr. 2008. Taiwan Arms Sales: Less Than Meet the Eye. *WebMemo 2098 on Asia*. Washington DC: The Heritage Foundation. www.heritage.org/research/reports/2008/10/taiwan-arms-sales-less-than-meets-the-eye accessed January 27 2014.

Tow, William. 1999. Assessing U.S. Bilateral Security Alliances in the Asia Pacific's "Southern Rim": Why the San Francisco System Endures. Presented at Asia/ Pacific Research Center, Institute for International Studies, Stanford University, 1–36.

Trachtenberg, Marc. 1999. Making Grand Strategy: The Early Cold War Experience in Retrospect. *SAIS Review* 19(1): 33–40.

Tronto, Joan. 1993. *Moral Boundaries: A Political Argument for an Ethic of Care*. London, UK: Routledge.

Tu, Wei-ming. 1993. *Way, Learning, and Politics: Essays on the Confucian Intellectual*. Albany: State University of New York Press.

Tu, Wei-ming. 2001. The Ecological Turn in New Confucian Humanism: Implications for China and the World. *Daedalus* 130(4): 243–264.

Tu, Weiming. Ed. 1994. *The Living Tree: The Changing Meaning of Being Chinese Today*. Stanford, CA: Stanford University Press.

Tull, Dennis. 2008. China in Africa: European Perceptions and Responses to the Chinese Challenge. *SAIS Working Papers in African Studies*. Washington DC: African Studies Program, The Johns Hopkins University, Paul H. Nitze School Advanced International Studies.

Turner, Jonathan and Jan Stets. 2006. Sociological Theories of Human Emotions. *Annual Review of Sociology* 32: 25–52.

Tzou, Jiing-wen. 2001. *Lee denghui zhizheng gaobai shilu [An Account of Lee Tenghui in Power]*. Taipei: Ink Publishing Co., Ltd [Yinke chubanshe].

Uhl, Christian. 2009. Displacing Japan: Takeuchi Yoshimi's Lu Xun in Light of Nishida's Philosophy, and Vice Versa. *Positions* 17(1): 207–237.

US Naval War College. 2010. *Syllabus Strategy and Policy, March 2010–June 2010*.

Vaisey, Stephen and Omar Lizardo. 2010. Can Cultural Worldviews Influence Network Composition? *Social Forces* 88(4): 1595–1618.

van der Putten, Frans-Paul. 2013. Harmony with Diversity: China's Preferred World Order and Weakening Western Influence in the Developing World. *Global Policy* 4(1): 53–62.

Van Ness, Peter. 1970. *Revolution and Chinese Foreign Policy: Peking's Support for Wars of National Liberation*. Berkeley, CA: University of California Press.

Van Ness, Peter. 1985. *Civilizer States: America and China in the Modern World*. Unpublished paper. Denver.

Van Ness, Peter. 2004. Conclusion. In Melvin Gurtov and Peter Van Ness. Eds. *Confronting the Bush Doctrine: Critical Views from the Asia-Pacific*. London, UK: Routledge, 260–269.

Vasilaki, Rosa. 2012. Provincialising IR? Deadlocks and Prospects in Post-Western IR Theory. *Millennium* 41: 3–22.

Vital, David. 1967. *The Inequality of States: A Study of the Small Power in International Relations*. Oxford: Clarendon Press.

Vrasti, Wanda. 2013. Universal but not Truly 'Global': Governmentality, Economic Liberalism, and the International. *Review of International Studies* 39(1): 49–69.

Vuving, Alexander. 2006. Strategy and Evolution of Vietnam's China Policy: A Changing Mixture of Pathways. *Asian Survey* 46(6): 805–824.

Wall Street Journal. 2017. WSJ Interview Exerpts: China, North orea, Ex-Im Bank, Obamacare, Bannon, More. *Wall Street Journal*, April 12, https: //blogs.wsj.com/washwire/2017/04/12/wsj-trump-interview-excerpts-china-north-korea-ex-im-bank-obamacare-bannon/ accessed 30 May 2017.

Wallace, Alan. 2013. Introduction: Buddhism and Science—Breaking down the Barriers. In B. Alan Wallace. Ed. *Buddhism & Science: Breaking New Ground*. New York: Columbia University Press, 1–30.

Waltz, K., et al. 2002. War with Iraq Is Not in America's National Interest. *The New York Times*. September 26, op-Ed. http: //mearsheimer.uchicago.edu/pdfs/P0012) pdf, accessed 24 July 2013

Waltz, Kenneth. 1979. *Theory of International Politics*. Reading: Addison-Wesley Pub. Co.

Wang, Ban. Ed. 2017. *Chinese Visions of World Order: Tianxia, Culture, and World Politics*. Durham, NC: Duke University Press.

Wang, Guangya. 2006. A Peaceful Role Player in World Affairs. *Beijing Review* 20: 16–17.

Wang, Hongying and James Rosenau. 2009. China and Global Governance. *Asian Perspective* 33(3): 5–39.

Wang, Jianwei. 1999. Managing Conflict: Chinese Perspectives on Multilateral Diplomacy and Collective Security. In Yong Deng and Feiling Wang. Eds. *In the Eyes of the Dragon: China Views the World*. Lanham, MD: Rowman & Littlefield Publishers, 73–96.

Wang, Jisi. 2005. China's Search for a Grand Strategy: A Rising Great Power Finds Its Way. *Foreign Affairs* 90(2): 68–79.

Wang, Jisi. 2005. China's Search for Stability with America. *Foreign Affairs* 84(5): 39–48.

Wang, Xiao-tao. 2015. Economic Integration: Silk-road Nations Develop New Motive Power. http: //hk.crntt.com/crn-webapp/search/allDetail.jsp?id=103965562&sw=%E4%BA%9A%E6%B4%B2%E5%9F%BA%E7%A1%80%E8%AE%BE%E6%96%BD%E6%8A%95%E8%B5%84%E9%93%B6%E8%A1%8C, accessed 27 October 2015.

Wang, Yi. 2013. Japan Should Admit There is a Dispute over Diaoyu Islands'. www.bbc.com/zhongwen/trad/china/2013/09/130921_china_japan, accessed 27 October 2015.

Wang, Yi. 2013. Jiandingbuyi zou heping fazhan daolu [Walk the Road of Peace and Development with Determination]. *People's Daily* [*Renmin Ribao*], November 22: 16.

Wang, Yiwei. 2014. Jiangqingchu Zhonguo meng de guoji neihan [Clarifying the International Implications of the China Dream]. *People's Daily* [*Renmin Ribao*], January 14. http: //theory.gmw.cn/2014-01/14/content_10107474.htm.

Wang, Yuan-kang. 2010. *Harmony and War: Confucian Culture and Chinese Power Politics*. New York: Columbia University Press.

Wang, Zefei. 2012. Jianchi buganshe nei zheng, zhongguo bu shu li [Sticking with non-intervention in internal politics, China would not be beaten on reason], April 27. http: //big5.fmprc.gov.cn/gate/big5/www.fmprc.gov.cn/zflt/chn/zfgx/ t926892.htm accessed 25 May 2014.

Ward, D. Michael, Randolph M. Siverson and Xun Cao. 2007. Disputes, Democracies, and Dependencies: A Reexamination of the Kantian Peace. *American Journal of Political Science* 51(3): 583–601.

Ward, Lee. 2006. Locke on the Moral Basis of International Relations. *American Journal of Political Science* 50(3): 691–705.

Watson, Gay. 2001. *The Resonance of Emptiness; A Buddhist Inspiration for a Contemporary Psychotherapy.* Delhi: Jainendra Prakash Jain at Shri Jainendra Press.

Watts, John. 2009. Copenhagen Summit: China's Quiet Satisfaction at Tough Tactics and Goalless Draw. *The Guardian*, December 2. www.theguardian.com/environment/2009/dec/20/copenhagen-climate-summit-china-reaction accessed September 10, 2011.

Wei, Da. 2011. Cong Hu Jintao zhuxi fangmei kan zhongmei guanxi [Reviewing Sino-US Relations from Chairman Hu Jianto's Visit to the United States]. *China Talk* (21 January). www.china.com.cn/fangtan/2011-01/21/content_21789075.htm accessed 29 September 2017.

Wei, George C. X. 2012. The Taiwan Issue and the Taiwan Factor: Studying Cross-Strait Relations within the Global Context. In George C. X. Wei. Ed. *China-Taiwan Relations in a Global Context: Taiwan's Foreign Policy and Relations.* Oxon: Routledge, 1–12.

Wendt, Alexander. 1992. Anarchy is what states make of it: the social construction of power politics. *International Organization* 46(2): 391–425.

Wendt, Alexander. 1999. *Social Theory of International Relations.* Cambridge, MA: Cambridge University Press.

Wendt, Alexander. 2003. Why a World State Is Inevitable? *European Journal of International Relations* 9(4): 491–542.

White, Hugh. 2012. *The China Choice: Why America Should Share Power.* Melbourne: Black Inc.

Wich, Richard. 1980. *Sino-Soviet Crisis Politics: A Study of Political Change and Communication.* Cambridge, MA: Harvard University Press.

Wich, Richard. 1980. *Sino-Soviet Crisis Politics: A Study of Political Change and Communication.* Cambridge, MA: Harvard University Press.

Wight, Martin. 1966. Why is There No International Theory? In Herbert Butterfield and Martin Wight. Eds. *Diplomatic Investigations: Essays in the Theory of International Relations.* London, UK: Allen & Unwin, 17–34.

Wilkinson, Robert. 2009. *Nishida and Western Philosophy.* Farnham: Ashgate.

Williams, David.2004. *Defending Japan's Pacific War: The Kyoto School Philosophers and Post- White Power.* London: RoutledgeCurzon.

Williams, Michael C. 2001. The Discipline of the Democratic Peace: Kant, Liberalism and the Social Construction of Security Communities. *European Journal of International Relations* 7(4): 525–553.

Wills, John. 2009. How Many Asymmetries? Continuities, Transformations, and Puzzles in the Study of Chinese Foreign Relations. *The Journal of American-East Asian Relations* 16(1): 23–39.

Windsor, Philip. 2002. *Strategic Thinking: An Introduction and Farewell.* Edited with Mats Berdal and Spyros Economides. Boulder: Lynne Rienner.

Womack, Brantley. 2006. *China and Vietnam: The Politics of Asymmetry.* Cambridge, MA: Cambridge University Press.

Womack, Brantly. 2006. *China and Vietnam: The Politics of Asymmetry.* Cambridge: Cambridge University Press.

Wong, John. 1976. *Yeh Ming-chen: Viceroy of Liang Kuang (1852–1858).* Cambridge, MA: Cambridge University Press.

Wong, John. 1998. *Deadly Dreams: Opium and the Arrow War (1856–1860) in China.* Cambridge, MA: Cambridge University Press.

Wu, Guoguang and Helen Lansdowne. 2008. *China Turns to Multilateralism: Foreign Policy and Regional Security.* London, UK: Routledge.

Wu, Jianmin. 2013. Zhongguo meng bushi zhongguo yao lingdao shijie [The China Dream Is Not about Chinese Leading the World]. June 19. http: //theory.people.com.cn/n/2013/0619/c40531-21890559.html accessed July 21, 2013.

Wu, Yu-shan. 2011. The Evolution of the KMT's Stance on the One China Principle: National Identity in Flux. In Gunter Schubert and Jens Damm. Eds. *Taiwan in the Twenty-First Century: Domestic, Regional and Global Perspectives.* Oxon: Routledge, 51–71.

Wuthnow, Joel, Xin Li and Lingling Qi. 2012. Diverse Multilateralism: Four Strategies in China's Multilateral Diplomacy. *Journal of Chinese Political Science* 17(3): 269–290.

Xi, Jinping. 2012. Xi Jinping zong shuji shenqing chanshu Zhongguo meng [General Secretary Xi Jinping Elaborated 'Chinese Dream" Affectionately], November 30. http: //news.xinhuanet.com/politics/2012-11/30/c_124026690.htm accessed 15 September 2014.

Xi, Jinping. 2013a. Rang mingyun gongtong ti yishi zai zhoubian guojia luodishenggen [Let the Consciousness of Communities of Common Destiny Rooted in the Neighbouring Countries]. 25 October. www.gov.cn/ldhd/2013-10/25/content_2515764.htm accessed 2 September 2014.

Xi, Jinping. 2013b. Jieshou lamei san guo meiti lianhe shumian caifang [A United Written Interview with Three Latin American Media], 1 June. *Renmin Ribao* [*People's Daily*]: 1.

Xi, Jinping. 2013c. A speech given at the 80th anniversary of the Central Party School and the opening ceremony of the Spring semester. 1 March. http: //cpc.people.com.cn/n/2013/0303/c64094-20656845.html.

Xianfeng Yiwu Shimo (XF YWSM) [*The journal of alien affairs during the years of Xianfeng*].

Xin, Lijian. 2013. Zhongguo waijiao quefa dazhanglue [The Lack of grand strategy in Chinese foreign policy]. April 2. www.my1510.cn/article.php?id=95604.

Xiong, Tao. 2012. *The Declaration on the Conduct of Parties in the South China Sea: Origin, Plight, Future* [Nanhai gefang xingwei xuanyan de qiyuan, kunjing, yu chulu]. Master Thesis, Jinan University, China.

Xue, Fucheng 1879. Shang li boxiang lun hede buyi zongsi haifang shu" [Why Robert Hart Should Not Be Put in Charge of Coastal Defence], *Yongan wenbian* [*Yongan collection of literature*] 2 (10 August), 53–55.

Xue, Yu. 2005. *Buddhsim, War, and Nationalism: Chinese Monks in the Struggles against Japanese Aggressions (1931–1945).* Oxon: Routledge.

Yan, Xuetong. 2011. Ancient Chinese Thought, Modern Chinese Power. Eds. Daniel Bell and Zhe Sun. Transl. Edmund Ryden. Princeton, NJ: Princeton University.

Yan, Xuetong. 2013. Title n.a. *A lecture delivered at National Chengchi University* (Taipei), March.

Yan, Xuetong. 2014. 'From Keeping a Low Profile to Striving for Achievement. *The Chinese Journal of International Politics* 7(2): 153–184.'

Yang, Jiechi. 2010. Chinese FM Refutes Fallacies on the South China Sea Issue. *China Today*, 25 July, www.chinadaily.com.cn/china/201007/25/content_11046054.htm accessed 8 December 2013.

Yang, Jiechi. 2013. Zhongguo meng yu meiguo meng xiangrongxiangtong xiangde yizhang [Compatibility and Mutual Benefits between the China Dream and the

America Dream]. July 11, www.chinanews.com/gn/2013/07-10/5027540.shtml accessed 15 September 2014.

Yang, Kuo-shu. 1995. Chinese Social Orientation: An Integrative Analysis. In Tsung-Yi Lin, Wen-Shing Tseng, and Eng-Kung Yeh. Eds. *Chinese Societies and Mental Health*. Hong Kong: Oxford University Press, 19–39.

Yarbrough, Beth and Robert Yarbrough. 1986, 'Reciprocity, Bilateralism, and Economic "Hostages": Self-Enforcing Agreements in International Trade'. *International Studies Quarterly* 30, 7–21.

Ye, Zicheng. 2011. *Inside China's Grand Strategy: The Perspective from the People's Republic*. Lexington: University of Kentucky Press.

Ye, Zicheng and Hongjie Li. Eds. 2009. *Zhongguo da waijiao [Chinese Diplomacy]*. Beijing: The Contemporary World Press [dangdai shijie chubanshe].

Yeophantong, Pichamon. 2013. Governing the World: China's Evolving Conceptions of Responsibility. *Chinese Journal of International Politics* 6: 356–361.

Yi, Nai-ching, and Ming-yih Wang. 2000. Chien fu toulou xiao gushi jingguo xiansheng chengyi gandong li guang yao [Chien Fu Told a Short Story: Sincere Chiang Ching-kuo Moved Lee Kuan Yew]. *China Times [Zhongguo shibao]*, September 20, forums.chinatimes.com/special/singapore/89920s01.htm.

Yin Ching-yao, 1984. *Zhong gong de tong zhan waijiao [Communist China's Propaganda Diplomacy]*. Taipei: Youth Culture [Youshi wenhua].

Yin, Ching-yao. 1973. Zhong gong waijiao yu duiwai guanxi [*Communist China's Diplomacy and Foreign Relations*]. Taipei: Institute of International Relations.

Yolles, Maurice, B. Roy Frieden, and Graham Kemp. 2008. Toward a Formal Theory of Socioculture: A Yin-yang Information-based Theory of Social Change. *Kybernetes* 37(7): 850–909.

Yoon, Sukjoon. 2014. Xi Jinping's 'Monroe Doctrine': Rebuilding the Middle Kingdom Order?" *RSIS Commentaries*, 29 May, www.rsis.edu.sg/publications/Perspective/RSIS1022014.pdf.

Yoshimura, Stephen. 2007. Goals and Emotional Outcomes of Revenge Activities in Interpersonal Relationships. *Journal of Social and Personal Relationships* 24: 87–98.

You, Ji. 2001. China and North Korea: A Fragile Relationship of Strategic Convenience. *Journal of Contemporary China* 10(28): 387–98.

Young, Iris Marion. 2003. The Logic of Masculinist Protection on the Current Security State. *Signs* 29(1): 1–25.

Younger, Jarred, Rachel Piferi, Rebecca Jobe, and Kathleen A. Lawler. 2004. Dimensions of Forgiveness: The Views of Laypersons. *Journal of Social and Personal Relationships* 21: 837–885.

Yu, Chia-fang and Chang Teng-chi. 2011. Lilun yizhi huo chuangxin: xin ziyouzhuyi zai zhongguo guoji guanxi xuejie de fazhan (1998–2008) [Copying or Innovation: The Development of Neoliberalism in Chinese International Relations Scholarship, 1998–2008]. *East Asian Studies [Dong ya yanjiu]* 42(1): 46–83.

Yu, Jiyuan. 2002. Xiong Shili's Metaphysics of Virtue. In Chung-ying Cheng and Nicholas Bunnin. Eds. *Contemporary Chinese Philosophy*. Oxford: Blackwell. 127–146.

Yu, Keping. 2000. Jingji quanqiuhua yu zhili de bianqia [Economic Globalisation and the Transformation of Governance]. *Philosophical Studies [Zhexue yanjiu]* 10: 17–24.

Yuan, Chuan-wei. 1989. Indian Studies in Modern China (1900–1989). *China Report* 25(2) (May): 175–180.

Yuan, Jingdong. 1999. Culture Matters: Chinese Approaches to Arms Control and Disarmament'. In Keith R Krause. Ed. *Culture and Security: Multilateralism,*

Arms Control and Security Building. London and Portland: Frank Cass Publishers, 71–102.

Yuan, Jingong. 2000. Asia-Pacific Security: China's Conditional Multilateralism and Great Power Entente. Strategic Studies Institute, Asia-Pacific Security: China's Conditional Multilateralism and Great Power Entente. www.globalsecurity.org/jhtml/jframe.html; www.globalsecurity.org/military/library/report/2000/ssi_yuan.pdf accessed 10 March 2014.

Zahariadis, Nikolaos. 1994. Nationalism and Small-State Foreign Policy: The Greek Responses to the Macedonian Issue. *Political Science Quarterly* 109(4): 647–667.

Zhang, Feng. 2015. *Chinese Hegemony: Grand Strategy and International Institutions in East Asian History*. Stanford, CA: Stanford University Press.

Zhang, Lihua. 2014. zhongguo chuantong wenhhua jiazhi guan yu minzurentong [Chinese Views of Traditional Cultural Value and National Identities] (January 8) www.rwwhw.com/Rjwh/Mzsj/2014-01-08/11811.html accessed May 30, 2014.

Zhang, Yongjin, and Teng-chi Chang Eds. 2016. *Constructing a Chinese School of International Relations: Ongoing Debates and Sociological Realities*. Oxon: Routledge.

Zhang, Zhidong. Ed. 1880. Zuoshizi zhang zhidong zou Liuqiuan yishen huanji zhe fu shangyu" [Zhang Zhidong reports that the Ryukyu case should be prioritized]. *Qingji Waijiao Shiliao* 24 (November 3): 1–3.

Zhao, Tingyang. 2005. *The Tianxia System: An Introduction to the Philosophy of a World Institution*. Nanjing: Jiansu Jiaoyu Chubanshe.

Zhao, Tingyang. 2006. Rethinking Empire from a Chinese Concept 'All-under-heaven' (Tian-xia). *Social Identities* 12(1): 29–41.

Zhao, Tingyang. 2009. A Political World Philosophy in terms of All-Under-Heaven (Tian-xia). *Diogenes* 56(1): 5–18.

Zheng, Yongnian, 2013. *The Rediscovery of the Tianxia World Order. In Gilbert Rozman Ed. National Identities and Bilateral Relations: Widening Gaps in East Asia and Chinese Demonization of the United States*. Washington, DC: Woodrow Wilson Center Press, 27–152.

Zhu, Feng. 2011. Flawed Mediation and a Compelling Mission: Chinese Diplomacy in the Six-Party Talks to Denuclearise North Korea. *East Asia* 28: 191–218.

Zhu, Zhaohua. 2011. Zhong Mian Bianjie Zhuquan Jiufen De Lishi Yu Jingyan Tantao [The Historical and Empirical Discussion of Sino-Burmese Border and Sovereign Disputes]. *Window of Southeast Asia* [*Dongnanya Zhi Chuang*] 15: 28–32.

Zhu, Zhongbo. 2011. The Grand Strategy of China during the Ancient Great Power Period [Zhongguo gudai qiangsheng shiqi de da zhanlue]. *Quarterly Journal of International Politics* [Guoji zhengzhi kexue] 4: 5.

Ziegler, Charles. 2006. Energy Factor in China's Foreign Policy. *Journal of Contemporary China* 11(1): 1–23.

Zoellick, Robert. 2005. Whither China: From Membership to Responsibility? Remarks to National Committee on U.S.–China Relations. New York City, http://2001-2009.state.gov/s/d/former/zoellick/rem/53682.htm accessed 10 March 2014.

Index

Made in the USA
Coppell, TX
26 August 2021